The Organizational
Society

REVISED EDITION

Books by Robert Presthus

The Organizational Society, Alfred Knopf, 1962, Vintage Books, 1965; revised ed., St. Martin's Press, 1978.

Cross-National Perspectives: The United States and Canada (editor), Brill, 1977.

Public Administration, Ronald Press, 6th ed., 1975.

Elites in the Policy Process, Cambridge University Press, 1974.

Interest Groups in International Perspective (editor), American Academy of Political and Social Science, 1974.

Elite Accommodation in Canadian Politics, Cambridge University Press, 1974.

La Società Dell'Organizzione, Rizzoli, 1971.

Organisation und Die Individualische, Fischer Verlag, 1966.

Behavioral Approaches to Public Administration, University of Alabama Press, 1965.

Men at the Top: A Study in Community Power, Oxford University Press, 1964.

The Turkish Conseil d'Etat, Cornell University Press, 1958.

The Organizational Society

REVISED EDITION

ROBERT PRESTHUS

ST. MARTIN'S PRESS   New York

Acknowledgments

Excerpt from "Personality as a Factor in Administrative Decisions" by Mabel Blake Cohen and Robert A. Cohen, *Psychiatry* (1951) 14: 47–53. Reprinted by special permission of The William Alanson White Psychiatric Foundation, Inc. Copyright © 1951 by The William Alanson White Psychiatric Foundation, Inc.

Excerpt from *The Authoritarian Personality* by T. W. Adorno, et al. (New York: Harper & Row, 1950), pp. 248–250. Reprinted with permission of *The American Jewish Committee;* all rights reserved.

Excerpt from "Philanthropic Activity and the Business Career" by Aileen Ross. Reprinted from *Social Forces,* 32 (March 1954). Copyright © The University of North Carolina Press. Reprinted by permission of the publisher.

Excerpt from Timothy Leary, *Interpersonal Diagnosis of Personality: A Functional Theory and Methodology for Personality Evaluation,* Fig. 47, p. 407. Copyright © 1957 The Ronald Press Company, New York. Reprinted by permission.

Excerpt from "Friends, Enemies, and the Polite Fiction" by Tom Burns. Reprinted from the *American Sociological Review,* 18 (1953), 659–660. By permission of the American Sociological Association. Copyright © 1953 by the American Sociological Association.

Excerpt from "The Population Ecology of Organizations" by M. Hannan and J. Freeman. Reprinted from the *American Journal of Sociology,* 82 (1977), 931–932, by permission of The University of Chicago Press. Copyright © 1977 by the University of Chicago.

PREFACE

This book is an interdisciplinary analysis of modern organizations and their influence upon the individuals who work in them. Conceptually, the analysis operates at three distinct but interrelated levels: society as a whole; the big, rational organization; and the individual. Organizations are defined as "miniature societies" in which the dominant values of society are inculcated and sought in a more structured, spatially restricted context. A major object is to show how individuals work out an accommodation in this milieu, and to develop a theory of organizational behavior that posits three ideal types of accommodation to big organizations: "upward-mobiles," "indifferents," and "ambivalents." It must be said that I am under no illusion that the mass of evidence cited throughout the book validates this theory. Such evidence can only be illustrative.

The analysis and the theory draw upon several social sciences. My own discipline, political science, contributes the grounding in the democratic-humanistic values that provide the normative framework of the book. Political science also contributes a conception of power in its various forms, as well as considerable data about the structure and processes of political organizations. Economic theory and research provide the major source of information about the changing structure of our economy, including the rise of large-scale organizations; the separation of ownership from management; the decline of the traditional competitive economy; and its replacement by a system of "administered" prices and production. Sociological constructs and data are used to illuminate the structural aspects of big organizations, including specialization, hierarchy, oligarchy, rationality, centralized authority, status anxiety, role conflict, the displacement of values, and the emergence of "informal" centers of power, prestige, and communication.

Harry Stack Sullivan's interpersonal theory of psychiatry is turned to the analysis of individual behavior in big organizations. The compelling impact of society and culture upon individual personality is similarly put in an organizational context. The resulting "socialization process" suggests how personality is largely determined by the authoritative values of society. Specifically, I attempt to show how the organization enlists such attitudes as anxiety and deference toward authority in the service of its major goals. Psychological formulations are also used to isolate individual needs of security, recognition, self-realization, and autonomy; these needs in turn are set against the structural characteristics of the "bureaucratic situation" with its demands for loyalty, predictability, and conformity. While such a multifaceted analysis necessarily sacrifices some rigor, I hope the attempt is warranted by a clearer picture of organizational behavior and the meaning of work in contemporary society.

Robert Presthus

Ithaca, New York

PREFACE TO THE
REVISED EDITION

Almost two decades have passed since *The Organizational Society* appeared, and dramatic social and political traumas have occurred, yet on the whole time has dealt generously with the assumptions underlying the book. Perhaps a major qualification would be my belief that a significant proportion of Americans were deeply identified with their occupational role, and that most of them accepted the principle of meritocracy. Instead, leisure, travel, and spectator activities have become more salient, and meritocracy is under attack from both the right and the left.

On the other hand, the pervasive turn to off-work satisfactions seems to be receding, after reaching its height during the 1960s and early 1970s. Some evidence now suggests that young men and women are in a "conservative" mood, in which traditional values of achievement and professionalism are reasserting themselves. Following a decade or more of "equal opportunity" policies, assiduously promoted by the federal government, we have entered a period in which an "ethic of fairness," of equality of condition, is being challenged by the venerable equality of opportunity. In part this reflects a sobering realization that the problem of distributive justice is less tractable than thought. Meanwhile, Americans have become less optimistic about political solutions to critical problems. Unemployment and inflation have dampened the altruism of young majoritarians, as indicated by their claims of "reverse discrimination" against preferential hiring and university admission for minorities. Following the endless dialectic of change, we seem to have gone through a cycle that mooted certain bench-mark assumptions of this book on into a period when they have again become viable.

Whatever the current onslaughts against meritocracy, and with full awareness of its tendency toward intergenerational corruption, I still hold it as a critical value—not only as the most realistic and equitable instrument of individual opportunity, but equally as a functional requirement of society. I am impressed with the utopianism of many critics of bureaucracy and meritocracy. Insofar as they retain much faith in socialism as a solution for our ills, they seem merely naive. It is ironic that socialists continue to assert a corner on egalitarian and humanitarian rhetoric, yet if one looks at the hard social indicators, it seems that welfare capitalist societies have come much closer to making good on such claims. I have absolutely no normative animus against socialism, of the British variety; my conclusion is based on the pragmatic conviction that it simply will not work, in part because it rests upon a wildly optimistic assumption regarding the perfectability of man, aggravated by an invalid theory of human incentives.

The indictment of hierarchical institutions that informs this book continues to rest upon their tendency to displace meritocratic bases of recruitment and mobility with ascriptive ones. I have no illusions, however, that the trend toward size, concentration, and bureaucratic rationalization can be turned aside, given the imperative of economic growth to provide full employment and satisfy the claims of advanced and advancing societies for higher living standards and increased welfare bounties. It seems equally unrealistic to assume that more government intervention can meet such claims, if only because they require vast revenues that must ultimately be drawn from the private sector. For this very reason, governments are as fully committed to economic growth as private industry. Indeed political regimes are less able to sustain high levels of unemployment.

Democratic stability in the United States, as is sometimes forgotten, was insured largely by the ideal and the reality of social mobility, brought about mainly by industrial growth, technological differentiation, and a vastly expensive system of higher education. Government and politics, by contrast, may be regarded as part of the national infrastructure, to some extent riding along on (and, ironically, at times eroding) the reservoir of human energy and productivity released by the American doctrine of "possessive individualism." It is precisely this wide ambiance of achievement-based egalitarianism that sets America apart from the rest of Western society and often makes absurd the attempts to apply Marxian class analysis to our society. To some extent, such attempts are part of a nostalgic, class-born *resentissement* against the American version of meritocracy and the extension of material delights to mass publics.

Of course the achievement ideal is often violated and manipulated by self-conscious minorities; and clearly, the distribution of wealth in American society remains highly inequitable, despite several decades of so-called progressive taxation (again testifying to the limitations of politics). But one need only look at comparative figures on university admission and social mobility to appreciate the uniqueness of the American experience. The tragic waste of human talent through limited educational opportunity in Britain, Canada, France, and Germany suggests the social cost of educational elitism. Despite the costs in high drop-out rates and some lowering of standards, I would argue that this is one waste among our prolific catalogue of public and private wastes that remains eminently justifiable.

My own conclusion, then, is that we should work hard to improve the existing system, to iron out its obvious inequities, to curb the tragic waste attending the garrison state, and to divert some of those recaptured billions to refurbishing our urban centers and to providing legal and medical care to everyone, without bankruptcy. At present the political-economic system runs us; some way must be found to reorder that condition.

In preparing this revised edition, I have acquired a special debt to my colleague H. T. Wilson for the benefits of wide-ranging discussions of bureaucracy, rationality, and the interpretation of Weber's complex, and sometimes contradictory, generalizations. The analysis also benefited from the thoughtful criticism of Michael P. Smith of Tulane University, especially regarding the implications of recent changes in the way individuals react to the claims of organizations for loyalty and dependability. My research assistant, Sono Fujii, helped greatly by sifting through the mass of cross-disciplinary research produced during the past two decades. I accept the usual responsibility for inadequacies found in the analysis.

R. P.

Toronto, Canada
January 1978

CONTENTS

MODERN ORGANIZATIONS: DEFINITIONS AND DYSFUNCTIONS

This book concerns the influence of social values and bureaucratic structure upon the members of the complex organizations that characterize American society. More specifically, it attempts to define the patterns of individual accommodation that occur in the bureaucratic milieu. Contemporary organizations have a pervasive influence upon individual and group behavior, expressed through a web of rewards, sanctions, and other inducements that range from patent coercion to the most subtle of group appeals to conformity. Indeed, bureaucratic organizations often seem less concerned with the self-realization of their members than with the relevance of such individuals for organizational goals of size, power, and survival. Ironically, members often accept this instrumental bargain; and why they do so is a matter of central interest here. We shall also be concerned with the larger social consequences of organizations. Does organizational logic enhance the survival chances of our society, or does it limit our ability to meet the demands of change in a swiftly changing world?

The organizations we are concerned with may be defined as large, fairly permanent social systems designed to achieve limited objectives through the coordinated activities of their members. We are concerned with all organizations in which people spend their working lives. The boundaries of such organizations are relatively distinct. Membership and responsibility can be assigned and "organizational" activities, values, and expectations can be differentiated from those that are extraorganizational. Such organizations have both manifest and latent goals. The manifest goal of private corporations is to produce and sell certain products at a profit. Their latent or "unofficial" goals, however, include all the aspirations of their members for security, recognition, and self-realization. Such latent goals and the methods used to gain them are often regarded as aberrations. They seem to subvert organizational ends. However, we shall assume here that such aspirations and methods are not only legitimate, but that they often help the organization achieve its manifest goals.

The bureaucratic model used throughout this study has various structural characteristics, including specialization, hierarchy, oligarchy (that is, a tendency toward control by the few), and interpersonal relations that are explicitly differentiated by authority. "An organization is a system of roles graded by authority." Such characteristics appear most clearly in large organizations, which may be defined as those in which the sheer number of participants and the scale of operations prohibit face-to-face relationships among most of their members. Size by itself introduces a pathological element in organizations that eases the problem of analysis by dramatizing their other characteristics. Although hierarchy appears in both the small group and the army, its intensity and effects are more sharply evident in the larger system.

In our analysis the terms "organization" and "bureaucratic structures" are synonymous. The total environment provided by such institutions will be called the bureaucratic situation. The classical analysis of bureaucratic organization is by Max Weber, who attached no invidious connotation to the term but indeed believed that bureaucracy was absolutely essential for both the modern state and the corporation. "The decisive reason for the advance of bureaucratic organization has always been its purely technical superiority over any other form of organization."[1] "Precision, speed, unambiguity, knowledge of files, continuity, discretion, strict subordination, reduction of friction and of material and personal costs—these are raised to the optimum point in the strictly bureaucratic administration."[2] Ideally, this system eliminates "from official business love, hatred, and all purely personal, irrational, and emotional elements which escape calculation."[3]

According to Weber, bureaucracy has the following characteristics: fixed and official jurisdictional areas, which are regularly ordered by rules, that is, by laws or administrative regulations; principles of hierarchy and levels of graded authority that ensure a firmly ordered system of super- and subordination in which higher offices supervise lower ones; administration based upon written documents; the body of officials engaged in handling these documents and files, along with

[1]Max Weber, "Bureaucracy," in Hans Gerth and C. Wright Mills, eds., *From Max Weber* (New York: Oxford University Press, 1946), p. 214.

[2]Ibid., p. 214.

[3]Ibid., p. 216.

other material apparatus, make up a "bureau" or "office"; administration by full-time officials who are thoroughly and expertly trained; governance by general rules which are quite stable and comprehensive.[4]

The position of bureaucratic officials has the following characteristics. Their job is a permanent vocation, a career for which they have been specifically trained. In most societies its conditions include a certain social esteem. Ideally, officials are appointed to their jobs by some superior authority. Bureaucratic demands for subordination and discipline would be fractured by election which would deflect responsibility to those outside the organization. Normally, individuals have life tenure which encourages "a strictly objective discharge of specific official duties." Finally, officials receive a regular, money salary, determined by their rank and length of service.[5]

Weber's analysis provides a good beginning, but it has certain limitations for the kind of study proposed here. Not only are the psychological consequences of the model for individuals ignored, but their latent goals are regarded as deviations that necessarily subvert the organization's rational means and ends. The critical distinction and the inevitable tension between the authority of position (hierarchy) and the authority of skill are unexamined. The influence of informal groups and the organization's part in socialization are similarly neglected.

Inevitably, Weber's analysis cannot include the distinctive ideological climate of America in recent times. Clearly, the 1960s have left a legacy that has sharply modified the context in which organizations exist. The continuing demand for equality has its organizational counterpart in somewhat utopian designs for organizations without hierarchy, oligarchy, and even specialization. The transformation of the merit principle brought by the demands of minorities and women for a redress of ancient grievances provides a new departure. Demands for greater participation by those in the lower reaches of the bureaucratic world are similarly germane. Finally, the expanding tolerance for individual autonomy, and even deviance, in American society has probably made some inroads upon the stereotypical behaviors traditionally seen inside big organizations. The institutionalization of protest, symbolized by such groups as Common Cause, has brought a new capacity for oversight that probably limits the discretion of even the most powerful organizations. Hopefully, the following analysis treats such new conditions adequately while at

---

[4]Max Weber, *Theory of Social and Economic Organization,* trans. A. M. Henderson and Talcott Parsons (New York: Oxford University Press, 1947), pp. 333–336.

[5]Ibid., p. 203.

the same time recognizing the strain toward continuity that bureaucratic structures reveal.

In sum, Weber deals almost exclusively with the formal, manifest functions of bureaucracy and gives little attention to their unanticipated consequences, both functional and dysfunctional. This orientation is explained in part by the social context in which he lived and wrote, namely, Germany at the turn of the century, with its patent class stratification, its patriarchal family structure, its extreme respect for authority, and its highly disciplined military and governmental bureaucracy. In the next chapter we outline a bureaucratic model that rests upon Weber yet includes the latent, "informal" aspects characteristic of organizations in contemporary American society.

When they occur together, as they usually do in large bureaucratic systems, hierarchy, specialization, and authority produce a distinctive psychological climate. Members are expected to be loyal to the organization, to behave consistently and rationally according to technical and professional criteria, and to defer to the authority of the organization's leaders. The social and psychological basis of this accommodation is the major concern of this book.

A basic assumption throughout is that cultural values and institutions largely mold individual personality and behavior. This occurs through a process called socialization. Society, in effect, provides a web of values and expectations that mainly determines the individual's character, his ethical beliefs, and his ideas about progress, success, and failure. People may, for example, be born with an impulse to dominate others, but values such as our democratic ideal of equality determine the manner and extent to which this impulse can be gratified. When people choose, they choose within this context of socially determined values. While our society provides a broad scope for individual choices, organizational influences traced here have significantly changed the conditions under which they are made.

Organizations impose socialization through their patent authority systems, their rational procedures, and their limited objectives. In this context organizations will be defined as miniature social systems in which the mechanics and the consequences of socialization are sharply defined. The organization resembles a school or a church in that it inculcates approved ideals, attitudes, and behavior, all calculated to enhance the organization's survival value. This educational function is apparent in the organization's authority system which encourages members to accept uncritically its legitimacy and rationality. The tensions arising from such organizational conditions are sharper than those existing in the larger society where differences in status and income are more fluid, transitory, and generally less invidious. In the United States, social and political stability have been achieved essentially by the ideal and the reality of upward mobility, often achieved inter-generationally.[6]

The organization's socializing influence and the individual's accommodations to its claims are, however, usually worked out through interaction with other people. This condition will be analyzed by using an interpersonal theory of behavior. Interpersonal theory insists that personality and indeed most forms of individual behavior are the result of one's perceptions of oneself in relation to others. Personality is mainly the result of social interaction rather than of biological impulse. In organizations such interactions often occur in a highly structured context in which authority, rank, power, and status are clearly differentiated. This accounts for the consistency of behavior seen in the typical bureaucratic setting.

The specialization and discipline of big organizations have both functional and dysfunctional consequences. Their gains in material rewards, industrial efficiency, and military power are clear enough. Their dysfunctions are more subtle and pervasive, raising problems of individual autonomy, integrity, and self-realization. Prominent among them today is a displacement of value from the intrinsic quality of work to its by-products of income, security, prestige, and leisure.[7] This displacement stems from the impersonality, the specialization, and the group character of work in the typical big organization. Its larger significance may appear in an alienation (defined as a sense of powerlessness or estrangement) from work, resulting from such factors as the economy's frequent concern with essentially trivial products or the monotony arising from the modern assembly line. The organization's capacity to meet the demands of change may suffer, since criticism and innovation tend to be muffled by its demands for conformity.

Such organizational conditions and expectations have fostered the growth of certain personality types whose skill and behavior reflect the demands of the organizational society. We shall define three such types as the *upward-mobiles,* the *indifferents,* and the *ambivalents.*[8] The

[6]Peter Blau and Otis D. Duncan, *The American Occupational Structure* (New York: Wiley, 1967), p. 76.

[7]Robert K. Merton, *Social Theory and Social Structure* (Glencoe, Ill.: Free Press, 1957), pp. 197–202; and "The Unanticipated Consequences of Purposive Social Action," *American Sociological Review,* Vol. 1, pp. 894–904.

[8]While lending themselves to oversimplification and misinterpretation, such types have a long and distinguished intellectual history, beginning in the Western world with Plato's "philosopher-kings," "guardians," and "workers," and Aristotle's "democratic" and "oligarchic" types of political states. More recent examples include Pareto's "lions" and "foxes," Mosca's "ruling class," Tonnies' "Gemeinschaft" and "Gesellschaft," Weber's "charismatic" and "bureaucratic" leaders, Veblen's "financiers" and "engineers," Lasswell's "political administrators" and "political agitators," Riesman's

upward-mobiles now tend increasingly to gain control of the efforts and rewards of professionals, scientists, and other highly trained personnel. Thorstein Veblen's separation of engineers and financiers, with its attending dysfunctions, is being repeated in many organizations—economic, educational, artistic, religious and military. The unexpected consequences include the alienation of the professionals, the aggrandizement of administration, a tendency toward oligarchy, and to some extent, impaired survival power of both organizations and society as the quality of decisions suffers from lack of participation by those who are best qualified to make them. It is important to add, however, that in comparison with such countries as Britain and Canada, the latter problem is eased in the United States by the "specialist ethos," which honors expertise, contrary to the generalist tradition which assumes, with demonstrably unhappy consequences, that liberally educated amateurs can manage the modern industrial state.[9]

It is important to discuss further the kinds of organizations with which this book is concerned. Essentially, we mean systems that have a large number of employees and operate in large-scale terms. A good example would be the 500 largest industrial corporations in the United States, which in 1975 had a net worth of over 600 billion dollars, employed over 14 million people, and ranged in total assets from over 44 billion dollars (Exxon) to a mere one and one-half billion (Lockheed Aircraft).[10] The global industrial hegemony of the United States is dramatically evident in the fact that twenty-three of the largest fifty corporations in the world are American, including five of the top six: Exxon, General Motors, Texaco, Ford, and Mobil Oil. Such organizations are a common instrument of modern society, featuring scientific procedures, standardization, objective recruitment, impersonality, machine operations, an exquisite division of labor, a hierarchy of authority and status, and a tendency to demand complete loyalty from their members. They dominate basic industry, finance, and utilities, and they have made deep inroads into educational and artistic areas. The indexes of size include number of employees, capitalization, proportion of total production, and the amount of capital required for entry into a given field. But an enter-

---

"inner-and-other-directed" men, Merton's "locals" and "cosmopolitans," and Mills's "abstracted empiricists" and "grand theorists." Psychology of course is replete with typologies, including Jung's "introverts" and "extroverts," James's "tender-minded" and "tough-minded," Adorno's "authoritarian" personality, as well as the gamut of psychopathological categories of mental illness. Used judiciously, such types have the great virtue of helping one order the infinite complexity of the real world.

[9]See, for example, on Britain, Max Nicholson, *The System: The Misgovernment of Modern Britain* (London: Hodder and Stoughton, 1967); and on Canada, Paul Mathias, *Forced Growth* (Toronto: Samuels, 1971).

[10]*Fortune,* May 1976, p. 318.

prise need not have all these characteristics to be classified as huge. Financial enterprises, for example, may control vast concentrations of capital, yet their total number of employees is relatively small; similarly with self-conscious public agencies like the Foreign Service and the Marine Corps. Although it is difficult to reach agreement on definition, in this book the organizations we shall analyze include the largest of our some 3,000 universities and colleges, which in 1970 had almost 20 percent of about 4 million students. They include enterprises like General Motors with 681,000 employees, Ford with 416,000, Rockwell International with 122,000, General Electric with 375,000, Exxon with 137,000, ITT with 376,000, the big insurance companies, and the dominant banks like the Bank of America and Chase Manhattan. Government departments, of course, are the epitome of such institutions.

The Small Business Administration, whose clientele is determined by size, defines an organization as large if it has over 1,000 employees. However, this figure varies with employment size and with dollar-volume standards, which change from industry to industry. Independent ownership and competitiveness in their field are the Administration's main qualitative standards for small businesses. In the end one must probably rely on certain general attitudes about bigness in our society. Certainly there is a consensus that General Motors and U. S. Steel are huge industrial organizations; that our seventy-odd billion-dollar corporations are big; that New York University and the University of California are huge academic organizations; that the AFL-CIO is a giant labor organization; and that the Farm Bureau Federation and the Farmers' Union are the giants among agricultural interest groups.

As one descends the scale from these obvious examples, disagreement will increase. However, the importance of size for our purposes is that large numbers of employees and large-scale operations usually result in a bureaucratic situation whose structural characteristics and psychological climate evoke certain patterns of individual accommodation. If this is true, it is not necessary to set down a precise index of size. We can define "large organizations" as all bureaucratic systems whose size prevents face-to-face interpersonal relations among most of their members. Regardless of their product, such organizations tend to operate quite similarly. They all arrange individual skills and relationships in order to secure continuity and stability. They all develop standardized methods to handle their major activities. They all exhibit a built-in conflict between authority based upon position and authority based upon skill. They are consciously designed to achieve a major purpose, that is, to produce steel, automobiles, public service, news, educated men, entertainment, and the like.

A common problem in organizational analysis is where to draw the boundaries of one's inquiry. In the present study, organizations are conceptualized as satellites of the larger social system; the behavior of their members is largely shaped by its values. Such organizations now provide the major arena in which individual claims for success, income, and security are resolved. But one cannot understand organizational behavior unless he brings to bear upon it the insights of several disciplines. Cultural psychology shows us how social values mold personality; sociology deals with the structure and consequences of social institutions; political science deals with power and with the resulting allocation of scarce values. Economics, the most systematic of the social sciences, analyzes the institutions and the incentives that produce wealth. Each treats of individual and group behavior. Together, they provide the theoretical basis for this book.

If social structure is critical in molding individual behavior and personality, the organization can usefully be conceived as a small society whose characteristics of specialization, hierarchy, and authority have a similar influence upon its members. The mechanisms that society employs to inculcate its values may be seen at work within the organization. The organization, in a word, socializes its members in a way similar to that of society. It co-opts the learned deference to authority inculcated by institutions such as the family and the church. We may assume that the patent authority and prestige structure of the typical organization enhances the effectiveness of the authority-deference mechanism.

Such a mode of analysis clearly requires the insights and conceptual tools of several disciplines. But the existing structure and values of the intellectual marketplace inhibit such an approach. Each discipline tends to define organizations in terms of its own image, with the result that organizational phenomena are divided into political, economic, sociological, and psychological compartments. Professional commitments and power struggles among university departments discourage the integration of social-science theory and methods. The reasons for this situation are found in the conditions of participation set down by academia today. They provide ironic evidence of our major theme by illustrating the extent to which organizational expectations and rewards influence individual behavior.

Unless one has experienced graduate training and apprenticeship in American higher learning, the stress involved in broadening one's approach beyond a single discipline is hard to imagine. Academic training instills a compelling inhibition against venturing beyond a given segment of knowledge. The underlying reason is the passionate specialization of university organization. All the dynamics of training, of values, and of professional recognition push one toward restricted fields of analysis. As a result, trained incapacity, technical introversion, and bureaucratic infighting are characteristic of most university departments. Each discipline carves out for itself a narrow segment of human behavior, concentrates mightily on developing it through research, theory, and immaculate terminology, and in the process accumulates such a bewildering array of facts and fables that the apprentice is virtually submerged by what is called the "basic knowledge in the field." To presume to go beyond this revealed wisdom is to risk the most crushing label in the academic lexicon: dilettante.

The dilemmas of specialization are aggravated by competing "schools" within each discipline, each having opposing conceptions of the field, its scope, and the proper ways of doing research. And, of course, each "school" has its priests, acolytes, and true believers. C. Wright Mills has shown that American sociology is sharply divided between at least two such schools, the "grand theorists" and the "abstracted empiricists," representing broadly a division between rationalists and positivists.[11] The implications of academic claims for "appropriate" professional behavior are suggested by the fact that some reviewers of Mill's work concluded: "Here is a man who will never be president of the American Sociological Association." Political science is similarly divided among those who regard the field as an aspect of political and moral philosophy and those who define it as a potential "science" resting upon empirical analyses of electoral behavior, political attitudes, leadership, etc. Attending conflicts tend to give academia a rather humorless quality and a competitive impulse that does credit to an Oriental bazaar.

In studying organizational behavior one can thus be eclectic not only about the disciplines to which he turns but also regarding method. Certainly the kinds of questions raised in this book require both the "traditional" and "scientific" conceptions of inquiry. Also, one cannot ignore the pressing normative questions that are engaged here. The autonomy of the individual in an organizational society is too important an issue to be stifled by methodological inhibitions. The present analysis will enlist all sources that seem helpful in understanding bureaucratic structure and individual accommodations to it.

We can now consider some of the tools that help us order the bureaucratic world. One is an analytical fiction known as the "ideal type," a concept that recognizes the diversity of modern organizations yet enables one to study them with the hope of building generalizations. Max Weber called this tool a "generalized rubric within which

[11]C. Wright Mills, *The Sociological Imagination* (New York: Oxford University Press, 1959), Chs. 2–3. For evidence that established scientific fields tend to suppress ideas that challenge conventional formulations, see Thomas S. Kuhn, *The Structure of Scientific Revolutions* (Chicago: University of Chicago Press, 1962).

an indefinite number of particular cases may be classified." As the term suggests, an "ideal type" is actually an illusion, a sort of Platonic ideal or composite of all cases in a given class. The assumptions of classical economics provide an example. To analyze behavior in the marketplace, economists posited a fictitious setting in which men were always rational, saved their money, and enjoyed the luxury of free choice in a competitive, self-regulating system. Most theorists knew, although their apostles sometimes forget, that such conditions existed mainly in their own minds. But the ideal made the real more understandable by providing a model against which to set the existing system.

Our "ideal type" is a generalized model of all large-scale organizations. Such a tool gives us a bench mark against which we can measure "an indefinite number of particular cases." This model, the main elements of which will be set down in the next chapter, provides the framework for chapters 6, 7, and 8, where we characterize the three bureaucratic types already mentioned: the upward-mobiles, the indifferents, and the ambivalents. The upward-mobiles are those who react positively to the bureaucratic situation and succeed in it. The indifferents are the uncommitted majority who see their jobs essentially as mere instruments to obtain off-work satisfactions. The ambivalents are a small, perpetually disturbed minority who can neither renounce their claims for status and power nor play the disciplined role that would enable them to cash in such claims.

Like the economist's classical model, these types are oversimplified and idealized, but they have a similar value as conceptual tools. Most research begins with similar premises that permit one to study complex institutions or events. The student of organizational behavior does not reason in a vacuum, but instead develops constructs that help in the selection and classification of information. In addition to bureaucratic structure and types, our guides include a number of democratic-humanistic values against which the consequences of modern organizations can be set. They include equality of opportunity, freedom of thought and expression, and self-realization. The consequences include the remarkable concentration of social, political, intellectual, and economic power characteristic of American society today. This concentration, documented in chapter 3, is evidenced by the size and proportion of markets, number of employees, percentage of total capital investment, and the social power that organizations now exert in many areas.

But such organizations are more than mere devices for producing goods and services. They have critical normative consequences. They provide the environment in which most of us spend most of our lives. In their efforts to rationalize human energy they become sensitive and versatile agencies for the control of human behavior, employing subtle psychological sanctions that evoke desired responses and inculcate consistent patterns of action. In this sense, as Max Weber feared, they push us toward the "iron cage" of history. Organizations are a major disciplinary force in our society. Their influence spills over the boundaries of economic interest or activity into spiritual and intellectual sectors; the accepted values of the organization shape the individual's personality and influence his or her behavior in extravocational affairs.

Because such values are supported by organized power, they become reinforced not only for those immediately concerned but for society generally. They provide the operational criteria of personal worth, success, and power. Increasingly, as concentration pervades every sector, such values can be achieved only in large organizations. Meanwhile, the latters' drive for efficiency and control, their long-run goals, and their precious self-images compel them to demand wider and deeper loyalty from their members. Such demands are usually justified by honorific abstractions such as "the good of the organization." Many individuals accept such demands, and some become as disciplined as the organization itself. Most of their interpersonal relations and their social life are bent toward career ends. Organizations therefore become instruments of socialization, providing physical and moral sustenance for their members and shaping their thought and behavior in countless ways.

These human consequences are the result of the growth of science, technology, and specialization in our society during the past century. Structural changes in the economy during that period and the growing size and power of organizations had striking implications for the traditional ideals of individual autonomy that had characterized a simpler society. While new conditions brought new opportunities based mainly upon economic growth and the specialization of labor, such opportunities existed in a different context that demanded new skills and discipline. Ironically, instead of bringing contentment, new opportunities often encouraged insecurity. A vague dissatisfaction persisted as people became afraid that the job they had was not as good as the one available. With one eye focussed on the main chance, the individual tended to lose the intrinsic satisfaction of work; work tended to become a mere means to other ends. When products are designed to become obsolete, when novelty becomes decisive, it becomes difficult to retain the instinct of workmanship. The specialization and impersonality of bureaucratic tasks were further causes in the estrangement of people from their work, which increasingly became a means of buying escape in the form of organized recreation and entertainment.

Modern organizations have nevertheless brought impressive gains in American living standards and national power and have become models for economic development in poorer countries. Our society is deeply committed both to the gains and to the instruments that have helped make them possible. This analysis implies in no way, therefore, a preference for anarchy or a longing for a rural utopia. It seeks instead to raise questions about the social and psychological impact of organizations and, by implication, to suggest greater discrimination in their use. It maintains that their impersonal, long-range objectives, patent control mechanisms, size, and tendency toward absolutism may have dysfunctional, anxiety-producing results for their members. Injustice may result as organizations bring their collective sanctions to bear against those who dissent. Such by-products, the unanticipated consequences of the bureaucratic situation, become most clear when organizational claims are set against democratic ideals of free expression, individual worth, and spontaneity.

For example, the bureaucratic situation tends to foster an adaptive personality type who develops the ability to play "tough-minded" rules, that is, those rules that give the organization's collective claims priority over any conflicting demands, such as loyalty to friends or to personal ideals. The "good of the organization" becomes the highest value. Such behavior is often unhealthy, encouraging self-alienation and anxiety, primarily because of its exploitative and manipulative character. In many occupational contexts, moreover, the individual has little choice as personal encounters are shaped essentially by a pecuniary impulse.

The size and impersonality of organizations may also encourage anxiety. Feelings of helplessness and of frustration occur as organizational power and demands checkmate the individual's claims for autonomy. Personal freedom and growth, in terms of effective choices and real participation in decisions that affect one directly, tend to be submerged by the centralized power and decision making that characterize organizations. Because success and psychic ease often require an uncritical acceptance of such conditions, security is often purchased with conformity. But the attending decline of personal responsibility in favor of collective irresponsibility may result in a subtle corrosion of integrity.

Such results may be the price for technical efficiency and material progress; but one must ask, what are the consequences for individual freedom and development? Writing in the 1830s, Tocqueville could say, "I know of no country in which there is so little independence of mind and real freedom of discussion as in America."[12] One must

---

[12]Alexis de Tocqueville, *Democracy in America* (New York: Alfred A. Knopf, 1954), Vol. 1, p. 263.

again ask, how has the organizational society affected this condition? Although we admire dispatch and productivity, the organizations that symbolize these tend to weaken the humanistic ideal that men must be treated as ends rather than as means. The effects of organizations in such terms are only vaguely felt, and understandably so, because they are subtle and cumulative.

Where the trend toward bigness has been analyzed, mainly in government and economics, conclusions have differed widely. Some deplore the rise of big government, big labor, and big agriculture on the grounds that it stifles competition and prevents equal access to raw materials and capital, while dampening individual incentive. On the other hand, economic concentration is sometimes regarded as a healthy by-product of the liberal theory of competition, providing a countervailing force that prevents exploitation by any single Leviathan.[13] However, there is no doubt that the consumer can be hurt by collusion among the giants, as seen in such practices as price "leadership" and built-in obsolescence. Meanwhile, smaller firms competing against the giants in any given field are greatly disadvantaged by their relative lack of capital and by their attending inability to influence major decisions in the industry. This latter eventuality can pertain even where smaller firms still outnumber the big ones.

Studies of concentration and size have usually been restricted to structural and competitive change, often attempting to show that the competitive market remains viable. There has been little concern with the normative implications of such trends. The effects of organizational tools, such as authority and status anxiety, upon individual self-realization have not been carefully traced. Such problems tend to be repressed, one suspects, because they underscore the disparity between organizational power and democratic ideals. Our liberal ethic avoids the problem of power because it happily assumes that self-interest necessarily ends in community advantage. Yet, unequally distributed power insures the unequal distribution of social opportunity and rewards. The resulting decline of personal autonomy often proves inadmissible in a society bred on individualism. The conception that the power of organizations must be matched by an equal measure of social responsibility is resisted.

We tend moreover to restrict our thinking about individual freedom to government, concluding that freedom is assured when public power is controlled. But somehow the logic of freedom, so compelling in this public context, is often neglected where private power is concerned. There, despite the intimate relationship between conditions of work and of self-realization, the implications of the

---

[13]John K. Galbraith, *American Capitalism* (Boston: Houghton Mifflin, 1956).

concentrated power now characteristic of our society have usually been ignored. The extension of material equality has been uncritically accepted as insuring the freedom necessary to make good our democratic ideals. The truth is that both public and private centers of power now tend to have a constricting effect upon many such ideals. In such ways, organizations threaten the social equilibrium that makes democracy possible.

As chapter 3 will suggest, bureaucratic logic has invaded areas far removed from the industrial world where it first appeared. For this invasion, our idolatry of size and our faith in technical solutions for human problems seem mainly responsible. As a result, artistic, educational, and spiritual activities have embraced bureaucratic organization, seeking efficiency and confusing size with grandeur as fully as their industrial and political counterparts. In adopting the techniques of commerce, they have inevitably adopted some of its values, and their character has changed accordingly. In terms of quality and of human values, the effect of modern organizations on art, liberal education, and mass communications is a disturbing question.

Such changes in the character of the work place tends to change the character of work. Here, the altered role and status of the professional is of particular interest. Professional standing becomes precarious in organizations where power, loyalty, and status rather than skill are increasingly the source of influence. It seems clear that the traditional independence of professionals and their style of work are being undercut. They have often become employees in a huge organization which alone can provide the capital plant, the laboratory, and the instruments necessary for the use of their skills. They become part of an intensely pragmatic bureaucratic structure. Since they no longer work for themselves, it becomes increasingly difficult for them to set their own pace, to decide how their energy will be spent, and to work in terms of knowledge rather than of time. Such changing conditions of work are patent in the contemporary union movement among university faculties. Although the trend is most marked in marginal institutions, in which instructors tend to define themselves essentially as teachers in a bureaucratic milieu, it is probably symptomatic of a secular decline in the autonomy that Western universities have enjoyed.[14]

The decline of the independent professional is matched by the rise of the administrator. Often possessing little technical knowledge beyond a somewhat intangible ability to organize others, administrators now control the allocation of the organization's resources. Since their

---

[14]Seymour M. Lipset and Everett Ladd, *The Divided Academy* (New York: McGraw-Hill, 1975), pp. 243–296.

role involves coordinating and arbitrating the conflicting demands of specialists, they tend to regard specialists in terms of power and strategy. Specialists are themselves not entirely innocent of the tactics of survival. But the administrators' own constant power orientation reinforces their perception of the specialist as an introverted "fact grubber." (This alienation may be subtly reinforced if they have abandoned their own technical or research aspirations.) Where administrative posts are a reward for professional achievement, as in a few eminent universities, this schism is eased. However, loyalty and seniority, qualities hardly calculated to inspire professional enthusiasm, have become the main bases for succession to administrative posts in big organizations, including academic. Combined with the higher prestige and income of administrators, this condition disenchants some professionals and intrigues others, with unfortunate results in either case.

In business and industry, the administrator's role was shaped mainly by the change in ownership structure that began early in this century. The risk-taking entrepreneur who dominated American industry from 1875 to 1910 was replaced by a salaried, professional executive. His was a management job in which "human relations" was among the critical skills. The rise of specialists in market analysis, tax policy, advertising, design, finance, and engineering brought diffused decision making. The ability to work effectively in committees and small groups took on a new significance. While the executives' main job was one of coordinating specialists, they also became "industrial statesmen." Aware that economics and politics were inextricably joined and that most people knew it, they kept in touch with publics who influenced the political framework in which their organization operated. Since they personally initiated less policy, while group decision making enabled them to share responsibility, taking risks became less appealing. Science, planning, market research, human inertia, and the creative wonders of advertising provided some insurance against fluctuations in demand. In sum, the counsel of their scientific entourage and their company's financial resources reduced both the need and the appeal of individual responsibility and risk taking.

Although such innovations brought new opportunities, they were often accompanied by a new dependence. Increasingly the organization set the conditions for individual work. Technicians required an organization to accommodate their talents. Without its physical plant, its administrative and capital resources, their skills were useless. Their prestige was a function of the organization's prestige. In academia, for example, evaluations of their scholarly work by publishers and critics were influenced by the eminence of the institution which employed them.[15] Undefined by such tangible indexes, they tended to count for less. This left them exceptionally vulnerable. The relatively small number of power centers in many sectors of society made possible a swift and far-reaching control. Like the radio actors and the screen writers blacklisted for political indiscretion, offenders could be disciplined on a national scale.[16] Their trained incapacity meant that they could turn to alternative work only at considerable financial sacrifice. And here again, diffused responsibility was clearly apparent. Those who expelled them were remote and evasive, unknown clients who worked through advertising agencies and interest groups often unknown to the public.

The increasing relevance of political and personal criteria in the career arena changed individual orientations toward work. The self-realization assumed by the creation of a finished product had been impaired by specialization. Now the loss of intrinsic joy in work encouraged a preoccupation with means. Conviviality, "personality," and dependency became important career skills. As C. Wright Mills found, "Our society has become a great showroom in which the individual must merchandize his personal wares if he is to compete successfully."[17] Like other commodities, the individual found that standardization had its sales value. One refrain runs throughout the well-known *Fortune* interviews with executives and their wives: the fear of being thought different. One must be "common," nonintellectual, and above all, "able to put others at ease." One must realize the importance of "constructive friendships," that is, friendships that have career utility. This ethic reflects in part existing group theory and the "adjustment" theme of mass education. The group decides and the individual conforms.

As Thorstein Veblen showed, such dominance relationships permeate every aspect of social life. With characteristic insight, he notes how "manners" are functionally related to status and dominance: "Manners . . . are symbolical and conventionalized survivals representing former acts of domination or of personal service or of personal contact. In large part they are an expression of the relations

---

[15] Diana Crane, "Scientists at Major and Minor Universities: A Study of Productivity and Recognition," *American Sociological Review*, Vol. 30, pp. 699–714; also Stephen I. Abramowitz, et al., "Referee Bias in Manuscript Review," *Journal of Applied Social Psychology*, Vol. 5, pp. 187–200. As the authors say, "The probability that the paper would receive a very firm publication endorsement was a good deal greater when it was sent out to an ideologically sympathetic referee . . . than to an unsympathetic one" (p. 196).

[16] John Cogley, *Report on Blacklisting*, 2 vols. (New York: Fund for the Republic, 1956).

[17] The process of "adult socialization" is treated in C. Wright Mills, *White Collar* (New York: Oxford University Press, 1951), pp. 182–188.

of status—a symbolic pantomime of mastery on the one hand and of subservience on the other."[18]

Similar demands are made by most organizations, often, one thinks, without realizing their larger implications. A report on standards of conduct for international civil servants prepared for the United Nations provides an example. "The international civil servant must accept special restraints in his public and private life. . . ."[19] "Integrity, international loyalty, independence and impartiality, and the subordination of private interests to the interests of the organization, are daily requirements."[20] Moreover, "integrity" is defined as the individual's capacity to regulate "his conduct with the interests of the international organization only in view."[21]

The private life of the staff member is also covered.

In principle, the private life of the international staff member is his concern and should not be intruded upon by his organization. At the same time, in order that his private life will not bring his organization into disfavor, he must set himself a high standard of personal conduct. . . . He must bear in mind that his conduct, whether connected or unconnected with official duties, must be such that it will not infringe upon any demonstrable interests of the organization he serves, bring it into discredit, or offend the community in which he lives. Such restraint must be exercised even in the use of rights recognized by existing legislation if this use is likely to reflect unfavorably upon the organization. Not only must the international civil servant be careful and discreet himself, but he should impress upon members of his household the necessity of maintaining a similar high standard of conduct.[22]

Although the present analysis obviously favors individual self-realization over organizational claims, the writer does not accept the Freudian view that people are inevitably in conflict with society and its institutions. Social organizations, on the contrary, often enhance their freedom and opportunity. In this respect every social institution—the family, the church, the university, the union, and the corporation—has a Janus-like character. On the one hand, it encourages individual autonomy by inculcating the skills and values necessary for self-realization. On the other, it demands conformity with its ends and the

[18]Thorstein Veblen, *The Theory of the Leisure Class* (New York: Macmillan, 1953), p. 48.

[19]International Civil Service Advisory Board, *Report on Standards of Conduct in the International Civil Service* (New York: United Nations, 1954), p. 15.

[20]Ibid., p. 14.

[21]Ibid., p. 4.

[22]Ibid., p. 15.

means used to achieve them. Striking a balance between these claims has always been difficult. But today it seems that organizational demands often receive a higher priority than individual ones.

While affirming one's belief in individual autonomy is something like coming out in favor of an early spring, the fact remains that a vital measure of a democratic society is the respect and freedom it provides the individual. Today, however, organizations tend to view people instrumentally. Their acquisitive demands restrict individual discretion; they subordinate individual values and aspirations to their major purposes. They dispense great rewards, but these are always distributed in terms of collective values which the individual must accept if he is to compete for them. Administrators often try to reconcile the organization's interests with those of the individual, but they tend nevertheless to view human beings as instruments designed to achieve ends considered to be more important than those of any individual person. As a result, collective values become the bench mark for evaluating and rewarding the individual. Humans, in effect, are made for the organization. They may succeed and prosper within it, but the organization, reflecting in turn the dominant values of society, always defines the terms of success. Yet, given their dignity as human beings and their capacity for reason and discovery, people ought not to be viewed as instruments. As Dostoevsky insisted: "The whole purpose of man surely consists in proving to himself that he is a man and not a cog in a machine."

THE | 2
BUREAUCRATIC
MODEL

We now turn to a review of the structural characteristics of the typical organization. While organizations obviously differ in technology, product, age, and tradition, they are quite similar in form, procedure, and the claims they make upon their members for loyalty and consistency. Most of them have the following characteristics: large size, specialization, hierarchy, status anxiety, oligarchy (rule by the few), co-optation (selection of their own successors by organizational elites), "efficiency," and rationality. The bureaucratic model to be described here is an ideal type. It has no exact counterpart in the real world. However, although every organization may not exhibit all these characteristics, we can safely assume that most of them will. Such organizations provide a distinctive psychological climate in which authority, power, and status are nicely differentiated. As a result, behavioral expectations are clearly prescribed; interpersonal relations occur in a structured context. Ideally, there is very little ambiguity in bureaucratic settings.

Although all the characteristics of the bureaucratic model are mutually reinforcing, size is among its most significant features. "Size," of course, has many dimensions, including the organization's scale of operations, volume of work, extent of capital resources, number of clients or customers, and the geographical scope of its activities. However, since our interest is precisely in the influence of the organization upon its own members, we are concerned here with organizations in which the number of members is large enough to prohibit face-to-face relations among most participants.

Durkheim has shown that as societies increase in size, density, and urbanization, the division of labor increases rapidly. Like suicide, specialization is a function of increasing civilization. This is because the members of the undifferentiated society find themselves in too intense competition. They therefore turn to a division of labor which will permit each segment to pursue its own goals with a minimum of conflict. "The division of labor . . . is a result of the struggle for existence."[1] Showing that organisms "prosper more when they differ more," Darwin found 200 species of insects living upon one tree, some feeding upon its leaves, some upon its fruit, and others upon its bark and roots. "Men submit to the same law," Durkheim observed. "In the same city different occupations can coexist without being obliged to destroy each other, for they pursue different objects."[2]

Organizations reveal similar motives and degrees of specialization. Specialization was one of the main weapons of the scientific management movement in its drive for greater productivity in industrial organizations. To some extent man undoubtedly becomes more proficient as he confines himself to a given field or activity. The organization of university departments along disciplinary lines and the impetus this gives to the accumulation of knowledge is an example. Perhaps as recently as 100 years ago, a scholar was often competent in two or three fields. Francis Bacon's major role was that of lawyer, but his reputation rests in philosophy. Today, the sheer volume of knowledge and the complexity of civilization mean that the productive intellectual is almost always limited to a single discipline, and perhaps to only one of its major subfields.

As organizations grow larger, we may say with Durkheim that they necessitate a greater division of labor. This differentiation attracts and accommodates the different interests and abilities of individuals, enabling each to find his place. In sociology today, for example, one finds a bewildering variety of special fields, including the sociology of religion, politics, industry, women, blacks, deviance, medicine, law, elites, mass, the media, science, the military, society, conflict, consensus, and policy making. Each provides a niche for expertise, new journals, grants, and exclusive career avenues.

In economic systems specialization permits those displaced by mergers to continue as parts of the new combination. "The small employer becomes a foreman; the small merchant becomes an employee."[3] And, we may add, the farmer-owner becomes a skilled worker in a nearby city. As the highly developed role of specialists and middlemen in our economy attests, specialization permits the survival of a great number of individuals who in simpler societies "would be condemned to extinction."

[1]Emile Durkheim, *The Division of Labor in Society* (Glencoe, Ill.: Free Press, 1952), p. 270.

[2]Ibid., p. 267.

[3]Ibid., p. 269.

Some qualification of Durkheim's assumption that specialization is generally beneficial seems required. Within many organizations, there is an inherent tension between those in hierarchical positions of authority and those who play specialized roles. This tension may be conceptualized as a conflict over the legitimacy of the two bases of authority. The specialist deplores the fact that those in hierarchical roles have largely appropriated to themselves the definition and the accoutrements of success in our society. In the university, for example, the major rewards in prestige and income go to those in administrative (hierarchical) positions. The most eminent faculty members must usually become administrators if they are to secure larger shares of these values. In industrial and academic research organizations specialists must convince the administrator to secure the resources necessary to carry out their technical work. This is especially frustrating because it means that in allocating such resources authority based upon hierarchy takes precedence over authority based upon knowledge.

On the other hand, those in hierarchical positions often find the specialists difficult. Rarely can they be persuaded that their own department does not deserve the lion's share of the organization's resources. Their "trained incapacity" makes it difficult for them to see that the administrator's role is inevitably one of achieving compromise among competing units within the organization. The conflict is often one between the organization-wide view of the administrator and the restricted perspective of the specialist. Moreover, specialists disturb the equilibrium of the organization by fighting among themselves about resources and recognition. In large organizations such conflicts are less amenable to accommodation based upon personal association and friendship. Each department or division tends to become a world in itself. Indeed, there are political and professional sanctions against collaborating with the enemy, because the internal discipline and unity of each subunit becomes so important in its competitive success. In this sense, size and attending specialization can become pathological.

The dysfunctions of specialization have inspired many innovations in the recent past. These include restructuring of the production line in automobile plants, where the disenchantment of workers with the traditional pattern of highly differentiated task specialization has resulted in high absenteeism, turnover, and strike action. Here, the essential problem is not one of productivity or objective rationality, since the *process* itself is widely regarded as "efficient." The problem lies in its human by-products. Among the most thoughtful and widely publicized of such innovations is Volvo's Kalmar plan, which includes a basic redesigning of the plant itself, to introduce a system comprising a mobile "assembly group" including twenty-eight stations, each with work groups of fifteen to twenty people.[4] The object is to structure the work so that each group can feel that they have done a complete job, such as installing the electrical system or the motor. Cars are routed on carriers, computer controlled for speed, on which workers can, although this rarely occurs, ride along the subsequent stations in order to follow the fabrication process as it develops. Twelve cars per hour move along the line, permitting workers ten minutes rest per hour. The main object is to replace traditional job specialization with a holistic work milieu.

Rivalry among the companies introducing such innovations (including Saab and Renault) plus the public relations incentives behind the Volvo scheme, makes evaluation difficult. On the one hand, the costs of capital plant apparently run 10 to 30 percent higher than those for traditional plants, in part because more space is needed to accommodate the assembly group concept. On the other, the morale of workers is heightened by the very fact that management is concerned about the problems of monotony and resentment resulting from assembly line production. It is suggestive that a Detroit worker team that spent several weeks in the experimental plant, concluded that it preferred the traditional American system because such required less thought and concentration. One suspects that the introspective drift among Swedes, their concern with self-realization made possible by a generalized affluence, may explain this difference between American and Swedish workers in similar industries using very similar technologies.

The size of modern organizations brings related dysfunctions. We often find that as size increases morale decreases.[5] While the relationship is less consistent, lower productivity and absenteeism are also positively associated with organizational size. This is apparently because members find it difficult to identify with the sheer number of people found in the typical organization. While small-group membership eases this problem, it does not necessarily improve the individual's rapport with the larger organization. Individuals tend to feel unimportant and somewhat alienated by its size, anonymity, and power. The pecuniary nexus between the organization and the individual may contribute to this self-perception. In mass-production industry, the highly rationalized work process encourages estrange-

[4]*Economist,* December 25, 1976, pp. 68–69.

[5]James C. Worthy, "Organizational Structure and Employee Morale," *American Sociological Review,* Vol. 15, p. 173; R. Marriott, "Size of Working Group and Output," *Occupational Psychology,* Vol. 23, pp. 47–57; David Hewitt and Jessie Parfit, "A Note on Working Morale and Size of Group," *Occupational Psychology,* Vol. 27, pp. 38–42.

ment by reducing the skill demands of the job. Such attitudes toward the organization, which are characteristic of the "indifferent" type, will be more fully developed in chapter 7. There is also considerable evidence that size contributes to hierarchy.

Hierarchy may be defined as a system for ranking positions along a descending scale from the top to the bottom of the organization. Ordinarily hierarchy refers to "line" relationships rather than to those among "staff" specialists who presumably do not give orders. Although this distinction may become tenuous because of the influence of specialists, certainly the main decisions in organizations are made by line officials. Hierarchy, which is as old as history, is of religious origin where it referred to the ranking of the officialdom set up to administer religious values.[6] As Weber shows, the change from charismatic authority, based upon revelation or magic, to bureaucratic authority, occurred in both religion and politics. This "routinization of charisma" brought rules and officials to administer them. The discretion of each official was necessarily limited, however, and the power he exercised was not personal but legal. Therefore, "a hierarchy of superiors, to which officials may appeal and complain in an order of rank, stands opposite the citizen or member of the association. . . . This situation also holds for the hierocratic association that is the church."[7] Hierarchy, then, is the result of the separation of personal, charismatic authority from official authority.

Nevertheless, as Victor Thompson finds, charismatic authority remains strong in modern organizations.[8] This is because hierarchy and the prestige attaching to it are often more easily maintained when a person's roles are not clearly defined. This ambiguity is one of the essential differences between hierarchical and specialist roles. It is well known that the farther away one is from those in high organizational posts the greater the tendency to hold them in awe, to attribute to them charismatic or magical powers. Hierarchical differences in authority, power, and income reinforce this perception. The higher one ascends in the hierarchy the more one's activities become differentiated and unamenable to precise evaluation. Contrast this situation with the role of the specialist who is assigned responsibility for a

---

[6]Max Weber, "Bureaucracy," in Hans Gerth and C. Wright Mills, eds., *From Max Weber* (New York: Oxford University Press, 1946), p. 282. Both Weber's conception of ideal types and the historical evolution of organizations from "charismatic" to "bureaucratic" bases of operation may have been influenced by Ferdinand Tonnies, whose earlier (1887) work contained both concepts, *Community and Association,* trans. C. P. Loomis (London: Routledge and Kegan Paul, Ltd., 1955).

[7]Weber, "Bureaucracy," p. 295.

[8]Victor Thompson, *Modern Organization* (New York: Alfred A. Knopf, 1961), pp. 493–497.

given functional task. Communication barriers between elite and rank and file aggravate this condition. In sum, the deference accorded those in major hierarchical positions is highly charged with charismatic implications. Such deference validates the individuals' need to impute superiority to those above them. It also honors the American creed which holds that there are significant differences in ability between those who succeed and those who do not.

Hierarchy is perhaps best illustrated by military organization. Ranks and authority are nicely graded from the top to the bottom of the organization. Ideally, this apparatus provides a chain of command extending throughout the entire system, in which each person from commanding general to buck private is under the control of the man immediately above him. At the same time he is himself the supervisor of the person directly below him in the hierarchy. It is not only positions that are ranked in terms of authority, but relative amounts of authority, status, deference, income, and other perquisites of office are ascribed to each position. Such perquisites are allocated disproportionately. They tend to cluster near the top and to decrease rapidly as one descends the hierarchy. This inequitable distribution of scarce values is characteristic of all big organizations; it provides a built-in condition of inequality and invidious differentiation. Hierarchical monopoly of the allocative systems augments the power of those at the top since rewards can be assigned so as to reinforce elite definitions of "loyalty," "competence," and so on. A related objective of this inequality is to reinforce the organization's status system, which in turn reinforces the authority and legitimacy of its leaders. Such consequences of the bureaucratic situation will be considered in chapter 5.

Hierarchy gives those at the top control of the formal communication system whose channels follow hierarchical lines. Since information is obviously a prerequisite for participation, this control enables the elite to manipulate both the issues and those who help resolve them. Hierarchy permits elites to determine what kind of issues will be raised for organizational consideration. Potential solutions can be delimited by hierarchical control of meetings. By proposing only a few alternatives and by indicating their preference among them, formal leaders can exercise disproportionate influence. The conditions of individual participation, that is to say, are always affected by hierarchy. Often, the places that individuals take around a conference table are an accurate index of their rank and status in the organization. The ensuing discussion tends to follow such rankings, with senior members dominating. As in other contexts, the weight attched to propositions is often a function of the formal status of their originator. The informal groups that appear in organizations are similarly structured by the relative influence, skill, seniority, and conviviality of their members.

Perhaps the main function of hierarchy is to assign and to validate authority along a descending scale throughout the organization. The resulting allocations surely constitute the basic authority structure of the organization. However, any discussion of authority in organizations must recognize that there are several bases for legitimating it. The whole burden of this book is upon the generalized deference to authority of many kinds that characterizes most individuals. We have seen that hierarchical authority has charismatic elements. But the greatest deviation from the hierarchical system of dominance is the authority that specialists enjoy by virtue of their technical skill and training. The steady accumulation of knowledge which characterizes modern Western society underlies this development. New skill groups arise and demand recognition of their expertise; a self-consciousness born of knowledge, introversion, and the desire to control the market for their skills brings professionalization. Soon specialists attempt to redefine the conditions of organizational participation. While hierarchical elites insist that the question of "what should be done" remains their prerogative, specialists insist that they are entitled to a larger role in substantive policy. Knowledge, in a word, challenges hierarchical legitimations of authority and role.

The resulting competition often leads to considerable legerdemain whereby mock recognition is given to line authority when in fact a decision has been made by specialists. Such fictions permit the traditional image of hierarchical supremacy to remain unchallenged by the relentless advance of scientific knowledge. Perhaps the best current example is the management of federal atomic weapons and missile research by high-ranking military officers whose experience has been restricted to the command of an army division or a ship. Equally germane is the experience in federal research funding in which Congressmen gave carte blanche to the leaders of the physical science community between 1940 and 1970, with some untoward consequences for balanced programs of teaching and research in America's major universities.[9]

The legitimation of authority by rapport or personal empathy has also become critical in organizations. This development has come about in part as a result of human relations techniques, which rest upon deep-seated individual needs for friendship and recognition. Moreover, as bureaucratic conditions of work become more common and more standardized, the primary distinctions among white-collar

---

[9]See Daniel S. Greenberg, *The Politics of Pure Science* (New York: New American Library, 1967)

jobs often include such subjective factors as sympathetic work relations. In this way the interpersonal skill and the work climate provided by organizational leaders and supervisors become a basis for individual acceptance of their authority. One suspects that the effects of this condition vary according to the degree of identification with one's substantive role. Research also shows that both the amount of influence that leaders exert and the amount they attempt to exert increase with group acceptance of them as people.[10] There is some evidence, moreover, that executives rarely fail because of lack of substantive knowledge; inadequate personal relations are more often the cause.

Despite the challenges of expertise and emotion, hierarchy remains a critical basis of organizational authority. From the human side, hierarchy is a graded system of interpersonal relationships, a society of unequals in which scarce values become even scarcer as one descends the hierarchy. Some tension inevitably results since freedom, rewards, and influence are unequally shared by those in the organization. This condition is aggravated because the career chances of any given individual rest in the hand of his or her immediate superior. This provides serious obstacles for those at lower ranks in the form of the innumerable veto barriers which requests for rewards or promotion must penetrate. Not only can the request be denied at any level, but if such requests are negated some distance up the hierarchy, those concerned may never learn the reasons for the veto nor at what point it occurred. This built-in veto power tends to increase the common feelings of remoteness and powerlessness among members of organizations.

Hierarchy has other functions. By delegating authority to the point where the skill necessary to carry out tasks resides, hierarchy may link authority with skill. By monopolizing the allocative system, elites increase their control of those in the organization. Individuals in organizations therefore tend to exhibit an "upward-looking" posture and a certain anxiety. When this atmosphere is set against democratic values of individual autonomy and self-realization, considerable tension may result. A serious operational dysfunction may occur as individuals, forced to choose between initiative and risk on the one hand and clearance and safety on the other, tend to choose the latter. They resist delegation. Those in higher positions are also reluctant to delegate because this makes them responsible for the potential errors of others. Such resistance is explained by the organization's drive to increase control, but since control is achieved only by limiting delegation, the organization tends to slow down. This unanticipated conse-

[10]John R. P. French and Richard Snyder, "Leadership and Interpersonal Power," in Dorwin Cartwright, ed., *Studies in Social Power* (Ann Arbor: University of Michigan Institute for Social Research, 1959), pp. 118–149.

quence refutes the claim that power must be centralized if big organizations are to act expeditiously: the gap between those who make decisions and those who carry them out remains.

Closely articulated with hierarchy in organizations is the status system. Status refers to the allocation of different amounts of authority, income, deference, rights, and privileges to the various positions in the hierarchy. Prestige is the deference attached to each position, and generally it follows hierarchy. The largest amounts of deference are assigned to those at the top of the hierarchy, and the relative amounts decrease at a disproportionate rate as one descends. Ideally, both status and prestige are accurate indexes of a person's contributions to the organization. As we have seen, however, the existing system of distribution insures that those in hierarchical "line" positions receive disproportionate rewards in comparison with those in specialist roles. The status system's functional consequences include concrete recognition of individual worth and achievement. Its dysfunctions include invidious comparisons of individual contributions, comparisons which are not always objectively based. Perhaps its main operational consequence is to reinforce the authority of those at each hierarchical level in the organization.

We can now consider the social and psychological bases of status. It seems clear that the current emphasis upon status symbols reflects a change from an economy of scarcity to one which Veblen called "conspicuous consumption." But conspicuous consumption is difficult today in America because mass production has made the symbols of material success available on so large a scale. The resulting disenchantment of elites is patent in the Middle East where the range of material benefits is being slowly extended through industrialization and inflation. Elites feel deprived as a result of the loss of indexes that once differentiated them from the masses. In the United States the decline of such psychic income means that status aspirations will be shifted to other areas, and that subtle, nonmaterial distinctions will become more highly valued since they are more difficult to establish. The importance of power and personal influence in society seems in fact to nourish a neurotic drive for any symbol that will enhance one's status. This drive, however, must not be dismissed as a search for mere invidious distinction. It reflects deeper needs for the recognition of one's personal worth in a society where organization and technical imperatives increasingly depict people in an instrumental role. Challenging such depersonalization becomes an incentive for status differentiation.

The social anatomy of status also suggests that its symbols become a substitute for values no longer attainable. The difficulty of achieving independence through owning one's business, a difficulty which reflects the trend toward bigness and concentration; the employment of the "independent" professions on a bureaucratic, salaried basis; the devaluation of the term "professional"—all seem conducive to increased status anxiety and striving. In a larger context, the whole trend toward hyperorganization is involved, in the sense that size and anonymity result in sustained attempts by the individual to preserve status in compensation for the loss of autonomy. C. Wright Mills speaks of the "status panic" that characterizes life in the white-collar world.

Also related is the mock "professionalization" of ordinary jobs through increased educational requirements. Ludicrous efforts to borrow prestige by substituting status-laden titles for socially devalued jobs: "news analyst" for reporter; "mortician" for undertaker; the crisp term "executive," (for example, "sales executive" for salesperson); the title "engineer" for all sorts of routine jobs; the co-optation of the honored symbol, "professional"—all suggest the effort to achieve status by word magic. In a deeper sense this trend may reflect decreased occupational mobility. If one cannot asscend the ladder as easily as before, why not enhance the status of that which is obtainable?

The American assumption of upward mobility generation by generation (often based upon empirical experience) is thus related to status idealization. A comparison with class-bound European and Middle Eastern societies suggests that sheer age, the maturing of the economy and declining personal autonomy in the United States will increase status consciousness, and that a greater emphasis will come to be placed upon artificial, bureaucratic distinctions as more objective claims to status become more difficult to achieve. A free and easy democracy requires a unique social and economic situation with relatively equal access to abundant natural resources. The organizational society checkmates this situation as the strategies of power are learned by many groups and as their countervailing power results in a rough equilibrium between major social interests. In this milieu, big organizations naturally turn to subtle status rewards as compensation for economic and personal dependence and limited mobility. The honoring of seniority is an obvious example. The small gap between initial and upper-level incomes in the bureaucratized professions further encourages the use of psychic rewards such as graduated ranks, titles, name plates, and "atmosphere."

Members are clearly differentiated according to their role and status. Types of sanction, forms of communication, dress, and conduct in off-work activities are often determined by one's position in the organizational hierarchy. As a rule those who deal with the public enjoy exceptional status reinforcements, including large, well-appointed offices, expense accounts (and hence greater social mobility), more staff and secretarial assistance, and those mechanical and human props that formalize access, create an impression of preoccupation with important matters, and encourage attitudes of deference. Such behavioral consequences of the status system will be considered in detail in chapter 5 under the psychological aspects of organizations.

The assignment of authority, legitimacy, and status along hierarchical lines means that the conditions of participation in formal organizations are determined by a minority. This characteristic of the bureaucratic model may be called oligarchy, which means "rule by the few." Although oligarchy has usually meant rule by the wealthy, modern oligarchs are often salaried employees whose status and power are based upon their control, not their ownership of great organizational resources. Although the power of such elites is limited in their external relations by the power of similar minorities elsewhere, our main concern is with the internal aspects of organizations where oligarchy seems relatively unrestrained. This is not to say oligarchy is inevitable, but merely that it is a highly probable feature of large organizations.

One must qualify the oligarchic generalization in other ways. Constraints against oligarchy vary from one kind of organization to another. From casual observation we may assume that the tendency toward oligarchy is probably greater in industrial organizations than in political ones. The constituencies (the potential opposition) in the industrial context are relatively limited in number and interest, in contrast to political organizations which usually include members representing a variety of interests. Such members, moreover, have at their disposal critical sanctions, such as the failure to vote for the party in question or to provide the funds or volunteer efforts necessary to keep the association solvent. Again, in a broad social context, the extent of oligarchy will vary with the degree of literacy and participation existing among members of the community. The skills and interests required for true bargaining between leaders and led vary considerably across different societies. Oligarchy, as a result, will be more probable in underdeveloped societies where political and organizational skills are the monopoly of relatively limited groups. There, in Pareto's phrase, the "circulation of elites" occurs within a small group. In Western society, on the other hand, relatively high literacy rates and greater participation in a larger number of associations mean that the skills which make oligarchy possible are more widely distributed. As a result, its effects are somewhat modulated.

It is always necessary to add that while "oligarchy" means the power of the few over the many, this does not mean that the majority is powerless. Even Machiavelli's Prince was admonished to have due regard for popular myths. The important point is that such power is unequal. The concept of power assumes reciprocity, but there is always a difference between the power of one actor and another. Obviously all elites are to some extent limited by their assumptions about mass reactions to their policies, but an oligarchy is characterized by the *preponderance of power* it enjoys. Oligarchy, then, assumes inequality of power, nothing more.

Oligarchy is apparent in the fact that decisions in big organizations are usually made by a minority. When organizations become large, communication is difficult, and the power of decision tends to be restricted to a few leaders. Some elites enhance their power by concealing information; but in any event the problems of disseminating information and of providing for widespread participation present almost insuperable obstacles. The pressure of demands for quick decisions often makes consultation impracticable. The highly technical character of many decisions tends furthermore to limit participation to those who have the requisite skills and knowledge—this despite the fact that the ramifications of the decision may extend throughout the organization. Thus the intensity of oligarchy probably increases in some sort of geometric ratio to organizational size. We know, for example, that the atomization of corporate stock ownership encourages oligarchy. The more dispersed the stockholders become, the greater the power of the controlling minority. And it is usually control, not ownership, that counts in modern organizations.

Robert Michels, the most authoritative student of oligarchy, found that it was characteristic of large organizations rather than of all.[11] In his view, organizations become oligarchic for technical and psychological reasons. The sheer number of members prohibits communication; and the resulting ignorance and inertia encourage direction by the few. Meanwhile, innovation and the claims of specialists increase the tendency toward oligarchy, because new skill groups gain

[11]Robert Michels, *Political Parties* (Glencoe, Ill.: Free Press, 1949). Almost a half century after Michels wrote, Charles P. Snow found oligarchy to be similarly characteristic of organizational life: "One of the most bizarre features of any advanced industrial society in our time is that the cardinal choices have to be made by a handful of men: in secret: and, at least in legal form, by men who cannot have a first-hand knowledge of what those choices depend upon or what their results may be. . . . And when I say the 'cardinal choices,' I mean those which determine in the crudest sense whether we live or die. For instance, the choice in England and the United States in 1940 and 1941, to go ahead with work on the fission bomb: the choice in 1945 to use that bomb when it was made: the choice in the United States and the Soviet Union, in the late forties, to make the fusion bomb: the choice, which led to a different result in the United States and the Soviet Union, about intercontinental missles." *Science and Government* (Cambridge: Harvard University Press, 1960), p. 1. The dynamics of oligarchy are dramatically apparent in the experience of the Russian Communist party, which before 1917 functioned with a large central committee. Once the revolution was successful, however, the need for control, action, and dispatch thrust power into pitifully few hands. As Barrington Moore says: "Just before the November Revolution on October 23, 1917, a small nucleus was created with the Party Central Committee at the suggestion of Dzerzhinsky, later chief of the secret police. The original members were

access to strategic points in the hierarchy and acquire an impetus to rule. Public relations people, for example, are apparently among the top policymakers in many organizations. Thus size, numbers, and the need for expertise are among the technical reasons for minority control.

These "causes" of oligarchy are reinforced by psychological factors, including the desire for power encouraged by the dominant values of our society. Although oligarchy is often justified by the need for control and the pressure for action it also reflects individual drives for power. The fulfillment of this drive is sometimes encouraged, furthermore, by the "true believer's" need for some omnipotent leader or myth. Subordinates may need the person of power to displace the burden of individual responsibility and to receive in return the benefits of certainty. Although its psychic nuances cannot be treated here, a significant by-product of oligarchy must be mentioned: the selective process in organizations tends to bring the power seeker to the top. Moreover, power and its dividends increase as one ascends the hierarchy. A fusion of psychology and personality often follows. While the logic and rewards of organization encourage the drive for power, its criteria of selection ensure that those who rise possess an exceptional urge to dominate. The implications for responsibility are sharpened by Michels' conclusion that control of any elite can come only from outside the organization. Max Weber, too, it may be recalled, insisted that only charismatic political leaders could galvanize modern bureaucracies into new directions.[12]

Michels developed his "iron law of oligarchy" by observing socialist political parties in Western Europe. Despite their lip service to equality, he found them oligarchic in operation. Power was centered in a core of permanent officials who typically made policy and presented it full-blown to the members for ratification. It is similarly ironic that organizations in the United States also exist in a democratic context and employ a liberal rhetoric, but are often nevertheless

---

Lenin, Zinoviev, Kamenev, Trotsky, Stalin, Sokol'nikov and Bubnov. The main task envisaged at this time appears to have been little more than the management of the details of the November uprising. Nevertheless, the idea of concentrating decision-making powers in the hands of a very few leaders persisted, owing to the continuing need for immediate and far-reaching decisions in the crises directly following the Revolution. By March 1919 the Eighth Party Congress set up, as a permanently acting body, a Political Bureau consisting of five members, who were 'to decide on questions which do not permit delay,' and to report bimonthly on all its work to a regular plenary session of the Central Committee. At that time the Politburo consisted of Lenin, Trotsky, Stalin, Kamenev and Bukharin. At no time during the period from 1919 to 1946 did the membership of the Politburo, including candidates, exceed seventeen individuals . . . its functions covered almost the entire scope of political, economic, social and cultural problems in Soviet life." *Soviet Politics: The Dilemma of Power* (Cambridge: Harvard University Press, 1950), p. 141.

[12]Max Weber, *The Theory of Social and Economic Organization* (New York: Free Press, 1947), pp. 360–362.

oligarchic. This is not only confusing but also somewhat inhibiting insofar as analysis is concerned. The problem of power is often ignored as an uncomfortable aberration. As a result, one must often cut through a haze of cheerful rationalizations concerning manifest power disequilibria. One such rationalization is the notion that authority in organizations is essentially a matter of consent, depending upon the acceptance of those who are subject to it.[13] This view must be qualified, however, mainly because it fails to ask *why* authority is accepted. When the question of learned deference to authority is raised, the motives for "acceptance" become clearer.

Obviously, individuals "accept" authority for many reasons and many possible reactions exist, ranging from eager cooperation to reluctant obedience. Confronted with an order, average individuals will estimate the consequences of various alternatives and adopt the one that seems in their own interest, insofar as they are able to identify it. In this restricted sense authority is no doubt "accepted," but to suggest, as this thesis does, that it is commonly within the individual's range of discretion either to accept or to reject is misleading. Rejection is usually impractical. Moreover, such a view fails to recognize the propensity to obey induced by socialization and by hierarchy, both of which tend to institutionalize obedience and to redefine "acceptance" by creating an expectation of compliance.

Floyd Hunter's study of power in Atlanta, Georgia, suggests the locus and the tactics of oligarchy.[14] While Atlanta may be unique, and while some recent research raises questions about elitist assumptions of community power structure, this remains an impressive study. He found a weblike pattern of power and influence ultimately residing in a half dozen members of an old-family elite. Viewed from the outside, power appeared to be more widely diffused, since many of its agents were obviously not members of the inner circle. But this illusion reflected the need to organize and to delegate power, particularly the need for a means of enlisting the energies and great expectations of those at the periphery. The vital decision to act or not to act remained in the inner circle although the responsibility for organizing, articulating, and carrying it through was necessarily shared with others. The latter exercised influence, it is true, but theirs was a borrowed, temporary influence. In effect, this group administered the power of the industrial, banking, legal, and social elite, and enjoyed the façade of power that such participation gave them.

[13]Chester I. Barnard, *Functions of the Executive* (Cambridge: Harvard University Press, 1938).

[14]Floyd Hunter, *Community Power Structure* (Chapel Hill: University of North Carolina Press, 1953); on oligarchy, see also Robert and Helen Lynd, *Middletown*, rev. ed. (New York: Harcourt, Brace & Co., 1959); and Frank A. Stewart, "A Sociometric Study of Influence in Southtown," *Sociometry*, vol. 10, pp. 11–31, 273–286.

The structure of oligarchy thus consisted of an inner elite supported by an aspiring, co-opted outer circle which dealt with an apathetic ratifying majority. Although the inner elite remained behind the scenes, reaching policy decisions at informal meetings, respondents were apparently able to differentiate nicely between the "real" power holders and the contenders at various levels. Hunter found (as Agger, Goldrich, and Swanson, the Lynds, Warner, Hollingshead, Vidich and Bensman, and Baltzell had found)[15] that the elite influenced various kinds of decisions and was relatively homogeneous, since the wealth, social position, and organizing skills of the minority were similar. While an outsider might occasionally be co-opted, usually through a romantic or a pecuniary nexus, admission to this circle was extremely limited. I found a similar tendency toward elite domination in a study of two communities in New York, where a socially advantaged group, constituting about 1 percent of all adults played an active role in ten major local issues.[16]

A similar tendency toward oligarchy is visible in most large groups, regardless of their function and ideology. In Congress, for example, party control is much stronger in the House of Representatives than in the Senate, in part because the House is five times as large. Within Congress the selection and the influence of committees encourage government by minority. As one observer concludes:

> Congressional Committees have lacked any definite responsibility. Their control over legislation submitted to them has been almost unlimited. They can amend or rewrite bills to suit themselves. They can report bills or pigeonhole them. They can initiate measures they desire and bury or emasculate those they dislike. . . . In short, congressional government is government by the standing committees of Congress.[17]

Perhaps the most powerful of such committees is the House Rules Committee which mainly determines the form and content of legislation that reaches the floor of the House. Here again, the size variable is critical, for it is generally agreed that in the Senate, only one-fifth as large, committees are less powerful and legislation coming from them

[15]See, respectively, Robert Agger, Daniel Goldrich, and Bert Swanson, *The Rulers and the Ruled* (New York: Wiley, 1964); Robert and Helen Lynd, *Middletown in Transition* (New York: Harcourt, Brace & Co., 1937); W. Floyd Warner, *Yankee City*, abr. ed. (New Haven: Yale University Press, 1963); August B. Hollingshead, *Elmstown's Youth* (New York: Wiley, 1949); Arthur J. Vidich and Joseph Bensman, *Small Town in Mass Society* (Princeton: Princeton University Press, 1961); E. Digby Baltzell, *Philadelphia Gentlemen* (Glencoe, Ill.: Free Press, 1958).

[16]Robert Presthus, *Men at the Top: A Study in Community Power* (New York: Oxford University Press, 1964).

[17]George B. Galloway, *Congress at the Crossroads* (New York: Thomas Y. Crowell, 1946), p. 184.

is subject to a much more incisive scrutiny. An example of the oligarchic power enjoyed by the Rules Committee is its handling of the school-aid bill during the Kennedy regime.[18] The 1977 House pay raise increasing salaries from $44,600 to $57,500, plus a variety of fringe benefits including an annual staff allowance of $255,144, did include a limitation on outside income, but as *Time* magazine reported, public opinion was greatly disenchanted, especially by the method of pushing the raise through which enabled members to avoid a vote on the controversial issue.[19]

Although the locus of their power is state and local rather than national, our political parties are similarly controlled by a professional minority.[20] Even a casual appraisal of the preliminary tactics of presidential nominating conventions reveals the power of the active minority. As Erwin D. Canham says, "Party organization, county, state, and national committees, should be made less oligarchical." But here again the majority plays its traditional role, namely, the ratification of choices made by others.[21]

Similar behaviors appear in academic and professional associations, in labor unions, corporations, and universities. The "causes" are the same: the need for the organizing skills of permanent officials; the development of bureaucratic systems of leadership, before which the unorganized majority is virtually powerless; and the size and specialization of contemporary groups, reflecting modern innovations in political tactics and communication. The desire for power and the discipline of those who hope to rise, as well as the apathy or disenchantment of the majority, are also at work.

The post-Watergate reaction has almost certainly brought an unprecedented degree of alienation among American citizens, only 54

---

[18]See the *New York Times* summary (September 28, 1961, p. 32) of President Kennedy's difficulties during the first session of the Eighty-seventh Congress, in which "most of the Administration's major setbacks came in House committees, several of which . . . bottled up a number of high-priority Administration bills and drastically modified some others." Then follows an account of the Rules Committee's part in the defeat of the school-aid bill.

[19]*Time*, March 14, 1977, pp. 12–13.

[20]On the character of party organization, Maurice Duverger concludes: "the organization of political parties is certainly not in conformity with the orthodox notions of democracy. Their internal structure is essentially oligarchic; their leaders are not really appointed by the members, in spite of appearances, but co-opted or nominated by the central body. They tend to form a ruling class, isolated from the militants, a caste that is more or less exclusive. In so far as they are elected, the party oligarchy is widened without ever becoming a democracy." *Political Parties: Their Organization and Activity in the Modern State* (London: Methuen and Co., 1954), p. 422. See also Moisei A. Ostrogorski, *Democracy and the Organization of Political Parties*, vol. 2 (New York: The Macmillan Co., 1902), chs. 6, 7.

[21]Even so sympathetic an observer of the American scene as Denis W. Brogan states:

percent of whom voted in the 1976 presidential election. Polls reveal considerable popular disenchantment with the political system and particularly, the integrity of those who are elected to Congress.[22] Despite the indictment (augmented by a number of forced resignations) of fourteen of its members (1972–1976), Congress resisted new legislation that would eliminate one flagrant source of conflicts of interest: the maintenance of law practices while serving in office.[23] Meanwhile, high-level appointees to federal regulatory agencies, such as the Interstate Commerce Commission and the Federal Trade Commission, came under attack by a study group, commissioned by a joint House-Senate Committee which found considerable evidence of conflicts of interest. More than half of all appointees to nine of the Commissions came from the industries they were named to regulate.[24]

The role of co-optation in enhancing organizational discipline and continuity must also be emphasized. Co-optation is the process by which those in power designate their successors. This prerogative is part of the monopoly of scarce values that hierarchy assigns to the organization's elite. Since their successors are chosen by existing elites, it can be assumed that they will personify traditional values. In this way sanctioned behaviors and expectations are transmitted through agents selected after what tends to be, given the remarkable tenure of oligarchs, a lengthy apprenticeship. As Arthur Stinchcombe writes:

> Such a feeling of awe, wonder, and worship toward powerful people—Tsars, millionaires, geniuses, stars, or bosses—tends to make them into models or ego-ideals which children, adolescents, and schizophrenics model themselves after. . . . Power makes a man extraordinary and people imitate extraordinary men, thus regenerating institutions over the generations. By selection, socialization, controlling conditions of incumbency, and hero wor-

"The basic defect of the Convention system is the imperfect representative character of the assembly. The delegates represent at least as much the wishes of the political leaders, pressure groups, city, county, and state 'machines' as they represent the wishes of the rank and file voters." *Politics in America* (New York: Harper and Brothers, 1954), p. 220. One may recall too Bryce's conclusion as to why great men are so rarely chosen president which rests in part upon this facet of our political system, i.e., "the method of choice does not bring them to the top." *The American Commonwealth*, Vol. 1 (New York: Macmillan Co., 1907), p. 84, pp. 78–85 passim. For detailed analyses of presidential nominating politics, see Judith H. Parris, *The Convention Problem: Issues in Reform of Presidential Nominating Procedures* (Washington, D.C.: Brookings, 1972).

[22]Cf. Nathaniel Beck and John Pierce, "Political Involvement and Party Allegiances in Canada and the United States," in Presthus, ed., *Cross-National Perspectives: United States and Canada* (Leiden: E. J. Brill, 1977), pp. 23–43; Roy S. Bryce-Laporte and Claudewell S. Thomas, eds., *Alienation in Contemporary Society* (New York: Praeger, 1976).

[23]*New York Times*, November 7, 1975, p. 3.

[24]*New York Times*, ibid., p. 14.

ship, succeeding generations of power-holders tend to regenerate the same institutions.[25]

Meanwhile, the impact of co-optation extends beyond those immediately affected. Each promotion provides an opportunity to dramatize the terms under which rewards are allocated. The indexes of success are reaffirmed, and the upward-mobiles receive another impetus to rise. For various reasons, including the search for internal unity and discipline, loyalty seems to have become the main basis for bureaucratic succession. Like seniority, loyalty enjoys the advantage of wide acceptance, for it is a quality almost everyone can aspire to.

Oligarchy and co-optation are apparent in union leadership, which becomes a sinecure despite periodic elections and an emphasis upon democratic values. Samuel Gompers served a thirty-eight-year term as president of the American Federation of Labor. After his death in 1924 the reins were held by William Green for almost three decades. Daniel Tobin led the Teamsters for virtually half a century; Hutcheson led the Carpenters for thirty-five years and, upon retirement, was succeeded by his son. John L. Lewis was president of the United Mine Workers for over forty years. George Meany has been president of the AFL-CIO since its inception. Such tenures and the resulting control of policy make possible tremendous concentrations of power. As Kermit Eby has said:

> The modern trade union, like the modern corporation, is monolithic; one huge human shaft of power directed from the top. Its conventions are attended by professionals—"pork choppers"— whose present and future security depends on the maintenance of the power hierarchy. Decisions which affect the rank-and-file worker are increasingly removed from his hands in both time and space. The decisions which must be made are technically so complicated that only the expert or the leaders advised by the expert are competent to make them.[26]

Oligarchy as an "organic necessity" is the result of technical demands for internal direction, unity and consistency, control of market conditions, leadership skills, public relations, and lobbying. It is often rendered necessary, in short, by the need for someone to give coherence and continuity to the vague, often conflicting aspirations of the majority. Given the role of unanticipated consequences in human affairs, the implications of oligarchy may come as a shock to those who exercise it, assuming that such considerations ever arise. Doubts,

---

[25]Arthur Stinchcombe, *Constructing Social Theories* (New York: Harcourt, Brace and World, 1968), p. 111.
[26]Kermit Eby, "The 'Drip' Theory in Labor Unions," *Antioch Review*, Vol. 13, pp. 95–96.

however, are probably resolved by the assumptions of infallibility that characterize most oligarchs—self-images which are nourished by their isolation and power.

Power to initiate, to communicate, to reward, to sanction, to shape public opinion—these are the prerogatives and tactics of oligarchy. As a result, policy and orders flow from the top downward, limiting the rank and file to an essentially passive role. Having neither the power of initiation, which permits the oligarchy to decide what shall be done and when, nor of choosing the avenues of consultation, which can be used to ensure favorable reactions to their policies, nor the control of patronage, which ensures discipline, the majority can only ratify. When such actions sharply violate their expectations, the mass may exercise a veto power, but such contingencies seem remote since they occur only if the minority loses the tactical skill that brought it to power in the first place.

In democratic societies the tendency toward oligarchy stands out most sharply in crises, when the use of arbitrary methods for democratic ends becomes acceptable. An obvious example is the way in which military and security imperatives are accepted during wartime. Most of us regard such invasions as a temporary inconvenience, a necessary tribute to national survival. Similarly, during wartime certain individuals shelve ideals which previously had seemed irreducible.

As is well known, the cold war ethos and the Vietnam conflict were designed and administered by men whose personal lives and integrity seemed impeccable. Indeed, they were the "best and the brightest."[27] Yet, they assumed decisive roles in a tragic misadventure that ultimately deceived those who made the major sacrifices, wasted the lives of some 60,000 young Americans and billions of dollars in a tragic and demoralizing war. Its architects included not only military strategists such as General Maxwell Taylor, but Ivy League academics such as Walt Rostow, Arthur Schlesinger, Jr., McGeorge Bundy, and Henry Kissinger, who rationalized the United States' political and military position. A host of unknown intellectuals, housed in government agencies such as the Rand Corporation and the Stanford Research Institute provided the strategical back-up for political and military leaders, designing schemes such as the "pacification" program whose irrationality was matched only by the euphemistic terminology used to characterize them. Their physical remoteness and intellectual detachment from the tragic consequences of their decisions made it possible for men raised in a liberal-democratic political culture to adopt such destructive and ultimately cynical means. At its

[27]Among others, see David Halberstam, *The Best and the Brightest* (New York: Random House, 1972); John C. Donovan, *The Cold Warriors; a Policy-making Elite* (Lexington, Mass.: Heath, 1974).

worst, organizational logic encourages such collectively irresponsible behavior.

Hierarchy and oligarchy seek rationality, another common structural characteristic of large-scale organization.[28] Rationality may be defined as the capacity (or at least the search) for objective, intelligent action. It is usually characterized by a patent behavioral nexus between ends and means. While rationality is always limited by human error, inadequate information, and chance, within these limits the rational person applies intelligence, experience, and technical skills to solve his problems. In an ideal-typical organization, rationality is sought by organizing and directing its many parts so that each contributes to the whole product. Specialization, careful recruitment, job analysis, and planning are among the obvious means to this end.

Rationality, of course, is a complex and elusive goal. It is necessary to think of it as occurring at various levels and in various degrees. Just as even the most sophisticated engines produce some friction, so human organizations may function at considerably less than optimal levels. We may say, with Herbert Simon, that behavior is only "intendedly rational." Limitations of cognition, energy, information, experience, and time reduce our capacity for logical, goal-directed behavior. For such reasons, it seems useful to qualify individuals' rationality with such terms as "subjective" when they maximize desired values relative to their actual knowledge of the subject. It is thus possible, one may assume, for individuals to fail completely in some endeavor, yet to be deemed to have been subjectively rational, simply because their failure was the result of ignorance of some essential contingency. At the margins, of course, it is not difficult to make judgments about the rationality of individual and organizational behavior in given situations. An individual's behavior is "consciously rational" when means are knowingly articulated to ends. A particular decision may be called "objectively rational" if in fact it is the correct behavior for maximizing given values in a given situation.[29]

An organization may be conceptualized as a system for enhancing the probabilities that decisions will be rational. By bringing a collective, focused goal-orientation and its paraphernalia of technical and organizational instruments to bear, modern organizations probably enhance rationality considerably. It can be seen that both the indi-

---

[28]The following comments on rationality and specialization in organization are based mainly on Max Weber, *Theory of Social and Economic Organization* (Glencoe, Ill.: Free Press, 1957); Robert Merton, "Bureaucratic Structure and Personality," *Social Forces*, Vol. 17, pp. 560–568; Hans Gerth and C. Wright Mills, *From Max Weber*, pp. 115, 225.

[29]Herbert A. Simon, *Administrative Behavior*, 2nd ed. (New York: Macmillan, 1957), pp. 76–77.

viduals' rationality and their normative preferences may become subordinate in this perspective.[30]

It seems that society tends to produce individuals who possess its dominant characteristics. The intended rationality of the organization is similarly instilled in its members. Not only are its structure and procedures designed to enhance predictability, but individuals too become, insofar as possible, animated instruments. Individual discretion is limited by regulations and precedents that cover all anticipated events and such regulations tend to become ends in themselves. As a result, individuals try to find written authority for every action and to avoid action when such cannot be found. The ability to interpret rules and the search for authority to act (or not to act) become valued skills. Knowledge of the rules and how they can be bent gives individuals security and a share of organized power. They thus develop a vested interest in preserving the rules against change.

Rationality is also sought through the division of labor and through recruitment on a scientific basis. Job requirements, including both technical skill and emotional qualities, are determined by men selected for their ability to determine such qualifications. Ideally, at least, skill and character are matched with such specifications, ensuring that placement is as objective as possible. This rational distribution of human effort is reinforced by the fact that organization units are also set up on a specialized basis.

Even the specialists' isolation contributes to their skill because they find satisfaction in the complete mastery of their roles. Denied an understanding of the larger scheme, they magnify the limited insights and satisfactions that are within their grasp. They are, as it were, driven to this end. Objective, impersonal standards become all the more acquisitive because they are often unaware of their implications. They think everyone lives that way. One is reminded of the Prussian staff officer who spent a lifetime seeking ways to reduce mobilization time by one half-hour.

Another significant by-product occurs: the decision-making process becomes highly diffused, the product of a collective organizational mind. Organized irresponsibility follows. Decision making in the big organization becomes abstract and impersonal, the instrument of an anonymous, fragmented intelligence.[31] Each decision is the result of various technical and personal considerations, the sum of the contributions of everyone involved in the deciding process. This dif-

[30]H. T. Wilson, "Rationality and Decision in Administrative Science," *Canadian Journal of Political Science*, Vol. 6, pp. 271–294.

[31]This aspect of bureaucratic systems is compellingly portrayed in the novels of Franz Kafka, *The Castle* (New York: Alfred A. Knopf, 1941) and *The Trial* (New York: Alfred A. Knopf, 1957).

fusion means that "everyone" (that is, no one) is responsible. In extreme cases the condition may lead to arbitrary and immoral behavior, particularly when compounded by intense personal identification with some political ideology, the state, the party, the church, or the "organization." In every case, the probabilities that the organization may act unjustly are increased by the weakening of individual responsibility. Only "the system" is responsible.

The modern culmination of this system was seen in the Nazi apparatus. As Albert Camus describes it:

> The crime is handed down from chief to sub-chief until it reaches the slave who receives orders from above without being able to pass them on to anybody. One of the Dachau executioners weeps in prison and says, 'I only obeyed orders. The Führer and the Reichsführer, alone, planned all this and then they ran away. Gluecks received orders from Kaltenbrunner and, finally, I received orders to carry out the shootings. I have been left holding the bag because I was only a little Hauptscharführer and because I couldn't hand it on any lower down the line. Now they say that I am the assassin.'[32]

This suggests why organizations more often cause a crime of logic than one of passion, to use Camus's phrase.

Stereotypical procedures and attitudes are often necessary to handle the volume and diversity of activity in modern organizations. Methods for handling each type of problem are prescribed, with each specialist contributing to the decision on the basis of his or her encapsulated skill and jurisdiction. This overriding technical ethos increases the probability that personal factors will be minimized. Ideally, there is no way that such elements can affect the decision process. The specialists' loyalties are to the work process and to their own technical skill, rather than to any mitigating aspects of a case. As Weber shows, to do otherwise would evoke considerable anxiety, so strong are the demands of precedent and procedure.

The organization, in sum, is rationally planned to achieve its ends. Like the human organism, it has a directing center that transmits cues to the entire apparatus. Authority, rewards, and sanctions are allocated in ways that try to ensure that its members work together. As we have seen, hierarchy and oligarchy are perhaps the main instruments for so doing. The first assigns authority, responsibility, status, income, and deference in a descending scale from top to bottom, providing a chain of graded interpersonal relationships that mediates the delegation of all sanctioned impulses. Oligarchy makes its contribution by monopolizing power and the distribution of the organization's

[32] Albert Camus, *The Rebel* (New York: Random House, 1959), p. 182.

scarce values. People work for status, income, recognition, and security; oligarchy permits the organization's elite to determine the conditions under which such values are allocated.

All this is highly idealized, of course. Even the most careful research finds it impossible to sort out the effects of technology and structure upon organizational control, particularly at the individual level.[33] Informal centers of power compete with the elite for influence in determining how resources are to be distributed. Meanwhile, unanticipated consequences subvert the organization's formal goals. Individuals persist in giving their personal objectives priority over organizational claims. An interesting case occurred early in the Carter administration when a young diplomat, Brady Tyson, of the United States Delegation to the United Nation's Human Rights Commission, expressed the "profoundest regrets" for the U.S. role in Chile while the Allende government was in power. Within a few hours, his remarks were repudiated by the President and deplored by the State Department, which recalled him from Europe in order to provide him additional training in the arts of diplomacy.[34]

We consider finally two common assumptions about big organizations: that they are characterized by "efficiency" and "freedom from conflict." Both assumptions need to be qualified. Despite the fact that organizations exude an aura of "efficiency," being highly organized to achieve their goals by means of the structural characteristics outlined above; and despite the fact that individuals, hired on the basis of training and expertise, pursue their specialties with authority and discretion and in accordance with prescribed rules; and despite the fact that everyone is briskly competent and appears to know exactly what he or she is doing, the belief in the "efficiency" of bureaucratic organizations is almost impossible to sustain. Not only is the very concept of "efficiency" virtually impossible of definition, except in some gross, tautological sense such as "the achievement of organizational goals with the minimum expenditure of resources," but no competent research exists demonstrating the "efficiency" of the bureaucratic model compared with some alternative. While some of its characteristics, such as specialization and oligarchy, probably increase productivity and discipline, it is fair to conclude that a rigorous demonstration of its "efficiency" has not yet been made.[35]

As Karl Mannheim has said, the advantages of modern organiza-

---

[33]Gary Stanfield, "Technology and Organizational Structure as Theoretical Categories," *Administrative Science Quarterly*, Vol. 21, pp. 489–493. See also Lawrence Hvebiniak, "Job Technology, Supervision and Work-Group Structure," *Administrative Science Quarterly*, Vol. 19, pp. 395–410.

[34]*New York Times*, March 9, 1977, p. 1.

[35]Karl Mannheim, *Man and Society in an Age of Reconstruction* (New York: Harcourt, Brace & Co., 1941), pp. 244, 293–295.

tions lie mainly in their tendency to increase group rationality by placing power and authority in relatively few hands. This permits the organization's major policies to be determined with limited conflict and considerable finality. Once this has been done, the energies of the entire organization can be devoted to the task of carrying them out. Centralized authority and the conclusive resolution of the essential value question, "What is to be done?" is thus the major operational advantage. But this leaves unanswered questions about its operational "efficiency," the effect of oligarchic decision making upon morale, and about the caliber of decisions reached without full participation. In the American economic sector, while productivity is perhaps the highest among Western nations, limited competition in many sectors, high overhead costs, and the tendency to pass costs along to the consumer in the form of constantly rising prices, raise questions about the "efficiency" of the typical corporate structure. In government, of course, while a great deal of lip service is paid to "management techniques," in-service training for executives, and the like, "efficiency" is essentially a casuistic symbol, enjoying perhaps, the same operational relevance as another honorific spook, "the public interest."

The other characteristic often imputed to the bureaucratic model is its "conflict-free" nature. This assumption is rarely analyzed, yet it is directly related to whatever "efficiency" the model achieves. Despite the high market value of conflict during the 1960s in American society, the dysfunctions of aggressiveness as a personal bureaucratic skill remain. If one assumes that centralized authority is required to achieve order and continuity in the organization, it follows that conflict must be muted and confined to the organization's elite. Once decisions are reached at this level, further argument is prohibited. As in the British Cabinet, an administered consensus occurs, ensuring "collective responsibility" and a united front before the organization and the outside world. That executives who disagree strongly with policy decisions must resign if they feel unable to accept the institutional decision, suggests the intensity of this demand for consensus.

The "conflict-free" assumption also provides psychological gains, reinforcing authority by the implication that the revealed decision is the "one best way," scientifically achieved in line with the experience, inside information, and knowledge possessed by the organization's leaders. Patent conflict, by contrast, suggests that since equally wise and expert people can disagree on an issue, there is some question about the very existence of objectively superior alternatives and of the organization's ability to uncover them. In this sense, the basic premises of organizational logic and effectiveness are challenged by conflict.

The strategic advantages of conflict repression are also apparent in the internecine struggles among the various units of the organization. Here, too, dissent is confined within the unit, enabling the latter to present a united front in its endless competition for a larger share of the organization's resources. Elites have a direct stake in such consensus because any inability to maintain equilibrium and its attending competitive advantages brings disapproval from higher echelons which also desire to convey upward an image of cohesion within their larger sphere. The weight of such expectations is shown by the fact that the gravest offense in bureaucratic society is to go over the head of one's superior, to reveal conflict to outsiders.

The "conflict-free" assumption is also undercut by the inherent tension between authority based upon hierarchy and that based upon the expertise of the many specialists found in the typical big organization. Each element tends to define its own role as the ultimate basis for authority. Those in hierarchical positions will insist that final authority must reside at the top, because the disparate skills, training, and professional introversion of specialists require some disinterested and superior coordinating presence. On the other hand, specialists will not always grant that those in formal positions of authority fully merit the authority which they usually possess.

While the intensity of this conflict varies, it is to some extent a built-in characteristic of all bureaucratic settings. Instead of defining organizations as "conflict free," one might better regard them as arenas in which conflict is endemic. Nevertheless, the system of centralized authority and the administered consensus found in modern organizations undoubtedly results in certain operational advantages. As Max Weber concluded, bureaucratic structures are the most effective instrument ever designed for handling large-scale activities.

TOWARD THE | 3
ORGANIZATIONAL
SOCIETY

When Henry Adams returned to America in 1871, he remarked that size and "an increased facility of combination" had become striking characteristics of the economy. Although the emerging pattern was clearest in industry, the bureaucratic model and its values also invaded other areas, extending the control of both human and material resources. By the 1930s the trend had culminated in the "organizational society." In economic terms, competitively determined prices, wages, and production had been displaced by an imperfect market, a market characterized by government intervention, negotiated decisions between labor and management, "sticky prices," and relatively few sellers in basic sectors of the economy such as automobiles, steel, and oil. A similar trend occurred in nonindustrial sectors. Power, growth, and security provided common motives, and the means of achieving them became increasingly alike.

Thus a "prebureaucratic" society of small organizations and unbridled competition was replaced by a more rational bureaucratic society. Obviously, complete rationality and control did not follow. In fields such as retail sales where capital requirements remained small, many small units flourished and competition remained lively. In all areas, the unanticipated consequences of human behavior remained as numerous as their intended objectives; and chance, error, and irrationality still influenced events. But, broadly speaking, the calculated direction of social affairs increased steadily from 1865 to the present. The federal government's manipulation of consumer and commercial credit suggests the expanding periphery of control over matters once left to chance. The obsolescence of the "laws" of supply and demand was dramatically revealed in the mid-1970s by the indictment and conviction of several hundred corporation executives for making secret pay-offs to agents of various foreign nations in order to secure business contracts. More conventionally, the molding of public opinion and the manufacture of favorable popular images by advertising and public-relations firms marks the advance of calculated operations. The development of integrated enterprises, mainly in steel and oil, which controlled their product from raw material to consumer, provides another example of the trend.

As a result, traditional ideals and theories became dated. In economic analysis, for example, the laissez-faire ideal of the competitive, self-regulating economy remained viable long after our major economic areas (investment banking, steel, copper, oil, automobiles, rubber tires, aluminum, tin containers, as well as liquor and cigarettes) had become typically oligopolic. A few sellers possessing vast financial and technical resources dominated a vast market. The myth of the typical American as an independent, self-employed, profit-making individual persisted, largely unaffected by evidence that size and technology had greatly increased the proportion of *employees* in the labor force. Despite the rise of national unions, the fiction of the individual workers bargaining for themselves, moving about freely seeking a higher wage, remained current.

This laissez-faire model, based on certain eighteenth-century assumptions of Smith, Ricardo, and Bentham, was strained in an attempt to explain the facts of "imperfect competition." If price competition was outlawed by tacit agreement, brand and advertising competition (based on technical innovation and a great deal of pure rhetoric) was enlisted to reinforce the limping theory. The depression of the 1930s brought the first systematic modification when Chamberlin and Robinson analyzed the disparity between the model and the real world. Four decades later, however, it still could not be said that their theory of imperfect competition dominated economic discourse in the United States.

The iconoclasm of Keynes, who gave government an equilibrating role in economic affairs and demolished some of the central assumptions of classical theory, was reluctantly accepted. Some economists insisted that the model had been misused, that it was never meant to describe actual conditions but merely to ease analysis and prediction. Although a model is by definition a caricature, its major task is nevertheless to help us understand reality. If it fails to do this, its validity must be questioned. Others maintained that even though the economy was no longer competitive, everything worked out as well as if it had been.

Laissez-faire economic theory was of course more than an economic philosophy. It was the unifying element in the American scheme of values. And since values are usually impervious to facts, popular views were little affected by the economic revolution. Certainly among the public and in those areas where few sellers and many buyers had become typical, and where demand and production had little to do with price, the pure theory of competition remained vigorous. Only a few professional economists faced the implications of the new economic structure for traditional theory and analysis. The dominant myths began to be questioned, however, by young university graduates whose career preferences revealed their own acceptance of the organizational society. Despite widespread defections during the turbulent 1960s, by mid-1970s they increasingly chose security in one of the depression-proof giants.

This chapter is concerned with our evolution from a primarily rural, agricultural, competitive, and rather individualistic society to an urban-industrial complex whose major social activities are carried on by huge bureaucratic structures in which the typical individual's role is one of instrumental dependence. Although each sector will be handled separately, there was a similar pattern of bureaucratic development among all the great interests—industry, labor, government, mass communications, and so on. The politics of survival demanded that each close ranks against the other contenders for power and plan its strategy accordingly. This competition partly explains the ubiquity of large-scale organizations.

In the formative years of American capitalism, extending roughly from 1865 to the turn of the century, business enterprise was typically owner-operated and controlled. The system was highly personalized. Owners risked their own money, played an active role in management, and competed wholeheartedly with their rivals. Neither through control of production, price, markets, large-scale operation, nor virtually unlimited capital and technical resources could they significantly influence the market. Although the early history of Standard Oil indicates that such efforts were made, the conditions permitting a fully administered economy did not as yet exist. Such an economy first appeared after the panic of 1873 when railroad consolidations were followed by widespread mergers.

An organizational society, however, requires concentrated power in various social areas. This rough equilibrium was not achieved until the 1930s when agriculture and labor gained the political strength that allowed them to manipulate their economic environment. Nor did these achievements result in more than a temporary equilibrium, since new conditions soon changed the balance of power. For example, financial interests suffered because the taxation and investment policies of big government reduced sharply their influence over industry by permitting corporations to set aside sufficient profits to meet their capital needs for expansion and replacement. Similarly, the alliance between government and labor during the New Deal period was shattered by the return of conservative government following World War II, as symbolized by the Taft-Hartley and Landrum-Griffin Acts.

The formative period from the Civil War to the first great merger movement, 1897 to 1904, began with an economic revolution. Before the war our economy was one of merchant capitalism. From 1820 to 1860 the first small factories appeared and manufacturing got its start with the use of coal for steam power, with the rise of railroads, and with the integration of factory units. But this was still the age of the speculative capitalist rather than of the manufacturer. Moreover, during the entire period from the Revolutionary War to the Civil War, agriculture dominated the economy. Manufacturing was done in the home by the "putting-out" system, or less frequently, in the small shop. Labor was provided by the family or by the proprietor and a few apprentices. The present factory system, depending on machine power tended by wage earners, is a post-Civil War phenomenon. Not until 1890 did the value of manufactures equal that of agriculture, but in another decade its value doubled that of its chief rival. Natural increase and immigration provided the manpower necessary to feed the growing economy. From 1820 to 1860 population grew from about 10 million to 31 million. Of equal significance for industrial development, the proportion of the urban population rose from 5 percent to over 16 percent. From 1860 to 1870 manufacturing establishments increased by almost 80 percent.

This emerging capitalism was dominated by a few entrepreneurs who possessed unusual skill in finance and integration. Carnegie in steel, Rockefeller in oil, Armour in packing, Stanford and Harriman in railroads, and Morgan in finance were among some of them. While their part in building industry has probably been overdrawn (without the rich human and natural resources of a young nation such progress would surely have been impossible), their philosophy and tactics set the pattern for the organizational society. Their careers symbolized perhaps the single quality most responsible for American industrial vitality: a freedom from tradition that welcomed technological change. Their genius for integration, their demonstration of the versatility of finance capitalism, their insight into the advantages of the oligopolic market—all provided a guide for those who followed.

Despite its survival as an honored symbol, laissez-faire existed for only a brief time. Our industrial revolution began after the Civil War, yet within thirty years the first great merger movement had begun. By 1897 consolidation to avoid ruinous competition and to capture market control and provide huge capital resources had become common. Thus the period in which the typical enterprise was operated in a competitive milieu by a single entrepreneur or family existed only briefly. The succeeding corporation era encouraged the development of huge organizations by making capital accumulation easier, by permitting risk sharing, and by divorcing ownership from management.

The architects of consolidation were versatile. Several variations on the corporation theme appeared between 1865 and 1900. The panic of 1873 brought the first great combinations in the form of "pooling" agreements by the railroads to ease the sharp competition that had brought on the debacle. Survival was ensured by dividing up the market. When pooling was declared illegal by the Interstate Commerce Act of 1887, an alternative was found in the form of "trusts." Here stockholders turned over controlling blocks of securities to trustees, receiving in exchange trust certificates. Enjoying absolute power, trustees created monopolies in sugar, lead, whiskey, and oil. However, successful prosecutions in New York and Ohio in 1890 and 1892 foreclosed this form of combination, too. The court decisions demonstrated again the subtleties of the law by voiding trusts on the grounds that charter rights had been violated, rather than on the grounds that monopoly undercut the "public interest."

Corporations next resorted to the "holding-company" device which made possible the great mergers that occurred between 1897 and 1904. Under this scheme, which is used by major corporations today, control of several companies is centered in a single organization. Despite possession in some cases of only a small proportion of its operating subsidiaries' stock, the holding company can appoint the subsidiaries' directors and officers, allocate their profits, and maintain general policy control.

The size and aggressiveness of the early corporations nicely suited the American milieu. A continental land mass, fertile and rich in mineral wealth, provided a basis for expansiveness. An endless frontier had ensured endless opportunity, and the shock of its eventual passing was cushioned by new technological frontiers. Wealth was still there for the taking, and men of vision and strength, imbued with an intensely pragmatic outlook, took it. Freed from the cramping influence of European class values, individualism and social mobility flourished, and size and growth itself became honored items in the national scheme of values. A spirit of optimism that equated change with progress because change often *was* progress achieved religious sanctity. While occasional protests arose from Populists and Progressives in the late nineteenth century and brought the Sherman and Interstate Commerce Acts, the power and technical efficiency of the industrial giants overcame most fears. It is often forgotten that the mass of Americans were not comparing their condition with some utopia but with the European experience from which most of them came. In the main, not until the impact of war and depression during the 1930s was there any serious questioning of the dominant laissez-faire theory or its corporate instruments.

It gradually became clear, however, that a basic change had occurred. As Calvin Hoover, former President of the American Economic Association, concluded: "We can say that by the beginning of World War I our economy had become sufficiently characterized by concentration in industry, imperfect competition, oligopoly, administered industrial prices, price leadership, and other departures from or modifications of the rule of the free, fully competitive market for us to consider the change fundamental."[1] Economic change was reflected in both social and organizational change. A society in which economic and social power were rather widely diffused was replaced by one in which power steadily became more concentrated and desired.

The equalization of power increased bureaucracy—that is, administration by rules—as self-conscious groups began to demand legal recognition of their work status. When, for example, trade unions insisted on contracts, a variety of informal conditions and practices, such as the ubiquitous coffee break, had to be covered specifically in the work bargain. Jurisdictional disputes similarly illustrate labor's new concern with legal relationships, and both labor and management began to operate in terms of *rules*. As a result, a new field of labor law evolved and unions were obliged to secure the legal and financial skills that would permit them to bargain intelligently with industry.

Traditional ideals were modified by the changing economic structure and its attending conditions of participation. Social mobility and economic independence, basic American values, were challenged by the restricted access to capital and raw materials that accompanied a concentrated, vertically integrated industrial economy. Inevitably, opportunities for self-employment declined as huge aggregates of capital and technical resources became necessary for entry and survival. From 1940 to 1970 the labor force increased by over 30 million, yet the number of self-employed workers and proprietors remained almost the same. Work specialization and the separation of the worker from his tools increased dependence and made centralized authority more necessary. Owner-operators were often replaced by

---

[1]Calvin B. Hoover, "Institutional and Theoretical Implications of Economic Change," *American Economic Review*, Vol. 44, p. 10.

professional executives whose behavior reflected their scientific-management, hired-hand role.[2] Stockholders, the absentee landlords of the twentieth century, were remote and uninterested, playing the only role that atomized ownership permitted—the calculation of dividends. Power shifted to those who could operate large-scale enterprises rationally and with proper regard for the new arts of human and public relations, which became more important as organizations became more impersonal and consumers became more critical of corporate behavior.

Social change created new skill groups, while others became obsolete. The risk-taking owner-operator of the nineteenth century was replaced by the general manager, surrounded by a technical staff and the advertising man, who boasted that he could create effective demand. It was price "leadership," excess-profits taxation, and consumer-protection legislation that brought the research laboratory and the advertising agency into existence. The new "environmental protection" rationale of industry punctuated the need for yet another skilled functionary, namely, the public relations expert. He was living proof that the creative role of ideas is equalled by their rationalizing function. Such innovations characterized the transformation of social organization and market conditions during this century.

Several conditions reveal the trend. In the field of labor, the rise of national industrial unions, the change in make-up of the labor force, the successful resort to politics under the New Deal, and the effort to influence the election of political candidates, marked the arrival of a new contender for social power. In agriculture, the indications include more effective use after 1933 of a built-in political advantage (rural over-representation in state and national legislatures), the changing pattern of farm size and ownership, the cultivation of a national image of the farmer as the symbol of Jeffersonian virtue, and the steady advance of mechanized, corporation farming at the expense of the family farm. Like labor and industry, agriculture's political tactics enabled it too to frustrate "economic law." In industry, indications include the smaller number and larger size of firms, the increasing difficulty of entry, the frequent mergers, the increasing proportion of total business held by one or a few firms, and the precarious rate of survival among small enterprises.

At the outset it is useful to review the general pattern of corporate holdings during the first half of this century. The classic source of information here is the Temporary National Economic Committee

[2] It is possible that this trend was exaggerated somewhat. For a careful analysis of the continuing significance of family-owned enterprise, see Philip Burch, *The Managerial Revolution Reassessed: Family Control in America's Large Corporations* (Lexington, Mass.: Lexington Books, 1972).

which found in 1934 that the 200 largest financial corporations held about half the national industrial wealth. About the same time Berle and Means found that less than 1 percent of some 300,000 nonfinancial corporations controlled about half the total corporate wealth. Nearly half the corporate wealth in the United States was in the hands of 200 corporations, one of which, the American Telephone and Telegraph Company, controlled "more wealth than is contained within the borders of twenty-one of the states." Berle and Means concluded: "A society in which production is governed by blind economic forces is being replaced by one in which production is carried on under the ultimate control of a handful of individuals."[3]

Such concentration was achieved mainly through industrial and financial mergers. As we have seen, the first great combinations occurred from 1897 to 1904. World War I was followed by another wave of consolidation, and the prosperity following World War II again brought a similar development. Mergers occur, apparently, in good times when conservative public opinion eases antipathies toward monopoly and encourages corporations to protect their gains or to spread their risks by merger. The first merger period, from 1897 to 1904, aimed at vertical integrations in order to control the market. By 1904, 318 industrial combinations had been formed, capitalized at about 7 billion dollars and comprising 5,288 plants. According to the U.S. Industrial Commission on Trusts and Industrial Combinations, the average share of the total domestic market controlled by twenty-two of the most important mergers was 71 percent.

After World War I a significant revival of consolidation occurred. From 1919 to 1930 nearly 12,000 public utility, banking, manufacturing, and mining concerns disappeared. The total number of mergers was about 2,100, five times the number during the period from 1877 to 1904. By 1925 the sixteen largest public utilities controlled over 50 percent of the total national generating capacity.[4] In 1921 the total number of banking establishments was over 30,000; ten years later the number had been reduced by almost one-third. At the same time, the urge to expand appeared in other fields such as retailing. The A. & P. Chain, which had some 5,000 stores in 1922, had added 12,500 more by 1928.[5]

The conditions that had encouraged earlier merger movements were again evident following World War II, namely, prosperity, conservative government, apathy, or disenchantment toward antitrust

---

[3]Adolph A. Berle, Jr., and Gardner C. Means, *The Modern Corporation and Private Property* (New York: Macmillan, 1933), p. 46.

[4]Federal Trade Commission: *Electric Power Industry*. 70th Congress, 1st Sess., Senate Doc. 46, p. 176.

[5]Harry W. Laidler, *Concentration of Control in American Industry* (New York: Thomas Y. Crowell, 1931).

legislation, in addition to a rather sophisticated justification of bigness by the mass media and trade journals. In this environment the postwar merger movement was bound to surpass its predecessors. *Fortune* magazine estimated that during the period from 1945 to 1953 there were 7,500 mergers important enough to be noted by the financial journals. The value of the companies involved was about 10 percent of total corporation assets. As William B. Harris said: "It is certain that the merger movement has resulted in whittling down the population of independent corporations in the one-million-net-worth league and in increasing the size of larger companies."[6] Meanwhile, in January 1955, the trend was dramatized by the merger of the Chase National Bank and the Bank of the Manhattan Company, two giants in commercial banking. The resulting enterprise became the nation's second largest bank with resources of about 8 billion dollars. (California's Bank of America was first with combined assets of 10 billion dollars.) Labor too contracted the merger fever, and a long-heralded fusion of the AFL and CIO occurred in 1955.

Mergers in industrial corporations involving "larger" acquisitions (those of 10 million dollars or more) grew steadily following 1953, reaching a "crescendo" in the late 1960s.[7] From 1948 to 1966 there had been a total of 784 such, involving 28 billion dollars, but from 1967 to 1969, 447 "large" takeovers occurred, amounting to just over 31 billion dollars. In 1968–1969, among the giant firms, Jones and Laughlin, Commercial Credit, Sinclair Oil, Glen Alden, and Youngstown Sheet and Tube were affected, all "megacorporations" in the 250 million dollar category. Historically, mergers had involved giant firms taking over small companies; now the giants were taking over each other. Table 3.1 presents the merger trend during the past quarter-century.

The reasons for such combinations exphasize both the advantages of large-scale organizations and the social changes outlined in this chapter. Since market conditions favor size, an incentive is always present for firms to expand by new acquisitions both horizontally and vertically. In a society where size *qua* size is highly valued, consolidation for sheer growth will always be a powerful motive. Horizontal mergers reflect the fact that growth in a given business or industrial area must end when that field is exhausted. Thus successful firms look for new areas to conquer and for ways of diversifying risk. Excess-profits taxes also encourage mergers by providing "cheap

---

[6]This and the following comments on mergers are mainly from "The Urge to Merge," *Fortune*, November 1954, p.102 *passim*.

[7]Phillip I. Blumberg, *The Megacorporation in American Society* (Englewood Cliffs, N.J.: Prentice-Hall, 1975), pp. 47–50. For details of the effects of size and concentration upon innovation, profitability, and economic power see this careful study.

Table 3.1. Large Acquisitions in Manufacturing and Mining by Firms Ranked Among the 200 Largest Manufacturing Firms in 1971 (by year, 1948–1972)

Year	Total large acquisitions[1]		Large acquisitions by 200 largest firms[2]		Percentage of total large acquisitions by 200 largest firms	
	Number	Assets (millions)	Number	Assets (millions)	Number	Assets
1948	4	$ 63.2	4	$ 63.2	100.0	100.0
1949	6	89.0	4	45.3	66.7	50.9
1950	5	186.3	1	20.0	20.0	10.7
1951	9	201.5	4	114.4	44.4	56.8
1952	16	373.8	6	174.7	37.5	46.7
1953	23	779.1	12	397.4	52.2	51.0
1954	37	1,444.5	15	930.2	40.5	64.4
1955	67	2,168.9	32	1,199.5	47.8	55.3
1956	53	1,882.0	28	1,260.8	52.8	67.0
1957	47	1,202.3	20	703.7	42.6	58.5
1958	42	1,070.6	20	721.1	47.6	67.4
1959	49	1,432.0	20	806.2	40.8	56.3
1960	51	1,535.1	23	871.1	45.1	56.7
1961	46	2,003.0	22	1,499.7	47.8	74.9
1962	65	2,241.9	25	1,052.5	38.5	46.9
1963	54	2,535.8	33	1,867.3	61.1	73.6
1964	73	2,302.9	31	1,055.7	42.5	45.8
1965	62	3,232.3	24	1,845.4	38.7	57.1
1966	75	3,310.7	29	1,953.6	38.7	59.0
1967	138	8,258.5	59	5,751.7	42.8	69.6
1968	173	12,554.2	83	8,225.7	48.0	65.5
1969	136	10,966.2	49	5,963.8	36.0	54.4
1970	90	5,876.0	29	2,670.0	32.2	45.4
1971	58	2,443.4	17	960.6	29.3	39.3
1972[3]	56	1,748.8	17	646.8	30.4	37.0
Total	1,435	69,902.0	607	40,800.4	42.3	58.4

[1]Acquired firms with assets of $10 million or more.

[2]Ranked by 1971 total assets.

[3]Figures for 1972 are preliminary.

Note: Not included in above tabulation are companies for which data were not publicly available. There were 311 such companies with assets of $7,080.1 million for period 1948–72, of which 109 companies with assets of $2,653.6 million were acquisitions by the 200 largest firms.

Source: Bureau of Economics, Federal Trade Commission.

dollars" for such investments. Meanwhile, those small companies confronted by three or four giants, the typical pattern in basic industry today, may feel that their survival chances are increased by merger.

The current wave of mergers is also motivated by the desire to gain access to new markets. Buying into an existing enterprise that produces the same commodity or provides an attractive new market has become common practice. New products, such as frozen foods and solar heat, will also attract the attention of established corporations who wish to share in the advantages of technical innovation. In this context, small firms, like minor political parties, often play an innovative role, developing new products or techniques that are co-opted by larger firms once their feasibility is proved. Extensive research indicates that large firms are probably less innovative than their smaller counterparts.[8]

For our purposes, however, the knotty question of the effect of mergers on innovation and competition is secondary. The main point is that mergers tend to increase concentration, which in turn tends to increase the size of organizations and the pervasiveness of bureaucratic conditions of work. On a commonsense basis, mergers do seem to increase concentration. This is not always so, however, because as in the case of U.S. Steel, the size of the total market may become so large that even a rapidly growing firm may over a period of time control less of the market. Nevertheless, when two or more firms merge, both concentration and size have probably increased, in the short run at least.

A related factor is the high survival values of size. In most industries the failure rate among giants is substantially less than that among small and medium-sized firms. There is evidence too that after an initial shakedown period our economy has achieved considerable stability in basic areas such as steel, oil, and electrical equipment. Among the hundred largest corporations in the period from 1909 to 1948, for example, sixty-three disappeared during the first twenty years, but only six disappeared during the following eighteen years.[9] Huge capital resources, experience, and good will enable established forms to survive. Failure rates support this interpretation, showing that small firms have a very high failure rate, while big enterprises rarely fail. In time such a pattern probably increases concentration.

Concentration is certainly apparent in the structure of our major basic industries. In most of them three or four giants account for about one-half of total production, while a substantial number of small firms share the remaining output. The resulting market situation is neither purely competitive nor purely monopolistic, but lies somewhere in between. Chamberlin called the attending economic

[8]Cf. Dean Worcester, *Monopoly, Big Business and Welfare in the United States* (Seattle: University of Washington Press, 1967); James M. Utterback, "Innovation in Industry and the Diffusion of Technology," *Science,* February 15, 1974, Vol. 183, p. 620.

[9]Morris A. Adelman, "A Note on Concentration and Merger," *American Economic Review,* Vol. 44, pp. 392–393.

behavior "imperfect competition," and it has since become known as "oligopoly," or competition among the few. With minor exceptions, such as soft coal, such quasicompetitive relations are the rule in basic industry and are also characteristic of cigarettes, motion-picture production, and commercial aviation. In 1947, for example, the three largest firms in automobiles, agricultural machinery, rubber tires, meat products, liquor, cigarettes, copper, tin containers, and office machinery did two-thirds or more of all business in their respective fields. A high degree of concentration also exists in steel, glass, dairy products, industrial chemicals, gasoline, cement, fertilizers, and milk distribution.

It seems at present that market concentration is becoming stable, despite the wave of mergers since 1950 and the restriction of entry by huge capital requirements and the experience of established firms. The share of the leading producers in the total sales of an industry has been defined as concentrated when the four largest firms account for 50 percent or more of the output.[10] In the period 1947 to 1966, four-firm concentration ratios increased in eighty-eight industries and declined in seventy-eight. In forty-seven industries, there was little or no change. From 1966 to 1970, however, concentration increased somewhat among the "concentrated" sector.[11]

Where penetration has occurred—in aluminum, automobiles, and steel, for example—the capital and the impetus were often provided by government, which alone has the capital and risk potential. After examining twenty large, basic industries, Joseph Bain concludes: "Absolute capital requirements for an efficient plant in all the manufacturing industries examined are large enough to restrict seriously the ranks of potential entrants."[12] Bain's calculations as to the capital required for "one efficient plant" are as follows: steel, 265 million to 665 million dollars; petroleum refining (including transportation facilities), 225 million to 250 million dollars; automobiles, 250 million to 500 million dollars; tractors, 125 million dollars; tires and tubes, 25 million to 30 million dollars; cement, 20 million to 25 million dollars; and cigarettes, 125 million to 150 million dollars. The smallest amount required was 500,000 dollars, in shoe manufacturing. These figures, moreover, do not include "shakedown losses" that may be "large and prolonged." Nor do they include the increases brought by inflation since Bain wrote.

[10]John Blair, *Economic Concentration* (New York: Harcourt Brace Jovanovich, 1972). Cited in Blumberg, *Megacorporation*, p. 67.

[11]Blumberg, *Megacorporation*, pp. 67–71.

[12]Joseph Bain, "Economics of Scale, Concentration, and Entry," *American Economic Review*, Vol. 44, p. 37; see also Ralph L. Nelson, *Merger Movements in American Industry* (Princeton: National Bureau of Economic Research, 1959).

Although industry was the first group to gain decisive national power through consolidation and political influence, other interests soon adopted similar tactics. A survey of the changing work force in labor, agriculture, and government suggests the way in which a rough power equilibrium was attained by the 1930s.

The trend in all areas was toward scientific, technical, semiskilled, and clerical employment, with a *relative* decrease in the "skilled" and "self-employed" categories. A persistent anomaly followed. The economic values of a society composed mainly of wage-earning employees were expressed in terms of "profit making." Meanwhile the number of small stockholders in our population and the decline of entrepreneurial status indicate that "profit making" is actually a highly restricted activity. In 1953 the total labor force, consisting of 63 million, included only 4 million entrepreneurs (excluding farm proprietors), while only 6.5 million persons owned stock in publicly held companies. By 1960, 12 million individuals owned stocks and, by 1972, a peak of 32.5 million were in the market. The *rentier* ideal remained tenuous, however, because of the striking concentration of ownership: the 1 percent of families with the largest personal income accounted for 47 percent of all dividends received and 51 percent of the market value of all family-owned stock while the 10 percent of families with the largest income accounted for 71 percent of dividend income and fully 74 percent of market value.[13]

An analysis of the labor force reflects the changes taking place, particularly in the development of industry and manufacturing, in the growing role of science and technology, and in the rise of big organizations in business, finance, agriculture, and labor. The trends can best be shown statistically. In 1870 our total population was 40 million; by 1970 it had risen to over 200 million. Beginning with 1870 when, as we have seen, the present industrial society began to take shape, agriculture dominated the economy with 6,730,000 workers of a total labor force of 12,920,000. Manufacturing and hand trades were a poor second with 2,130,000, while educational and professional services required only 330,000. Trade, including finance and real estate, employed 850,000. Transportation (including public utilities) with 580,000 employees was also significant.

By 1900, however, a new trend had appeared. Of a total labor force of 29 million, agriculture remained vital with 10,880,000, but manufacturing had sharply risen to 13,027,000. Professional services had

[13]Marshall E. Blume, Jean Crockett, and Irwin Friend, "Stockownership in the United States: Characteristics and Trends," *Survey of Current Business*, Vol. 54, pp. 17–19; James D. Smith, *The Personal Distribution of Income and Wealth* (New York: National Bureau of Economic Research, Columbia University Press, 1975); J. Keith Butters, et al., *Effects of Taxation on Investment by Individuals* (Cambridge: Harvard Business School, 1953), p. 26.

increased to almost 8 million. Transportation and other public utilities had also increased considerably.

By 1930 agriculture had lost its lead, having declined to only 10,321,000 in a labor force of 48,686,000. Manufacturing, with 24,044,000, far surpassed agriculture. Trade had doubled its numbers. Educational workers had increased to 1,650,000, while other professional services numbered 1,760,000. By another decade the disparity between agriculture and manufacturing had increased further. In 1940 gainful workers numbered 51,742,000, of whom agriculture took only 9 million, a decrease of almost one and one-half million during the depression decade. Meanwhile, manufacturing continued its gains, employing almost 27 million workers. Among other categories, only professional services and trade increased significantly during this period.

Agriculture, in sum, suffered a relative decline from 1870 to 1940 as shown by its decreasing share of the total labor force. The dividing point for agriculture is 1870; before this time it had always provided at least one-half of the total working force. Although its relative position had declined steadily, in 1870 agriculture still retained 53 percent. By 1940 its proportion had fallen to only 17 percent. Put another way, whereas agriculture had provided 50 percent of the labor force in 1870 and manufacturing only one-sixth, by 1940 agriculture's share had decreased to about one-sixth, while manufacturing had increased to almost one-half.

In virtually every occupational sector a similar trend continued following World War II. The most dramatic increase occurred among white-collar workers who rose from only 17 percent of the work force in 1900 to 31 percent in 1940, and to almost 50 percent in 1970. Among them, clerical and professional-technical workers showed the largest gains. Blue-collar workers actually decreased, climbing slowly from 45 percent in 1900 to 49 percent in 1940, and falling off slightly to 47 percent in 1970. The upsurge in the proportion of service workers symbolized the evolution of a highly rationalized and productive postindustrial society. In 1900, service workers comprised only about 3 percent of the labor force, but by 1940 they had grown to 12 percent, and by 1970, accounted for about 14 percent. Farm managers and workers, on the other hand, suffered a sharp decline, from just over one-third of the work force in 1900 to less than one-fifth in 1940, and to only 4 percent of the work force by 1970. This changing occupational structure is summarized in Table 3.2.

Another dramatic change is the increase in professional, clerical, and managerial jobs. In 1910, over 23 percent of the labor force was self-employed, but by 1970 this proportion had fallen to about 6 percent. Meanwhile, the secular increase in semiskilled, clerical, and

Table 3.2. Changing Composition of the National Work Force, 1910–1970

Year	Total	Professional	Farmers	Man-agers	Clerical	Skilled	Semi-skilled
1910	37,317	1,632	6,132	2,446	3,804	4,363	5,489
1920	41,236	2,049	6,387	2,792	5,682	5,570	6,631
1930	48,598	2,945	6,012	3,652	7,936	6,282	7,972
1940	52,020	3,381	5,274	3,958	8,923	6,104	10,918
1950	56,239	4,910	4,309	5,018	10,820	7,782	11,146
1960	68,579	7,162	2,898	5,443	9,768	8,870	12,363
1970	78,627	11,140	3,126	6,128	13,714	10,158	13,909

SOURCE: *U.S. Statistical Abstracts* (Washington, D.C.: U.S. Government Printing Office), see U.S. Department of Commerce, *Historical Statistics of the United States*, 1975, p. 139. For "skilled" workers, I have used the "craftsmen, foremen, and kindred workers" category; for "semiskilled," the "operatives and kindred workers" category. While there will be some disagreement about these selections, they do reveal the secular trend which is my major concern.

professional jobs reflected the demands of giant organizations for more white- and blue-collar workers. The turn to machine power and the reduced need for craftsmen was visible in the relatively slower increase of skilled workers after 1920. This trend was accompanied by a rise in the proportion of semiskilled workers, from 14 percent of the labor force in 1910 to 21 percent in 1940, leveling off at about 18 percent in 1970.[14] A more detailed representation of the job categories is shown in Table 3.3.

Thus by 1970 fewer than 10 percent of Americans worked for themselves; the remaining 90 percent were employees. Roughly half of them, perhaps as many as 40 million, worked in environments that can be called "bureaucratic settings." The conditions of their work often included large size, standardization, impersonality, exquisite specialization, hierarchy, and dependence. Such organizations, moreover, could buy the research and management skills that intensify these conditions still further.

The bureaucratized labor force is now spread around the economy. By 1975 its members included some 14 million public servants, civilian and military, in local, state, and federal governments. Some 15 million of them work for our 500 largest industrial corporations, nineteen of which have over 100,000 employees and one of which, General Motors, has 681,000.[15] Many work for private utilities like American Telephone and New York Telegraph whose assets of 80

[14]Such changes were attended by a vast increase in administrative workers. During this half century, production workers in manufacturing increased by only 87 percent, while production workers in administrative kinds of work increased by 244 percent, Seymour Melman, "The Rise of Administrative Overhead in the Manufacturing Industries of the United States 1899–1947," *Oxford Economic Papers*, Vol. 3, p. 62. Frederic W. Terrien and Donald L. Mills, "The Effect of Changing Size Upon the Internal Structure of Organizations," *American Sociological Review*, Vol. 20, pp. 11–13.

[15]The survival value of size is suggested by the fact that only thirty-three corporations were displaced from the 1974 list; in almost all cases they ranked in the lowest quartiles in terms of sales.

Table 3.3. Major Occupational Groups in the Labor Force, 1900–1970*

Major occupation group, both sexes:	1970	1960	1950	1940	1930	1920	1910	1900
Total:	79,802	67,990	59,230	51,742	48,686	42,206	37,291	29,030
White-collar workers	**37,857**	**27,028**	**21,253**	**16,082**	**14,320**	**10,529**	**7,962**	**5,115**
Professional, technical, and kindred workers	11,561	7,090	5,000	3,879	3,311	2,283	1,758	1,234
Managers, officials, and proprietors	6,463	5,708	5,096	3,770	3,614	2,803	2,462	1,697
Clerical and kindred workers	14,208	9,431	7,132	4,982	4,336	3,385	1,987	877
Sales workers	5,625	4,799	4,025	3,450	3,059	2,058	1,755	1,307
Manual and service workers	**39,419**	**33,377**	**29,749**	**26,666**	**24,044**	**20,287**	**17,797**	**13,027**
Manual workers	*29,168*	*25,474*	*23,733*	*20,597*	*19,272*	*16,974*	*14,234*	*10,401*
Craftsmen, foremen, and kindred workers	11,082	9,465	8,205	6,203	6,246	5,482	4,315	3,062
Operative and kindred workers	14,335	12,254	11,754	9,518	7,691	6,587	5,441	3,720
Laborers, except farm and mine	3,751	3,755	3,774	4,875	5,335	4,905	4,478	3,620
Service workers	*10,251*	*7,902*	*6,015*	*6,069*	*4,772*	*3,313*	*3,562*	*2,626*
Private household workers	1,204	1,817	1,492	2,412	1,998	1,411	1,851	1,579
Service workers, exc. private household	9,047	6,086	4,524	3,657	2,774	1,901	1,711	1,047
Farmworkers	**2,450**	**4,132**	**6,858**	**8,995**	**10,321**	**11,390**	**11,533**	**10,888**
Farmers and farm managers	1,428	2,528	4,325	5,362	6,032	6,442	6,163	5,763
Farm laborers and foremen	1,022	1,604	2,533	3,632	4,290	4,948	5,370	5,125

*In thousands of persons 14 years old and over, except as indicated. Census data for 1900, June 1; 1910, April 15; 1920, January 1; 1930–1970, April 1.
Source: *U.S. Statistical Abstracts* (Washington, D.C.: Government Printing Office).

billion dollars and 939,000 employees overwhelm the others in its field. They also work in the transportation industry, mainly for such giants of transportation as Penn-Central with 78,539 workers, Trans World Airlines with 78,600, and Southern Pacific with 43,300.

Some are found in great financial houses like California's Bank of America, New York's Chase Manhattan and Citibank, each of which is capitalized at over 40 billion dollars and has 30,000 or more workers. Others serve the giants of life insurance where the fifty largest firms do over 80 percent of the business, leaving the remainder to be shared by 1,000 other companies. Of these fifty, two giants, Metropolitan and Prudential, have combined assets of 75 billion dollars and a labor force of over 100,000. Yet others are clerks in vast retail empires, including Sears Roebuck (377,000), Woolworth's (202,402), and J.C. Penney (186,000). A few work for the thirty largest universities which in 1970 had 1,270,000 full-time students, over 30 percent of a total of over 4 million presumably studying in 1,145 accredited four-year institutions across America. These statistics indicate roughly the extent of bureaucratization in our society.

The trend toward increased size among organizations is equally apparent in other sectors. In agriculture, for example, the average size of farms increased steadily during this century, while the total number decreased slightly. As *The New York Times* reported in 1955, "The traditional family-type farm is disappearing rapidly and is being replaced by large-scale and highly mechanized projects."[16] In 1900, there had been 5,737,000 farms, which increased to 6,560,000 by 1916, and to 6,812,000 by 1935, the high point in American history. By 1945, however, this number had decreased by about one million. Five years later the total number of farms had declined further to 4,884,818. The trend continued and by 1975 the number of farms was 2,808,000. From 1900 to 1975 our population increased from 76 million to over 200 million. The farm-production index increased by almost 50 percent, from 85 in 1910 to 123, while gross farm income rose from 7,352,000 dollars to 54,226,000,000 dollars. The earlier pattern of dominance of the market by the few repeated itself: 17 percent of all farms received 61 percent of all farm income. At the other end of the scale, 25 percent of all farms shared only .9 percent of all such income, that is, less than $2,500.[17]

Technology and the capital required for highly mechanized, commercial farming brought results similar to those seen in basic industry. In 1949, for example, 484,000 farms, less than 10 percent of the total, produced over 50 percent of all farm products, and 9 percent of the nation's farms earned more than the remaining 91 percent. By 1976, 81 percent of all farms earned less than $20,000 per year, while 1.9 percent earned $100,000 and over.

Meanwhile, the size of farms increased steadily. In 1900 farms of 1,000 acres and over numbered 67,405; by 1940 they had increased to 100,531, and by 1945 to 112,899. The trend toward size is also apparent in the next smaller category, farms from 500 to 1,000 acres. In 1920 the number had been 149,819. By 1940 such farms numbered 163,694, and by 1945, they reached 173,777. Hired workers on all farms during this quarter of a century decreased from 2,883,000 to

[16]*New York Times*, December 20, 1955, p. 22.

[17]Harold Breimyer, "The Changing American Farm" in F. Clemente, ed, *The New Rural America, Annals of the American Academy of Political and Social Science*, Vol. 429, p. 20.

2,117,000. Following World War II, the decline continued and by 1975 such workers amounted to only 1,290,000, while the number of farms of 500 to 1,000 acres had risen to 216,000. Meanwhile, total farm income reached the hundred billion dollar mark. Thus the family-type farm, which had produced the Jeffersonian ideal of the sturdy yeoman, faded before the corporation farm, often owned by an absentee landlord who sought a place in the country and perhaps a way to take advantage of generous tax write-offs by refurbishing a rundown farm.

Another incentive was the price-support program of the government which attempted to guarantee farm prosperity. Despite the disapproval of agricultural economists and the dismay of neoclassical theorists, support at fairly high levels began to look more and more like a permanent policy. Commercial farmers made it clear that the government "ought" to help them in this and other ways. Here again the disparity between economic fact and economic theory was strange and wonderful. The spectacle of the farmer competing successfully with business in the struggle for subsidies violated liberal economic theory, but the lessons of organization had been well learned. By 1970, direct annual federal payments to farmers amounted to 3,717 billion dollars for conservation, sugar, and cotton programs alone.

The global reach of technology and bureaucratic rationalization is most dramatically evident, however, in multinational agribusiness, which has created a "Global Farm" to serve a "Global Supermarket."[18] Production sites have been established in underdeveloped countries where labor and land may cost as little as 10 percent of American costs. High-value items, fruit, flowers, meat, and vegetables, are increasingly grown outside the United States, co-opting land and resources often used to grow food used by indigenous populations. In the resulting world market, every item has its price, which is determined by what the Supermarket's best-off customers can pay. The by-products include greater concentration within the United States as farmers and workers lose their jobs. About ten billion dollars of agricultural products are imported annually, two-thirds of which are estimated to compete with home-grown products. Meanwhile, as seen in industrial and commercial spheres, government derives another impetus to support existing political and economic structures abroad that sometimes distort local economic development. The consequences include a "most-favored" position for agricultural exports. Governments exclude such enterprises from land-reform schemes.

[18]Francis M. Lappe and Joseph Collins, "Four Myths about World Hunger," *The Guardian,* May 22, 1977, p. 18; see also, Richard J. Barnet and Ronald E. Müller, *Global Reach: The Power of Multinational Corporations* (New York: Simon & Schuster, 1974), pp. 179–184.

Food produced for local consumption declines as producers shift to export crops. The wages of agricultural workers tend to be kept low in an effort to increase the competitive strength of exports.

The pattern of union membership and the rise of huge, monolithic structures in labor also confirm the advance of large-scale organization. Survival in a managed economy required collective discipline, the deemphasis of the individual worker, the turn to government, and "cooperation" with industry. Although membership fluctuated with changing economic conditions, with labor legislation, and with the impact of war, from 1900 to 1960 the trend was upward, amounting to about 5 percent increase annually. In 1900 only 3 percent of a labor force of 29 million was unionized. By 1935 membership had risen to almost 9 percent while the total labor force had increased by less than half. By 1953 the proportion of union members to total working force reached almost 27 percent, but by 1974, it had dropped slightly to 25.8 percent. In round numbers, the totals were as follows: 1900, 791,000 members; 1935, 3,728,000; and in 1953, between 16 and 17 million; in 1974, 21,643,000, but in 1975, just over 20 million. This increase, however, masks the fact that membership as a proportion of all nonfarm workers has suffered a secular decline from 32 percent in 1950 to just over one quarter in 1975. While gains have continued in several areas, such as teamsters, auto workers, retail clerks, and strikingly, civil servants, white-collar workers have continued to resist unionization. Their impetus is undercut by the fact that their own pay raises are articulated with those of unionized workers.

The causes of this pattern are varied. The economic cycle has always been basic, with membership usually rising in good times and decreasing during periods of unemployment. Exceptions occurred, however, and doubts came to be raised about the old theory that the business cycle was the independent variable insofar as union membership was concerned. Unionism suffered its worst decline in the eminently prosperous years from 1921 to 1923 and was fairly stable during the period from 1927 to 1929. Allied with economic conditions was sympathetic legislation such as the National Labor Relations Act. When this Act was passed in 1935, union membership was less than 4 million; two years later it had more than doubled. By 1941, even before the war-inspired spurt, membership had jumped to 10,489,000. From 1942 to 1945 union membership increased from 10,762,000 to 14,796,000, a gain of about 36 percent. Since 1930, it seems, unions have benefited most from emergencies, such as war and depression. Once crisis provided an opportunity for entry, they consolidated their gains, which included not only increased numbers but also a foot in the door that served them well as time and organization brought new opportunities. Among such new opportunities, mentioned elsewhere, is a union movement among college and university teachers. However, as noted, the union's share of the total work force is now declining.

Perhaps government best symbolizes the rise of the organizational society. The trend is apparent in the number of public servants, in the size of the national budget, and in the magnitude of public indebtedness. It can be shown that public employment has increased at a disproportionate rate. In 1870 there were only 49,000 federal employees. By the turn of the century the number had increased to 256,000. With the exception of sharp rises during World War I, growth from this time until the early 1930s was steady but unspectacular, with employees approximately doubling from 1901 to 1930. The Great Depression, however, brought a sharp upsurge which was further accelerated by World War II. During the 1930s public employees doubled from about 550,000 to over 1 million. But this increase was far surpassed during World War II, which began with 1,370,000 civil servants and ended with 3,569,000. After 1945, however, federal jobs (excluding the military) declined steadily until 1950 when the total began to rise from 2,117,000 to its present level of about 2,900,000 (over 1 million of these work in the Defense Department).[19] This increase, however, is modest compared with state and local growth which expanded from a postwar level of only 3,181,000 (including teachers) to a grand total of over 10 million in 1975. California's monthly payroll for its 484,000 civil servants was almost 600 million dollars; in New York, 375,000 bureaucrats collected 386 million dollars. Although sustained borrowing can postpone the day of reckoning, New York City's 1975–1977 financial debacle indicated that deficit financing has its limits. Swollen payrolls, financially irresponsible pension schemes, uncontrolled expenditures in the welfare sector—all combined to reduce the city to a crises-ridden suppliant for federal and state and private bailouts. The city's total outstanding debt (1975) was over 14 billion dollars, and its huge annual outlays went mainly for salaries for its some 400,000 employees and its educational, welfare, and debt-service programs.

The vast number of employees underscores government's expanding role during our lifetime. War, depression, and the threat of war have combined to project government into practically every aspect of

[19]This leveling off may be related to the increasing use of consulting firms by the federal government. Very little is known about this subject, but it seems that although ideally the firms are hired for their expertise, the relationship involves patronage and political loyalty, mediated by class-affected "old boy" networks. The competence of such firms is apparently moot, as suggested by an extensive catalogue of disasters, Daniel Guttman and Barry Willner, *The Shadow Government* (New York: Pantheon, 1977).

national life. The erosion of laissez-faire by big agriculture, big labor, and big industry has been accelerated by big government's efforts to control the economy. The Great Depression brought great popular disenchantment with laissez-faire and an unprecedented acceptance of economic planning. The change has been somewhat obscured by the use of an "emergency" label, and by our national tendency to regard what has become permanent and normal as an aberration.

Public spending also dramatized changing popular expectations. In 1860 total federal expenditures were only 63 million dollars, but by 1870 the Civil War and increased veterans' benefits had brought the national budget to 309 million dollars. This was the high point of federal expenditures for thirty years, not exceeded until 1890. From that time on expenditures climbed steadily, and 1917 brought the first billion-dollar budget. The cost of modern war was reflected in a twelvefold increase in 1917 and 1918, rising to a total of 18 billion dollars, an amount not to be exceeded until World War II. By 1945 public spending reached what seemed a staggering total of over 100 billion dollars. Following the war some retrenchment occurred: the budget was cut to 60 billion dollars in 1946; to 39 billion dollars in 1947; and to 33 billion dollars in 1948. Subsequently, however, consensus among American political and economic elites that the Soviet Union was not prepared to meet the conditions of peaceful co-existence, in addition to the need for sustaining a purchasing power equal to the 50 percent increase in national productivity since 1939, brought rearmament and foreign aid programs that boosted expenditures sharply.[20] By 1966, the federal budget amounted to 135 billion dollars, of which 56 billion dollars was for defense; by 1971, it had risen to over 200 billion dollars, including 77 billion dollars for defense; and by 1975, the total was 350 billion dollars, of which about 112 billion dollars involved defense spending. Essentially, such spending reflects the growing capacity of great interest groups to co-

[20]The incentives for the ensuing "cold war" rationale were of course mixed, encompassing political, economic, and moral-ideological components. American political and economic leaders were agreed that an aggressive international posture was required to rebuild shattered European powers, to enable them to resist communist influence, and to reestablish their economies on a capitalistic basis. The moral imperative came from the attending belief that collectivist alternatives to free enterprise brought totalitarian regimes. These three incentives are explicit in the comment of Joseph M. Dodge, a Detroit banker who had a critical role in shaping the postwar policies of the United States: "The world political problem today is the extent to which government controls of ownership will replace free enterprise. . . . Underlying these problems and trends is the ultimate fact that the expansion of socialism and government control and ownership finally leads toward some form of totalitarianism." "The General Economic and Political Problem . . . " L. M. Dodge Papers, Detroit Public Library, 1947, cited in Joyce and Gabriel Kolko, *The Limits of Power* (New York: Harper & Row, 1972), p. 93.

opt government largesse, aggravated no doubt by inflation, and the structural imperatives of the political system which dictate that politicians must secure campaign funds to insure their tenure. The unrestrained allocation of subsidies, estimated at 62 billion dollars annually, follows inevitably.[21] The monumental weight of such imperatives is suggested by the experience of Richard Nixon, who came to office pledged to reduce government spending, but incurred the largest nonwartime deficits in history, amounting to 23 billion dollars in 1972 and rising to over 30 billion dollars in 1973. By 1977, the White House financial staff was planning for a deficit of some 60 billion dollars. The essentially political, often irrational character of public spending is suggested by the following judgment:

> The defense budget, while susceptible to rational analysis, remains a matter of political resolution. Choices of this order can be made in only one place: the political arena. There the relative importance of values can be decided by the relative power brought to bear on their behalf. There the distribution of power can decide matters that the distribution of fact and insight cannot.[22]

Given hindsight, we can now see that depression spending, which was widely heralded as the beginning of the end, was actually mild. The national debt, which had been 24 billion dollars in 1924, increased to only 28 billion dollars in 1935, the middle of the depression. The grand expenditures began in the late 1930s with rearmament. But even these amounts, reaching 40 billion dollars in 1939, appear relatively insignificant beside subsequent wartime spending. In the four years from 1942 through 1945 the debt rose as follows: to 72 billion; to 136 billion; to 201 billion; and to 258 billion dollars. Moreover, the demands of defense (about 112 billion dollars for 1976) and debt service (around 18 billion dollars per year) had by 1970 raised the figure to 382 billion dollars. Since we have enjoyed unequalled prosperity and are still unable to reduce the debt, it can be assumed that it will remain near this figure indefinitely, a built-in in-

---

[21]Taylor Branch, "Government Subsidies: Who Gets the 62 Billion," *Washington Monthly*, Vol. 4, pp. 9–27.

[22]Warner R. Schilling et al., *Strategy, Politics and Defense Budgets* (New York: Columbia University Press, 1962), p. 15. See also, Charles L. Schultze, *Setting National Priorities* (Washington, D.C.: Brookings, 1972). The resulting conditions, some of which are virtually beyond comprehension, include the following: Over $300 billion is spent annually by all nations for military weapons and forces, more than worldwide expenditures on education or health, and about the same as the combined income of the poor countries that contain half the world's population. See, among others, Alva R. Myrdal, *The Game of Disarmament* (New York: Pantheon, 1977); Don Oberdorfer, "Disarmament: Sincerity or Illusion," *The Guardian*, March 20, 1977, p. 18.

centive to inflation. In sum, throughout the entire period, war and defense have been the principal factors in high public expenditures and indebtedness.

Government's financial legerdemain was aggravated by some of its substantive programs. Whatever the value of their distributive aims, one of the effects of such efforts as the "Equal Opportunity" program was to contribute to the decline of achievement-oriented norms of recruitment and mobility in American society.[23] Insofar as such norms have been one of the most energizing and democratic distinctions between our open society and class-bound Europe, this may be an expensive innovation. The policy is mainly a product of the black revolts in major cities during the 1960s and the attending disenchantments of other minority groups, particularly Mexican-Americans. Essentially, it seeks to ease our national legacy of slavery and discrimination against members of minority groups and women by systematically favoring them in recruitment and promotion in government (particularly the military), business, and industry. In addition, similar measures have been introduced in university and college admission and grant programs.

Perhaps inevitably in a period of high unemployment among graduates, such programs have resulted in inequities for some members of some majority white groups who have labeled the programs as examples of "reverse discrimination" and maintained with some justice that they have lowered academic standards in higher education. The issues involved and the resort to the courts by disadvantaged individuals are well illustrated by *Bakke* v. *the Regents of the University of California,* now in the United States Supreme Court on appeal by the Board of Regents following an adverse 1976 decision in the California State Supreme Court. The state court held that the "two-track" admissions policy of the University of California–Davis Medical School was unconstitutional because it discriminated in favor of minority groups and against the white race, in violation of the Fourteenth Amendment which guarantees equal protection under the law.[24]

Paul Allan Bakke is a young graduate engineer who spent four

---

[23]For an influential analysis of the problems involved in easing inequality, see John Rawls, *A Theory of Justice* (Cambridge: Harvard University Press, 1971). For a critique of Rawls' treatment of equality, including the judgment that he exhibits a latent meritocratic bias, see also, Crawford B. Macpherson, *Democratic Theory* (New York: Oxford University Press, 1973) and H. T. Wilson, *The American Ideology* (London and Boston: Routledge and Kegan Paul, 1977), chap. 9.

[24]Robert Lindsay, "White, Caucasian, and Rejected," *New York Times Magazine,* April 3, 1977, p. 47. For a similar case involving the University of Washington Law School, see *De Funis* v. *Odegaard,* 94 U.S. 1704 (1974).

years in the Marine Corps, including seven months in a combat unit in Vietnam. Subsequently, while working in the space program near Palo Alto, he came into contact with physicians working on problems of radiation and the effects of space travel on the human body. Galvanized by a deep interest in medicine, he began courses in chemistry and biology to meet premed requirements; he also worked as a hospital volunteer. In 1972, he applied to the new Davis Medical School. His undergraduate grades averaged 3.51 on a 4.0 scale; he had excellent recommendations. On tests of scientific knowledge, quantitative analysis, verbal ability, and general information, he ranked in the 97th, 96th, 94th, and 72nd percentiles, respectively. He performed well in his personal interview and was recommended for admission by the faculty member who interviewed him. However, because of illness in his family, Bakke's application and interview came late in the year and he was rejected, despite the fact that his points under the evaluation system totalled 468 out of a possible 500, and that scores of 479 had been designated at Davis as the threshold of "automatic admission." Among the unhappy aspects of this case is the fact that the Davis Admissions Officer, Peter Storandt, aged 30, who became convinced that Bakke had indeed been patently disadvantaged, revealed that "some of the prize slots in the freshman medical class were being given—at the order of senior medical-school officials—on the basis of friendship and political connections." He was subsequently fired.

Meanwhile, the sixteen minority applicants selected by a special committee had undergraduate grade averages of 2.88 compared with 3.49 for applicants admitted through the regular stream. In scientific knowledge, whereas regular applicants ranked at the 85th percentile, the special students ranked in the 35th percentile.[25]

After unsuccessful efforts at getting his case reconsidered, Bakke turned to the courts, with the results indicated earlier. Our concern here is less with the political and ameliorative aspects of the government's program, which can obviously be justified on historical and humanitarian grounds, than with its objective consequences in terms such as the capability of critical national programs and the disenchanting effects of a policy that directly controverts meritocratic norms. The pervasiveness of this assault is seen in university faculty recruitment where subjective criteria are now prescribed. The job announcement bulletin of the American Political Science Association, for example, includes the following regulation regarding nepotism: "Institutions employing political scientists should abolish nepotism rules, whether they apply departmentally or to the institution as a

[25] Ibid.

whole. Employment and advancement should be based solely on professional qualifications without regard for family relationships."[26] There is of course an inherent contradiction between these two sentences, which constitute a linguistic miracle. In the real world, departments are often obliged to make a package deal in order to recruit the preferred member (in some cases the female partner) of such immaculately professional unions.

The size and concentration now seen in government and the major economic sectors have inevitably affected other institutional sectors. Interest groups, for example, have grown phenomenally and have harnessed the most sophisticated tactics to their drive for political influence, essentially in response to government's expanding control over the economy.[27] Today, such groups are exquisitely varied, ranging across the whole spectrum of national activities. Most recent among them are groups representing disadvantaged sectors of American society, such as senior citizens, minority groups, the poor, women, blacks, Indians, Eskimos, and those in total institutions, such as prisons and asylums. Indeed, it is difficult to find any social activity or interest that does not have such representation. This is not to say, of course, that they are all *equally* represented. Substantial variations exist in their political and organizational resources, with business-industrial and professional groups tending to monopolize the instruments of political influence, both in number and resources. If labor unions are defined as "voluntary groups," they too enjoy annual budgets, vast memberships, and research facilities that give them considerable power at every level of government. Yet, in part because of the class selectivity of legislators and higher civil servants, labor does not enjoy the legitimacy ascribed to business, industrial, or professional groups.

When one analyzes the relative political effectiveness of interest groups, business-industrial types tend to rank highest. This is largely because they have the greatest amounts of resources, including the exceptional legitimacy that governmental elites ascribe to economic actors. As a result both access and influence vis-à-vis legislators and high bureaucrats are easier for them to obtain, compared with welfare or ethnic groups. The central place they occupy in the national economy is indicated by the fact that such groups comprise almost one quarter of all group types in the United States. Not only are their budgets the largest among all groups but their permanent heads, located mainly in Washington, D.C. and New York City,

[26]*American Political Science Association, Personnel Newsletter*, Vol. 21, p. 17.
[27]See Robert Presthus, *Elites in the Policy Process* (New York and London: Cambridge University Press, 1974).

possess the greatest amounts of such political resources as university education, middle-class-and-higher social origins, high salaries, high levels of felt political efficacy, frequency of access to governmental elites, and high levels of lobbying effectiveness.

The increasing role of interest groups has several effects. Certainly, from the standpoint of democratic participation they have increased the sum total of public influence on government policy. One problem, however, is that such groups (with the exception noted of poverty and minority groups) tend to represent social interests that are already highly advantaged. To some extent, they put government in the position of protecting the strong against the weak. The obvious solution is to somehow organize society on a more widely representative basis, yet the hard fact of inequitable resources remains and tends to insure a perpetuation of the status quo.

From our immediate perspective, such groups have accelerated the rise of the organizational society. They have enhanced the validity of the definition of politics as essentially a struggle between highly self-conscious groups, engaged in a competitive struggle for their own advantage. Any larger community interest tends to become essentially an honorific symbol, often used as an instrument in their competition for ever larger shares of government's largesse. Such groups increase the parameters of the bureaucratic situation, as they enlist every known organizational weapon to serve their ends of security, income, and influence—often for narrowly limited ends. In this sense, they have substantially increased the pace at which we are moving toward a society of increased rationality and control.

A suggestive example is the pervasive and sometimes disturbing role of professional associations.[28] Historically, such organizations have been instrumental in upgrading the quality of service provided the public in their various spheres. They have undoubtedly deepened occupational commitment and group solidarity among their members. They have also provided an occupational alternative that enables many individuals to escape the personal dependency attending work in the giant collectivities in which most Americans spend their working lives. At the same time, certain untoward consequences have attended the rise of professionalization. Artifically-induced certification and protectionism are often visible. Analytically, of course, it

---

[28]For an incisive critique of professional values and behavior, see Burton Bledstein, *The Culture of Professionalism: The Middle Class and the Development of Higher Education in America* (New York: Norton, 1977); see also Corinne L. Gilb, *Hidden Hierarchies* (New York: Harper & Row, 1966); regarding the emerging "semi-professions" and their search for legitimacy, see Amitai Etzioni, *The Semi-Professions and Their Organization* (New York: Free Press, 1969).

is difficult to determine whether such anomalies are a consequence of professionalization itself or of bureaucratic organization. My assumption is that the two conditions are inseparable because of the extent to which professionals have structured themselves into bureaucratically-designed organizations. The behaviors we shall describe are products of self-conscious professionalization, organized along bureaucratic lines and articulated through traditional interest group structures. Some of the resulting dysfunctions need to be reviewed. They illustrate well the "two faces" of complex organizations.

As other collectivities, professional association tends to demand total loyalty and a uniformly positive endorsement of the established norms and values of a discipline. Thus it is that the manifest associational function of enhancing the interests of members is reinforced by a less happy capability—the displacement of sanctions vis-à-vis dissidents within their ranks.

Such activities may appear in conjunction with the association's role as a mediator between its members and the foundations and government. The association acts as a gatekeeper between its members and the sources of funding from related organizations. It plays a legitimating role. Partly as a labor-saving device, government agencies and foundations "clear" research and fellowship applications with the appropriate association. Here a pervasive interlocking directorate, similar to that found in the corporate world, may be seen. Members designated by each association serve on the relevant committees of private foundations and such government granting agencies as the National Science Foundation.[29] Communication among such networks is typically informal and provides a useful instrument for allocating rewards and deprivations. In most cases, such clearances may be pro forma; reasonably objective standards may apply, always subject to the kinds of "halo images" cited elsewhere.

In other circumstances, candidates may be rejected on essentially subjective grounds. One might assume that foundations would have the independence and the expertise to make judgments on the grounds of the usual evidence, including a candidate's vitae and letters of recommendation from his peers. Such evidence, however, may at times become tangential, subordinated to the endorsement of elites from the relevant association, using ascriptive criteria. Thus a form of blacklisting may occur, typically rationalized in professional language of marginal scholarship, research interests that are too esoteric, too traditional, and so on. Despite the vast size and scope of American

---

[29]For an account of the symbiotic links existing among prestigious individuals in the universities, foundations, and the federal government following World War II, see Daniel S. Greenberg, *The Politics of Pure Science* (New York: New American Library, 1967).

academic disciplines, it seems that the penumbra of control and legitimacy narrows sharply, permitting the sanctioning of individuals on a national and indeed an international scale (the latter because members of international committees are similarly designated by elites in the various national associations).

Meanwhile, preferment or the hope of preferment will insure that most association members, through commission or omission, endorse this system. Insofar as their present condition represents mobility from lower middle-class origins, academic men are especially likely to defer to the collective power of associations. They do have something to lose. Here, ironically, is the other face of the American ideal and reality of social mobility. One might deplore the weakness of philanthropoids who default on their own obligation to determine the conditions of awards, but their behavior seems characteristic of the collective irresponsibility inherent in modern bureaucratic settings. In the case of the Stanford Center for the Advanced Study of Behavioral Science, for example, despite its terms of reference which prescribe the development of behavioral studies by funding scholars of demonstrated achievement in this area, its fellows have included established scholars, academic statesmen, recent undeveloped Ph.Ds, and most interestingly, individuals whose interests are nonbehavioral if not anti-behavioral. This condition suggests that the Center's criteria of admission are at best an amalgam of ascription and achievement.

The sanctions available to professional associations and their interlocking foundations are exquisitely varied. These include ineligibility for appointment to major departments, having one's books reviewed unsympathetically or not at all (the editors of the various journals in the various subfields of a discipline typically meet annually to discuss matters of mutual concern), having one's research grant applications denied. Control of editorships of the several journals insures considerable influence over the direction of research in a discipline and the selection of manuscripts for publication, which is critical for a scholar's professional advancement. The selection of reviewers for manuscripts and books makes possible some control of the type of evaluation received. Since editors do not select in a vacuum, ascriptive criteria may intrude. Faced with a manuscript from a Big Ten department and another from some lesser institution, there is a tendency to favor the former. As Logan Wilson put it, "Papers from major universities look better to editors. . . ."[30] Allocation of the typical association's rewards such as its presidency through co-opta-

---

[30] *The Academic Man: Sociology of a Profession* (London: Oxford University Press, 1958), p. 171; also Diana Crane, "Scientists at Major and Minor Universities: A Study of Productivity and Recognition," *American Sociological Review*, Vol. 30, pp. 699–714.

tion rather than election, the rule until quite recently, provides another basis for ascriptive criteria. It is ironic that the American Economic Association offered its presidency to Thorstein Veblen, perhaps America's most seminal thinker, only at the very end of his career. This should not have astonished Veblen, however, since he remained an assistant professor at the University of Chicago for sixteen years, during which he wrote two classics, *The Theory of the Leisure Class* and *The Engineers and the Price System.* Meanwhile, perhaps the most productive American political scientist of his generation labors at a far Western university of no particular distinction. One can say of him, as was said of C. Wright Mills, here is a man who will never be president of his association.

So compelling are ascriptive incentives that certain lower-rank Ivy League departments tend to recruit "rejects" (i.e., individuals not selected for tenure) from Harvard, Yale, and Columbia in preference to superior candidates from less prestigious institutions. Whereas such behaviors may appear suicidal in the long term, their dysfunctions are muted by the fact that even the most self-conscious departments require a work force comprising only about 20 percent of productive scholars, complemented by a large contingent of academic statesmen, all of whom are great teachers. The multiple activities of the typical university department mean that such individuals can remain busy across the years, carrying out mundane chores and academic ceremonials, meanwhile validating the Parkinsonian dictum that work expands to fill the time available to perform it.

The sanctioning mechanisms of associations are reinforced by the structure of universities, which mirror the concentration noted earlier in industry. In American political science, some twenty departments have long monopolized prestige, power, publication, and the production of graduate students. The ties of mutual reinforcement among them are constantly fed by a meticulous system of exchange.[31] The currencies are quite varied, including promising young faculty and graduate students, prestigious senior posts, lectures, chairmanships, participation in panels at annual meetings, uniformly enthusiastic reviewing of books, reciprocal citing of each other's work, support for foundation grants, posts in the association hierarchy, and so on. The self-conscious cohesion underlying these exchanges permits the effective allocation of sanctions vis-à-vis outsiders, carried out through the informal network existing among senior members of such depart-

---

[31]The latent assumptions underlying the system of exchange in elite universities are explicit in Theodore Caplow and Reece McGee, *The Academic Marketplace* (New York: Basic Books, 1959), and E. Digby Baltzell, *The Protestant Establishment* (New York: Random House, 1964), especially ch. 15.

ments (and their graduates stationed around the country), who control entry to privileged sanctuaries within academia. Typically, as in the South, where the best people were never directly involved in lynching, vendettas are usually carried out by acolytes, some of whom have visions of being brought back to the eminent departments which conferred their *rites de passage*.[32] Such demonstrations of complete loyalty have had career utility since an early political scientist first gave advice to his prince. In a way that makes the Committees of Correspondence seem inept, the punitive impulse is sped around the strategic centers, achieving a remarkable continuity.

The Byzantine ethos is ramified by the confidentiality of recommendations and the indirection made possible by a liberal education. Some awkwardness was introduced in academia by the mass democratic thrust of the 1960s which forced the public announcement of positions that traditionally had been kept hidden, in part to insure that ascription might retain an appropriate role. Now, "chairpersons" are obliged to dissimulate in a more oblique way, the usual ploy being some variation on the theme that a blundering legislature has inexplicitly called back funds thought available, that it has proved impossible to find a person adequately suited to the department's needs, or (as in one case brought to my attention) that the deadline for applications has unfortunately passed. Some chairpeople simply fail to answer inquiries regarding the very posts they have advertised.

One suspects that such sanctions vary across disciplines, but social science surely contains its share of Establishmentarians who long for place and power in the real world of politics, and thus find an adequate reservoir of arguments justifying them. When professional record or personal ideology fail as disqualifying stigmata, social criteria can be marshaled to serve a similar end.[33] Here, even the cohesion of the first twenty may be strained as the preferences of Ivy League scholars and teachers tend to shut out what may be called Big Ten types. It is not entirely a matter of the class origins of the individuals concerned, since socialization and the fact of regional social elitism tend to preserve the distinction being made here.[34] Despite any potential anachronism in a technological age, the model of the

---

[32] This phenomenon has been labeled "The Silver Cord" by Caplow and McGee, *The Academic Marketplace*.

[33] As one faculty member in an elite university put it, we prefer a "good social person, nice person, happily married; you let some shit in, or someone with marital problems, Christ knows what'll happen." *The Academic Marketplace*, p. 137. Or again, "He played the recorder. That was the reason we hired him. [Interviewer]: "Because he played a recorder?" "Yes, we thought that would be nice." Ibid., p. 141.

[34] Cf. E. Digby Baltzell: *Philadelphia Gentlemen: The Making of a National Upper Class* (Glencoe, Ill.: Free Press, 1958).

English gentleman persists in the Ivy ambiance. This often attractive model tends at times to disqualify Big Ten types who may lack the grace, civility, and dependency that may characterize those socialized in more self-conscious milieux. Some discontinuity is introduced, of course, by the onslaughts of universalistic recruitment upon the Ivy arena, as well as by the imperative of the "productive minority" which even the most hallowed department must enlist to preserve a semblance of the reality upon which its mystique rests. But even the most primitive urbanite can be smoothed out in the hierarchical, deferential authority structures of Ivy League departments. Meanwhile, alternatives remain available, in the form of Continental, British, and Canadian recruits who do well in the Ivy milieu since they personify the residual ideal.[35]

The remarkable continuity of the British-Ivy model is inexplicable, however, without the existence in the American hinterlands of a huge reservoir of aspirants, educated in Ivy departments which (unfortunately in this context) produced until quite recently the great majority of American Ph.Ds, socializing them into a self-conscious image of the appropriate academic role that could only bring disenchantment since market conditions effectively foreclosed the possibility of realizing their desire. Such is the discipline nourished by hope and ambition, however, that many such individuals continue to honor the ideal, collaborating happily in its institutionalization, treasuring the occasional honor thrown their way, and in the case of the "true believer" colluding in the occasional injustice required to preserve and enhance their association and its reputation among political and economic elites.[36]

Here again American pragmatism, its respect for power and success, is decisive in mediating the personal dependency and manipulation of self that may attend this conception of professional behavior. Such conditions of participation also reflect the growing complexity of American society and particularly the specialization accompanying it which constricts the operational boundaries of each domain, bringing greater dependence along with often superior performance. Sunk costs of time and knowledge aggravate the resulting dependency. In the process, the potential scope of selective sanctioning increases. We are confronted with an organizational triumph, the rather remarkable situation in which in a nation of 220 million people, each occupa-

[35]For an account of the facility with which aliens can fit into established power structures, see Lewis Coser, "The Alien as a Servant of Power: Court Jews and Christian Renegades," *American Sociological Review*, Vol. 37, pp. 574–581.

[36]See, for example, the account of the career of C. Wright Mills in Dan Wakefield, "Taking It Big," *The Atlantic*, September 1971, pp. 65–71.

tional hierarchy is able quickly to identify and discipline individuals in perhaps the most salient of their life spaces. The centralized shaping of dominant norms in a given association reinforces the effects of specialization. An effective blacklist can be authoritatively mounted and disseminated from this governing center, whose permanent officials, as Robert Michels found, enjoy decisive influence vis-à-vis the members designated for one- and two-year positions in the association's official apparatus and its apathetic rank and file.[37] The co-optation process whereby those in elite roles designate their successors tends to ramify the acceptance of the official, monolithic code of the association. Given the ongoing pragmatic orientation, ambivalents will stand condemned as quixotic, and probably stupid as well, for their demonstrated incapacity to confirm and affirm the going system. Indeed, one suspects that the flushing out of such ambivalent types is not entirely unwelcome, since it enhances in some unknown measure the competitive potential of those remaining. As other politicians, academics are intendedly quite rational and, following Harry Stack Sullivan, we may assume that their characteristic dependency sharpens their capacity to elect pragmatic, anxiety-reducing accommodations.

Cohesion among the sanctioning agents in associations, foundations, and government agencies is probably enhanced by their common liberal ideology and tendency to work out their careers in overlapping roles. Thus foundations tend to provide a comfortable sanctuary for deposed university presidents and business school deans, as well as for high government officials perhaps seeking to escape responsibility for such foreign misadventures as Vietnam.[38] Such rotating portfolios tend to encourage continuity and cohesion among those who allocate their largesse to properly qualified academics. As suggested here, clearances are required from gate keepers in a discipline, as well as from permanent officials of associations, with the effect that the nominally responsible heads of foundations and agencies often exercise an essentially de jure role in the process of selection and rejection. As often happens in organizations, those who seem to be responsible are not really responsible, and just who is often remains problematic.

Professional associations and foundations, in effect, are characterized by many of the dimensions found earlier in the ideal-typical

---

[37]Michels, *Political Parties.*

[38]The extent of such interlocking relations among the American foreign-policy-making elite since World War II is traced in Donovan, *The Cold Warriors* and Halberstam, *The Best and the Brightest.*

bureaucracy: hierarchy, considerable tension between ascriptive and achievement norms, oligarchic co-optation in the circulation of elites, patterns of official secrecy, conventionalism and a demand for complete loyalty, and a Kafkaesque diffusion of responsibility.

Meanwhile, other critical sectors have been affected by the spread of bureaucratic norms and rationalization. And here again such imperatives as science, technology, and changing economic values have made a revolution. Newspaper ownership, for example, reveals a secular trend toward size and combination similar to that in basic industry. From 1909 onward the number of independent dailies steadily declined. Despite the increase in literacy and in population, the number of dailies peaked in 1920, when 2,600 newspapers existed, with a total daily circulation of 24 million. By 1939 the number had been reduced to about 2,000 and by 1976, only 1,500 daily papers remained, with a daily circulation of 62 million. Only one city out of twelve having daily newspapers shows competition in this field; only in our large metropolitan centers do readers enjoy the diversity of opinion that competition brings. Once again, the owner-operator had been replaced by new corporate forms, this time by nationwide newspaper chains. Such chains, including the Hearst, Thomson, Knight-Ridder, Scripps-Howard, Gannett, and McCormick-Patterson interests, now control 63 percent of total newspaper circulation. Control is sharply concentrated within the twenty largest chains, with Gannett at the top with 54 dailies, followed by Thomson Newspapers with 53, Knight-Ridder with 32, Newhouse with 30, and Freedom Newspapers with 24. Early in 1977, moreover, Gannett announced an agreement to merge with the Speidel Newspaper chain, which would push the Gannett total to 70 dailies, spread across 28 states. Seventy-two newspapers changed ownership during 1976 in what *Business Week* characterized as the "frenzied bidding war now raging among newspaper publishers."[39] In the early 1970s the largest ten chains accounted for one quarter of the total industry revenue of $2.2 billion.[40] The difficulties of entry and the resulting concentration are suggested by the fact that around 10 million dollars is required to launch a big city paper. In a medium-size city of 50,000 the investment required is around 750,000 dollars. Insofar as newspapers

[39]*Business Week*, February 21, 1977, p. 56. See also, Stephen R. Barnett, "Merger Monopoly and A Free Press," *The Nation*, January 15, 1977.

[40]Ernest C. Hynds, *American Newspapers in the 1970s* (New York: Hastings House, 1975), pp. 130–132. Of the 1,500 dailies remaining across the United States, one-half belong to one or another of 155 chains. The definition of a "chain" or "group," moreover, is not very stringent, since it means the ownership of only two or more papers. As in other industrial sectors, there is a great deal of concentration within this structure.

depend heavily upon advertising revenue (about two-thirds of total income), concentration reflects the press's declining share of total advertising income; by 1976, for example, regarding total *national* advertising volume, newspapers accounted for only 20 percent of the total, amounting to 2 billion dollars, while television received almost half, or 5 billion. In terms of total advertising revenue, newspapers did better, retaining 32 percent of all expenditures in 1975, compared with just under 20 percent for television. However, television's billings grew steadily following World War II, from only 8,700,000 dollars in 1948 to over 5 billion in 1975.[41]

Such structural and financial conditions mean that newspaper publishing has become big business. The decline of competition brings substantial economic rewards. According to Otis Chandler, owner of the Times-Mirror Company, a noncompetitive newspaper "gives you a franchise to do what you want with profitability. You can engineer your profits. You can control expenses and generate revenues almost arbitrarily."[42]

Perhaps inevitably, some cost in editorial autonomy and popular understanding occurs. Although the quality and coverage of news production is often excellent, access to the public media has been curtailed and there is a disturbing tendency for even the best papers to become agents of the government, even to the extent of suppressing news for *raisons d'état,* as in the Bay of Pigs affair or as in Vietnam, where wildly optimistic official versions of political and military reality were far too long accepted.[43] It is only fair to add that reassuring exceptions exist, as in the case of the Pentagon Papers, published by *The New York Times,* despite the opposition of the Nixon Administration. In critical areas involving, for example, such issues as political alternatives to the going system of welfare capitalism, the press no longer serves as a marketplace for opposing ideas. As the distinguished Committee on Freedom of the Press concluded: "The owners and managers of the press determine which persons, which facts, which versions of the facts, and which ideas shall reach the public."[44]

News distribution became more structured as a few major news

---

[41]Standard and Poor's, *Industry Surveys,* October 1976, p. c–69.

[42]*Business Week,* February 21, 1977, p. 59. See also, Donald McDonald, "The Media's Conflict of Interests," *The Center Magazine,* November-December 1976, p. 21, and Suzanne de Lesseps, "News Media Ownership," Editorial Research Reports, Vol. 3 (Washington D.C.: *Congressional Quarterly, Inc.,* March 1977).

[43]Gay Talese, *The Kingdom and the Power* (New York: World Publishing Co., 1969), pp. 4, 5, 7, 18, 23, 116, 317; Halberstam, *The Best and the Brightest.*

[44]Robert D. Leigh, ed., *A Free and Responsible Press* (Chicago: University of Chicago Press, 1947), p. 16.

services assumed control of selecting, writing, and disseminating national and international news.[45] Standardized opinion received another fillip as the same story with the same interpretation appeared in newspapers across the country, if not internationally. The resulting decline of individual criticism was aggravated by the syndicated columnist whose interpretations provided a predigested opinion for millions of readers. Both diversity and quality languished under a system that featured manufactured news and mass appeal. Standardization received yet another impetus as newspapers acquired radio and television outlets, culminating in 1975 in a new rule by the Federal Communications Commission forbidding such cross ownership, and breaking up some of the existing combinations but leaving untouched 79 others.[46] Reporters understood the realities of power, and the expectations of their publishers were clear enough. The dominant rationale held that since the publisher owned the newspaper, which was after all a business, its editorial policy was properly his to determine.

Book publishing, in which relatively small capital requirements have traditionally eased entry, also succumbed to the merger fever. Giant conglomerates acquired publishers as part of their own move toward diversification. Gulf and Western, which owns Paramount Pictures and some dozen other companies, took over Simon and Schuster, which in turn owns Pocket Books, the softcover publisher. CBS bought one of the largest small operations, Fawcett Publications, which publishes thirty magazines' and endless paperbacks. It also owns Holt, Rinehart & Winston. Doubleday now owns the Literary Guild, Dell Paperbacks, and Delacorte Press. MGA, another entertainment giant, owns G. P. Putnam's Sons and its paperback subsidiary, Berkeley Publishing. The conflicts of interest that may arise from such dual ownerships are suggested by the suit brought by Alex Haley against Doubleday, in part because it allegedly sold the paperback rights of his best seller *Roots* to its own subsidiary at a nominal price that injured Haley who, as author, received one-half of such proceeds.

Radio Corporation of America not only owns NBC but acquired Random House, Alfred A. Knopf, Pantheon Books, and Ballantine Books. Warner Communications owns Warner Books. *The New York Times* owns several magazines, as well as Quadrangle Books. The *Los*

---

[45] Jerome A. Barron, *Freedom of the Press for Whom?* (Bloomington: University of Indiana Press, 1973); Ben H. Bagdikian, *The Effete Conspiracy* (New York: Harper & Row, 1972); David J. Leroy and Christopher H. Sterling, *Mass News: Practices, Controversies, and Alternatives* (Englewood Cliffs, N.J.: Prentice-Hall, 1973).

[46] de Lesseps, "News Media Ownership," p. 193.

Angeles Times now owns the New American Library paperback house, and Hearst Corporation owns Avon Books. Time, Inc., of course, produces *Time, Life,* and *Fortune,* but in addition it owns Little, Brown and Company.[47] It is difficult to say what if any impact such ownership structures have on the selection and production of books. One suspects that the very size and multifarious activities of the conglomerates insures considerable latitude for the managers of the publishing firms; only when their profit and loss statements become an issue would the parent executives be likely to intervene directly. The effects on increased concentration are clear enough.

Radio and television followed the trend as the major networks, their clients, and the advertising agencies dominated local stations, aided by the latter's need for "name" programs and advertising revenue. Here again, programing reflected science, specialization, and the pecuniary nexus. Responsibility was atomized, masked, and unequally shared by clients, agencies, and networks. Television, which was hailed as a new opportunity for experimentation, quickly fell into the organizational pecuniary mold. As John Crosby, whose frank and intelligent critiques of television make him unique among his guild, commented on this development:

> Television is suffering from the same ailment that afflicts the rest of the country—bigness. Today three networks control what 180,000,000 people are going to look at. Even if the program heads who wield this vast power were all high-minded, this would be a narrow bottleneck through which to pour all the creative energy of the country. But they're not high-minded men. . . . When an independent producer brings a show to a network, the network's first query is: "What's my cut?" The going rate is thirty per cent. If the producer doesn't cut the network in for that much, he's not likely to get air time.[48]

Although such practices indicate that programing responsibility is shared among sponsors, advertising agencies, and networks, it is not equally shared. The advertising agencies, which are the least visible to the consumer, have the most control over program content. As early as 1930, in the words of one executive, "much of the original glamour and mystery of radio had vanished, and men had to take a more realistic approach. The Ayer firm rapidly developed the view that an agency must start with the client's sales program, determine whether radio could help, and then devise a program which will

[47]*St. Louis Post-Dispatch,* March 20, 1976, p.27.
[48]*New York Herald Tribune,* July 29, 1960.

achieve specific ends in terms of sales."[49] By 1976, according to *Fortune,* total annual expenditures on advertising in the United States were 32 billion dollars.[50]

The volume and concentration of advertising billings and the attending influence of relatively few agencies and sponsors are suggested by the following data. Among the three big networks in 1944, CBS had thirteen clients who bought over 1 million dollars of time each; and of these, three spent over 4 million dollars. NBC's million-dollar clients numbered eleven; ABC's, nine; and MBS's, three. Among the advertising agencies, J. Walter Thompson bought over 13 million dollars worth of time from the three networks, Young and Rubicam bought 10 million dollars, and Dancer, Fitzgerald, 7 million dollars. Three agencies, that is, bought one-fourth of the total time sold by the three major networks. In 1945, moreover, only seven sponsors and six agencies provided fully one-half of CBS's $6,724,362 worth of billings.[51]

By 1958 a relatively small number of sponsors continued to dominate media advertising and to share with the agencies the major responsibility (or lack of it) for program content. The one hundred leading network-television advertisers did 93.4 percent of total billings, which amounted to $527,641,094. Moreover, the first ten among them accounted for 42 percent of this huge sum.[52]

By 1975 the impact of television, with billings something like two-and-one-half times those of radio, had radically altered the distribution of media advertising. Some 3,500 advertising agencies handled a total of 7 billion dollars' worth of billings in radio and television. Of these agencies the eighty-seven largest did over 25 million dollars' worth of billings, over 1,000 of the remaining 2,476 did fewer than 1 million dollars, while another 1,127 did between 1 million and 5 million dollars.[53] In the past, the first position had been held by soap companies, followed by the big firms in food products and automobiles. By 1975, these rankings had changed as tobacco manufacturers assumed the lead, followed by toiletries, automotives, consumer service, and liquor—all of whom spent very similar amounts for that year. Sharp fluctuations occur among these product lines, since ad-

[49]Quoted in Llewellyn White, *The American Radio* (Chicago: University of Chicago Press, 1947), p. 56.

[50]*Fortune,* August 1976, p. 136.

[51]Ibid., pp. 57–58.

[52]*Broadcasting,* Yearbook Issue (1959), pp. D62–D74; *Printers' Ink,* October 30, 1959, pp. 304–305, 361–362.

[53]*Standard Directory of Advertising Agencies,* National Register Publishing Co., October 1976, p. A–5.

vertising expenditures closely follow consumer spending. General Mills, for example, had a dramatic 130 percent increase from 1975 to 1976, attended by 49 percent increases for General Foods and R. J. Reynolds Tobacco. Corporations generally spend an average of 1 percent of sales for advertising, ranging from a low of 0.1 percent among mining firms to highs of 3.7, 3.4, and 3.3 percent in tobacco, motion pictures, and chemicals, respectively.

The effects of such structural variables on program content and the shaping of American values seem clear enough. Since the advertising agencies' aim of maximizing the audience is shared by the sponsor who provides the money, programs are bound to be standardized. The networks, licensed to control the air in the public interest, in effect sublease their concession to unknown occupants, the agencies, who assume the major role in program design. Here again the scientific paraphernalia (market research, program ratings, motivational research, etc.) of a new bureaucratic skill group exerts its influence. Although the sponsors will not buy any "package" indiscriminately, their main objective is to increase sales, and it is the "engineers of consent" who tell them how. Their consumer research proves that comedians are preferable to symphony; so the same entertainers labor the same tired routines for decades. Here the lack of competition is painfully apparent. Although critics insist that radio has not had a new idea in twenty-five years, the success of the existing formula provides little reason for change. Thus the pecuniary values, the harnessing of social science to merchandizing, and the resulting search for standardized commodities seen in newspaper publishing tend to be duplicated in radio and television.

In motion pictures a succession of antitrust suits aimed at divorcing production from exhibition and at block booking indicates that the managed market exists there also.[54] Control of the environment from producer through consumer is achieved through vertical integration and through the shaping of consumer demand by unrestrained advertising. Under the block-booking system, the theater owner is obliged to contract for films in groups, sometimes forty to fifty at a time. In effect, to qualify for a few "A" films the owner must accept several "B" pictures or worse.

Motion-picture ownership has been highly concentrated, with five major companies enjoying an "overwhelming superiority" in capital resources, volume, profits, and power. Before 1940 the Big Five—Metro-Goldwyn-Mayer, Paramount, R.K.O., Twentieth-Century Fox, and Warner Brothers—"controlled 70 percent of first-run theaters in

---

[54]The landmark cases are two: *United States* v. *Paramount Pictures*, 334 U.S. 131 (1948) and *United States* v. *Loew's*, 371 U.S. 38 (1962).

the ninety-two largest cities."[55] The "majors" also included Columbia, United Artists, and Universal. In 1938 these companies were sued by the Department of Justice, which charged them with monopolistic practices, citing their vested interest in both production and distribution and their ownership of theaters. In addition to block booking, their offenses included blind selling, overbuying, and clearance protection. Blind selling is related to block booking; the exhibitor contracts to buy films which are often not yet produced. Overbuying also attended block booking because the exhibitor was obliged to contract for many films, sometimes including short subjects and newsreels in order to secure those he wanted. Clearance protection sets time limits before pictures shown by a certain type of house can be shown by others in the same zone. This system protects the first-run theaters, which are 80 percent affiliated and are often owned or controlled by the major film companies. Following extensive litigation, these practices were modified under a "consent decree."

While landmark court decisions "have destroyed the nationwide combination that controlled the motion picture industry,"[56] the decisions did not provide for sustained regulation among those who make, those who distribute, and those who show its product. Some observers feared that the industry, which in the words of one judge, has "shown a marked proclivity for unlawful conduct . . . ," might resume its old ways once the courts' watchdog role, established in the Paramount case, came to an end.[57] Market structure and the pattern of film allocation remain far from the competitive model. Distributors retain potential monopoly power through their copyright of popular films. The circuits of motion-picture houses, some of which were divorced from producer ownership, were not broken into small enough units. United Paramount theaters, for example, retained some five hundred houses, while National Theaters and Stanley Warner emerged with three hundred each. When such circuits are concentrated in specific areas, as the larger ones tend to be, they may again permit strong bargaining for preferential treatment.[58] As Michael Conant concludes: "The circuits should have been destroyed."

Some of these conditions have been obviated by post–1960 developments in the industry. Television, of course, brought near disaster, of-

[55]Ruth A. Inglis, *Freedom of the Movies* (Chicago: University of Chicago Press, 1947).

[56]Michael Conant, *Antitrust in the Motion Picture Industry* (Berkeley: University of California Press, 1960), p. 218.

[57]Ibid., p. 209.

[58]Ibid.

fering a broader, often more realistic entertainment menu with less expense and inconvenience. In 1946, weekly attendance at movie houses reached a peak of 80 million. By 1963, the figure had shrunk to only 21 million and by 1975, it had fallen to 18 million. Gross revenues dwindled by 25 percent. The industry is now producing about 150 feature films a year, compared with 1935 when the total was 700 films. For the most part the studios are grinding out TV serials, TV specials, and TV commercials. M-G-M, in 1973, withdrew completely from the business. Box-office miracles still occur occasionally, including *The Sound of Music* (gross 100 million dollars) and *The Godfather* (150 million dollars), but essentially the industry now relies upon its sales to television for economic survival.

Some aid and comfort came to the industry from certain Warren Court decisions[59] that "made it possible for films exploiting sex, nudity and violence to flood the screen."[60] A substantial number of suits charging obscenity, defamation, and violation of privacy were launched. The advent of the more conservative Berger Court brought considerable tightening up as censorship was viewed more favorably and in 1976, made contingent upon local discretion in an effort to meet community variations in taste.[61] Meanwhile, relationships between the producers and television were beset with legal difficulties concerning copyright, distribution rights, and a bizarre situation in which a flourishing black market existed in stolen films. On the positive side, there is some indication of an upturn in attendance, beginning about 1972. The financial trials of the industry have been eased by takeovers of some majors by such conglomerates as Gulf and Western and Trans-America Corporation. Although one shudders to think of the image of America transported abroad by most films, financially at least, they have been vital. The return from them has been estimated at about one-half of total industry income, easing greatly the impact of competition from TV.[62]

This brief account of "noneconomic" areas indicates similarities between the structure and tactics of the mass media and those of the major basic industries. Vertical integration in order to control production, distribution, and demand is a common feature, attended

---

[59]Among others, the Carmen Babtz case, *Rabe* v. *Washington,* 405 U.S. 313 (1972); *United States* v. *I am Curious (Yellow),* 404 F. 2d 196 (3d Cir. 1968).

[60]Alexander Lindey, *Entertainment, Publishing and the Arts: Agreements and the Law,* Vol. 1 (New York: Clark Boardman, 1975), p. 272.

[61]Cf. "The Devil in Miss Jones" case, *Vergari* v. *Pierre Productions, Inc.,* 43 App. Div. 2d 950, 352 N.Y.S. 2d 34 (1974); *People* v. *Wrench,* 73 Misc. 2d 434, 341 N.Y.S. 2d 985 (1973). For the "Deep Throat" case, see *United States* v. *Marks,* 520 F. 2d 913 (1975).

[62]Michael Mayer, *The Film Industries* (New York: Hastings House, 1973), p. 202.

by size and concentration. The planning and effort required to gain such control is an impressive tribute to human ingenuity. But the imperatives of economic organization, such as the need to secure a safe return on a huge, fixed capital outlay, encourage violent standardization and a pervasive "don't-take-a-chance" mentality. A related dysfunction is the high money costs of maintaining the overhead apparently necessary to control such complex systems. In 1976, for example, American Broadcasting Company lists total receipts of 1.64 billion dollars, yet emerges with a net profit of only 17 million dollars. Its expenses include 32 million dollars in advertising costs.

This overview suggests the emergence of the bureaucratic model as the major organizational form in our society. Beginning about 1875, social, economic, and political trends in the United States prepared the way for the "organizational society," characterized by large-scale bureaucratic institutions in virtually every social area. The master trends included the separation of ownership from management; increasing size and concentration in business, industry, and eleemosynary fields; the decline of competition as the financial resources required for entry in almost every sector became prohibitive; the development of a political economy; and the emergence of an employee society. We now turn to the sociopsychological basis of personality as a preface to an analysis of individual behavior in this changed organizational context.

THE | 4
SOCIOPSYCHOLOGICAL
BASIS OF
ORGANIZATIONAL
PERSONALITY

We can now consider how personality is formed largely through the process of socialization. Once this process has been examined in a broad social context, its formulations will be applied to the typical bureaucratic organization, which we have defined as a miniature of the larger social system. For this purpose we shall rely mainly upon Harry Stack Sullivan's interpersonal theory of psychiatry and the two disciplines upon which it rests, social psychology and cultural anthropology.[1]

There are of course many psychologies and many theories of personality, each differing somewhat in its conception of the critical variables that shape personality and human behavior. Sullivan's interpersonal theory, however, provides a most fruitful basis for examining behavior in a bureaucratic setting. What follows depends explicitly upon his formulations, particularly those dealing with anxiety, authority, and the social and developmental basis of personality. The utility of these concepts for organizational analysis should become clear as they are applied in this and subsequent chapters.

A major assumption of interpersonal theory is that humans are social beings; their motivating values and behavior are mainly determined by the dominant values of a given society. This cultural matrix outlines their aspirations and provides the very symbols and concepts with which they think. Although the notion that mind possesses

---

[1]Harry Stack Sullivan, *Interpersonal Theory of Psychiatry,* H. S. Perry and M. L. Gawel, eds. (New York: Norton, 1953), pp. 16–18.

supersensory powers is as old as Plato, who denied that sense perceptions were real, medical research has shown that mind is actually the product of a particular state of knowledge at a given time. As F. S. A. Doran concludes: "Mind is an expression of brain function. . . . Its contents are largely determined by the social force of tradition, and by the fears, beliefs, prejudices, and values of those with whom it comes in contact."[2]

In sum, social conditions define knowledge. People do not think in a vacuum; reason occurs instead within a given framework of cultural values that is rarely questioned, because it is the only reality one knows. This framework becomes a cherished emotional and intellectual repertory and will be so retained until shattered by powerful conflicting experiences. Such personal and social value systems give meaning and order to the phenomenal world. They play a labor-saving role by providing "givens" that facilitate perception and appropriate behavior. Such value systems are systematically instilled by society, which employs compelling rewards and sanctions to insure that individuals internalize them.

A major assumption of this study is that we may validly conceive of big organizations as microcosms of the larger social system. This formulation permits us to apply the concepts of socialization and interpersonal psychiatry to the analysis of organizational behavior. Organizations are indeed miniatures of society. They have a hierarchy of status and of roles, a system of myths and values, and a catalogue of expected behaviors. They are probably more significant than most voluntary associations because of their concern with economic and status needs and with the discipline that results. Such organizations are defined here as miniature social systems that meet many of the most basic needs of their members and expect in return loyalty and conformity.

A caveat is required. Although the values inculcated by society and its many organizations are perhaps inevitably conflicting, we shall confine ourselves here to an analysis of the socialization *process* itself, and to the kinds of values that seem functional in terms of *work* organizations. In later chapters we shall consider the problem of value incongruity and attending personal strains, as seen for example in the conflict experienced by middle-class children who are taught to be quietly aggressive and competitive outside the home while remaining generous and cooperative within the family.

Sullivan's interpersonal theory is concerned with individual and group relations, their social context, and their critical role in shaping

[2]Francis S. A. Doran, *Mind: A Social Phenomenon* (New York: William Sloane Associates, 1953), p. 169.

personality. Whereas psychiatry in the past had focused primarily upon the unique individual, Sullivan conceived of personality as mainly the result of *social interaction*. "Psychiatry is the field of interpersonal relations under any and all circumstances."[3] "Personality is manifest in interpersonal relations, and not otherwise."[4] This conception was based upon two decades of experience with neurotic and schizophrenic patients, which convinced him that "not sick individuals but complex, peculiarly characterized *situations* were the subject matter of research and therapy."[5] Personality and mental aberrations were the result of the individual's accommodation to people who were significant to him. Psychiatry was compared and linked with social psychology. Psychiatry, however, approached the study of human relations through aberrant behavior, which Sullivan insisted was usually an example of extreme or "unduly prolonged instances of relatively universal behavior."[6] Psychoneuroses were merely an exaggerated manifestation of conventional behavior.

Although a member of the "cultural" school of psychiatry, Sullivan built into his interpersonal theory the biological elements of personality. This is clearly apparent in his developmental conception of personality in which unfolding biological needs, such as the sex instinct during adolescence, bring about significant modifications of personality. But the expression of such needs is always largely determined according to existing social values *imposed through interpersonal contacts*. In this conclusion he followed Mead, Cooley, and Simmel, who found earlier that "personality traits are determined in large measure by sociological and cultural conditions."[7] His psychiatry, then, is essentially a cultural psychiatry, drawing upon social psychology and anthropology which had demonstrated the critical role of given social values and institutions in shaping personality.

In the present analysis organizational behavior is similarly viewed as the result of interpersonal liaisons in a "complex, peculiarly characterized [bureaucratic] situation."

For our purpose, Sullivan's conception of anxiety is especially critical. From birth onward the individual is subjected to group norms that over a period of time mold his personality. Personality is defined as a consistent way of reacting or accommodating to interpersonal situations. The *reduction of anxiety* by compliance with the perceived wishes of authoritative persons, such as parents, teachers, and supe-

---

[3]Sullivan, *Conceptions of Modern Psychiatry* (New York: Norton, 1953), p. 4.

[4]Dorothy R. Blitsten, *The Social Theories of Harry Stack Sullivan* (New York: William-Frederick Press, 1953), p. 58.

[5]Ibid., p. 21.

[6]Ibid., p. 23.

[7]Ibid., pp. 19–20.

riors, is a critical mechanism in this process. Interpersonal psychiatry asserts that most behavior is the result of the individual's search for relief from tension by conforming to authority. Anxiety is seen as the most compelling of such tensions, and much of behavior is explained by efforts to escape its painful effects. Apart from certain psychological needs, the bases of tension are socially derived. Children learn that "good" behavior is rewarded, while "bad" behavior is punished. They learn to seek the sanctuary of approval because anxiety evoked by the disapproval of authority figures is unpleasant. Such learning and reinforcement are most clearly seen in childhood when parents manipulate their affection to control them. Although it is sometimes difficult to decide just who is manipulating whom at this stage, the parents usually win out. "Socialization" has occurred; the children have learned the culture; they accept socially approved patterns of behavior.

The end result of the process by which individuals learn to maintain security in interpersonal relations is called the "self-system." This system may be defined as a characteristic way of reacting to others. Unlike needs based upon the physiochemical structure of the individual, the self-system "is derived wholly from the interpersonal aspects of the necessary environment of the human being; it is organized because of the extremely unpalatable, extremely uncomfortable experience of anxiety; and it is organized in such a way as to avoid or minimize existent or foreseen anxiety."[8] The self-system, however, does not necessarily guarantee functional accommodations. Its characteristic security operations may result in failure. Such accommodations are characteristic of our ambivalent type.

Because the socialization process is essentially a function of learning, we must briefly consider learning theory. Here again an outsider must decide which specific theory is most useful for his purposes, for as in the case of psychology, there are several theories of learning. In what follows, the work of so-called Stimulus-Response (SR) theorists such as Thorndike, Pavlov, Skinner, and Mowrer will be drawn upon.[9] These men believe that the learning of anxiety follows a basic Pavlovian principle: an individual associates a given stimuli with a certain response. They also stress the reduction of anxiety as a reward of reinforcement for certain kinds of learning. Both concepts seem useful in explaining behavior in the authority-structured bureaucratic situation.

Learning may be defined as a modification of the nervous system resulting from exposure to a certain kind of stimulus. Its effectiveness

---

[8]Sullivan, *Interpersonal Theory of Psychiatry*, p. 190.

[9]Bergen R. Bugelski, *The Psychology of Learning* (New York: Holt, Rinehart & Winston, 1956), chaps. 1, 4, 5.

depends upon the number and strength of existing habits, upon one's perceptual facility, and upon the strength of the drive or need evoked by the stimulus. *Perception* is the process of becoming acquainted with the environment. Its basic motive appears to be curiosity, but anxiety and an apparently instinctive tendency to use our sense organs are also involved.[10] Observation suggests that we appraise new situations in an effort to orient ourselves, to decide what role is appropriate. Perception defines the behavioral limits of a situation in the sense that its accuracy determines the effectiveness of our response. Evidence will be presented later to show that a certain level of anxiety facilitates perception. However, as Sullivan and others have shown, anxiety may also distort perception, culminating in exaggerated, "neurotic" responses.

It is clear that perception is affected by the environment, which provides the potential stimulus field. In some situations stimuli are obvious and highly differentiated. There is little ambiguity, therefore, about the behavior expected. The bureaucratic situation has these characteristics, and a major assumption based on experimental psychology can now be stated: *in organizations both perception and conditioning are sharpened by the manifest, authoritative nature of the stimuli. The bureaucratic situation will therefore be called a "structured field."*

Reinforcement is also vital to learning, since it eases conditioning through rewards and punishment. We know that reinforced responses will be quickly learned and will, over a period of time, change one's personality. Individuals develop certain tensions (anxieties) that reflect needs for food, water, sex, recognition, power, and security. Actions that satisfy these needs are reinforced because they reduce tension generated by the need. The reduction of anxiety is thus an unusually powerful reinforcement. Learning is also affected by attitudes, that is, by predispositions to act in certain ways. We learn things that agree with our preconceptions (our personality) much more easily and retain them longer than those that seem alien.

The psychological field of organization and the way it affects behavior can be suggested by two classic studies. Pavlov and Skinner have shown how problem solving in dogs and rats can be conditioned through the manipulation of stimuli and through the use of rewards and punishments.[11] Pavlov's experiments demonstrated the conditioned response by adding a new stimuli, a bell sound, to the usual situation causing salivation in dogs. Normally dogs salivate only upon

[10]Stanley S. Stevens, *Handbook of Experimental Psychology* (New York: Wiley, 1951), pp. 357–358.

[11]Ivan P. Pavlov, *Conditioned Reflexes* (London: Oxford University Press, 1927); B. F. Skinner, *The Behavior of Organisms: An Experimental Analysis* (New York: Appleton-Century-Crofts, 1938).

seeing food, but after the bell was rung several times just before feeding. Pavlov found that the sound itself caused salivation. The animal had become conditioned to the bell sound.

Skinner's experiments suggest the importance of reinforcement (using the reward principle) in learning. A hungry rat, placed in an empty box equipped with only a lever, will in time depress the lever. Since this releases food, the consequent reduction of hunger increases the chances that the rat will repeat the action, illustrating the need-reduction principle in behavior. Reinforcement and motivation, building upon needs and satisfactory ways of meeting them, thus lead to learning and to habit formation.

Different patterns of learning (socialization) result in different modes of perception. The bureaucratic situation, for example, is not "seen" in the same way by all its members. While some individuals perceive the organization as a favorable place in which to assert their career claims, others view its systems of authority and status as threatening. Each structures reality into a discrete mold. As our three modal types suggest, each adopts interpersonal accommodations that meet his or her own needs.

Socialization, however, is more than a process; it is also a system for inculcating certain approved values and excluding others. Both the process and the values have a lasting influence upon personality. Margaret Mead found a striking example in the Balinese custom of teasing and playing with the child until it became excited, whereupon the mother breaks off play without further gratification. This practice produced withdrawn adults, unable to achieve close emotional relations with others.[12] Kardiner found similarly that the mother is a frustrating object to the child in the Marquesian and Alorese societies.[13] Neglect and rejection characterize mother-child relations among the Marquesians, but since the father assumes a protective role, the children tend to develop independent, outgoing personalities. In Alor, however, both parents reject the child, a practice which apparently accounts for the suspicion and hostility of the Alorese. Among the Comanche, on the other hand, parental care was found to be consistently sympathetic, resulting in self-confident, cooperative adults.[14]

The effect of social structure on personality is suggested by Erich Fromm's analysis of German character in *Escape From Freedom*.[15] He

---

[12]Margaret Mead, *From the South Seas* (New York: Morrow, 1939).

[13]Abraham Kardiner, *The Psychological Frontiers of Society* (New York: Columbia University Press, 1945).

[14]Ibid.

[15]Erich Fromm, *Escape From Freedom* (New York: Rinehart & Co., 1941). The extension of the family system to political systems in non-Western cultures is analyzed in

maintains that dislocations following World War I prepared German society for totalitarian government. Highly respected institutions, the army, the patriarchal family, political control by miltary and upper-class elements, and a rigid class system collapsed following the war. The democratic Weimar Republic, inflation, impoverishment of the middle class, the growing political influence of the working class, mass unemployment, the father's inability to support the family, the defeat of the hallowed army, all brought the disintegration of old values and a state of psychological shock that resulted in a desire "to escape from freedom." Submission to the political and racial myths of National Socialism provided the major avenue.

Not only was the individual German's personality shaped by such values, but German institutions reflected and reinforced them. The well-known German respect for authority molds and reflects an authoritarian social structure. Such social influences were reinforced by the individual's projection of his conscience upon German institutions. Money-Kyrle argued (on the basis of interviews following World War II) that the German bureaucrat's idealization of the state indulged his own authoritarian inclinations.[16] His dependency permitted him to accept its directives even when they were immoral. At the same time, the rigid class system nourished power-oriented attitudes that well suited the demands of the state. The individual's subordination to such imperatives as racial purity, and the feelings of helplessness that followed, were compensated for by dividends of shared power.

American values and institutions also shape personality in distinctive ways. There have, of course, been many analyses of the so-called American character; those by foreigners such as Bryce and Tocqueville may be best because they are less culture-bound. Although cross-cultural generalizations are always subject to error, societies are different, and such differences mean, as Newcomb said, that "there are many aspects of personality which are, so to speak, standard equipment in one society."[17] In our culture such equipment probably includes a distrust of theory, considerable respect for size and quantitative standards, respect for power, an unchallenged belief in a high degree of social mobility (based upon the ideal of equal opportunity), great disparity in consumption levels (validated by *personal* success or failure), and a pragmatic ethic that often makes success the test of truth. Although often regarded by Europeans as the product of

Robert A. LeVine, "The Role of the Family in Authority Systems: A Cross-Cultural Application of the Stimulus-Generalization Theory," *Behavioral Science,* Vol. 5, pp. 291–296.

[16]Roger E. Money-Kyrle, *Psychoanalysis and Politics* (New York: Norton, 1951).

[17]Theodore Newcomb, *Social Psychology* (New York. Holt, Rinehart & Winston, 1950), p. 340.

considerable naïveté, these values probably reflect our youth, wealth, and relative freedom from intense religious and political differences.

More important, they are bound up with a pervasive *need to be liked.* This single impulse, it seems, explains much about our affinity for group action. We are trained to get along with others and to honor this value highly. Exceptionally sensitive to majority norms, we are good at cooperation, although this fact is somewhat obscured by the rhetoric of competition and by the notion that we are unusually "individualistic." Here our emphasis upon competitive athletics probably has a myth-fulfilling function, sustaining a faith that has become tenuous in more important areas. In major industries such as steel, automobiles, and electrical equipment, a competitive shadowboxing goes on; but concentration and difficulty of entry seem to have culminated in a watered-down advertising competition among firms that produce commodities similar in both quality and price.

These changing terms of competition among organizations have changed the terms of competition *within* organizations. Personal competition remains lively, but it is worked out in an organizational context that requires different values and behavior. An obsolescence of individualism is apparent in a general preference for conformity and adaptability. Well-rounded men who can "play on the team" are sought in most fields,[18] including the universities, where one might have thought that diversity would have been nourished.[19] This condition is aggravated by hierarchy, which insures that one's career chances are mainly dependent upon his immediate superior. Needless to say, the latter's judgment is always an amalgam of personal, technical, and professional considerations, including such subjective indexes as loyalty, dependency, and conviviality. The typical American is assumed therefore to be a group-oriented individual, anxious to be liked and afraid to be different. With some exceptions to be noted later, socialization tends to produce individuals who function well in group situations.

The manipulation of affection and approval begun by parents is continued by the school, the church, and the professional association. Each invokes the mechanisms of learned behavior and anxiety to cash in on its claims. Over a period of time, the characteristic ways of accommodating to such claims shape the individual's personality. The intensity of needs for approval vary individually, just as the values that evoke anxiety vary within cultures in terms of class, vocation, religion, and race. But everyone tends to develop certain satisfactory

[18]William H. Whyte, Jr., "The New Illiteracy," *Saturday Review Reader,* No. 3 (1954), p. 160.

[19]For academic stereotyping, see Theodore Caplow and Reece McGee, *The Academic Marketplace* (New York: Basic Books, 1959).

methods of accommodation, of avoiding anxiety, and of gaining approval.

Anxiety is among the most compelling human drives. As Sullivan maintains: "I believe it fairly safe to say that anybody and everybody devotes much of his lifetime, and a great deal of his energy . . . to avoiding more anxiety than he already has, and, if possible, to getting rid of some of this anxiety."[20] Although anxiety is a hypothetical construct, because we can only infer that it "causes" behavior, the present analysis rests squarely upon this conception of anxiety's role. The internalization of approved values creates a built-in capacity for anxiety as the desires of the individual collide with society's expectations.

Abnormal or neurotic anxiety, however, is different from the fairly common kind of uncomfortable, often unspecific feeling that all of us have when we lack adequate control of situations that are important to us. Anxiety occurs along a continuum ranging from incapacitating, free-floating dread to mild uneasiness. In the present analysis our main concern is with functional anxiety, a moderate degree of tension or sensitivity that tends to sharpen the individual's perception of behavioral alternatives appropriate to a given situation and to their probable consequences. In organizations functional anxiety insures greater sensitivity to the nuances of interpersonal situations and to the varied roles demanded by the nice gradations of status and authority in the bureaucratic work place.

Anxiety appears when something threatens the individuals' relations with persons important to them. Sullivan insists that anxiety is so pervasive that our interpersonal relations are always affected by it. Social psychologists, too, recognize the central role of anxiety in explaining behavior and personality, since the threats and uncertainty associated with it evoke powerful motivations. Among successful business executives, for example, the fear of failure may lead to compulsive attempts to achieve security by controlling one's environment and by achieving ever greater success.[21]

Among young children, the weight of social expectations is increased by the inability to judge their validity; they necessarily accept prevailing values on the basis of faith. During this stage, Sullivan maintains, the child "learns to chart a course by the anxiety gradient." Such interaction with society and its authority figures results in the "self-system," developed in an attempt to reconcile individual needs with those of society. As a style of behavior that evokes the approval of

[20]Sullivan, *Interpersonal Theory of Psychiatry*, p. 11, and *Conceptions of Modern Psychiatry*, pp. 19–23.

[21]Burleigh Gardner, "What Makes Successful and Unsuccessful Executives," *Advanced Management*, Vol. 13, pp. 116–125.

authority figures, this system becomes a way of meeting interpersonal situations with a minimum of strain. The resulting image is of an individual constantly seeking equilibrium and developing stereotyped patterns of accommodation. A continuous reinforcement occurs as functional methods are retained because they reduce anxiety, while dysfunctional ones are discarded.

In bureaucratic settings the mechanisms used to reduce anxiety include avoiding responsibility by dependency upon one's superiors. In studying anxiety among nurses in a 700-bed hospital, I. E. P. Menzies found that "tasks are frequently forced upwards in the hierarchy, so that all responsibility for their performance can be disclaimed. . . . We are struck repeatedly by the low level of tasks carried out by nursing staff and students in relation to their personal ability, skill, and position in the hierarchy."[22] The patent authority structure of the organization encourages this type of accommodation. This defense is often dysfunctional, however, because it reduces the ability of the nurses to handle anxiety realistically. Excessive dependence and evasion result, instead of an ability to tolerate and to deal more effectively with anxiety.[23] The resulting pressure toward regressive, childlike behavior makes some of the best students stop their training because they are "distressed about the inhibition of their personal development."[24] Insofar as authority relations are concerned, bureaucratic conditions of subordination and dependency may at times encourage infantile behavior.

The link between childhood experiences and organizational behavior is explicit in the following psychiatric study:

An adult person is seen as responding to people and situations in the present on the basis of modes of reaction which have been established at an early period in his life and which are relatively fixed and unchanging. In persons who have had favorable life experiences, the modes of reaction are, on the whole, rational and realistic. In those who have had unfavorable experiences, the modes of reactions are less rational and less realistic. For example, an employee may be observant of the way in which his boss greets him at the start of each day's work. If the boss smiles and speaks in a friendly tone, the employee feels that all is right with his world; he can now get down to work and look forward to a good day. If, however, the boss ignores him, or greets him with a preoccupied smile, the employee may interpret this as being due to the fact that the boss has a hangover, has quarrelled with his wife, is thinking

[22] Isabel E. P. Menzies, "A Case Study in the Functioning of Social Systems as a Defence Against Anxiety," *Human Relations,* Vol. 13, pp. 95–121.

[23] Ibid.

[24] Ibid., p. 117.

hard about how to make a sale to an important customer; or he may interpret it as meaning something is wrong in the boss's attitude toward him. The more rational person will, perhaps, look back over his performance record of the past few days to see if the boss has had any cause to feel unpleasant toward him; not finding anything outstanding in the way of cause for criticism, he concludes that the boss has something on his mind which is no concern of his. The less rational person will tend to conclude, without weighing the pros and cons, that the boss is dissatisfied with him; he will seek for the cause, and perhaps find some more or less trivial complaint which might be made against him. He will then decide that this is the reason for the lack of friendliness in the greeting.

The more rational person's thinking is based on a good general estimate of his own worth as an employee and a fairly accurate working knowledge of his boss. He would, for instance, have concluded from his past experience with the boss that he was a fair-minded person who did not tend to ride his employees for minor errors. The less rational employee does not have the same accurate estimation of his own worth, nor is he able to see the boss in terms of his previous experience with him. Instead, his evaluation of the current situation is distorted by the effects of early life experiences with arbitrary and unreliable authority figures (chiefly, of course, his parents) which have led him to conclude that all authority figures who he meets will behave similarly. In these early relationships, the person may have developed such techniques of dealing with these unreliable authorities as overemphasis on perfect performance, or the assumption of an attitude of compliance designed to placate them. In situations where the superficial manner of the boss reminds him of his extremely painful and unpleasant childhood experiences the defensive operations which were devised to take care of the childhood situation may be automatically evoked without the person's first stopping to determine whether the boss is, in fact, similar in attitude and behavior to the earlier authority figure. Because the employee's observation of the current person with whom he is in relationship is subordinated to the necessity to use these well-established defenses, his ability to learn or to convince himself that the boss is not like that is seriously impaired.

From this example, two of the basic propositions of interpersonal psychiatry can be seen. First, present day attitudes are based on previous experiences with people important in the person's life; second, where early experience has aroused severe anxiety, defense reactions take precedence over learning from new experiences. . . .

We offer four examples of the way in which personality structure affects administration. They are, naturally, oriented around the difficulties which arise because of some aspect of the administrator's character. There is one exception (Case A) in which the specific limitations of the administrator's character tend to make her a good administrator, at least within certain limits. Some, but not all of these examples, came from people who were patients. However, they were all successes in terms of doing their work, making their living, and so on.

Case A was a liaison officer between two agencies. She operated on a high level, participating in policy-making as well as in carrying out various projects. Her administrative contacts were largely with superiors and equals. Because of her special knowledge, she frequently suggested and sold ideas to her superiors and then sold them to those who were to carry them out. Her job did not carry a great deal of direct authority, but rather this was exerted through her superiors. Her job was largely determined by her own abilities. In fact, she had developed it far beyond any of her predecessors. Her particular ability was that of finding out what people wanted and then selling their ideas to others (or even to themselves). She seldom originated an idea; her greatest interest was focussed, not on the work itself, but on what those with whom she worked would think of her, and, indeed, her whole working day could be considered as a continuous effort to elicit approval from the people around her. Actually, she was a favorite daughter of a number of the superiors with whom she worked. Their attitude can be expressed: 'What would we do without A? She is so willing, so friendly, so hard-working, so reliable.' Her relationships with her equals were not very close or warm. They, of course, suffered from contrast with this paragon, and there was some tendency on the part of A to help her superiors to notice this contrast. Naturally, since A's interest was so centered on approval, she did not have time for casual friendly contacts with her colleagues; also she feared their envy, and sensed that she deserved it. Occasionally, she was much in the limelight as the result of being singled out for recognition. Such situations gave rise to feelings of fear almost to the point of panic, since she dreaded the resentment both of those she outcompeted among her equals, and those she overtook among her superiors. . . .

This interest in and skill at eliciting approval dated from her childhood. Her mother was a severely critical, demanding person who was always in the limelight at home. She used such tactics as illness and depression, as well as the emotional dependency of the children upon her, to force the whole family to give her constant cheerful attention, approval, openly demonstrated affection, and reassurance. The needs of A were disregarded, both by the mother who dominated her and by the father who was forced to ignore her through fear of the mother's jealousy.

In her administrative work, A was occupied, first, with trying to please the superiors and, in a sense, to get from them the approval she failed to receive at home; second, with placating the always threatening figure whose good-will might be but an evanescent thing, which could give way to rage and attack; third, with avoiding any serious threat to the superior in the way of knowing more or having any greater ability. She both sought the limelight, for the reassurance it gave her of being approved of, and feared it, for the retaliation it brought from the envy of others.

It can be seen that A's approach to her work had one serious defect. While she did an outstanding job, what she did depended to a dangerous extent on her immediate superior. She tended to take up and carry out any ideas presented to her by a person whose approval she valued whether it was good or bad, practical or not. The combination of her great energy and selling ability on the one hand, and her lack of critical judgment resulting from her dependency on approval on the other hand, resulted in the danger of unleashing this dynamo of energy in a direction which might be shortsighted or even harmful.

Case B was, again, a government official who had held a variety of administrative positions. He had been at the head of a staff of perhaps one hundred and fifty workers, being in turn responsible to a higher departmental head. He then became something of a management expert, and revised the procedures of a whole department, involving many thousands of workers. A comment of one of his fellow workers was illustrative of his difficulties in the latter job: 'B, you are always getting new ideas, writing them up, selling them, and then going on to something else without following them through.' A further side light on B's problems came from the fact that this comment seemed funny to him, an expression of his fellow worker's jealousy. The trouble with B as an administrator was that he was not interested in administration; he was not concerned with the work itself, or with the comfort or efficiency of his subordinates, or with the recognition of his superiors. His concern was with showing how clever he was. If he were cleverer than his fellow worker or his boss, that made him feel good, and he seldom hesitated to let the other person in on it. Since he was in actuality an exceedingly intelligent and able chap, he had a good deal of success. But as he moved up in the hierarchy of administration, his lack of genuine interest in the work introduced an increasing deficiency. . . .

His performance in his work was also clearly derived from his childhood experience. His father was a clever ne'er-do-well, full of bright ideas and ingenious schemes; his mother was a martyred soul who earned the family's living and tried to elicit from B some of the dependability and affection the father lacked. The boy found his life at home so painful that he managed never to be around. He worked on the school newspaper, played in the band, went out for baseball, joined the Boy Scouts; and since his afternoons and evenings were filled with such activities, he was seldom at home. In this way, he did not have to take part in the struggles between the parents and spared himself the painful emotional demands of the mother, while acquiring considerable feeling of achievement from his scholastic abilities and the prominence that his activities brought him. In his current life too, the great defect was his inability to tolerate emotional relationships with others; he was not a filial and co-operative subordinate, a friendly and companionable fellow worker or husband, or a kindly and concerned superior. He was, rather, a clever and isolated person, full of bright ideas and unaware of his emotional emptiness.

The third illustrative case, C, was a top-level administrator in a government agency. Despite his high position, he had two major weaknesses as an administrator. First, he was unsure of his authority and tended to regard differences of opinion as insubordination. Instead of permitting open discussion by his staff which could finally culminate in a considered decision by him, he became tense and angry and ended discussion with an arbitrarily stated edict often arrived at too hastily. Second, he was exceedingly anxious to be a well-liked boss and this need made him too readily inclined to listen to one person's point of view and agree with it even though it might not correspond with his better judgment. The overauthoritative behavior occurred when a difference of opinion arose in a group; the overagreeable behavior, when he discussed a problem with just one other person. C's conflictful attitudes obviously put a premium for his staff on making private arrangements with him rather than decisions in which the whole administrative group participated. This, in turn, led to lack of communication from one co-worker to another, as well as to a somewhat inconsistent collection of projects and plans, not all of which were compatible.

To illustrate the kind of difficulties C's conflict gave rise to: His executive assistant came to him to discuss the problem of a junior technician in the agency, a personable young man who seemed to be a constant focus of dissension among the clerical staff and also among his fellow technicians. It appeared that he was actively involved in flirtations with two of the stenographers, and in addition he went to considerable trouble to charm all of the young and attractive girls in the office. He played the two whom he was involved with off against each other, with the result that they were not speaking and refused to co-operate in their work. Several of the less involved girls had taken sides, and the morale and efficiency of the office had dropped considerably. The young man's fellow technicians were angry with him and collaborative work between them suffered. C's assistant suggested that the young man be discharged; C agreed, expressing his confidence in his assistant's judgment and his feeling that the decision was wise.

Immediately after he was told of his discharge, the young man came to see C. With his usual charm and plausibility, he told his side of the story, and C succumbed to his appeal and reversed his assistant's decision. This, of course, meant a serious blow to the assistant's pride and, as well, an undermining of his prestige with the workers whom he supervised. Perhaps most serious of all was the doubt which he now had of the advisability of taking the responsibility for making decisions in the future which might expose him to a repetition of this rebuff.

C was the only child of a stiff and reticent college professor and a socially prominent mother who was cold, authoritarian, and yet overindulgent to her son. Association with his father's intellectual friends, his mother's society friends, and great emphasis in his rearing on his special destiny combined to set him apart from his juvenile confreres. He did not have the experience of group life and give-and-take with equals which would have given him some idea of the place he could win in a group by virtue of his own ability. He came to think of himself as destined to do great things, while he lacked the self-esteem upon which leadership must be based. His conception of leadership had the connotation: a leader must be able to make himself obeyed. It also had the connotation: a leader must be loved by his men. To combine authority with friendliness requires that a person be able to tolerate differences of opinion and resentment when the subordinates are not pleased with his decisions. Made anxious by differences of opinion, which called into question his intellectual ability, his worthiness in the eyes of his father; made anxious also by others' resentment of his authority, which stirred up frightening echoes of his resentful feelings toward his mother's authority—he was unable to find any securely consistent position which would enable him to deal with such conflicts. . . .

Case D, again a government administrator in charge of several hundred workers, was handicapped by the dislike which his subordinates and, to some extent, his equals and superiors felt for him. While he was a person of outstanding ability, perhaps the most gifted of the four mentioned, he had been the least successful in his work. His assistants were not motivated to please him or to make the activities that he planned and directed into successes; some of them, indeed, probably rejoiced in seeing this haughty and distant man defeated. His superiors were inclined to judge him according to the strict letter of the law, and when an error occurred, saw to it that he took the consequences.

The dislike for him was based on his arrogant, superior manner. He felt that each should do his work according to the rules and that there was no excuse for sloppiness, inefficiency, or any personal element. If the rule is that employees are to get to work at 8:30, then arriving at 8:31 is an infraction which carries consequences. He felt that if one does good work, that should be its own reward and there should be no need for praise.

Despite these consciously held ideas, D was extremely sensitive. When he was not appreciated by his superiors or when his subordinates disliked him, he felt hurt and could not understand it. He wished his subordinates to consider him a good leader, and had difficulty in recognizing that this required some evidence of concern for them on his part.

To illustrate with an example: Over a period of a year he had become increasingly critical of the attitudes of his subordinates, even though their performance equalled or excelled that of a parallel unit. He felt that they had become too self-centered; they demanded too much for themselves and did not recognize their place in the scheme of things as *he* had done when on *his* way up the ladder. Finally, when the employees organized a grievance committee, which was an accepted practice in other similar units, D became incensed, refused to recognize the committee, and became so bitter in word and action that the efficiency level of his unit fell to a very low ebb.

Some of D's difficulties can be traced back to the way in which the problem of affection was handled in his upbringing. He was the elder of two sons of a very stern, forceful, and reserved father and a somewhat passive, ailing mother. An outstanding athlete in his youth, his father had suffered an industrial accident which to most men would have been severely disabling. However, instead of accepting a pension, or even a more sedentary inside job, the father had bulled his way to success in a job calling for hard physical exertion. D was reared in this Spartan tradition, and accepted as his own his father's standards of grim persistence and acceptance of fate, even at the expense of suppressing artistic and creative interests of his own. D had a younger brother who did not adhere to the father's standards—instead he was lazy and self-indulgent. When refused a request by the father (a request which D would never dream of making), he would throw a temper tantrum so violent that the sick mother would intervene to have his request granted. Thus the brother was granted much for which D had longed as a youth. But instead of feeling envious of the brother and resentful of the inconsistency of his parents, D felt rage at the younger brother whom he regarded as too self-centered, demanding, and lacking in respect and consideration for his elders. In other words, he was unaware that he, too, craved affection and indulgence as his younger brother did. . . .

In concluding, two points derived from the psychiatric study of administrators seem to . . . warrant considerable further study.

First, those who choose administrative work for a career and who succeed in it seem to have certain personal motivations for making the choice and certain personal traits which account for their success. (We are not including in this statement those who become administrators by chance or by outliving their competitors.) The motivations have something to do with deriving a sense of well-being and security from knowing how to get others to do things that one decides are worth doing. Success in achieving this has something to do with finding out in the early years, when dealing with parents and siblings, how to get other people to want to do what you wish. It is easy, for instance, to think of the contrast between the stereotype of the college professor, a person who is highly intelligent and capable of formulating excellent plans but who has not a ghost of a notion as to how to go about interesting or inducing anyone else to carry out his ideas; and another kind of person who handles with ease and spontaneity the problems of relationship with those who are involved in the work. This personality difference is what we refer to as having been in large part determined by the nature of a person's early relationships. . . .

The second point is that success in administration on higher levels has one significant difference from that on lower ones— namely, that there is no superior to please or to manipulate when one reaches the policy-making top. Therefore, for the top man, the motivations and skills must be at least in some ways different from those of the men who work under him. He must, for one thing, have a considerably greater degree of maturity and independence of judgment. There is a large, and open, question as to whether these traits will be found at the top in the event that they are lacking on the way up the ladder. Further, as illustrated by Cases A and B, there is considerable doubt whether the personality characteristics contributing to success in climbing up the ladder, are always conducive to good leadership once a man has arrived at the top.[25]

These cases suggest the links between childhood experiences, personality, and organizational adjustment. They illustrate Sullivan's interpersonal theory as a way of explaining organizational behavior. Since interpersonal relations are largely a function of individual needs to reduce anxiety, the objective situation is only one part of the field; individual perception and personality always play their part in determining how a given situation will be handled. But perception is the product of a "self-system" reflecting the individual's experience from childhood onward.

Interpersonal theory emphasizes both the social situation and personality. The situation, however, plays the major role. As Sullivan concludes: "The human organism is so extraordinarily adaptive that not only could the most fantastic social rules and regulations be lived up to, if they were properly inculcated in the young, but they would seem very natural and proper ways of life."[26] Certainly it is clear that man can live under many different ethical and political systems. Cultural anthropology has revealed the range of behavior that characterizes so-called instinctive drives. It is not surprising therefore that Sullivan and the others should build their theory around its major assumptions.

Anthropological research destroyed some cherished illusions. Freud's theory was shown to depend in part upon his definition of certain sexual behaviors and attitudes as being *instinctive,* when in fact they reflected his own nineteenth-century, European, middle-class values. Similarly, the competitive impulse that most Americans accepted as primeval was shown to be culturally determined. The Hopi, for example, exhibited none of the so-called competitive instinct, and a similar "aberration" was found in Japan following World War II when school children resisted competitive innovations. In regard to pugnacity, the Arapesh and Dobu tribes were sharply different, suggesting again the weight of social structure in shaping "inherent" tendencies.

The human susceptibility to socialization is in part explained by the individual's long period of biologic and economic immaturity. While lower animals become self-sufficient shortly after birth, Western men and women are dependent for some two decades before they strike

[25] Mabel B. Cohen and Robert A. Cohen, "Personality as a Factor in Administrative Decisions," *Psychiatry*, Vol. 14 (1951), pp. 47–53. Copyright © 1951 by The William Alanson White Psychiatric Foundation, Inc. Reprinted by special permission of The William Alanson White Psychiatric Foundation, Inc.

[26] Sullivan, *Interpersonal Theory of Psychiatry*, p. 6.

out alone. During this time they are dependent upon those who provide their emotional and physical sustenance. At the same time, it appears that even as a child they become aware that they have some power. When toilet training, walking, and speech begin, they learn that they can defy their parents in matters that are obviously important to them. Here again we see that biological impulses are always conditioned by cultural patterns that differ from society to society. Even the Oedipus complex, which Freud believed to be instinctive, is now thought by some anthropologists to be culturally specific, the result of a monogamous, patriarchal family structure.

The family and other authority figures measure the individuals' "growth" largely in terms of their adjustment to social norms. Such norms include national traditions and mythology, religious beliefs, economic and political values, in fact, the whole cultural web that sustains us throughout life. These norms include the parents' perception of the kinds of skills and attitudes required by children for success in our organized society. As a result, individual personality tends to reflect the social structure. The dominant values of society become a superego controlling the individual through approval and anxiety. As Erich Fromm observes: "Society must tend to mold the character structure of its members in such a way they will want to do what they have to do under the existing circumstances."[27]

As we have seen, the individuals' successive experiences with authority figures result in a "self-system," a way of relating themselves to the world. This system becomes a framework for accepting or rejecting the vast number of stimuli that impinge upon them. Millions of sensory fibers transmit such stimuli through their nervous systems. Certain reflexes become reinforced and linked together, providing the basis for habitual patterns of behavior. *Both individuals' perceptions and their behavior become, so to speak, structured.* They develop a time-tested way of organizing reality, and their reactions become stabilized accordingly. This relatively consistent pattern of behavior is commonly defined as "personality." Moreover, the personality continually reinforces itself by a selective process that tends to accept only approved impressions which are in turn incorporated into the existing value system. Conflicting stimuli tend to be rejected, and when individuals reject most conflicting stimuli, we say that they have a low tolerance for ambiguity.

How this process of organizing reality becomes stereotyped is suggested by the so-called "authoritarian-personality" type, that is, one who scores high on a scale of attitudes that include militarism, chauvinism, antiradicalism, exceptional conventionality, deference for au-

[27]Erich Fromm, *Man For Himself* (New York: Rinehart & Co., 1947), p. 241.

thority, a poor view of human nature, belief in force and "toughness," and a general power orientation.[28] The well-known California F scale, which measures authoritarian attitudes, includes nine attitudinal categories and several descriptive statements of each. The "authoritarian personality" is one who selects a large proportion of such statements as being compatible with his own attitudes. The significance of the scale is that many of these attitudes seem congruent with those of the upward-mobile type.

AUTHORITARIANISM SCALE[29]

CONVENTIONALISM: *Rigid adherence to conventional, middle-class values.*

Obedience and respect for authority are the most important virtues children should learn.

A person who has bad manners, habits, and breeding can hardly expect to get along with decent people.

If people would talk less and work more, everybody would be better off.

The businessman and the manufacturer are much more important to society than the artist and the professor.

AUTHORITARIAN SUBMISSION: *Submissive, uncritical attitude toward idealized moral authorities of the in-group.*

Obedience and respect for authority are the most important virtues children should learn.

Science has its place, but there are many important things that can never possibly be understood by the human mind.

Every person should have complete faith in some supernatural power whose decisions he obeys without question.

Young people sometimes get rebellious ideas, but as they grow up they ought to get over them and settle down.

What this country needs most, more than laws and political programs, is a few courageous, tireless, devoted leaders in whom the people can put their faith.

[28]Among others, Theodore W. Adorno et al., *The Authoritarian Personality* (New York: Harper & Row, 1950); Erich Fromm, *Man For Himself;* J. Jahoda and Richard Christie, *Studies in the Scope and Method of "The Authoritarian Personality"* (Glencoe, Illinois: Free Press, 1954), pp. 226–275; Jack Block and Jeanne Block, "An Investigation of the Relationship Between Intolerance of Ambiguity and Ethnocentrism," *Journal of Personality,* Vol. 19, pp. 303–311; Abraham H. Maslow, "The Authoritarian Character Structure," *Journal of Social Psychology,* Vol. 18, pp. 401–411; Richard Christie and John Garcia, "Subcultural Variation in Authoritarian Personality," *Journal of Abnormal and Social Psychology,* Vol. 46, pp. 457–469; Milton Rokeach, "Generalized Mental Rigidity as a Factor in Ethnocentrism," *Journal of Abnormal and Social Psychology,* Vol. 43, pp. 259–278; Rokeach, "Narrow-Mindedness and Personality," *Journal of Personality,* Vol. 20, pp. 234–251; Rokeach, "Prejudice, Concreteness of Thinking and Reification of Thinking," *Journal of Abnormal and Social Psychology,* Vol. 46, pp. 83–91.

[29]Theodore W. Adorno et al., *The Authoritarian Personality,* pp. 248–250. Used by permission.

No sane, normal, decent person could ever think of hurting a close friend or relative.

Nobody ever learned anything really important except through suffering.

AUTHORITARIAN AGGRESSION: *Tendency to be on the look-out for, and to condemn, reject, and punish people who violate conventional values.*

A person who has bad manners, habits and breeding can hardly expect to get along with decent people.

What youth needs most is strict discipline, rugged determination, and the will to work and fight for family and country.

An insult to our honor should always be punished.

Sex crimes, such as rape, and attacks on children, deserve more than mere imprisonment; such criminals ought to be publicly whipped, or worse.

There is hardly anything lower than a person who does not feel great love, gratitude, and respect for his parents.

Most of our social problems would be solved if we could somehow get rid of the immoral, crooked and feeble-minded people.

If people would talk less and work more, everybody would be better off.

Homosexuals are hardly better than criminals and ought to be severely punished.

ANTI-INTRACEPTION: *Opposition to the subjective, the imaginative, the tenderminded.*

When a person has a problem or worry, it is best for him not to think about it, but to keep busy with more cheerful things.

Nowadays more and more people are prying into matters that should remain personal and private.

If people would talk less and work more, everybody would be better off.

The businessman and the manufacturer are much more important to society than the artist and the professor.

SUPERSTITION AND STEREOTYPE: *The belief in mystical determinants of the individual's fate; the disposition to think in rigid categories.*

Science has its place, but there are many important things that can never possibly be understood by the human mind.

Every person should have complete faith in some supernatural power whose decisions he obeys without question.

Some people are born with an urge to jump from high places.

People can be divided into two distinct classes: the weak and the strong.

Some day it will probably be shown that astrology can explain a lot of things.

Wars and social troubles may someday be ended by an earthquake or flood that will destroy the whole world.

POWER AND 'TOUGHNESS': *Preoccupation with the dominance-submission, strong-weak, leader-follower dimensions; identification with power figures; over-emphasis upon the conventionalized attributes of the ego; exaggerated assertion of strength and toughness.*

No weakness or difficulty can hold us back if we have enough will power.

What youth needs most is strict discipline, rugged determination, and the will to work and fight for family and country.

An insult to our honor should always be punished.

It is best to use some prewar authorities in Germany to keep order and prevent chaos.

What this country needs most, more than laws and political programs, is a few courageous, tireless, devoted leaders in whom the people can put their faith.

People can be divided into two distinct classes: the weak and the strong.

Most people don't realize how much our lives are controlled by plots hatched in secret places.

DESTRUCTIVENESS AND CYNICISM: *Generalized hostility, vilification of the human being. Human nature being what it is, there will always be war and conflict.*

Familiarity breeds contempt.

PROJECTIVITY: *The disposition to believe that wild and dangerous things go on in the world; the projection outwards of conscious emotional impulses.*

Nowadays, when so many different kinds of people move around and mix together so much, a person has to protect himself especially carefully against catching an infection or disease from them.

Nowadays, more and more people are prying into matters that should remain personal and private.

Wars and social troubles may someday be ended by an earthquake or flood that will destroy the whole world.

The wild sex life of the old Greeks and Romans was tame compared to some of the goings-on in this country, even in places where people might least expect it.

Most people don't realize how much their lives are controlled by plots hatched in secret places.

SEX: *Exaggerated concern with sexual "goings-on."*

Sex crimes such as rape and attacks on children deserve more than mere imprisonment; such criminals ought to be publicly whipped, or worse.

The wild sex life of the old Greeks and Romans was tame compared to some of the goings-on in this country, even in places where people might least expect it.

Homosexuals are hardly better than criminals and ought to be severely punished.

When combined with certain other typical values and behaviors of successful executives isolated by Gardner, Henry, and Warner, the "authoritarian personality" findings provide a highly tentative but suggestive hypothesis, namely, that bureaucratic structure and its behavioral demands provide a sympathetic environment for the authoritarian type, who may, in turn, be equated with the typical upward-mobile. For example, note the similarity between the following values found to be characteristic of successful business executives, and these items from the F scale: low identification with one's mother and close attachment to one's father; condescending attitude toward subordinates and a close positive identification with superiors; admiration for powerful, decisive, and prestigious superiors.[30]

As suggested, the conditions of participation in big organizations place a high value upon power, status, prestige, order, predictability, easy acceptance of authority, hard work, punctuality, discipline, and conventionality. The authoritarian personality scale includes several categories and their definitive attitudes that seem to be consonant with such values, including the following:

Conventionalism: "Obedience and respect for authority are the most important virtues children should learn." "If people would talk less and work more, everybody would be better off."

Authoritarian Submission: "What this country needs most, more than laws or political programs, is a few courageous, tireless, devoted leaders in whom the people can put their faith."

Authoritarian Aggression: "What youth needs most is strict discipline, rugged determination, and the will to work and fight for family and country."

Anti-Intraception: "The businessman and the manufacturer are much more important to society than the artist or the professor."

Power and "Toughness": "People can be divided into two classes: the weak and the strong." "No weakness or difficulty can hold us back if we have enough will power."

The authoritarianism research concludes that certain individuals have personality needs that include dominance, submissiveness, and

[30]W. Floyd Warner, *American Life: Dream and Reality* (Chicago: University of Chicago Press, 1953), pp. 188–189; Burleigh Gardner, "What Makes Successful and Unsuccessful Executives"; William Henry, "The Business Executive: The Psychodynamics of a Social Role," *American Journal of Sociology*, Vol. 54, pp. 286–291.

rigidity. Our analysis suggests that such individuals have an affinity for the ideal-typical bureaucratic structure. We also know that values are related to occupational preference. In a word, to some extent individuals are attracted by vocations that suit their personality.

Such alignments are suggested by research showing that men can be divided into two broad categories, extrovert and introvert. William James called these "tough-minded" and "tender-minded," for reasons which will soon become apparent. Not only are traits in each category surprisingly uniform, but they reflect vocational interests. Extroverts are usually realistic in their perception and adjustment to events. They accept conditions as they are, believing that existing values and institutions are probably necessary and proper. They accept the rationality and legitimacy of the existing system. In general, they are oriented toward absolute categories, custom and ceremony, hierarchy, and obedience.[31]

On the other hand, introverts have rather different values. They tend to measure institutions by some ideal standard and to believe that human intelligence can remove their inadequacies. Having an optimistic view of people, they prefer an "open society" to one where status is determined by birth or tradition. They prefer complexity in geometric and art forms and regard problems as multifaceted rather than as simple and clear cut. Not only is the world seen as unordered, but its values and institutions are regarded as relative and changing. Unlike the extrovert who is outward looking both in conception and interest, introverts are highly self-conscious. Emotionally and artistically oriented, they often reject majority norms. According to Jung, this dichotomy is also apparent in the kinds of mental illness to which each type is susceptible. The extrovert is subject to hysteria and psychopathy, disorders that have few moral implications; the introvert's illnesses include anxiety, depression, and compulsion, which often mirror value conflicts.

Such conclusions enable us to define personality types and to trace the relation between society, personality, and vocation. We turn first to personality traits and job preference. The German psychologist, Spranger, suggested that individuals could be divided on the basis of interest into several categories.[32] Two of these are useful for our purposes: the *theoretical* and the *economic*. The theoretical person, who resembles the introvert, is empirical, rational, and critical, mainly concerned with discovering truth. Vocationally, he is a scientist,

---

[31] Hans J. Eysenck, *The Psychology of Politics* (London: Methuen, 1954); *The Structure of Human Personality* (London: Methuen, 1953); Theodore W. Adorno et al., *The Authoritarian Personality*.

[32] Eduard Spranger, *Types of Men*, 5th German ed. (New York: Hafner Publishing Co., 1928), cited in Hans Eysenck, *The Psychology of Politics*, pp. 159–161.

philosopher, or academic. Opposed to this is the economic type, a utilitarian, who honors that which is useful. Consequently, he tends to reject art, theory, and esthetics. Successful administrators are usually the pragmatic type; among their other calculations, they must to some extent view individuals as means to organizational ends.

Spranger's theory provided the basis for linking occupation with values. H. E. Brogden, for example, found a consistent dichotomy between "practicality" and "idealism," which conformed nicely with the "tough-minded" and "tender-minded" categories.[33] "Idealistic" items include a preference for reading the lives of Plato, Aristotle, and Socrates rather than those of Alexander, Caesar, or Charlemagne. Idealists would rather be politicians, mathematicians, or ministers, than businessmen or sales managers. Their friends are introspective and interested in social questions rather than being industrious, practical, or endowed with leadership qualities. On the other hand, the "practical" individual accepts a business society's terms, placing a low value on theoretical and esthetic activities. Unlike idealists, who are concerned with how things "ought" to be, they accept things as they are and work out a scheme of action within this framework.

This dichotomy between the practical and idealist types carries over into vocational preferences, as demonstrated by the Strong Vocational Interest Inventory. The Strong test assumes that individuals who succeed in certain occupations have similar interests and values. *Ability* is not a factor in the test; *interest* is the main consideration. Patterns of interest for many vocations have been established, with the result that one can determine which one fits. Once the vocational patterns were analyzed, several conclusions emerged. Thurstone, for example, found four major interest factors: science, language, people, and business. Interest in business was characteristic of the "tough-minded," while interest in people-oriented vocations characterized the "tender-minded." A positive association was thus found between values and vocational preferences.

A related study may now be mentioned. Barron found that "yielders" (those who conformed to group opinion) preferred simple designs, whereas "nonyielders" (those who retained their opinions regardless of majority pressure) preferred complexity in designs.[34] In this study the idealist-complexity independents (introverts) had the following traits. They valued creative work, original ideas, the indi-

[33]Hubert E. Brogden, "Primary Personal Values Measured by the Allport-Vernon Test, 'A Study of Values,'" *Psychological Monographs,* Vol. 66, No. 16, pp. 1–31, cited in Hans J. Eysenck, *The Psychology of Politics,* p. 163.

[34]Frank Barron, "Complexity-Simplicity as a Personality Dimension," *Journal of Abnormal and Social Psychology,* Vol. 48, pp. 163–172.

vidual, integrity over personal appeal, some uncertainty, and free communication of inner feelings. They disliked taking orders, integrating with a group, discipline, or devotion to a leader.

While conclusions drawn from such disparate studies must be highly tentative, they do suggest a basic personality difference between an idealistic type and a pragmatic one. Applying this hypothesis to the bureaucratic situation, we assume that idealistic personalities tend to avoid structured, collective situations in which personal or hierarchical authority is the source of legitimacy. Their value preferences seem inapposite to typical organizational demands, such as uncritical acceptance of the organization's manifest goals, structured interpersonal relations, collective decision making, and diffused responsibility.

On the other hand, we can assume that the bureaucratic situation provides a sympathetic work place for the pragmatic types who seek accommodation through certainty and power. Obviously, organizations include other types, and a definite range of behavior characterizes this particular type; but the upward-mobiles will probably find the bureaucratic milieu generally compatible. In Sullivan's terms, their self-system and its time-tested security operations prove functional in the "complex, peculiarly characterized" interpersonal relations that occur in big organizations. Such upward-mobile types personify organizational values. The true "bureaucratic personality," they accept the organization's latent goals of power, growth, and survival. They define and express its values to the outside world. Although other members may reject its collective values, the upward-mobiles are often deeply committed to them. If they are to succeed, they must accept such values uncritically. They are intensely subject to organizational discipline. If, as the Indian proverb says, to be free is to be without desire, they are not free, because they desire power and its derivative rewards.

While the extent to which individuals legitimize organizational claims varies considerably, the pragmatic types seem well adapted to such accommodations. Certainly their easy acceptance of authority is functional. Such claims are reinforced by the organization's "conditional love," which (like parental love) is often contingent upon obedience. Here again the anxiety syndrome seems basic. Approval and acceptance tend to be exchanged for loyalty and conformity. Deprivations may occasionally be required, but such expectations are usually met on the basis of tacit understanding. Accommodation is also eased by middle-class child-raising practices and extended education, which honor authority and self-discipline.

As suggested earlier, pragmatic types have high dominance and submission tendencies, exceptional conventionality, and a low tolerance for ambiguity. They believe in firm leadership, in differentiating the weak from the strong. They honor respect for parents and obedience in children. Having this orientation, they believe that most problems can be solved by vigorous action. Here again, it seems, the bureaucratic situation provides an appropriate milieu for individuals with some of these tendencies. Their dominance-submission needs, for example, enable them to play the dual role of deference to those above and dominance toward those below. As Maccoby, Gardner, Henry, and Warner found, *successful executives have an intensely personal attachment to their superiors, accompanied by a detached and impersonal feeling toward their juniors.* [35]

While the pragmatic types' style of accommodation increases their life chances, we can assume that the idealists have lost ground. Their toleration for ambiguity and preference for personal autonomy have proved less amenable to organizational demands. The scientist, technician, engineer, scholar, and artist, i.e., the professional-employee class, are now directed by the upward-mobile. The latter's values are critical because they shape the ends and conditions under which their skill and knowledge are expressed. Since elite values tend to become bench marks for popular behavior, the upward-mobile's influence seems likely to increase.

Significantly, this perception of the changed conditions of occupational success directly influences socialization. The family now receives many of its child-rearing cues from organizational elites whose influence and life styles provide the daily fare of the mass media. These individuals most dramatically personify the change from an economy of saving to one of consumption. They validate the "success" aspirations of our society. While training in such values may occur almost unconsciously, it is often systematically built into the child's personality by parents whose education, insight, and expectations give them an awareness of functional norms and behaviors in a bureaucratic society. As Miller and Swanson found, urban child-rearing practices directly reflect existing social and economic organization:

> Bureaucratic parents train their children for this new world and treat them in terms of its values. For most parents this will not be a matter of self-conscious planning. Their methods of child care will simply reflect the values these fathers and mothers have learned from living in a bureaucratized society. . . . The confident, smooth relations of the great organization of which he must be-

[35] Michael Maccoby, *The Gamesman* (New York: Simon and Schuster, 1976); W. Lloyd Warner, *American Life*, pp. 188–189; Burleigh Gardner, "Successful and Unsuccessful Executives"; William Henry, "The Business Executive."

come a part will require him to get along well with other people and to take their feelings as well as his own into account with skill and confidence. . . . [The] child will need to be taught that superiors are not hateful figures to be challenged but men of skill and feeling whom he should emulate.[36]

In highly over-simplified form, the following developmental process tends to occur. Socially validated beliefs and behavior are instilled in the young through the anxiety-conformity-approval syndrome. In this way "culturally defined and interpersonally imposed patterns of behavior come to motivate human beings as imperiously as biologically determined requirements."[37] This process, moreover, persists throughout life as the socialization role of the family is reinforced by the small group, the school, and the church. Success now requires extended university training, and such training is the prerogative of middle-class families who employ child-rearing practices that give their children the inside track by emphasizing striving, punctuality, and the suppression of unprofitable emotions. These attributes prove functional in big organizations, now among the main sources of mobility, status, and prestige. As a result, those who possess these attributes assume power and tend to replace themselves with men who reflect their own image. In such ways the socialization process is tuned to the demands of modern society and its organizations for consistency, conformity, and the muting of conflict.

[36]Daniel R. Miller and Guy E. Swanson, *The Changing American Parent* (New York: Wiley, 1958), p. 55; see also, Rosabeth M. Kanter, "The Organization Child: Experience Management in a Nursery School," *Sociology of Education,* Vol. 45, pp. 186–211.

[37]Blitsten, *The Social Theories of Harry Stack Sullivan,* p. 53.

THE PSYCHOLOGY | 5
OF COMPLEX
ORGANIZATIONS

We now turn to the psychological bases of organizational behavior. How are individuals conditioned to accept the legitimacy of authority? What are the conditions of participation set down by the organization for its members? An essential proposition is that the bureaucratic situation constitutes a "structured field," comprising three discrete systems: *authority, status,* and *small groups.* Psychologically, a structured field is one in which stimuli are patent, stable, and compelling. Such a field eases perception and learning by providing cues that guide and limit individual choices. The individual's learned deference toward authority is evoked and interpersonal relations are ordered in ways that honor organizational claims for loyalty, consistency, and dispatch. Organizations are composed of a congeries of small groups that have a similar influence on behavior. They inculcate majority values in their members; they reward compliance and punish those who resist their demands. In many cases, group values contribute to the organization's manifest goals. In others, they conflict with them. But in every case, small groups have a pervasive socializing function. In sum, the three systems of authority, status, and small groups provide the major conditions of participation.

Here, an important qualification must be made. In addition to the systems just mentioned, every bureaucratic situation includes a fourth system, namely, that of technology. This system consists of the technical process that participants must use to achieve their purpose. Consider for example the operating room in a hospital where a group of specialists is about to perform an operation. Factors of authority, status, and small groups are obviously at work, but these are augmented by technical imperatives, the "laws of the situation," which govern perhaps even more imperiously the behavior of doctors, anesthesiologists, and nurses. Similar task requirements provide the framework for most interpersonal contacts in modern organizations. Despite the difficulty of separating this technical system from the other systems, the major focus of our analysis is upon the latter; the inherent and infinitely varied technical context is treated as a "given."

We saw earlier that organizations are systems of roles graded by *authority*. Ideally, there is very little ambiguity in interpersonal relations. Each position is differentiated by fairly precise assignments of authority and prestige. Such assignments outline the repertory of expected behaviors attached to each position. While personality differences will obviously affect the resulting accommodations, these conditions encourage stereotypical responses. The authority system is a critical factor in this context.

Authority can be defined as *the ability to evoke compliance.* Unlike power, which is a broader concept with connotations of force and the ability to impose one's will regardless of opposition, authority usually rests upon some official position. Although it has several bases of validation, authority is typically legitimated by formal, hierarchical position. Chester Barnard has argued that authority must be "accepted" by those who fall within its penumbra. This conception of authority is useful, but one must note that the word "acceptance" has many nuances, and that "acceptance" is only the final expression of many complex motivations, affected by the bureaucratic situation and the personality of the individuals concerned. The question remains, why does the individual "accept" bureaucratic authority.

To say that authority is defined by "acceptance" suggests that the individual has a real choice between acceptance and refusal, that authority is an "either-or" proposition. But this assumes too great a degree of free will and too simple a social situation. As we have seen, individuals are trained from birth onward to defer to authority. They develop a generalized deference to the authority of parenthood, experience, knowledge, status, and so forth.

Moreover, in any given authority situation, factors other than the immediate interpersonal relationship are involved. So many degrees of compliance exist, ranging from enthusiasm to resignation, that explicit rejection becomes a crude and unlikely alternative, particularly among highly socialized individuals. (Bureaucratic individuals will often be highly socialized, that is, sensitive to the built-in expectations of interpersonal situations, because of the extended education often required to acquire the necessary technical skills.) The secular increase of women in the work force (almost half of all wives are now working outside the home) may augment this condition, given their early role socialization that emphasizes persuasion, indirection, and the repression of conflict in interpersonal relations. We can assume that compliance will be normal. In organizations, people rarely withhold consent. Rather, they evade, procrastinate, "misunderstand," "forget," or project the unwelcome task upon someone "better qualified."

For these reasons, the probability of hierarchical authority being rejected is remote. In organizations where authority and its symbols are organized and obvious, and where sanctions exist to encourage "acceptance," we have left the level of mere "influence" for a more authoritative context. The essential distinction is one of *sanctions:* bureaucratic authority is reinforced by rewards and punishments, while mere influence operates without such sanctions. This difference underlies the assumption that bureaucratic interpersonal relations are more often "authoritative" than "influential." This is not to say that individuals in organizations do not use influence. With the possible exception of the military, authority usually has at least a facade of permissiveness, but those concerned are rarely unaware of the structure of authority in a given situation. Moreover, aside from other motivations—such as ambition, the need to reduce anxiety, and the desire for group approval—the mere fact that an order emanates from a superior tends to induce "acceptance" based on an assumed legitimacy of the superior's role. Thus the very structure of modern organizations creates a tendency to comply.

Authority does not always operate hierarchically. In addition to informal centers of power, there is the fact that technical skill demands recognition. A superior may defer to a specialist when technical questions are conclusive. Yet, as the experience of the atomic physicists suggests, the control of specialists in terms of recruitment, rewards, and programs is usually exercised by those in hierarchical positions.

Any appraisal of authority must also note that organizations are composed of many subhierarchies, each bound together by authority, interests, and values in a way similar to the total organization. Each has its power structure headed by a leader who is decisive within his or her own system, but who is a subordinate when viewed from the perspective of the larger hierarchy. This devolution of power has important consequences. It insures discipline since the life chances of those in each subhierarchy are usually determined through representations made to the elite on their behalf by such subleaders. As a result, an upward-looking posture characterizes the whole organization. Moreover, the will of the elite is transmitted downward through the organization by the subleaders, again reinforcing their authority and status within their own subsystems.

Here, the ambiguity of goals in organizations may be seen. To retain their position and preserve the hope of future rewards, subleaders must honor organizational values and at the same time retain the loyalty of their own group by defending the group's interests against competitors within the system and against neglect by the elite. Although they are torn between such conflicting demands, their own careers are in the hands of their superiors, and we can assume that they will usually give priority to the latter's claims. Superiors will measure the subleaders by the loyalty, dispatch, and affirmation with which they carry out their policies. Thus the price that subleaders pay for marginal power and great expectations is loyalty upward.

In considering the premises underlying bureaucratic promotion, Henri de Man reveals other tensions of authority. While employees prefer that their superior be chosen on the basis of technical skill and bargaining ability, the manager who delegates authority has quite different qualifications in mind.

> In large-scale industries . . . characterized by extreme division of labour, he usually knows little about the craft competence of the worker he promotes to a foreman's job. What he wants is a "trusty" man, this meaning one whom he can regard as being devoted to the profit-making aspect of the undertaking and fully convinced of the importance of maintaining the employer's authority. [This system] rests on the psychological assumption that bureaucratic and quasi-military discipline is the best sort of discipline for an industrial enterprise.[1]

Organizational authority, in sum, is composed of legal, moral, psychological, and skill ingredients, whose relative weights vary in terms of how manifest and compelling the stimuli are in a given situation. Organizations are systems in which stimuli are exceptionally patent and compelling. In addition, they are relatively constant. Authority and its symbols are hierarchically structured so that the individuals who personify authority may change, but the *system* of authority remains. Indeed, the organization may be defined as a relatively permanent system of authority relationships. Ideally, there is little ambiguity about rights and obligations. In comparison with other forms of social power, which are often vague and transitory, bureaucratic power is obvious and definable. The principle of hierarchy ensures that it usually follows the formal structure of the organization. Moreover, insofar as organized behavior is group behavior, the weight of authoritative stimuli is increased by sheer numbers. The acceptance of organizational values by the majority fosters a consensus that makes dissent seem quixotic. Both the upward-mobiles who embrace such values and the indifferents who tolerate them become anchoring stimuli who encourage the acceptance of group norms. Only the ambivalents find authority threatening. This leads us to a major proposition: *reactions to authority constitute the most critical variable in organizational accommodation.* Each of our types reacts somewhat differently to authority, and these differences mainly account for their discrete patterns of adjustment and mobility.

[1] Henri de Man, *Joy in Work* (London: Kegan Paul, 1929), pp. 204–205.

Authority relationships thus mediate personality and the ability to estimate the consequences of alternative responses to organizational claims. Although attitudes toward authority are largely derived from early experiences with one's parents, cultural values provide the raw material from which socialization is built. In a patriarchal, highly structured society such as the Middle East, deference to authority becomes ingrained and automatic. Its legitimation will typically be ascriptive, resting on the father's ancestral dominance and the tradition-based authority of religious and secular notables. In a more mobile and individualistic society, authority must rely to a greater extent on objective bases of skill and rationality to make good its claims. Here again, we see the weblike pattern of culture, family, and individual, each acting upon the other.

Given the interplay of such situational, psychological, and cultural factors, we can assume that the bureaucratic setting produces exceptional probabilities that individuals will defer to authority based on hierarchical position. The formal possession of authority, the mere occupancy of a superior position, encourages deference in others. Indeed, the positive assumption of authority on whatever grounds enhances compliance. Haythorn found that "when one member of a group was aggressive, self-confident, interested in an individual solution to a task, and showed initiative, other members of the group showed less of such behavior than they normally did."[2] This tendency was based upon the group's desire to avoid conflict, as well as the common "levelling effect" of a collective situation.

As Donald Calhoun has suggested, organizations try to establish their legitimacy by rationalizing authority in terms of ethical and ideological principles.[3] All organizations, of course, strive to find some basis other than sheer power for their authority. Evocative symbols and rituals, usually idealistic, patriotic, or "service-oriented," are enlisted to inspire loyalty to the organization. If loyalty is to be merited, the values, motives, and routine behavior of the organization must be seen as selfless; if possible the organization must appear as the embodiment of certain universal ideals that are beyond criticism.

Max Weber posited three bases of legitimacy for bureaucratic authority: legal-rational, traditional, and charismatic. The first is based upon the assumption that the organization functions impersonally and objectively in terms of duly enacted laws, rules, and regulations.

---

[2]Cited in L. F. Carter, "Leadership and Small Group Behavior," in Muzafer Sherif and M. O. Wilson, eds., *Group Relations at the Crossroads* (New York: Harper & Row, 1953), p. 273.

[3]I am indebted here to D. C. Calhoun's, "The Illusion of Rationality," in R. Taylor, ed., *Life, Language, Law; Essays in Honor of Arthur Bentley* (Yellow Springs: Antioch Press, 1957).

Traditional legitimacy rests on the belief that the organization and its values are hallowed by age and experience and ought not be challenged by any time-bound individual. Charismatic legitimacy is based upon an irrational faith in leaders who are assumed to have magical powers. Charismatic personalities inspire among their followers a desire for sacrifice and devotion. Traditional and charismatic authority are essentially prebureaucratic; over a period of time, both tend to be replaced by legal-rational norms. The process is not linear, however; the charismatic bases of authority remain viable in modern organizations, especially in party organization.

Most organizations enlist all of these legitimations in justifying their claims to obedience, and the appeals are usually articulated in terms of the general welfare. However, it is necessary for organizations and their elites to simplify what is really happening, since their objectives are actually more complex and less disinterested than this. While elites do seek to advance the common good, they are at least equally concerned with perpetuating the organization and its personal prerogatives and with mediating conflicting interests within it. However, as Calhoun says, if mass loyalty is to be maintained, all three activities must be rationalized in terms of the first objective. Since it is impossible to define the general welfare, much less to achieve it, the organization must often invoke another ideological resource, the myth that it is founded upon unquestionable, unchanging principles.

Once such principles are accepted, it becomes possible to attribute any patent shortcomings, blunders, and injustice to the organization's members, leaving its ideals intact. If individuals achieve something noteworthy, it is an institutional triumph; if they fail, it is a personal aberration. This behavior is seen in the dramatic "confessions" that occur in the Communist party, but sacrificial mechanisms that differ mainly in degree are evident in most organizations. Necessity demands that failures of theory and practice be personalized, projected on some individual in a way that shows human error was involved rather than organizational legitimacy. Certain highly self-conscious systems, among which one can safely include the Marine Corps, the medical profession, and the Foreign Service, exhibit this collective idealization, often evoking exceptional loyalty from enchanted members. By contrast the "outsider" feels ineffectual. The continuity, power, and rituals of bureaucratic structures reinforce this self-perception.

As we have seen, this side of the bureaucratic coin appears to suit a pragmatic personality type who has unusual need for certainty, authority, and mystical helpers, marked, for example, by such beliefs as "Science has its place, but there are many things that can never be understood by the human mind," and "Every person should have complete faith in some supernatural power whose decisions he obeys without question." The claims of the organization to legitimacy, rationality, and loyalty are reinforced by associating it with eternal wisdom. We saw earlier that the hierarchical distance between elites and the rank and file encouraged a tendency to endow leaders with charismatic qualities. Elite monopolization of authority, status, and income reinforces this tendency.

Another psychological tactic of organizational elites is the promotion of an illusion of unanimity among members. Internal differences of interest and opinion are muffled in an effort to present a public image of discipline and unity that will enhance the organization's authority and its competitive chances. Dissent and criticism are repressed or confined within the organization. Once a decision has been hammered out, everyone must accept it since further discussion would impair the desired solidity. In part, organizations restrict participation in order to avoid the appearance of internal disharmony that true participation often entails. The common requirement that speeches and publications be cleared through a "public-information" agency is germane. Unfavorable reports can easily be dismissed as irresponsible or unauthorized, the implication being that the organization's elites are its only responsible spokesmen. These are the priests who represent the organization before the public, interpret its catechism, and explain away any disparity between its high ideals of service and its routine behavior.

To increase the probability that its members will endorse the unanimity principle, various incentives are used. These include appeals to loyalty, sacrifice, perpetuation of the organization's ideals, and so forth. Negative sanctions, on the other hand, are powerful yet latent, depending upon the social sensitivity, the anxiety-reduction needs, and the ambition of the individual. Such mechanisms reduce the need for crude sanctions, and since the majority of members are "indifferents" who merely tolerate organizational demands, followed by the "upward-mobiles" who eagerly embrace them, only a small residue of "ambivalents" remain as subjects for discipline.

Such accommodations have their basis in socialization. The successive authority relationships that begin in childhood and continue throughout one's life culminate in a "self-system" that normally includes a *generalized* deference toward authority. This orientation is continually reinforced because it reduces anxiety by insuring the approval of those who are important to us. Organizations provide many opportunities for anxiety reduction through such deference. In the process certain typical values and forms of behavior are instilled in their members. Consider, for example, the universal values of professional military organizations and the stylized behavior of their members. Discipline, "honor," "obedience," respect for authority, patent social distinctions (symbolized by such gems as "officers and their ladies, enlisted men and their wives"), an orientation toward physical power—*all are internalized and become personal norms of conduct.*[4]

The resulting pattern of "anticipated reactions" is the main basis upon which organizations function. An obvious example is the effect of rank insignia in the military. The mere sight of a high-ranking officer, identifiable at twenty paces, evokes a whole battery of conditioned responses from his subordinates. The accommodation is reciprocal, moreover, in that both actors know their proper roles. Levels of deference, degree of familiarity, tone of voice, indeed, the whole interpersonal situation is mediated with ease and dispatch by this single cue. The operational effect of such signals seems clear: the more patent and authoritative the stimulus, the more prompt and certain the response.

Anxiety's role in reinforcing organizational authority is explicit in an account of the experience of a new plant manager:

> Before being handed the reins . . . Peele was called to the main office for a "briefing." The main office executives told Peele of his predecessor's shortcomings, and expressed the feeling that things had been slipping at the plant for some time. They suggested that . . . the former manager who had recently died, had grown overindulgent with his advancing years, and that he, Peele, would be expected to improve production. . . . Peele, therefore, came to the plant sensitized to the rational and impersonal yardsticks which his superiors would use to judge his performance. As a successor, Peele had a heightened awareness that he could disregard top management's rational values only at his peril, for his very promotion symbolized the power they held over him. Since he was now on a new assignment, Peele also realized that he would be subject to more than routine observation by the main office. As a successor, he was "on trial," and, therefore, he was anxious, and anxious to "make good." Comments about Peele's anxiety were made by many main-office personnel, as well as by people in the plant who spoke repeatedly of his "nervousness."
>
> In turn, this anxiety spurred Peele to perform his new role according to main-office expectations. As one of the main-office administrative staff said, "Peele is trying hard to arrive. He is paying more attention to the plant." Peele also accepted top manage-

[4]G. Dearborn Spindler, "The Military—A Systematic Analysis," *Social Forces*, Vol. 27, pp. 83–88; Elizabeth G. French and Raymond R. Ernest, "The Relation Between Authoritarianism and Acceptance of Military Ideology," *Journal of Personality*, Vol. 24, pp. 181–191; for a fascinating historical study of military organization and mentality, see Cecile B. Woodham-Smith, *The Reason Why* (New York: McGraw-Hill, 1954).

ment's view of the plant out of *gratitude* for having been promoted from the smaller plant where he had been, to the larger one at Oscar Center. "I appreciate their confidence in me," he said, "and I want to show it."[5]

An interesting latent consequence of such behavior is an exaggeration of authority demands, which is often dysfunctional since it aggravates the fear of action and responsibility often seen in big organizations. This distorted perception reflects the anxiety of the individual to please his superiors and his impression of being relatively powerless vis-à-vis the organization's leaders. Since the elite is remote and its will cannot always be definitely known, the individual attempts to anticipate its expectations. As a result such expectations may seem more compelling than they are meant to be. The individual is not inclined in any case to underestimate them for fear of impairing his career chances. In this way organizational claims may be expanded beyond reason, not by the organization's elites, but by the individual.

The extent to which bureaucratic culture can include negative assumptions about human nature and its consequent tendency toward bizarre conditions of participation is patent in an experience of New York City's first consumer's counsel. After presenting certain job descriptions designed to recruit young lawyers interested in consumer affairs, the counsel had the following colloquy with the civil servant in charge of job descriptions for the city:

"We can't have people like that working for the city. We want career people, who will stay 20, 25 years, not these kids on their way through. Ya know why?"

"Actually, I don't," I admitted.

"Because in just one or two years they don't build up any equity in the pension fund."

Now I was mystified. "So what?"

"We don't want people with no equity in the pension fund," he said. "We want people who build up 10, 15 years' equity, a substantial amount of money due them from the pension fund."

"But what difference does that make?"

Schwartz answered slowly, beating his words out with one finger. "A man with 10 years' equity in the pension fund doesn't put his hand in the till, 'cause he can lose his pension rights."

"But these young lawyers aren't thieves!"

"Everyone near the till is a potential thief," said Schwartz. "That's

---

[5] Alvin W. Gouldner, *Patterns of Industrial Bureaucracy* (Glencoe, Ill.: Free Press, 1954), pp. 71–72; for additional evidence on the psychological bases of the anxiety-authority relation see Jack Block and Jeanne Block, "An Interpersonal Experiment on Reactions to Authority," *Human Relations*, Vol. 5, pp. 91–98.

why we have civil service. We lock 'em in; they have to stay with the city forever."[6]

Similar assumptions and reactions mediated by authority occur in many social contexts. Authority and prestige based on wealth, knowledge, role, technical expertise, social class, notoriety, or whatever the current values, elicit deference in all interpersonal situations. Communication between two individuals is always influenced by estimates of their relative status. In everyday affairs this is shown by the fact that the weight we attach to any opinion is largely a matter of the commentator's prestige. In organizations the tendency to defer exists simply because orders come from above, from superiors. By itself the formal distribution of authority creates a disposition to obey, essentially because such authority is assumed to be legitimate by those exposed to it. Hierarchy, the isolation or remoteness of the organization's elite, and its power to displace sanctions and allocate rewards reinforce this tendency.

Despite some untenable consequences, such a psychological situation is generally economical, insuring discipline and the reduction of overt interpersonal conflict. The organization's task is simplified by the fact that the reactions it evokes are already deep-seated. Since birth the individual has been conditioned to operate in an environment structured by authority. Noncoercive influences, including custom, mobility expectations, and potential rewards, practically eliminate the use of gross instruments of control. As will be shown later, the effectiveness of permissive measures is also a function of the social class and the anxiety potential of those concerned.

Because obedience becomes almost automatic, its significance is easily overlooked, or it may be repressed as an uncomfortable irony in a society where individualism is a pervasive ideal. Nevertheless, authority relations become institutionalized between parent and child, leader and follower, teacher and student, officer and enlisted man. Over time various stylized responses evolve, many of which have a remarkable survival value. For example, the contemporary military ritual whereby one moves two steps backward before turning away from a superior is apparently of feudal origin. Although such accommodations may be inspired by imperative cues, the mere presence of an authority figure is usually sufficient to evoke compliance. Since individuals tend to become conditioned to whole classes of stimuli, the respect for authority initiated by parents is generalized to the whole range of authoritative stimuli. With the exception of the ambivalent

[6]Philip Schrag, *Counsel for the Deceived: Case Studies in Consumer Fraud* (New York: Pantheon, 1972), pp. 32–34.

type, the entire socializing experience of individuals seems to prepare them for an organizational role.

We can now consider the psychology of the *status system*. This system may be defined as a hierarchy of deference ranks. The deference that is ascribed to organizational positions may be called status or prestige. While prestige is in part assigned to the person who occupies a given position, it is mainly ascribed to the position itself. We are concerned here with formal hierarchical status rather than with the status ranking attached to occupational roles of specialists. As noted earlier, status is disproportionately allocated in organizations. Its perquisites of income and prestige are concentrated at the top and decrease linearly as one descends the hierarchy. Status gradations are highly visible. They are marked off by appropriate titles, offices, equipment, secretarial assistance, and degrees of accessibility. Relative amounts of authority further differentiate status ranks. The rationale for such a distribution system is that one's status is roughly equal to one's ability and one's contribution to the goals of the organization.

Status systems in social and organizational life are typically geared into dominance-submission hierarchies. Such hierarchies vary considerably in shape and complexity. As Wilson reports, among animals, a simple despotism may exist in which one individual rules over all the others, with no rank differentiation among his subordinates.[7] A more common structure finds hierarchies made up of multiple ranks in a linear sequence in which one individual A dominates all others, his immediate inferior B dominates all others except A, and so on to the lowest individual on the ladder. In some cases, triangular structures of dominance are found, but these apparently tend over time to become linear. Among chickens, for example, straight-line hierarchies have been found to increase group effectiveness. Triads of hens feeding according to a linear dominance order consumed more than those arranged in a circular pattern. Among animals, once dominance hierarchies have been established, group cohesion and cooperation are enhanced because each individual tends to accept the resultant structure. Only in crises will the dominance pattern become visible. Wilson reports that baboon troops may interact for hours without revealing their hierarchic design; but when tension arises, often over a bit of food, the dominance pattern becomes graphically visible.

Among most primates, status signs exist that symbolize the dominance hierarchy. Among wolves, for example, the "leading male is unmistakable from the way he holds his head, ears, and tail, and the

---

[7]Edward Wilson, *Sociobiology: The New Synthesis* (Cambridge: Harvard University Press, 1975), p. 279.

confident, face-forward manner in which he approaches other members of his group. He controls his subordinates without any overt display of hostility."[8] Similarly, among rhesus monkeys the dominant male presents himself in an elaborate posture, signifying his rank: head and tail up, testicles lowered, body movements slow and deliberate and accompanied by unhesitating but measured scrutiny of other monkeys that cross his field of view.[9]

Status signs also include chemical signals. In male European rabbits, the development of the submandibular gland increases with the rank of the individual. By "chinning," that is, by rubbing their lower head against objects on the ground, dominant males mark the territory occupied by their colony with their own glandular secretions.[10]

Many of these status signals mark dominance patterns in modern bureaucratic settings. The "staging" instruments that denote and legitimate hierarchical rank in virtually all types of technical sectors include not only the obvious physical accoutrements of office. Individuals in dominant positions exhibit behaviors not entirely unlike those of the rhesus monkey and wolf leader mentioned above. The leadership style inculcated by the British public schools is apposite, including the easy assumption of superiority, commanding presence, upper-class speech forms, and the assumption of entitlement to preferential treatment.[11] The attributes usually included in ascriptive catalogues of successful individuals, such as "character," "good judgment," and "dependability," are similarly germane.

Although it is common in our time to deplore dominance hierarchies as illegitimate and undemocratic, research indicates that they often include functional consequences for the collectivity in which they occur. Here again, animal and insect behavior are suggestive. We note elsewhere that ape bands accept only the warning signals of experienced oligarchs. Reproductive advantages seem to be another product of dominance structures. Among anubis baboon females, selective breeding occurs, as they copulate only with the most dominant males during ovulation, while consorting with juveniles and lesser males at other times.[12] J. G. Frazer suggests that hierarchy brought

[8]R. Schenkel, "Ausdrucks-Studien an Wölfen," *Behaviour*, Vol. 1, pp. 81–129. Cited in Wilson, *Sociobiology*, p. 280.

[9]S. A. Altmann, "A Field Study of Rhesus Monkeys," *Annals of the New York Academy of Sciences*, Vol. 102, pp. 338–435. Cited in Wilson, *Sociobiology*, p. 280.

[10]R. Mykytowycz, "Territorial Function of Chin Gland Secretion in the Rabbit," *Nature* (London), Vol. 193, p. 799. Cited in Wilson, *Sociobiology*, p. 280.

[11]Rupert Wilkinson, *Gentlemanly Power: British Leadership and the Public Schools* (New York: Oxford University Press, 1964).

[12]B. Irven Devore, "The Evolution of Human Society," in John F. Eisenberg and Wilton S. Dillon, eds., *Man and Beast: Comparative Social Behavior* (Washington: Smithsonian Institution Press, 1971), pp. 297–311. Cited in Wilson, *Sociobiology*, p. 288.

the first peace known to early man.[13] Among the Yanomama Indians of Brazil, as Wilson reports, politically dominant males produce a "strongly disproportionate" number of the children because of the existing system of polygamy in which supplementary wives are traditionally the reward for male achievement.[14]

Aside from such social and genetic advantages, those in positions of hierarchical dominance enjoy certain personal benefits. Wilson suggests that the top-ranking animal is under less stress than his subordinates and may thus expend less energy in routine activities. At the same time, he is less likely to suffer from endocrine hyperfunction, which increases his effectiveness.[15]

In modern organizations, the status-dominance system provides a battery of signals and stimuli that conditions the behavior of subordinates. Multiple hierarchies exist that in some cases subject the individuals to subordination in several contexts, ranging from the structure of his small groups to the status hierarchy of the entire organization. At the same time, the specialization and fragmentation of large organizations provide him a certain independence. Regardless of their rank, the individual is relatively immune from the sanctions of those in other segments of the organization. He knows who his own supervisor is.

On the other hand, certain organizational conditions insure the individuals' dependency. Hierarchical control of status rewards and resulting status anxiety encourage the cheerful acceptance of existing patterns of distribution. The use of the co-optation principle in appointing successors and the fact that long tenure in a single organization is now the modal career pattern enhance dependency. Individuals become extremely sensitive to the opinions of their immediate superiors, who control their career chances. In some bureaucratic situations, including academia, apprentices must be sponsored by a patron who insures their advancement through assiduous (however muted) negotiations with other influential seniors. This system results in the somewhat anomalous spectacle of middle-aged people exhibiting dependency behavior quite similar to the parent-child relationship. Such sponsorships violate bureaucratic norms of impartiality and impersonality insofar as they reflect personality, class, and religion. The resulting personal dependency is a function of the long training and the indoctrination characteristic of technical fields, of the natural insistence of elites that successors mirror their own values, and of individual needs for status and security.

---

[13]James G. Frazer, *The Golden Bough,* abr. ed. (London: Macmillan, 1960).

[14]James V. Neel, "Lessons from a 'Primitive' People," *Science,* Vol. 170, pp. 815–822. Cited in Wilson, *Sociobiology,* p. 288.

[15]Wilson, *Sociobiology,* p. 289.

The repertoire of behaviors that mediate hierarchical relations rests in part upon phylogenetic (biological) residues in human and animal experience. Perhaps the relevance of such residues is suggested by the comments of one conglomerate president, "The executive is a lonely animal in the jungle who doesn't have a friend."[16] Others seem to be the result of ontological, that is, culturally derived, mechanisms. Here, it should be noted, we are qualifying somewhat Sullivan's theory that ontological experiences are the primal factor in the shaping of human behavior. Actually, while the predominance of cultural determinism is accepted, it is clear that certain patterns of behavior have a phylogenetical base. These are seen among certain species of birds who despite being raised from birth in an environment in which they are subjected to a great variety of bird-recorded songs, adapt to the song which is inherently appropriate to their kind.

As Konrad Lorenz has shown, among primates, who are the closest to humans, certain behaviors persist that enhance the survival potential of the groups concerned. Among ape bands, for example, a selective differentiation occurs whereby only the warning signals expressed by senior oligarchs become stimuli for protective action.[17] Frazer shows, too, that in the earliest times monarchy and its patent hierarchical system were similarly functional, reducing potentially destructive competition among class and status groups, ordering authority relationships, and generally reducing social ambiguity by invoking such mystiques as divine right.[18]

In modifying Lorenz's theory regarding the innately aggressive nature of humans, Eibl-Eibesfeldt has shown that phylogenetically-derived behaviors deflect conflict among animals and humans.[19] Among certain types of monkeys, it is common for those meeting for the first time to extend a hand, indicating recognition of status differentials and of friendship. The status-hierarchical imperative is seen in the fact that seniors sometimes respond by presenting a foot to the disadvantaged supplicant.

Among humans, such repertoires are more subtle and differentiated, in part because modern organizations may be characterized psychologically as a structured field in which the bench marks of status and hierarchy are patently designed to evoke organizationally-functional responses. It may also be that the blurring of individual differences attending mass production and stereotypical consump-

---

[16]Studs Terkel, *Working* (New York: Avon Books, 1975), p. 532.

[17]Konrad Lorenz, *On Aggression* (New York: Harcourt, Brace, 1967), pp. 40–45.

[18]Frazier, *The Golden Bough.*

[19]Irenäus Eibl-Eibesfeldt, *Love and Hate,* trans. G. Strachen (New York: Holt, Rinehart & Winston, 1972).

tion styles have nourished a compensating reaction in the occupational world, which attempts to ease the resulting blandness by a highly differentiated status apparatus.

In modern organizations individual status needs are often met by the nice articulation of status systems which include noneconomic incentives; these are experienced by employees as a source of job satisfaction. The dynamics of such needs are patent in the words of a secretary for a corporation president:

> I've been an executive secretary for eight years. However, this is the first time I've been on the corporate end of things, working for the president. I found it a new experience. I love it and I feel I'm learning a lot. I enjoy one thing more than anything else on this job. That's the association I have with the other executives, not only my boss. There's a tremendous difference in the way they treat me than what I've known before. They treat me as . . . on the executive level. They consult me on things, and I enjoy this. It stimulates me. I feel like I'm sharing somewhat of the business life of the men. So I think I'm much happier as the secretary to an executive than I would be in some woman's field where I could perhaps make more money. But it wouldn't be an extension of a successful executive. I'm perfectly happy in my status.[20]

Status systems tend to evoke *obedience*, which seems to be an innate characteristic. Both in society and in the organization, certain stereotypical patterns of behavior seem to have their origin in submissiveness. As Lorenz says regarding the function of polite manners, "a considerable proportion of the mannerisms enjoined by good manners are culturally ritualized exaggerations of submissive gestures most of which probably have their roots in phylogenetically ritualized motor patterns conveying the same meaning."[21] The acute attention paid to the words of a bureaucratic superior by his subordinates, often characterized by appropriate sounds or gestures of approval, seems germane.[22] The stylized behavior of the German *Beamte* who backs away from his superior, not turning away until some distance separates them is of similar interest. Thorstein Veblen, as noted earlier, has also shown how "manners" are functionally related to status and dominance: "Manners . . . are symbolical and conventionalized survivals representing former acts of dominion or of per-

---

[20]Terkel, *Working*, pp. 90–91.

[21]Lorenz, *On Aggression*, p. 77.

[22]A catalogue of such behaviors in various contexts is available in Ervin Goffman, *The Presentation of Self in Everyday Life* (New York: Doubleday, 1959); *Strategic Interaction* (Philadelphia: University of Pennsylvania Press, 1969); and *Frame Analysis* (Cambridge: Harvard University Press, 1974).

sonal service or of personal contact. In large part they are an expression of the relation of status—a symbolic pantomime of mastery on the one hand and of subservience on the other."[23]

The salience of hierarchically superior models for behavior is suggested by research involving chimpanzees, who tend to learn by imitating only higher-ranking members of their species. In one instance, a low-ranking member was taught a rather complicated routine for removing bananas from a feeding apparatus. However, when he performed this skill before the band, the other animals contented themselves with confiscating the fruit, making no effort to learn something from him. However, after the highest ranking chimpanzee was removed from the band and taught the same routine, the "other members watched him with great interest and soon learned to imitate him."[24]

Such learning is by definition culturally acquired. Deference to authority or obedience, on the contrary, is thought to be "a disposition innate to human beings."[25] Thus the dynamics of bureaucratic authority structure seem to rest firmly upon phylogenetic adaptations. Despite the contemporary decomposition of traditional authority structures and the relentless incursions of technology, rationality, and science upon charismatic authority, evidence reveals that obedience to hierarchical authority remains compelling. The acceptance of higher authority in wartime (Auschwitz, Dresden, Hiroshima, My Lai, for example) has been shockingly documented.

More recently, a dramatic experimental study indicates how competing claims of pity can be compromised by prior commitment to authority. The psychologist, Stanley Milgram, brought together 110 individuals from several occupations in a simulated learning experiment.[26] They were told that the objective was to test the effects of certain punitive stimuli on learning. They were shown a person in an adjoining room, strapped in a chair with electrodes connected to his arms. Their role, they were told, was to transmit electric shocks whenever he made a mistake. The strength of the shocks was to be increased from mistake to mistake, and the subjects were given a machine with a series of levers ranging from 15 to 440 volts. The higher voltages were labeled as "dangerous."

---

[23]Thorstein Veblen, *The Theory of the Leisure Class: An Economic Study of the Evolution of Institutions* (New York: Macmillan, 1953), p. 48.

[24]Cited in Lorenz, *On Aggression*, pp. 42–43.

[25]Eibl-Eibesfeldt, *Love and Hate*, p. 102.

[26]Stanley M. Milgram, *Obedience to Authority: An Experimental View* (New York: Harper & Row, 1974); "A Behavioral Study of Obedience," *Journal of Abnormal Psychology*," Vol. 67, pp. 372–378; "Einige Bedlingungen von Authoritatsgehorsam und seiner Verweigerung," Z. exp. u. angew. *Psychology*, Vol. 13, pp. 433–463.

A group of psychiatrists, asked to estimate the likelihood of the subjects completing the instructions, insisted that only 1 percent of them would carry the task through to the end. What actually happened was strikingly different. Even though simulated cries of protest and pain were heard from the test room, 62 percent of the subjects obeyed the instructor's directions. Their pity was evoked by the cries, and they suggested that they should stop. But when the instructor insisted that they must continue, they did so, often laughing hysterically and saying they would not accept responsibility. When the instructor left the room, the subjects cheated by pretending to administer the shocks in increasing volume. Nevertheless, as indicated, almost two-thirds complied when directed by the experimenter. The experiment indicates that innate dispositions to obey authority can override alternative cultural imprinting.

According to Milgram, the explanation lies in the anxiety evoked in respondents by the strain of being forced to reject authority if they refused to continue administering the shocks to the "victim." Such anxiety

> stems from the individual's long history of socialization. He has, in the course of moving from a biological creature to a civilized person, internalized the basic rules of social life. And the most basic of these is respect for authority. The rules are internally enforced by linking their possible breach to a flow of disruptive, ego-threatening affect. The emotional signs observed in the laboratory—trembling, anxious laughter, acute embarrassment—are evidence of an assault on these rules. As the subject contemplates this break, anxiety is generated, signaling him to step back from the forbidden action and thereby creating an emotional barrier through which he must pass in order to defy authority.[27]

Such dependency relations are thus linked to earlier patterns of individual socialization. As we have seen, anxiety is an integral part of the child's developing relationship with his parents. After two decades of clinical experience, Sullivan concluded that anxiety is uniquely an interpersonal phenomenon, with its origins in the extreme dependence of the infant upon his mother. This learned tension becomes a critical mechanism in personality formation as individuals meet threats to their self-esteem by compliance and receive reinforcement for such responses through the consequent reduction of anxiety. This early conditioning seems to be at work in the organizational situation where dependency is built into most interpersonal relationships by patent differentiations of status and authority. One's

[27] Ibid., p. 152.

career mobility and the perceived atmosphere of his work environment are determined mainly by the attitudes of his superiors toward him. He must secure their approval in order to obtain the resources necessary to carry out his tasks. His joy in work will be decisively affected by his perception of their evaluation of his performance. In the typical bureaucratic setting their very remoteness may inspire some distortion in this process. Such conditions mean that typical organization people will tend to be disciplined, anxious, and sensitive in their relations with others. They will understand that mobility requires the support of prestigious seniors, the gatekeepers who control the avenues of authority, status, and income.

Emotional security is also among the reinforcements, since socialization insures that finding a validation of one's values in the group is a prerequisite of satisfactory personal adjustment. The number and diversity of voluntary groups in American society provide a broad range of individual choice and accommodation, insuring some compensation for the individual's restricted occupational role. Relative status within the whole society is apparently less vital than a recognized status position in one or more of such groups. Fortunately, there is a status hierarchy for everyone, ranging from honored professions to the underworld. Even within prisons a subtle hierarchy exists, in which forgers rank near the top since they presumably work with their brains.

Despite the variety of such indexes and the several roles that each of us plays as a bureaucratic parent, citizen, marriage partner, and so forth, occupation has become the major status referent. Education, technical skill, and attending levels of consumption now seriously challenge property as status indexes. Since occupational roles are increasingly played in such arenas, organizations become important dispensers of status dividends. Both people's personal status and the status of their occupation can be augmented by the status of the organization in which they work.

The status system, however, has other functions. Perhaps the most important is to be seen in the fact that differential status allocations reinforce the authority of organizational leaders. Whether the system is consciously directed to this end is not at issue. We are interested in its objective results. The status system ramifies authority by validating the right of elites to exercise it. "Insignia and titles of status have the effect of credentials."[28] In our meritocratic society the system fosters the assumption that unequal rewards reflect objective differences in ability. However much this assumption has been undercut by the

---

[28]Chester Barnard, "Functions and Pathology of Status Systems in Formal Organizations," in William F. Whyte, ed., *Industry and Society* (New York: McGraw-Hill, 1946), p. 60.

federal government's program of "equal opportunity" for minority groups, with its introduction of particularistic bases of recruitment in many occupational sectors, workers still tend to believe that those in supervisory positions "know what they are doing." As the Survey Research Center's findings (1974) show, almost two-thirds of a cross-section of American workers in all occupations, men and women, feel this way.[29] No doubt this finding partly reflects their will to believe that universalistic standards underlie promotion, but one may assume that their opinion also reflects their on-the-job experience.

Status thus honors the principle of hierarchy and its allocation of authority throughout the organization. In effect, the legal, rational basis of authority is reinforced by personal, charismatic qualities imputed to those who exercise most of it. We saw earlier that the distance between elites and the rank and file encouraged the human tendency to ascribe exceptional competence to those of higher rank. Highly visible status differences aggravate this tendency.

In the process the learned tendency of the individual toward obedience is evoked. As Chester Barnard maintains:

> Men are eager to be "bossed" by superior ability, but they resent being bossed by men of no greater ability than they themselves have. So strong is this need of assigning superior status to those in positions of command that, unless the obvious facts preclude it, men will impute abilities they cannot recognize or judge. They want to believe that those of higher authority "know what they are doing."
> . . . This desire for the justification of subordination leads often to profuse rationalization about status and even to mythological and mystical explanations of it.[30]

It is only fair to note that Barnard's main emphasis is upon the rational aspects of status; he believes that the system effectively validates objective differences in ability and in the difficulty and importance of occupational roles. The problem of course is to distinguish between the rational and the charismatic bases of status.

Meanwhile, bureaucratic conditions of work aggravate status demands. They encourage anxiety by changing the basis of status ascription from objective criteria, such as the importance of the work itself, to subjective ones, such as charisma and hierarchical rank. Specialization, hierarchy, and impersonality encourage efforts to personalize jobs. The breakdown of work into simple tasks and machine processes seems to foster alienation which diverts attention away from work toward its by-products of status and prestige. Particularly in the mid-

[29]Robert P. Quinn and Linda J. Shepard, *The 1972–73 Quality of Employment Survey* (Ann Arbor: Survey Research Center, 1974), p. 200.

[30]Barnard, "Functions," pp. 60–61; also Hans Speier, "Honor and Social Structure," *Social Forces*, Vol. 12, pp. 74–97.

dle ranges of organizations, a "status panic" may occur in which employees make sustained and often pathetic efforts to recapture their individuality. Such efforts may arise as a counterpoise to the increasing rationalization of work. As C. Wright Mills says:

> In the white-collar hierarchies, individuals are often segregated by minute gradations of rank and, at the same time, subject to a fragmentation of skill. This bureaucratization often breaks up the occupational basis of their prestige. Since the individual may seize upon minute distinctions as bases for status, these distinctions operate against any status solidarity among the mass of employees, often lead to status estrangement from work associates, and to increased status competition. . . . Above all, the hierarchy is often accompanied by a delirium for status merely because of its authoritarian shape: as Karl Mannheim has observed, people who are dependent for everything, including images of themselves, upon place in an authoritarian hierarchy, will all the more frantically cling to claims of status.[31]

The demand for status may express itself in sustained efforts to borrow prestige from whatever source possible. Organizations of many kinds now "sell" prestige to their members, and employees borrow status from the company in which they work.

> If white-collar relations with supervisors and higher-ups, with customers or clients, become so impersonal as seriously to limit borrowing prestige from them, prestige is often borrowed from the firm or the company itself. The fetishism of the enterprise, and identification with the firm, are often as relevant for the white-collar hirelings as for the managers. This identification may be implemented by the fact that the work itself . . . offers little chance for external prestige claims and internal self-esteem. So the work one does is buried in the firm.[32]

In his analysis of union intellectuals, a sociologist notes the status-borrowing activities of a "careerist" type who is closely identified with the hierarchy of his union and is oriented toward a career within it. Having no ideological commitments, no nonorganizational goals, and "very little if any professional identification," his satisfactions center around the chance for social mobility through his position. "His union job means a chance to bask in the reflected glory of great men."[33]

---

[31]C. Wright Mills, *White Collar* (New York: Oxford University Press, 1951), pp. 254–255.

[32]Ibid., p. 243.

[33]Harold L. Wilensky, *Intellectuals in Trade Unions* (Glencoe, Ill.: Free Press, 1956), p. 146.

Similar behaviors may be seen in academia. As noted earlier, most departments exhibited a functional division of labor in which some 20 percent of members produced the research upon which any prestige claims of the department were based, while the remainder were occupied with administration, teaching, and academic ceremonials. Thus, even in the most self-conscious milieu (it may be recalled that Caplow and McGee found that all nine of the departments included in their study of faculty norms in elite universities ranked themselves at the very top of the prestige scale) a displacement of values tends to occur whereby the prestige claims of most academics are shifted from achievement to a parasitic alternative: the eminence of their department and university. More generally, it seems that those in hierarchical roles tend to be less concerned with the intrinsic character of work than with its by-products of status, prestige, and security. This is partly because such roles stress subjective, promotional, and human-relations skills and activities.

Following Sullivan, we assume that status anxiety contributes to the acceptance of organizational authority. Essentially, the status system reinforces authority by structuring interpersonal relations in terms of the relative prestige of the actors. Their roles are nicely defined. Subordination and superordination are prescribed. In this sense, the status system provides a form of "staging" that conditions behavior.[34] Interpersonal transactions are always held in the senior's office, which always contains patent indexes of his superior prestige. The subordinate asks for an appointment with the superior. It is clear whose time is at a premium. If the superior wishes, he can aggravate the resulting dependency by requiring that the subordinate wait. His secretary constitutes a fairly obvious prop, validating her boss's prestige claims by virtue of his preoccupation with important affairs.

Although some pathological results may follow, this milieu may also increase organizational effectiveness. By making authority relations highly visible, the status system prescribes the roles of all parties. Ambiguity and conflict are reduced. No time is wasted establishing dominance by informal gamesmanship. One can turn immediately to the business at hand. The limits of discussion and dissent are outlined. Since important decisions can rarely be reconciled by an objectively superior alternative, despite the prevailing scientism of "systems analysis," "social indicators," "T-groups," and the like, the capacity to decide on the basis of authority becomes all the more significant. Because conclusive proof is not forthcoming, debate might otherwise go on indefinitely. Decisions can, moreover, be conclusive since once su-

---

[34]Goffman, *The Presentation of Self in Everyday Life*, pp. 252–254.

perior authority has legitimated them, no further discussion of their merits is permitted, at least officially. Interpersonal relations can be smoothly negotiated if both actors play their roles skillfully, the senior by masking his dominance, the junior by discreet validation of the superior's prestige and wisdom. The interplay of staging and learned deference attitudes makes manipulation rather than command the common organizational currency. Such results are illustrated by the way that Navy recruits during World War II quickly accepted its "affirm-and-conform" rationale.[35] The organization's "structured field" molded behavior in desired ways. Tradition, authority, and status prescribed appropriate responses in most situations.

The status system enhances motivation and discipline by its promise of highly valued rewards and its immediate psychic income. As the displacement of value from work to its by-products has eroded the almost uniquely American emphasis upon achievement, status and prestige have become more highly valued in themselves. Following a kind of Hobbesian dialectic, men strive to validate their uniqueness by the acquisition of ever greater status and prestige. In part, those in hierarchical posts assign disproportionate weight to such values because their work offers less intrinsic satisfaction than that of specialists. The absence of objective criteria of performance in higher posts further aggravates status anxiety. Status perquisites are highly reinforced because they tend to reduce such tensions. Meanwhile, control of the status-distribution system gives elites a powerful sanction, providing compelling incentives for many of its members.

The distribution of such rewards, moreover, makes for sustained effort. Status expectations and potentials are perceived as virtually unlimited. The higher one ascends in the organization, the greater the relative amounts of status, prestige, and income he enjoys. There is a continuing incentive to strive. However, it must be noted that such striving varies with age and class. As Hollingshead and Redlich report, the career aspirations of upper-middle-class men in New Haven are quite different during their early and late career stages. "A young male looks forward to the time when he will . . . earn $15,000, $25,000, or as much as $50,000 a year and will help make decisions, not just carry out those made by others." But at fifty, men had begun to say: "My job is to hold on." Moreover, this class, over 70 percent of whom are members of national business organizations, was the most status conscious of the five class strata in the city. They "are extremely

[35]Arthur K. Davis, "Bureaucratic Patterns in the Navy Officer Corps," in R. K. Merton et al., eds., *Reader in Bureaucracy* (Glencoe, Illinois: Free Press, 1952). On the general question of individual fusion with the group, see Peter M. Blau, "A Theory of Social Integration," *American Journal of Sociology*, Vol. 65, pp. 545–556.

sensitive to how they must behave . . . in order to continue to move upward in the managerial hierarchy."[36]

We can now consider the psychology of small groups. Our concern here is with work groups that typically include ten to twenty members. Such groups carry out the critical tasks of the organization. They are the instrument that links the individual with the larger organization. Such groups are perceived quite differently by those who direct the larger organization and by the individuals who work in them. Organizational elites probably tend to regard work groups in a detached, instrumental way, with little differentiation among them qualitatively. Group members, on the other hand, tend to identify strongly with their own group, to regard it as more salient than the larger organization, which may seem to be remote and impersonal. The systems of authority and status discussed earlier impinge most directly upon the individual in this small group context.[37]

Technology is also vital at this level since the very structure of the work group, the design of its authority relations, the degree of control over the individual work process, the nature of supervision, among other factors, seem to be greatly influenced by the technical nature of the group's role. As noted elsewhere, however, research regarding the relative weight of technology on such variables as the structure of organizations, the closeness of supervision, and individual morale has been generally inconclusive. One compelling theoretical problem has been that both technology and structure are treated as being unidimensional variables when in fact they are complex aggregates. As yet, the problem of holding such variables constant in empirical research efforts has not been solved.[38] Nevertheless, one may safely conclude that technology is a critical element in small group behavior.[39]

The behavioral incentives of small groups are clearly of phylogenetic origin, typically reflecting such needs as survival and mating and care of young. A division of labor is also made possible. Animals of most species fight their own kind, and man is no exception, but there is much evidence that they also exploit the advantages of sociability. In this context, the small group may be thought of as a

[36]August B. Hollingshead and Frederick C. Redlich, *Social Class and Mental Illness* (New York: Wiley, 1958), p. 86.

[37]For a useful study of a hospital ward work group, see Peter M. Newton and Daniel J. Levinson, "The Work Group within the Organization: A Sociopsychological Approach," *Psychiatry*, Vol. 36, pp. 115–142.

[38]For a summary of such problems, see Gary G. Stanfield, "Technology and Organizational Structure as Theoretical Categories," *Administrative Science Quarterly*, Vol. 21, pp. 489–493.

[39]See, for example, Charles Perrow, *Complex Organizations* (Glenview, Ill.: Scott-Foresman, 1972).

compensation for the rationalization and impersonalization that characterize most bureaucratic settings. Once again, the incentives for group intimacy may be seen in extra-human societies. As Eibl-Eibesfeldt reports, animals and fish that become separated from their kind quickly seek to rejoin them.[40] The urge of fish to be with their conspecifics is particularly strong. They exhibit virtual panic as they swim about searching for their shoal. A primal incentive is self-preservation; apparently fish that prey upon them must single out a victim, but this is made more difficult by the constant alternation of targets caused by the collective movement of the shoal.

Among birds, flocking serves a similar function, enabling them to combine against a common enemy.[41] The aggressive instinct is harnessed to group needs as seen among passerine birds who stake out particular territories, defending them against other members of the species, with important consequences for survival. Birds are kept from nesting too closely together so that food-gathering is simplified and the rearing of young eased. Among the most suggestive results is that population growth is controlled: the spatial distribution of birds over some distance limits procreation because the possession of territory is a prerequisite of breeding.

The division of labor made possible by groups enables certain hunting wolves to chase their prey while others cut off and attack single victims. Among leaf-cutting ants in tropical South America, a very sophisticated specialization occurs: three different worker castes exist, each with a prescribed task. The largest ants defend the nest; medium-sized workers cut and carry pieces of leaves; while the smallest process the leaves into the compost which produces the fungi upon which the ants feed. Human social groupings probably rest upon somewhat similar needs, particularly the need of familial stability through marriage to perpetuate the species.

The group character of organization may be clearer when considered from the perspective of individuals. They usually perform a specific task in a group of specialists, organized in a hierarchy not unlike that of the larger organization. For individuals, this subunit often becomes *the* organization, since their work and their life chances are bound up with it. They may develop considerable loyalty to it, regarding other groups as competitors. They will probably form close personal ties with some of their fellow workers, and they will certainly evaluate their colleagues in terms of their technical skill and personal attributes. In this sense organizational be-

---

[40]Eibl-Eibesfeldt, *Love and Hate*, pp. 57–62.

[41]Eliot Howard, *Territory in Bird Life* (New York: Atheneum, 1964), cited in Eibl-Eibesfeldt, *Love and Hate*, p. 64.

havior is group behavior, and many of the generalizations of small-group theory apply, including the evolution of dominance-submission hierarchies.

Here again, biopolitics is useful in suggesting the pervasiveness of the need for group acceptance among humans in many different cultural contexts. As Eibl-Eibesfeldt says, "human beings possess a rich repertoire of gestures of appeasement and submission, most of them innate."[42] Among animals, such "behavioral analogies to morality" are equally common. People in the most different cultures weep and lament in very much the same way, using the same gestures and the same sounds. Even children who are born deaf and blind weep. Phylogenetic adaptations are visible in culturally defined gestures of obeisance and surrender: in submitting, one makes himself smaller by kneeling, bowing, or prostration. Among Bushman children, quarrels often end by children staring at each other until one finally capitulates by lowering the head. Among Australian aborigines, a small child might be pushed along in front of adults, since the presence of children tends to inhibit aggression.

A common but instructive example may be seen in behavior in railroad compartments. For reasons apparently having to do with territorial rights, precedence is given to the first occupant of the compartment. Subsequent arrivals will deferentially inquire (despite patent evidence to the contrary) whether "that seat is taken," whereupon the incumbent will grant permission to enter. The occupants then join in assuming possession of the compartment (they form a group) and the same ritual will be repeated as subsequent travellers enter their domain. Requests for permission to enter will be accompanied by signals of appeasement calculated to insure acceptance. Smiles,[43] friendly greetings, perhaps a slight nod, or in certain cultures, a bow.

It is well known that most individuals need recognition and a sense of belonging; the strength of this need is shown by the fact that exclusion is among the most painful of group sanctions. Indeed, some individuals develop such strong identification with their subgroups that intergroup rivalry is the rule in organizations. Meanwhile, the very conception of a common external danger increases group cohesion. Roethlisberger and Dickson found a highly protective attitude and great cohesion among a bank-wiring group; also, the very knowledge that they were being investigated increased the morale and the output

---

[42]Eibl-Eibesfeldt, *Love and Hate*, p. 96.

[43]The disarming impact of a smile is patent in the reported case of an American sergeant in Vietnam who suddenly found himself face-to-face with two Vietcong soldiers. His gun misfired and he smiled. In the moment during which mistrust was dispelled by this signal, he ejected the cartridge, reloaded, and shot both men.

of the group.[44] Other evidence shows that workers try to ease feelings of anonymity and impersonality by forming close personal relations, and that a permissive atmosphere may increase job satisfaction and even productivity.

The cohesiveness often found in small groups notwithstanding, sociometric analysis indicates that a scale of personal attractiveness or preference exists in many face-to-face groups, suggesting that some individuals will be regarded as outsiders with attending feelings of alienation (defined here as self-estrangement) from the group. Such rankings can occur regardless of the technology of the work group, although they may be related to it in the sense that an individual's sociometric ranking may be related to the performance of his or her work role.

A related, but distinct aspect is alienation from the work itself. Technology seems to have a curvilinear affect upon this form of alienation, which is least among individuals in craft activities, intermediate in machine tending, and highest among workers on assembly line technologies.[45] Two suggestive questions are the extent to which alienation from work is related to alienation from the larger society, a classical Marxian assumption, and whether the degree of felt powerlessness, a typical index of alienation, is related to type of work. A careful analysis by David Payne suggests a negative answer to both questions.[46] Another study looking essentially at two often assumed correlates of alienation concludes that in our "large-scale, capitalist system, control over the product of one's labor, ownership and hierarchical position has only an indirect effect on alienation, whereas control over work process (closeness of supervision, routinization, and substantive complexity) has an appreciable direct effect on powerlessness, self-estrangement, and normlessness."[47]

Certain limitations of group research may be mentioned. One problem is that its frequent use of experimental designs creates artificial situations. For example, one well-known study of decision making established a statusless group. Yet in human behavior one of the firm generalizations is that whenever people meet, age, experience, expertise, and power create status differences. Research from which status factors have been excluded has important limitations. Much of

[44]Fritz J. Roethlisberger and William J. Dickson, *Management and the Worker* (Cambridge: Harvard University Press, 1941).

[45]Robert Blauner, *Alienation and Freedom* (Chicago: University of Chicago Press, 1964).

[46]David Payne, "Alienation: An Organizational-Society Comparison," *Social Forces*, Vol. 53, pp. 274–282.

[47]Melvin L. Kohn, "Occupational Structure and Alienation," *American Journal of Sociology*, Vol. 82, p. 111.

the research also requires that participants be informed of the objectives and procedures of study, with the result that spontaneity is lost and behavior may be affected in unknown and perhaps unknowable ways. This disadvantage of social research is aggravated by the difficulty of securing accurate diagnoses when people themselves are the observers.

Despite such limitations, the findings of group research are very useful. Individuals behave differently in groups than when alone, and such differences have organizational consequences. An obvious example is seen in mob psychology where anonymity provokes behaviors that individuals qua individuals would not consider. Although crowd behavior undoubtedly reflects personal needs to release aggression, group situations also tend to encourage conformity. The hierarchical character of groups strengthens this tendency. If groups are to act, some structuring must exist. Even in antiauthoritarian associations, such as religious sects, the need "to achieve the imperative goals" of the organization insures bureaucratization and gradations of power and authority. While authority and power in such contexts lean more heavily upon charismatic legitimations, operational claims override equalitarian values.[48] In any informal group situation, once a goal is set, certain individuals gradually assume leadership, by virtue of skill, intelligence, the wish to dominate, or perhaps mere ignorance of their own limitations. The resulting pattern may become crystallized through group acceptance, apathy, and oligarchy, all of which place a monopoly of information and patronage in a few hands. In such situations there is a tendency for the individual to seek "consensual validation" of his views by comparing them with the "official line," which is assumed to reflect "inside" information, an institution-wide view, and so forth. That is, he will look elsewhere, to the group and to its authority figures, for cues that define approved opinions.

Group influence on the individual is thus partly the result of imitation. Much of learning and other social behavior is imitative. Examples include children copying their parents' speech, adolescents aping the dress and mannerisms of their peers, and adults incorporating as their own the opinions of prestigious figures on issues about which they have no firsthand information. The motivation is probably a desire for psychological security and a feeling of belonging. We imitate those we admire. The weight of such majority demands (which are often rationally determined and necessary) is suggested by the finding that people on conservative university faculties are more

[48]Paul M. Harrison, "Weber's Categories of Authority and Voluntary Associations," *American Sociological Review*, Vol. 25, pp. 232–237.

likely to become increasingly conservative with age than are members of less conservative faculties.[49]

The individual's deference to group norms has been established by many experimental studies, including a celebrated one by Sherif.[50] Using a common perceptual illusion that a fixed light in a dark room is actually moving about, he found that different individuals gave consistently different judgments as to the alleged movements. He next placed three such individuals together and found that under group influence each abandoned his earlier judgment in favor of a common evaluation.

Another experiment, involving a situation where a correct answer was possible, is equally suggestive.[51] Asch placed a small group (seven to nine members) in a classroom, explaining that they would be shown lines of different lengths and that their task was to match those of equal length. The lines were placed vertically on a large card, with an index line on another card placed alongside. Each student called out the number of the line he believed identical with the index line. Three trials were given. During the first two the experiment proceeded smoothly because the distinctions between the lines were obvious. But on the third trial one member began to call out numbers that were different from the others. Without his knowledge all the other students had been instructed to give unanimously a *wrong* answer.

Following the matching, this individual was questioned by the group. Was it likely that he could have been right and everyone else wrong? What were the reasons for his judgments? Finally he was told about the arrangement and its objectives. For our purposes the important thing is that despite the obvious length differences and the ease of matching them, after a series of tests one-third of the dissenting individuals accepted the judgment of the group. Asch divided these "yielders" into three categories: those who actually thought they saw what the majority saw; those who immediately decided, "I am wrong, they are right"; and those who were not much concerned with accuracy but suppressed their own judgment because of a need to conform.

A study by Coch and French dealing with resistance to change in a factory is also useful.[52] Following a slight change in her job, a machine operator produced at a reduced rate of 50 units per hour. Some ten days later, however, she reached normal production (about 65 units),

[49]Paul Lazarsfeld and Wagner Theilens, *The Academic Mind* (Glencoe, Ill.: Free Press, 1958), pp. 248–249.

[50]Muzafer Sherif and Carolyn W. Sherif, *An Outline of Social Psychology* (New York: Harper & Row, 1952).

[51]Solomon E. Asch, *Social Psychology* (Englewood Cliffs, N.J.: Prentice-Hall, 1952).

[52]Lester Coch and John R. P. French, Jr., "Overcoming Resistance to Change," *Human Relations*, Vol. 1, pp. 512–532.

and soon began to exceed the rates of her group. She then became the target of considerable abuse as a "rate-buster," whereupon her productivity decreased to the group's level. Three weeks after the change, the other operators were transferred, leaving this girl alone. Within four days she was turning out 83 units per hour and produced steadily at that rate thereafter. A classic example of group influence involved a bank-wiring group which set a standard for a fair day's work consisting of a certain number of completed units. Men who exceeded this rate were called "speed kings" and criticized severely by the group. On the other hand, those who failed to maintain the rate were called "chiselers" and were censored for violating the group's expectations.[53]

Compliance in organizations is thus encouraged by small group sanctions, most of which invoke the anxiety-conformity-approval syndrome but vary considerably according to the situation. In the industrial situations mentioned above, ridicule, censure, and even blows were used to punish nonconformists. On the other hand, in organizations engaged in highly technical work requiring considerable education and training (correlated in turn with middle-class drives for success), sanctions are rather more Machiavellian, and rewards meet status needs more often than economic ones. Organizations encourage the use of subtle deprivations. Decisions affecting an individual are sometimes made anonymously for reasons that remain unknown even to the subleaders of the group in which the individual works. Often the elite feels no compulsion to explain its actions, particularly if subjective or "political" reasons are involved. In such cases "the good of the organization" provides a sufficient rationalization. As a result individuals may not know for some time that they have been disciplined, while the actual reasons for it may elude them permanently. Here again, hierarchy, size, and the diffused responsibility of the organization are decisive.

Deprivation of response is a common reinforcement whereby the group disciplines individuals (and achieves discipline) by isolating them. This is at best a painful experience, since socialization insures that our emotional and physical needs are bound up with an accepted position in the group. An extreme case was reported in England recently when a crane operator, who had refused to join his union in a walkout, was given the "silent treatment" for several months. We saw earlier that professional associations command sanctions that may include ignoring or putting down the work of outsiders. In our society where personal "maturity" is usually equated with conformity and group acceptance, deprivations of this kind are probably excep-

---

[53]Roethlisberger and Dickson, *Management and the Worker*, pp. 419–421.

tionally painful. The need to be liked, which Europeans find one of our most noteworthy characteristics, is a powerful incentive to conformity.

Deprivation of response is most effective in highly self-conscious organizations, where desired behavior is induced by systematic conditioning. The uncanny ability of the Marine Corps' "boot-camp" program to instill loyalty and morale in recruits comes to mind, but this program differs only in degree from the indoctrination used by many organizations. One of the latent functions of tenure in universities is almost surely to provide an extended probationary period during which candidates can be properly socialized into the preferred value structure of a given department. Organizational loyalty will always be strained by the disparity between individual expectations and satisfactions, and by such training, organizations are in effect anticipating the future. When high morale persists despite the disenchantment that experience must bring, we can assume that a substantial proportion of members have internalized the organization's values. In so doing each becomes a positive stimulus, increasing the legitimacy of group norms, making defection less likely and deprivations more painful.

Drawing upon phylogenetical and culturally based adaptations, organizations provide a psychological climate that encourages compliance. Such responses prove rewarding because they reduce anxiety and increase mobility chances by insuring the approval of authority figures who control the organization's distribution system. Small groups play a similar socializing role. They use various rewards and sanctions to inculcate desired values in their members. Although their norms are not necessarily consonant with organizational goals, the significant result is that small groups provide stimuli that condition individual behavior in large, bureaucratic organizations.

The preceding chapters have attempted to set down the theoretical, institutional, and psychological framework for individual participation in the large-scale bureaucracies that dominate the work place in American society. I have been especially concerned to suggest that bureaucratic organizations provide a "structured field" in which the symbols of authority, status, and functional role tend to be exceptionally patent and compelling. Individuals tend to respond to this highly rationalized setting in terms of an anxiety-conformity-approval syndrome. However, variations in congenital residues and socialization mean that individuals will respond differently to this environment. Three discrete patterns of individual accommodation have been posited. In the next chapter, we turn to the first of these, the "upward-mobiles."

PATTERNS OF | 6
ACCOMMODATION:
UPWARD-MOBILES

When this book first appeared, one of its bench-mark assumptions was that a limited but significant proportion of individuals are highly committed to traditional values of hard work and success. Our upward-mobiles select themselves out of this highly motivated minority. To some extent, their commitment to work may be instrumental rather than intrinsic. It may be a means of achieving scarce values including security, influence, and high income. However, the operational effects may be similar since individuals must to some large extent perform optimally in their work if they are to succeed in their work settings. The crucial question here, however, is whether our initial assumption regarding the salience of work and success remains valid in the face of the onslaughts against traditional values during the past two decades.

Clearly, the contemporary thrust toward counter-culture life styles, the focus upon the occult, the ubiquity of chiliastic religious sects, the mass appeal of astrological lore, the spasms of irrational violence seen in bizarre "families," revolutionary brigades like the Weathermen— all must in part reflect the intensity of the human desire to escape the stereotyping brought about by middle-class, bureaucratic values that demand rationality, discipline, and deferred gratification. Such movements have obviously receded considerably since their apogee during the 1960s, but the traces that remain cannot be ascribed entirely to their proximate causes in Vietnam and Watergate.

We must ask then, is the protestant ethic of asceticism, hard work, and accumulation still viable? During the late 1960s a pervasive concern arose regarding the attitudes of workers toward their jobs. Disenchantment was not limited to blue-collar workers who typically have ranked near the bottom in job satisfaction surveys. Now middle-class salesmen, executives, and technicians were apparently questioning the intrinsic value of their roles, and one read daily about examples of abrupt "opting out" among individuals in the middle of their career stream. The "dehumanization of work" and "blue-collar blues" became common phrases in the mass media and in neomarxist analyses of "one-dimensional" man among intellectual circles. By 1973, such attitudes inspired federal legislative proposals such as the "Worker Alienation Research and Technical Assistance Act of 1973" (HR 2143 and Senate 736). Meanwhile, university programs, which had often been highly pragmatic and occupationally oriented, were being challenged by a variety of "soft" courses, including "black studies," "womens' studies," "the theory of revolution," and similar "culturally oriented" themes that often reflected student interest in third-world countries.

If these events were symbolic of a generalized rejection of traditional values and attitudes toward work, our assumption that a substantial proportion of highly motivated individuals could be found in the bureaucratic arena would either have to be sharply modified or abandoned.

One systematic way to answer this question is through sample-based surveys regarding secular changes in attitudes toward work and personal success during the past two decades. Such information is available. In 1973, the Michigan Survey Research Center published the results of a survey covering 33 indices of work conditions, including financial rewards, challenging conditions of work, the adequacy of technical resources on the job, health and safety and hours, and an omnibus "overall quality of work" category.[1] The survey covered a cross-section of American workers (N = 2,157, weighted), including men, women, blue-collar, white-collar, and management types, white and nonwhite, by education, age, occupation, and industry. When the results were compared with those of a previous study in 1969, "significant change (i.e., statistically significant change) was the exception, not the rule."[2] On the whole, not only had conditions remained much the same, but individual attitudes toward work were generally fairly optimistic. Responding to a crucial item regarding job satisfaction, "If a good friend of yours told you he was interested in working in a job like yours for your employer, what would you tell him?", 63.8 percent (63.1 percent in 1969) would "strongly recommend" their job.[3] Insofar as quality of supervision is a salient issue, 71 percent said their supervisor "knows his job very well."[4]

A better appraisal of trends is available through successive Gallup polls, dating back to 1958 and reported in the Survey Research

---

[1]Quinn and Shepard, *The 1972–73 Quality of Employment Survey*, pp. 241–243.
[2]Ibid., p. 260.
[3]Ibid., p. 55.
[4]Ibid., p. 200.

Center study. All of these surveys included a "roughly comparable" single-item question on job satisfaction. Here again, with the exception of the period 1962 to 1964, conditions remain unchanged, as measured by seven nationwide polls.[5] Such evidence permits us to conclude that our earlier assumption regarding the existence of a small but critical reservoir of "upward-mobiles" in the society can be retained. Evidence will be presented later regarding the motivations of the two remaining types of accommodation, the "indifferents" and the "ambivalents."

We now turn to the upward-mobile type of accommodation. Following interpersonal theory, we assume that individuals behave according to the perceived expectations of a given social situation. Over a period of time such responses become relatively consistent; they are continually reinforced because they meet compelling individual needs for security, recognition, and group acceptance. While such accommodations are always the result of interaction between the bureaucratic situation and personality, social and organizational values mainly determine the character of functional (anxiety-reducing) and dysfunctional (anxiety-producing) behavior in a given culture. Personality is worked out in a social and interpersonal context. As Sullivan observes, people gradually develop, through their relations with significant others, a self-system, a personal style of behavior that rejects anxiety-producing responses in favor of those that insure approval. The bureaucratic situation seems to evoke three kinds of personal accommodation, each associated with one of our three personality types, the upward-mobiles, the indifferents, and the ambivalents.

Writing early in this century, Max Weber could speak of the contempt with which Americans regarded bureaucracy. This observation seems less germane today. Not only has respect for big organizations increased, since they meet our pragmatic test of success, but demands for conformity have muted criticism based upon less tangible criteria. In many sectors, personal and ideological conventionality have become prerequisite for jobs that once required only technical skill and adequate performance. Here, perhaps, is an ironic consequence of our open system of higher education. The present oversupply of highly-trained graduates encourages the potential use of ascriptive criteria of recruitment. Contrast this condition with countries such as Canada where an elitist conception of higher education has meant an historical dependence upon immigration to provide the expertise required to build a modern society. The trend may also be associated with decreasing mobility, or at least with more structured conditions

[5] Ibid., p. 258.

of participation resulting from greater specialization, the increasing size of many work places, and an emerging career pattern of long service in a single organization.

Such changes brought the obsolescence of certain skill groups and their replacement by those who could meet the new conditions. Just as the guild artisan's craftsmanship yielded to mass production, the owner-entrepreneur was displaced by the corporation manager. An essentially "political" economy brought the need for new talents, such as "human relations," that could placate employees and clientele disenchanted by the size and impersonality of modern organizations. Someone was also required to interpret the rhetoric of "service" which now eased the traditional profit theme. Hence the public-relations expert. Significantly, the new skills were often concerned with subjective matters, as if the dominant technical passion required some modification. Among the most recent of such developments is the role of managers of multinational corporations. In addition to providing the management skills required to direct a swift structural adaptation to changing conditions in labor costs and world markets, such men have become greatly concerned with legitimizing their role. Insofar as this requires the decomposition of traditional political boundary lines and the conventional view that political and economic power are separate, they have developed a countervailing ideology.[6] The rationale includes the view that multinationals are integrating the rich and the poor nations, overcoming through mutual economic benefits so-called free and authoritarian regimes, and in general creating a world economy that will ultimately prove mutually beneficial to everyone concerned. From one standpoint the multinational corporation represents a triumph of organization over territory and, viewed disinterestedly, the dispatch and flexibility revealed by its swift accommodation to changed economic environment is impressive indeed. However, the political ramifications of this development are complex and often disquieting.[7]

The managers of multinationals provide a nice example of individual accommodation to structural change. This theory of adapta-

---

[6]Among others, see Richard J. Barnet and Ronald E. Muller, *Global Reach: The Power of the Multinational Corporations* (New York: Simon and Schuster, 1974), ch. 3.

[7]See, for example, Anthony Sampson, *The Sovereign State of ITT* (New York: Stein and Day, 1973); Jean-Jacques Servan-Schreiber, *The American Challenge* (New York: Atheneum, 1968); Richard Eells, *Global Corporations* (New York: Interbook, 1972); Robert Heilbroner, "The Multinational Corporation and the Nation-State," *New York Review of Books*, February 11, 1971; Richard J. Barnet, *Intervention and Revolution* (New York: Mentor Books, 1972); Edith T. Penrose, *The Large International Firm in Developing Countries* (Cambridge: MIT Press, 1968).

tion rests upon the findings of cultural psychology, which replaced earlier conceptions of a static human nature with the idea of a "marketing personality" who could nicely adjust to changing social and organizational expectations. In this context we can think of a "bureaucratic personality" as an adaptive type. However, since the members of any organization will always react somewhat differently, some qualifications are necessary. While three discrete patterns of accommodation seem to exist, the "upward-mobiles," the "indifferents," and the "ambivalents," each is an ideal type. The bureaucratic situation evokes various degrees of identification and a commitment. One "upward-mobile" may have compulsive success drives that are quite unrealistic, while another may retain a rational estimate of his or her own ability and of the rewards to be reasonably expected. With the "indifferents" and "ambivalents" a similar range of behavior exists. Our types must, therefore, be viewed as modal patterns of adjustment to the bureaucratic situation.

The existence of such types underscores an important theoretical assumption in this study, namely, that not everything that is significant about individuals can be explained by the group or occupation in which they live and work. While sociological theory provides a central basis for understanding behavior, it neglects to some extent the influence of individual personality. Human beings are not only social animals; they are also Hobbesian egoists whose unique personalities and life experiences influence their perception of interpersonal situations and resultant behavior. To this extent every definition of a social phenomenon is individual, and we can assume that responses will vary somewhat accordingly. Social structure and socialization are undoubtedly dominant in shaping personality, but the individual is more than a passive cultural phenomenon.[8]

It is suggestive, for example, that some of the traits apparently required for career success and dominance are biologically selected.

---

[8]The conception that human behavior occurs in the context of certain objective conditions and that a given individual's *perception* of these conditions is a vital factor in resultant behavior is often credited to W. I. Thomas. In his view, subjective experience is the intervening variable between objective conditions and individual behavior. For a summary and evaluation of his "situational approach," see Edmund H. Volkart, *Social Behavior and Personality: Contributions of W. I. Thomas to Theory and Social Research* (New York: Social Science Research Council, 1951). Note the similarity between this conception of behavior and that of Sullivan, whose personality theory rests essentially upon individual definitions of *"complex, peculiarly characterized situations,"* Dorothy R. Blitsten, *The Social Theories of Harry Stack Sullivan* (New York: William-Frederick Press, 1953), p. 21. (Italics added.) For an early attempt to apply psychology to the analysis of political behavior, see Harold D. Lasswell, *Psychopathology and Politics* (Chicago: University of Chicago Press, 1930), and *Power and Personality* (New York: Norton, 1948).

The eminent biologist, Edward Wilson, for example, cites evidence suggesting that "an 'upward-mobile gene' exists that can be rapidly concentrated in the uppermost socio-economic classes."[9]

If social structure alone were responsible for personality and behavior, our discrete types of accommodation would presumably not exist. The organization would evoke very similar accommodations in all of its members. But as we have seen, not only do different patterns of class socialization, and consequent differences in perception and reaction to interpersonal situations, characterize individuals, but the same pattern of socialization may evoke different responses among those subject to it. This combining of social and psychological theory is validated by the experience of Emile Durkheim who began his classic study of suicide with the intention of isolating the social roots of self-destruction, but who ended with an essentially psychological and individual cause, *anomie.*

Some prefactory observations should also be made about the extent to which women fit the upward-mobile profile. A survey of the evidence suggests that they are not typically found in the upper reaches of the occupational world. We know for example that no women are included among the 440 top executives analyzed in 1975 by Sturdivant and Adler (see p. 180). More ironically, given its vaunted program of equal opportunity formalized in the Equal Opportunity Act of 1967, and reinforced by a presidential executive order in 1972 explicitly prohibiting job discrimination on the basis of sex, in 1972 only 1.5 percent of some 12,000 federal officials at the GS–16 level and above were women.[10] Similar underrepresentation exists in the higher levels of most career milieux. About 40 percent of American wives are now in the work force, yet the great majority remain in the lower and middle ranges of certain sex-linked occupational hierarchies, including mainly what have been called the "semi-professions": teaching at the elementary and secondary school levels, nursing, librarianship, and sales, clerical, and secretarial work. Only about 20 percent of women are in professional and related fields; only 16 percent hold managerial and administrative positions, and among these only about 4 percent earn 15,000 dollars or more per year.[11] About 40 percent of the female work force is found in blue-collar, in-

[9]Edward O. Wilson, *Sociobiology: The New Synthesis* (Cambridge: Harvard University Press, 1975), p. 554; see also, Richard J. Herrnstein, "Quantitative Hedonism," *Journal of Psychiatric Research*, Vol. 8, pp. 399–412.

[10]Helene S. Markoff, "The Federal Women's Program," *Public Administration Review*, Vol. 32, p. 144.

[11]Laurily K. Epstein, ed., *Women in the Professions* (New York: D. C. Heath, 1975), p. 50. See also Valerie K. Oppenheimer, "The Sociology of Women's Economic Role in the Family," *American Sociological Review*, Vol. 42, pp. 387–406.

dustrial, and service jobs, with before-tax income (1972) of only 5,000 dollars.[12]

The proportion of women in these various categories has remained quite stable over the past quarter-century, despite increasing educational achievement among women.[13] University teaching appears to have offered perhaps the most equitable career avenue during the recent past. Not only has there been a special effort to recruit women, but they have apparently been provided equal pay and perquisites.[14] The disenchantment generally experienced by women who work finds impressive support in the traditional practice of discriminatory pay scales, in every sector of the economy. In 1973, for example, the annual median income of full-time working women was 6,335 dollars, compared with 11,186 dollars for men.[15] The disproportion across all job categories averaged 56.6 percent; that is, women's salaries were just over half of men's salaries, with those in professional and related ranks faring somewhat better, at 65 percent of men's salaries.[16]

Such evidence indicates that women will only infrequently be found among the upward-mobile types who tend to monopolize decisions and rewards in modern organizations. We now turn from the comfortable area of statistical information to the highly tentative one of explanations for this condition. Among the most common is simple job discrimination.[17] Men consciously seek to dominate the occupational world, reflecting traditional sex-linked family roles in which women have been confined phylogenetically to child-raising and home-making while men have been socialized into roles stressing power and dominance, including hunting, warfare, and competition.[18] Culturally-induced tendencies toward dependency, passivity, innerdirectedness, sensitivity, and so on are held to disqualify women from the tough, competitive behaviors said to characterize the occu-

[12]Pamela Roby, "Sociology and Women in Working-class Jobs," in Marcia Millam and Rosabeth Moss Kanter, eds., *Another Voice* (Garden City: Doubleday, 1975), p. 203.

[13]Abbott L. Ferriss, *Indicators of Trends in the Status of American Women* (New York: Russell Sage Foundation, 1971), pp. 108–114.

[14]Allan Cartter and Wayne Ruhter, *The Disappearance of Sex Discrimination in First Job Placements of New Ph.Ds* (Los Angeles: Higher Education Research Institute, 1975).

[15]Epstein, *Women in the Professions*, pp. xvi.

[16]Ibid., p. xvii. See also Larry E. Suter and Herman P. Miller, "Income Differences Between Men and Career Women," *American Journal of Sociology*, Vol. 78, pp. 962–974.

[17]Cf. Roslyn S. Willett, "Working in a Man's World: The Women Executive," in Vivian Gornick and Barbara K. Moran, eds., *Woman in Sexist Society* (New York: Basic Books, 1971), pp. 367–383.

[18]For this view, see Lionel Tiger and Robin Fox, *The Imperial Animal* (New York: Dell, 1972); for a more charitable view of man in nature, see Eibl-Eibesfeldt, *Love and Hate;* Judith M. Bardwich and Elizabeth Douvan, "Ambivalence: The Socialization of Women," in Gornick and Moran, ibid., pp. 147–157. For evidence that men are often successful in maintaining vested occupational and social interests against women in

pational world. Such a thesis is obvious and obviously valid as a historical statement of a condition which is changing, although apparently at a slower rate than assumed.

A more provocative thesis is that women tend to have a psychological inhibition to success in the competitive work arena. This disposition has been called the "fear of success."[19] This hypothesis has been challenged on both methodological and substantive grounds.[20] Other observers have argued that women tend to have a biologically and culturally based emotional set that tends again to inhibit their success in the rational, calculating *Gesellshaft* milieu of modern bureaucracies. They may, in effect, suffer greater role strain in the work milieu. If this is so, it may explain why some researchers have found that the costs of success are greater for women than for men. "The indication is that, unlike men, women who improve their position by increasing their expertise, by moving up occupationally, or by moving into positions of authority may also run the risk of losing friendship and respect, influence, and access to information. They can expect that the strains created by the work might increase, and almost none of this will improve with time."[21]

One other condition bearing upon the occupational status of women is the extent to which they are committed to their work role. Insofar as bureaucratic success often comes to those with great staying power, the finding that work is psychologically more central for men than for women may be relevant.[22] Any attending career dysfunctions are probably reinforced by male resistance to female dominance: a Harvard Business School survey (1965) found that two-thirds of the men surveyed preferred not to have a women boss, and indeed, that one-fifth of women surveyed felt similarly. Such conditions underlie our assumption that women will be highly underrepresented among upward-mobiles.

---

professional types of organizations, see Jon Miller, Sanford Labovitz, and Lincoln Fry, "Inequities in the Organizational Experiences of Women and Men," *Social Forces,* Vol. 54, pp. 365, 378.

[19]Matina Horner, "The Measurement and Behavioral Implications of Fear of Success in Women," in J. W. Atkinson and Joel Raynor, eds., *Motivation and Achievement* (New York: Halsted, 1974), pp. 91–117.

[20]Adeline Levine and Janice Crumrine, "Women and the Fear of Success," *American Journal of Sociology,* Vol. 80, pp. 964–971. Also, Vivian Gornick, "Why Radcliffe Women Fear Success," *New York Times Magazine,* January 14, 1973, pp. 10–11, 54, 56, 58–62.

[21]Miller et al., "Inequities in the Organizational Experiences of Women and Men," p. 378. See also Donald J. Treiman and Kermit Terrell, "Sex and the Process of Status Attainment: A Comparison of Working Men and Women," *American Sociological Review,* Vol. 40, pp. 174–200.

[22]Raymond G. Kuhlen, "Needs, Perceived Need Satisfaction Opportunities, and Satisfaction with Occupation," *Journal of Applied Psychology,* Vol. 47, p. 56.

With such qualifications in mind, we now turn to an analysis of the values and behavior of the typical "upward-mobile." Although his behavior may at times appear unappealing, we are concerned with it only as a form of accommodation to the bureaucratic situation.

Upward-mobiles are typically distinguished by high morale; their level of job satisfaction is high.[23] Indeed, the process and criteria by which they are selected tends to insure that they will have an unfailing optimism. The reasons for this are clear. They identify strongly with the organization and derive strength from their involvement. Their dividends also include disproportionate shares of the organization's rewards in power, income, and ego reinforcement. As we have seen, subjective inequality is a built-in feature of complex organizations and is rationalized on the basis of that equality of opportunity which has set the American experience apart from its European legacy. Power is moreover easily justified by those who have it, since it confirms daily their right to possess it. The upward-mobiles will not, therefore, seriously question a system that has proved its rationality. The system remains an internalized article of faith until, as in the case of Arthur Miller's hero in *Death of A Salesman,* the disparity between rhetoric and reality becomes irrepressible. But even then, self-punitive mechanisms may be invoked to preserve the myth: personal failure rather than the failure of the system provides a rationalization.

This ability to identify strongly with the system is highly productive in personal terms since it qualifies upward-mobiles for the organization's major rewards. (As we saw earlier, group influence and rank are a function of acceptance of the group's values.) The organization qua organization has meaning for them, evoking loyalty, affirmation, and a constant point of reference. Having accepted its legitimacy and rationality, they can act on the basis of its value premises. The capacity for identification has great strategic value today because social power is on the whole becoming more evenly divided among competing groups. This condition sharpens the organization's conflicts with competitors and puts a premium on loyalty and certainty among its members. The organization tends to resemble a church, which needs champions to endorse its values and to increase its survival power. No dissenters need apply. The demand is for conformity. A rational and

[23]Two empirical tests of my theory of accommodation indicate that the upward-mobiles' high level of job satisfaction is positively related to their strong desire for promotion. Dorothy N. Harlow, "Professional Employees' Preference for Upward Mobility," *Journal of Applied Psychology,* Vol. 57, pp. 137–141; Charles O'Reilly, Gene E. Bretton, and Karlene H. Roberts, "Professional Employees' Preference for Upward Mobility: An Extension," *Journal of Vocational Behavior,* Vol. 5, pp. 139–145. For another empirical test that generally supports the theory, see Henry Pruden, "The Upward-Mobile, Indifferent, and Ambivalent Typology of Managers," *Journal of the Academy of Management,* Vol. 16, pp. 454–464.

sustained attention to business is required; and the heterodoxy possible in a less organized, more secure society becomes a luxury because it impairs unity. A similar capacity for rational calculation has been found in a corporate role-type called "the gamesman," who is apparently quite willing to accept the constraints set down by Congress and the regulatory agencies provided that all other competitors do the same.[24]

Since they accept the legitimacy of the larger purposes of the organization, upward-mobiles find involvement easy. Their personalities, which may include authoritarian preferences, enable them to deal in oversimplification and idealization. They can act without an immaculate cause. They can overlook the contradictions in the routine operations of the organization, as distinct from its official myths. They are able to find certainty and consistency in an organization that is imperfect because it is real. In a sense, they must avoid reality by cultivating the illusion that its actions eventuate in perfect justice. This characteristic of perception calls to mind W. I. Thomas's observation: "If men define situations as real, they are real in their consequences."[25] The organization's values are internalized by upward-mobiles, and thus become premises of action. This psychic act provides them with an operational skill: the capacity for action despite conflicting alternatives and contradictory aims.

Here a distinction must be made between the upward-mobiles' values and their behavior. Their low toleration for ambiguity and their deference toward authority might seem to disqualify them for the versatile role-playing that organizations require. In a democratic society, for example, upward-mobiles must pay homage to democratic expectations of equality and impartiality, even though they know that some are born to lead and others to follow. However, they can usually assume the appropriate roles whether or not they identify with the underlying ideals. They manipulate the democratic consensus favoring permissive authority relations and recognize that "getting along with people" has career utility. Such role playing emphasizes the need for mock behavior in which polite fictions, irony, and banter are used to "get a message across" without disrupting the status relations of those concerned.

Ritualistic behavior is often used to conceal resentment or hostility that, indulged in, would paralyze interpersonal relations:

> One afternoon, a conversation with the manager led to his talking about the effects of promotion on different men in the factory, and

---

[24]Michael Maccoby, *The Gamesman* (New York: Simon and Schuster, 1977).

[25]William I. Thomas, *The Child in America: Behavior Problems and Programs* (New York: Alfred A. Knopf, 1932), p. 572.

eventually, to something of a diatribe against one particular person who had moved up into an executive position the year before. He had tried to get support for the promotion from everybody, had blackened the man who was leaving and whose position he hoped to fill, had gone into local politics on the same side as the divisonal manager, had displayed unpleasant anxiety when the time came for the decision. Now, despite his fulsome affability, he was unpopular with his colleagues, was looked on by those lower down as a tale-bearer, and so on. All this was delivered with gestures and emphasis distinctly more lively than earlier in the conversation, which ended with this episode, both of us returning to separate desks.

Later in the afternoon, he telephoned the man of whom he had been speaking; there was question of the allocation of a morning's time put in by a shiftworker. The whole manner of dispute was handled with the greatest mateyness and ease; first names were used, there was no sense of effort in maintaining the demonstration of friendliness; there was no overemphasis, nor, on the other hand, any discrepancy between facial expression and words or tone of voice; each other's account of the facts was fully accepted and agreement quickly reached.

Inside the space of one hour, my companion had displayed quite marked enmity and equally well marked friendship toward the same person. There was, as far as I judge, no suspicion of aware-ness that there was any incompatibility between the two episodes— both were acted through natural expression of two distinct roles.[26]

Such displays of the "marketing orientation" are among the condi-tions of participation at higher levels of bureaucracy. One point of view suggests that the rigidity of typical authoritarians sharply limits their ability to play such conflicting roles and thus disqualifies them for success in bureaucratic occupations. Although the upward-mobile type is often authoritarian and seems to fit well into authoritarian oc-cupations such as business, medicine, the military, police work, and religion,[27] their manipulative, "other-directed" ethic enables them to play the roles required for success. There is therefore no real conflict between our perception of upward-mobiles as potentially authori-tarian, yet at the same time as being able to adapt to several roles. No doubt they will occasionally experience considerable strain in adapt-ing themselves, but this problem is surely eased by the fact that most of the time they will occupy superior positions which meet their need for dominance in interpersonal relations.

[26]Tom Burns, "Friends, Enemies and the Polite Fiction," *American Sociological Review*, Vol. 18, pp. 659–660. Reprinted by permission.

[27]Don Stewart and Thomas Hoult, "A Social-Psychological Theory of the Authori-tarian Personality," *American Journal of Sociology*, Vol. 65, pp. 274–279.

In the main, their "self-system" enables them to accept manipulation both of themselves and of others as part of the vocational bargain. Although they may lack spontaneity, they strive to master the "human-relations" approach. They master the art of the calculated response, in which deference, warmth, enthusiasm, and disapproval are nicely weighted. Like the Navy's gentleman, the upward-mobile is never unintentionally rude. This is a luxury he cannot afford since, like firmly held views, such self-indulgence is of limited career utility.

The efforts of the upward-mobiles to master interpersonal relations are often eased by their associates, who will also play the roles prescribed by their respective positions. Their self-images, their needs, their degree of sophistication, and their level in the hierarchy will guide their behavior. Meanwhile, feedback insures that everyone's behavior will be affected by the perceived reactions of those with whom he communicates. Facial expressions, verbal responses, subtle unspoken expectations, provide the cues. Just as experienced lecturers sense when they are "reaching" their audiences, upward-mobiles read the signals their behavior evokes in others. Although this skill will vary among individuals, the distinguishing mark of upward-mobiles is that they *think* in such strategic terms and are able to modify their behavior accordingly. Such behavior is essentially rational and requires an ability to avoid passionate value attachments that might inhibit one's versatility.

We have seen that the power-oriented individual is likely to find the order and security of a bureaucratic career appealing, as opposed, say, to the uncertainty of writing or politics. It seems that our typical upward-mobile has an exceptional drive for power. This impulse is sometimes symptomatic of a basic insecurity; the fear of failure is common among successful executives. As the former president of a conglomerate put it:

> Fear is always prevalent in the corporate structure. Even if you're top man, even if you're hard, even if you do your job—by the slight flick of a finger, your boss can fire you. There's always the insecurity. . . . You're fearful so many things will appear on your record, stand against you. You're always fearful of the big mistake. You've got to be careful when you go to corporation parties. Your wife, your children have to behave properly. You've got to fit in the mold. You've got to be on guard.[28]

We may suppose that such anxiety provokes an exceptional need for control over the environment. Attempts to dominate others, to monopolize any discussion are common manifestations of this need. Whatever its source, anxiety explains some of the upward-mobile's

[28]Studs Terkel, *Working* (New York: Avon Books, 1975), p. 531.

discipline and energy. Certainly the relationship between compulsive striving and personal maladjustment is well known. In a test profile of 243 "best," "average," and "poorest" salespeople, Crafts found that the "best" group scored *lower* on "stability" and "self-sufficiency." He concluded that "too much" of these qualities was detrimental, "very probably because superiors must be relied on, catered to, and pleased, if the individual is to be successful."[29]

Dominance is often associated with sheer physical size and energy. As research in biosociology indicates, among certain animals and insects these attributes are empirically observable and seem to be genetically selected in the sense, for example, that dominant males enjoy preferential mating rights or a monopoly of females in polygynous societies, such as the Yanomama Indians of Brazil. Wilson notes that dominance by size is common.[30] We have reported earlier some of the dominance signals found among lower vertebrates and suggested their relevance for human behavior. The patent hierarchical structure and attending status and authority system of modern organizations provide a sympathetic setting for such tracking.

In the United States one finds that high bureaucratic positions are often held by men who are physically large or exceptionally forceful. Hollywood's idealization of the virile male, who solves most problems by a punch in the jaw, both reflects and molds American conceptions of the qualities required for success. Historically, political and economic power have often been grounded in sheer physical strength.[31] Allied with this physical component is a subjective ability to assume what Weber called a "charismatic" (magical) role. Commanding presence, effective staging, long-range views, an air of infallibility, the ability to dignify commonplace observations—these are typical upward-mobile postures. Their object is to inspire confidence, to appeal to the father-needs of those who find life uncertain. In this context, if the upward-mobile appears a fraud because he promises more than anyone can deliver, it must be admitted that there is a vast market for his fraudulence. Popular naïveté and insecurity provide a sympathetic background for this magical facet of his role. The rewards for the ability to inspire confidence are therefore great. The peculiar talent

---

[29]Leland W. Crafts et al., *Recent Experiments in Psychology* (New York: McGraw-Hill, 1938), p. 241.

[30]Wilson, *Sociobiology*, p. 296.

[31]For an example of such single-mindedness coupled with great physical strength, see Alex Gottfried, "The Use of Psychosomatic Categories in a Study of Political Personality," *Western Political Quarterly*, Vol. 8, p. 239 *passim*. An authority on executive recruitment reports that "industry generally won't hire sales trainees unless they are at least five feet ten inches tall." He attributes this practice to the belief that tall men possess dominant personalities that help them close sales. *Nation's Business*, Vol. 49, p. 19.

of the upward-mobile is that he recognizes and manipulates this latent human need.

Clinical research supports our hypothesis about the power orientations of successful organization men.[32] The Kaiser Foundation's experience with over 2,000 psychiatric patients and some 1,000 psychosomatic and normal subjects revealed that the "managerial personality," who achieves interpersonal adjustment through dominance, was the most common type among 3,000 cases. Over 600 such individuals supply the basis for the following generalizations. Their behavior is most suggestive. They often assume what has been called a "doctor's-helper" role, that is, they cannot admit that they really need help, but instead they deny their own symptoms and attempt to convince the therapist and others of their normality and excellence. Although they are the largest single group diagnosed, they do not tend to present themselves for therapy; and when they do, they rank lowest among all patients in the number of times they appear for treatment.

Significantly, and in accordance with the authoritarianism findings, these men tend to misjudge their interpersonal relations. They consistently attribute too much weakness to those with whom they interact. They tend to look down on others. Three times as many military officers exhibit such power-oriented accommodations as do the general run of patients who appear for treatment. The "managerial personality" also tends to be closely identified with his parents, a common quality among those ranking high on the Adorno F scale.

This type is also identified by characteristic illnesses. A high proportion have psychosomatic ailments such as ulcers and hypertension. Anxiety attacks are another typical symptom, apparently because the compulsive, energetic façade used to defend their self-image of control and power breaks down. The admission of anxiety or any form of weakness is a painful experience for this type, and the refusal to recognize it is in part responsible for their common "doctor's-helper" posture. As might be expected, such compulsive individuals tend to present themselves as right and strong; the neurotic person on the other hand presents himself as passive, guilty, and uncertain. In the American and German cultures, according to the early Timothy Leary, "successful, well-adjusted compulsives are generally respected by others for their diligence and organization. The notion of efficiency is heavily loaded with power connotations."[33]

In interpersonal terms, the managerial type accommodates by security operations that emphasize strength, efficiency, self-control,

---

[32]Timothy Leary, *Interpersonal Diagnosis of Personality* (New York: Ronald Press, 1956), p. 329 and ch. 20.

[33]Ibid., p. 328.

dominance, and compulsion. "Adjustment through power" provides him with security against anxiety by virtue of the control he achieves over situations and other people. "He gains a feeling of certitude and organization." "He wins awe, admiration and obedience from others."[34] His own needs and the power position to which they have driven him affect his interpersonal relations in predictable ways. "In general it will be found that rigid, autocratic individuals seek out docile, admiring followers. They are most comfortable when they are paired with those who symbiotically match their interpersonal reflexes—who flatter, obey, and respect them."[35] On the other hand, when such types must interact with those of similar character, a real power struggle may ensue.

The process whereby individuals who work together become "locked" into mutually satisfying relationships suggests the utility of interpersonal theory in organizational analysis. Here again, evidence from the Kaiser research provides the example. As Leary says, a "most common setting for rigid interpersonal relationships is the occupational."[36] He then traces his experience with a management group comprising four executives responsible for a manufacturing and distributing plant of a national corporation. Although the analysis began at the request of the firm's general manager, who was worried about the excessive drinking of one of the executives, it soon became apparent that this behavior was merely a symptom of rigid and destructive reactions among individuals in the group.

Each executive was given several tests, including a self-evaluation profile that enabled each to rate himself. All four rated themselves as strong, hypernormal, and responsible. They were also asked to rate each of their colleagues. After these ratings had been charted (see Figure 6–1) and combined with psychologists' evaluation of each individual's personality, a "self-deception" index was established. In each case there was considerable self-delusion about the character of each executive's interpersonal relations with other members of the group. While the production manager, for example, claimed to be strong and somewhat friendly, his associates saw him "as an extremely cold, hard, unfriendly, selfish person." The general manager, whom the psychologists regarded as the most effective member of the group, had the smallest perceptual disparity. While he was less sympathetic and friendly than he claimed, both his colleagues and the psychologists saw him as a "strong, forceful, nonhostile person. They clearly admire and respect him."

[34] Ibid., p. 325.
[35] Ibid.
[36] Ibid., p. 403 and ch. 25.

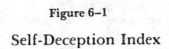

Figure 6-1

Self-Deception Index

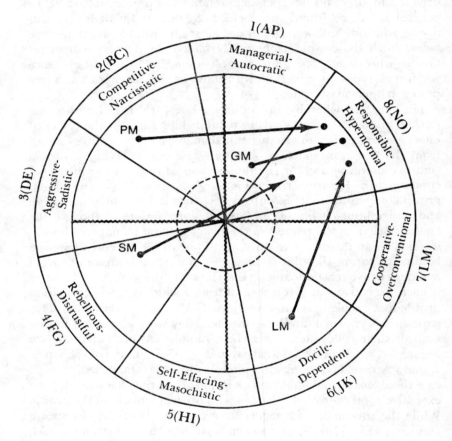

Social Stimulus Value of Four Executives; Plotted Indices of Self-Deception. *Key:* The labeled points (e.g., PM) represent the pooled Level I-S behavior of the subject as rated by others. The arrows link the Level I-S score to the subject's self-perception. The length of the arrow indicates how much self-deception exists. The direction of the arrow indicates what the subject misperceives.

SOURCE: Timothy Leary: *Interpersonnal Diagnosis of Personality: A Functional Theory and Methodology for Personality Evaluation,* Fig. 47, p. 407. Copyright 1957 The Ronald Press Company.

In terms of interpersonal theory, such misconceptions of self and others must result in strained, unproductive relations. Moreover, these relations tend to be reinforced by the dynamics of the situation. For example, the general manager is locked into a close and "mutually self-deceptive" relation with the personnel manager. "Although they both try to believe that they have a collaborative, friendly union of equals, actually an intense leader-follower association exists." This relationship meets the personal needs of each. Although neither is aware of its real character, the other members of the group are, and their perception of the situation further distorts the group's relationship. The production manager despises the personnel man for his dependence upon the general manager, while the sales manager is jealous of the general manager's approval of the personnel man. The latter, in turn, is terrified by the production and sales managers, who perceive him as weak and self-effacing.

The upward-mobile accommodation is worked out in similar interpersonal terms. Since upward-mobiles often get to the top of the organization and must deal with members at every level, the significance of their own values and behavior is clear. If these are marked by a need to ward off anxiety or to dominate others, organizational relations will be complicated. Since such compelling needs and the security operations they encourage are almost impossible to change, they may disrupt the organization.

This probability suggests one of the built-in dysfunctions of organizations, namely, the fact that the very qualities required for success, including great energy, dominance, and status consciousness can very easily distort interpersonal relations within the organization. However, organizations can take a great deal of punishment, and inertia itself often provides a substitute for leadership.

Bound up with the upward-mobile's capacity for action in ambiguous situations is an ability to view individuals in essentially detached terms. As Michael Maccoby found, the "gamesman's" concern for individuals is limited because he cannot afford to devote much time to personal problems unless these are directly related to the ends of the organization.[37] To some extent the successful organizer must view people as instruments. The intensity of this impulse varies from relatively innocuous forms, on the one hand, to the rigidity of a military leader who will sacrifice any number of men to take a strategic position. But the difference is probably one of degree; the mentality is often similar. Following a study of 473 executives from various fields, Burleigh Gardner says of their relations with others·

[37]Maccoby, *The Gamesman*, pp. 106, 188–190.

In general, the mobile and successful executive looks to his superiors with a feeling of personal attachment and tends to identify himself with them. His superiors represent for him a symbol of his own achievement and activity desires, and the successful junior tends to identify himself with these traits in those who have achieved more. . . . On the other hand, he looks to his subordinates in an essentially impersonal way, seeing them as "doers of work" rather than as people. This does not mean that he is cold and treats them casually. In fact, he tends to be rather sympathetic to their problems. But he still treats them impersonally, with no real or deep interest in them as persons. It is almost as if he viewed his subordinates as representatives of things he has left behind, both factually and emotionally. The only direction of his emotional energy that is real to him is upward and toward the symbols of that upward interest, his superiors.[38]

This suggests that the capacity to rationalize organizational claims is part of the value equipment of upward-mobiles. They may respect individual dissent and error, but the question is one of *priority,* and in the last analysis they will accept the organization's values. Their ability to appraise situations objectively and to act appropriately is bound up with their loyalty to collective values and abstractions. Since they identify with the organization, in a measure ranging from casual opportunism to complete surrender, they become an instrument of such values. They become *the organization* and can thus accept its logical imperatives without much regard for competing individual values. The wrongs inflicted in defense of institutionalized ideals are well known. To some extent they can be explained in terms of the total loyalty that organizations demand and some individuals seek.

In the context of Robert Merton's distinction, the upward-mobile is typically a "local."[39] Unlike the "cosmopolitan" who has a broad disciplinary or national perspective, the interests and aspirations of locals are tied to their own organizations. Always loyal, they regard its rules and actions as "the one best way" to handle large numbers of people. If the organization's claims occasionally result in injustice, this is inevitable in an imperfect world. Never doubting the supremacy of

[38]Burleigh B. Gardner, "What Makes Successful and Unsuccessful Executives", *Advanced Management,* Vol. 13, p. 118. Similar attitudes are traced in William Henry, "The Business Executive: The Psychodynamics of a Social Role," *American Journal of Sociology,* Vol. 54, pp. 286–291.

[39]Robert Merton, *Social Theory and Social Structure,* rev. ed. (Glencoe, Ill.: Free Press, 1957), pp. 393–395 and ch. 10; also, Alvin W. Gouldner, "Cosmopolitans and Locals: Toward an Analysis of Latent Social Roles," *Administrative Science Quarterly,* Vols. 2, 3, pp. 281–306; 444–480.

collective values, upward-mobiles enthrone administrative, keeping-the-organization-going skills and norms. This accounts in part for their ambivalence toward the specialist whose professional norms compete with his loyalty to the organization. In all this, they personify the "routinization of charisma" whereby organizations have tended historically to become more rational and monistic. People without a "calling," they bring little passion to their work. Rather, the upward-mobile tends to become, in Balzac's phrase, a "quill-bearing mammal," a dealer in means for whom the paraphernalia of organization outweigh claims of "mission," creed, and party. These tend instead to become instrumental, honorific abstractions used to evoke affirmation and loyalty among the rank and file.

Acceptance of the organization's goals commits upward-mobiles to conformity and to impatience with those who qualify and dissent. As a result, they tend to personalize opposition, finding it difficult to accept as a matter of principle or honest divergence, and attributing it instead to a querulous wish on the dissenter's part to be different for difference's sake. Their temperamental affinity for clear-cut causes and decisive action is relevant here. Their assumed low tolerance for ambiguity makes it difficult for them to understand those who fail to see what to them is so clearly evident.[40] The fact that their personal values are not always shared will escape or puzzle them. Their hostility toward heterodoxy may be sharpened by a natural resentment that others should escape the discipline and sacrifice that ambition has required of them.

The upward-mobile's preference for conventionality is functional because organizational claims now cover such matters. Political opinions, patterns of consumption, off-work activity, and so forth, tend to fall into the bureaucratic net. By honoring socially-legitimated values upward-mobiles not only reinforce the standards by which they themselves are measured, they also increase the probability that conformity will occur throughout the organization. This phenomenon is clearly apparent in countries, such as England, where a remarkable social control is achieved through each class's imitation of the one above it. In organizations a similar mechanism is apparent in the elite's personification of majority values and in the internalization of those values by ambitious subordinates.

---

[40]Empirical research raises some question about the assumption that upward-mobiles are characterized by a low tolerance for ambiguity. Testing the hypothesis that "promotional preference is negatively related to tolerance for ambiguity for individuals who have high job satisfaction," Charles O'Reilly and his colleagues found no significant relationship, "Professional Employees' Preference for Upward Mobility: An Extension," pp. 141–142.

Upward-mobiles define such necessities as virtues and accommodate themselves accordingly with a minimum of strain. In part this is because manipulation of self is perceived as a necessary instrument to preferred ends. On the other hand, they may not even think in these terms but may instead accept such behaviors as rational prescriptions that follow naturally from their career orientation. They may feel no sense of deprivation at being required to accommodate, because they feel no sense of conflict. As a result, they will not understand those who resist the acquisitive demands of the organization. This distinction between bureaucratic types is the result of basic differences in their perception of situations and by the strength of their personal need to ease anxiety. Their modes of accommodation differ accordingly.

Upward-mobiles idealize action and know that it requires oversimplification. Here their capacity for impersonal thinking is helpful since it enables them to separate out the parts of a problem and to handle each in turn without regard for their complexity or for their broader implications. Any self-deception involved here may or may not be consciously experienced. The ability to set aside the personal or idealistic factors of a problem permits "tough-minded" decisions that meet organization demands. As Goethe said, the "acting man" is often without conscience. But more than the mere recognition of the required measures is involved. Many individuals, one suspects, know what behavior is required in certain situations, but cannot fill the prescription. In such cases personality is involved, rather than strategy or information.

In all this we have undoubtedly exaggerated the upward-mobile's rationality and oversimplified the behavioral mechanisms involved. In suggesting that their accommodation is mainly a matter of pragmatic choice, we have narrowly avoided saying that everyone could become an upward-mobile if they wished. However, desire must always be reinforced by an awareness of the conditions of successful participation and the personality and the skills required to displace them. Our upward-mobiles include not only those who want power, but also those who have the self-discipline and the temperament necessary to achieve it.

Another characteristic of upward-mobiles is their status anxiety, often manifested in a compulsive concern with rank and the symbols of prestige. The term "anxiety" is deliberate since their concern with status and with its derivatives of power and prestige goes beyond mere sensitivity to define a general orientation.

A man wants to get to the top of the corporation, not for the money involved. After a certain point, how much money can you make? In my climb, I'll be honest, money was secondary. Unless you have tremendous demands, yachts, private airplanes—you get to a certain point, money isn't that important. *It's the power, the status, the prestige.* Frankly, it's delightful to be on top and have everybody calling you Mr. Ross and have a plane at your disposal and a car and a driver at your disposal. When you come to town, there's people to take care of you. When you walk into a board meeting, everybody gets up and says hello. I don't think there's a human being that doesn't love that.[41]

Again, as Donald Frey, chief executive of Bell and Howell puts it, "I just have to run a *whole* business. . . . In the crudest sense, you could say it's a need for power."[42]

Like the search for power, status enchantment is a constant element in the upward-mobile equation. The authoritarian-personality research found significantly that such an orientation is common among individuals who seem to find the bureaucratic environment congenial. As we have seen, status differentiation plays a critical role in organizations. It provides a psychological environment that is conducive to efficiency in operational terms, reinforcing authority, minimizing overt conflict, and structuring personal relations.

Status will be defined here as the prestige or deference attached to the role or position one holds in an organizational hierarchy.[43] Although status is not always conferred according to formal hierarchical role, since some members (such as our "ambivalents") will not accept hierarchical definitions of relative status, in the main status and prestige are assigned and rewarded by elites in terms of formal organizational position. In contemporary society high status is usually articulated with high office in some large-scale organization. The other major basis for status ascription is occupational role, which may in the case of such high-status occupations as physician or Supreme Court justice be played independently or in a small group. It is often distinct from hierarchical position.

It seems equally clear that status has obligations as well as rights and privileges. Those possessing large amounts of it enjoy preferential amounts of income, authority, and security; but in return they must behave in ways approved by the status-conferring group or organization. Such obligations, of course, discourage many (including our "in-

---

[41] Terkel, *Working*, pp. 538–539. Italics added.

[42] *Fortune*, September 1976, p. 140.

[43] Sociologists define "status" as the *position* an individual occupies in the social hierarchy, but I use it here in its popular connotation. Richard T. LaPiere, *A Theory of Social Control* (New York: McGraw-Hill, 1954); Kingsley Davis, "A Conceptual Analysis of Stratification," *American Sociological Review*, Vol. 7, pp. 309–321.

differents") from seeking higher status, since the rewards do not seem worth the effort. At the same time, a parasitic alternative may be used, the borrowing of status through association with prestigeful figures who do meet their obligations. This is not easy, however, since the latter are naturally reluctant to risk depreciation of their own status currency by sharing it with those who have smaller amounts. Status aspirations thus play an important part in behavior. By granting or withdrawing status and prestige, organizations reinforce our behavior. The effectiveness of status manipulation is based on the fact that status is the index for such highly prized values as security, recognition, income, and authority. In this sense, status is a function of the anxiety-adjustment-approval syndrome. We can assume that the intensity of status anxiety varies with individual needs for approval and self-esteem.

The status incentive is among the most powerful psychological weapons of modern organizations. In business, status acquisition and reinforcement have become the subject of rational calculation.[44] Standard Oil of California, for example, classifies executives from type 1, who merit drapes, wall-to-wall carpeting, private offices, walnut desks, and the like, to type 4, with no private office and oak desks. Although, as one president put it, "you'd expect executives to be more mature," corporations have found that if morale is to be maintained, office equipment for executives of identical ranks must be identical.[45] Some executives, it seems, have developed to a fine art the skill of being the first to acquire new status indexes, thus acquiring for themselves a sense of distinction. Such honor is only temporary, however, since their colleagues will quickly acquire the new index for themselves, even if this requires spending their own money.

Status preoccupation is useful in two ways. It meets the organization's demand for bench marks of authority that ease routine operations; and it also meets the individual's demand for recognition. As Thorstein Veblen saw, with characteristic prescience, the change from an economy of scarcity to one of consumption is involved. Life styles in an abundant yet anonymous society no longer differentiate individuals, resulting in a search for indexes that can set one apart in socially approved ways. Frustrated in meaningful areas, such needs may find expression in inconsequential, nonanxiety-producing activities. Veblen shows how the ownership of dogs and horses falls into this category, precisely because they perform no useful service and are valued mainly for sporting or honorific purposes: "The dog

[44]*Time,* January 24, 1955, p. 80.
[45]Ibid.

commends himself to our favor by affording play to our propensity for mastery, and as he is also an item of expense, and commonly serves no industrial purpose, he holds an assured place in man's regard as a thing of good repute. The dog is at the same time associated in our imagination with the chase—a meritorious employment and an expression of the honorable predatory impulse."[46] Similarly, "the horse, displaced almost entirely from utility, has acquired a new rarity value as an emblem of class dignity."[47]

The theme of unlimited opportunity for those who have what it takes also aggravates status anxiety, because there are never enough rewards to satisfy expectations. Bureaucratic conditions, moreover, reduce the opportunity for achieving status at the same time that they stimulate the desire for it. The separation of workers from their tools and the exquisite specialization of modern work tend to reduce the opportunity for individual independence and self-realization. At the same time, minute bureaucratic gradations in income, skill, and seniority intensify the desire to assert one's uniqueness.

In many cases the status anxiety of upward-mobiles is probably forced upon them by organizational demands. But here again their personalities encourage acceptance since status symbols provide the reference points of power. Because status is an effective means of validating their claim to better things, status sensitivity becomes part of the skill equipment of upward-mobiles. They had learned a great truth, namely that most of us are influenced by pretense and often confuse form with substance. They know that a little sorcery is necessary in human affairs, and that if they do not take themselves seriously, no one else will. The rigid upward-mobiles often lack such detachment, however, and play the status game with deadly seriousness. Indeed, upward-mobiles may be roughly defined as those who can take seriously the status systems of big organizations. As we have seen, they tend to adore power and are somewhat humorless in their dedication to majority values. Status sensitivity thus becomes merely a part of the whole organizational ethic, to which they pay an attention similar to that paid its other prescriptions.

The upward-mobiles' upward-looking mien and their conventionality reinforce this preoccupation. They will note that their seniors play the status game, and here as elsewhere become models for their conduct. If they are to play an expansive role, which they must, the necessary props must be enlisted to show that they too merit

---

[46] Thorstein Veblen, *The Theory of the Leisure Class: An Economic Study of the Evolution of Institutions* (New York: Viking, 1899), p. 141.

[47] Ibid., p. 142.

deference. Like the military officer, they will gear their social activities to those of equal or, if possible, higher rank. Since those above them will be playing the same game, their association with them will probably be limited to a few formal occasions which, it will be quite clear, are in the line of duty. Since co-optation by one's seniors is the main avenue to success, the disadvantaged accept such conditions gracefully, confident that their turn will come in time. A common example of such behavior is the use of the surname by seniors when addressing their juniors. (On certain social occasions, eased perhaps by liquor or bonhomie, given names may be used.) Such practices validate status and promote deference. In a democratic society they may entail some strain, but the upward-mobiles' remarkable self-discipline and their affinity for authority usually outweigh any conflicting values.

Personal status and organizational discipline are also reinforced by structured patterns of communication. Seniors communicate through secretaries who become their alter ego and often exaggerate the status factors inherent in the relationship. Seniors rarely visit their subordinates, since this would put them at a psychological disadvantage and reduce their control of the interpersonal situation. Normally the subordinate comes to the senior, and the latter sets the tone of the meeting. Displeasure can be nicely weighted. Tone of voice, form of address, length of the meeting, amount of time the subordinate is required to wait, whether interruptions for phone calls are permitted— all tend to define the relative status of the participants, and all can be manipulated to obtain desired consequences. The upward-mobile must become extremely sensitive in measuring out and receiving such dispensations. Versatile role-playing is therefore a vital career skill.

The preoccupation of upward-mobiles with status is functional because they are anxious to rise, and because a disciplined self-promotion is required to impress those above them with their suitability for bigger things. As the objective relationship between status and achievement becomes more difficult to establish, the collection of unearned status increments is encouraged. Here again the familiar displacement of goals can be seen. The acquisition of status and prestige becomes an end in itself rather than a derivative of some significant achievement. A common manifestation is the discreet cultivation of prestigious elders by young upward-mobiles in need of a patron. Such behavior is directly related to the co-optative mechanism which now governs bureaucratic succession. Significantly, it is also similar to the individual's early dependence upon authority-figures, mother, father, teacher, and so forth. Perhaps modern organizations speak of themselves as a "family" in order to evoke loyalties and responses deeply anchored in the individual's past.

Vigorous self-promotion may occur, often characterized by assiduous name dropping and by monopolizing those who can provide access to publicity, honorific offices, and other instruments of personal advantage. "Getting one's name known" is thus a bureaucratic skill, sometimes practiced without much reference to productive work. The manipulation of both self and others may become common as upward-mobiles analyze the prevailing means to success and set about achieving it. Some psychologists emphasize that negative results ensue, for example, self-alienation. C. Wright Mills concludes that the "personality market"

. . . underlies the all-pervasive distrust and self-alienation so characteristic of metropolitan people. Without common values and mutual trust, the cash nexus that links one man to another in transient contact has been made subtle in a dozen ways and made to bite deeper into all areas of life and relations. People are required by the salesman ethic and convention to pretend interest in others in order to manipulate them. In the course of time, and as this ethic spreads, it is got on to. Still, it is conformed to as part of one's job and one's style of life, but now with a winking eye, for one knows that manipulation is inherent in every human contact. Men are estranged from one another as each secretly tries to make an instrument of the other, and in time a full circle is made: one makes an instrument of himself, and is estranged from it also.[48]

A related upward-mobile skill is the careful avoidance of anything controversial. A major objective is to avoid prejudicing any further career opportunity, since even undesired opportunities can pay status dividends within one's own organization by judicious and casual mention. To avoid controversial matters, to create an aura of unlimited friendship, and to borrow status by discreet name dropping may appear rather negative, but these are significant criteria in the bureaucratic situation where "personality" and "working with the team" are vital. William H. Whyte, Jr., reports a survey of 150 personnel direc-

---

[48]C. Wright Mills, *White Collar* (New York: Oxford University Press, 1951), pp. 187–188. About 1887, on the basis of empirical research and observation, F. Tönnies made the following similar observation regarding the effect of German industrialization on interpersonal relations: "In the conception of Gesellschaft [an ideal type of modern, rational capitalistic society] the original or natural relations of human beings to each other must be excluded. The possibility of a relation in the Gesellschaft assumes no more than a multitude of mere persons who are capable of delivering something and consequently of promising something. . . . In Gesellschaft every person strives for that which is to his own advantage and affirms the actions of others only in so far as and as long as they can further his interest. Before and outside of convention and also before and outside of each special contract, the relation of all to all may therefore be conceived as potential hostility or latent war," *Community and Association*, trans. Charles P. Loomis (London: Routledge and Kegan Paul, 1955), p. 88.

tors of large companies who were asked to choose between an "adaptable administrator" and a man with "strong personal convictions who could make decisions." The directors voted three to one for the administrator.[49]

The status ethic means that all participants will demand that each contribute increments of equal value, thus insuring mutual benefits and sustained growth of the collective investment. Hierarchical principles of distribution insure that the elite controls the total status reservoir. Around every elite therefore may be seen a circle of aspirants awaiting the co-optative nod and seeking in various ways (including hard work) to enter the sanctuary. In our abundant society high reward potentials in status and income encourage such accommodations, as does also an increasing career commitment to a single organization. Such conditions emphasize middle-class skills and values such as discipline, the repression of aggression, and a long-run view.[50]

Upward-mobiles tend to analyze and to employ the status system rationally. Exceptionally sensitive to its implications, they evaluate social situations in status terms and manipulate interpersonal relationships accordingly. In practically every field achievement is now evaluated in terms of derived power and status. The intrinsic aspects of work tend to become secondary, while more tangible derivatives of prestige and income are decisive. When the divorce between work accomplishment and contrived status becomes widely acknowledged, a certain disenchantment follows for those who retain the puritan value that rewards "ought" to reflect objectively differentiable achievement. But this puritan ideal rests upon the premise that a set of shared values exists by which achievement can in fact be evaluated. Such agreement is precarious in the age of the publicist, of commercialized art and entertainment, and of the common-denominator sophistry of the mass media. Instead, a variant of Gresham's Law emerges in which the hard currency of achievement is devalued by the attending corrosion.

The orientation of upward-mobiles is thus often "procedural," as distinguished from the "substantive" attitude toward work traditionally regarded as decisive in career success. While they may possess the talent and inspiration to do creative work, this genial ethic en-

---

[49]William H. Whyte, Jr., *The Organization Man* (New York: Simon and Schuster, 1965), p. 160.

[50]Such values reflect differences in child-rearing practices that have apparently remained stable insofar as success aspirations are concerned. L. Richard Fave, "Success Values: Are They Class Differentiated?" *American Journal of Sociology*, Vol. 80, p. 161.

courages them to choose alternatives that promise greater reward in less time. Upward-mobiles are not necessarily those who lack talent and discipline; but it appears that they often consciously elect alternatives that lead more quickly to the ends they prefer.

Perhaps it should be emphasized that such a choice is not open to everyone. As noted earlier, temperamental affinity and self-discipline are always required. To sit through endless meetings; to consider gravely the opinions and suggestions of subordinates who neither know nor can be told that higher policy imperatives have so narrowed the range of alternatives that discussion is really beside the point; to endure the often pointless discussions into which committees often degenerate; to give way gracefully on small things; to suppress dislike and irritation; to treat unequals equally; to seriously propose expansive plans and programs, most of which are sure to be still-born; to waste ruthlessly the time of others in an effort to legitimate one's role of coordination; to discuss every issue at the level of principle, meanwhile keeping an eye on its implications for one's power and perquisites; to weigh proposals both in terms of their substantive rationality and in terms of the influence of those who propose them; to see progress and hope where neither exist—all require great staying power, the ability to bend reality into desired shapes, and an impregnable optimism. As Veblen said of the business executive and the university administrator: they have a "business-like facility in the management of affairs, an engaging address, a fluent command of language before a popular audience and what is called 'optimism'—a serene and voluble loyalty to the current conventionalities and a conspicuously profound conviction that all things are working out for good."[51]

The conditions of upward-mobility are also seen in the fusion of vocational and off-the-job energies. As the following comments suggest, business and professional success are nicely correlated with philanthropic activities.

Public relations head of large retail firm: If you study the lists of campaign workers, you will find an amazing parallel between the level a man holds in his place of business and the level he holds in the campaign. Thus, if you are working at the bottom part of some business organization, you will be ringing doorbells. You can't possibly head a campaign and deal with people who are the heads of large corporations. As you go up in the business world, you go up in phi-

---

[51]Thorstein Veblen, *The Higher Learning in America* (New York: Viking, 1918), p. 245.

lanthropy. If you are at the top in a business or financial corporation, you will appear at the top of the campaign.

President of firm: You will find that when a man first gets into this game he will be given some sort of minor campaign position depending on his business position. My own men have taken these positions; but as they have progressed with the firm, so they have taken on more responsibility in these campaigns. Furthermore they are helping themselves since I am watching them to see how they get along. They are ambitious, which is all to the good. They realize that we want them to do this work, and they will do a good job when we set them to it.

Lawyer: The top leaders have participated from year to year in the campaigns. They become part of it, and each year they become more and more experienced. They are just moved up to the vacancy above. Of course there is a sort of screening process which takes into account the respectability of the person and the type of occupation that will permit him to hold the position. The whole organization of philanthropic activity is arranged like a ladder. Once you start in the system, you slowly climb up—and if you have real and vital interest, you reach the top rungs.

General Manager, Trust Company: You don't just volunteer for these positions—it isn't done; you wait until you are asked. In fact, I don't know what would happen if you did volunteer! When asked, you are expected to say 'Yes,' but it is considered bad to show any eagerness. I am sure that if someone volunteered to be chairman of the next campaign he would be turned down.

General Manager, Bank Y: Training for philanthropy is a very important part of the training in our bank. It's our policy to drill into our men from the very beginning that they *must* take an interest in the community they're working in. Even if they're just a manager in a small town they *must* take an interest in the new hospital, or school, or whatever it is. We get reports each year on every clerk in every branch, and this shows whether they have taken an interest in their community affairs or not. They're reprimanded if they don't show this community interest. Stress right through is on this. And it's all for public relations. We *have* to do it—the competition between banks is so great. So we are all trained to take community responsibility. We expect to see the result of it somewhere in our balance sheet!

Professional Organizer A: Even the ordinary volunteer canvassers get to know people whom they would not ordinarily meet. I can give you an example of this. There was a cocktail party at a particular home here in Wellsville a few days ago for the various team captains and vice-chairmen. Many of these men would never have gone to that house for a cocktail party, and they probably never will again. But the campaign gave them a chance to see the inside of the house and meet other people whom they would not usually meet. That sort of thing goes on a lot. People know they will rub elbows with a lot of important people. They will make friends and contacts. A man makes acquaintances in his work and maybe at his club, but these campaigns are an opportunity for him to meet a lot of other people, and make a lot of friends. That's the way it works. You can see the friendships being made all around you.

Professional Organizer E: He is the center of all publicity. The spotlight is on him for a long time and he is placed before people's eyes. It certainly helps him in his business or profession.[52]

Social and philanthropic activities are thus subject to bureaucratic rationality. They may become manipulative, since they are frankly directed toward acquiring status values that have direct career and organizational benefits.

Consumption styles are also a means of validating and indexing career achievement. In exceptional cases they may become a subtle way of communicating to the elite any obvious disparity between social status and career position. The implication is that an individual's style of life and social skill "should" warrant greater recognition in terms of prestige and income. Since social status usually follows occupational role, there is something paradoxical about one who is a member of the elite in a social context but not in the other. Since they deny their own values, such deviations may produce anxiety among conventional upward-mobiles. Aspiring upward-mobiles are perceptive enough and skillful enough to rig such expectations. This proposition assumes considerable rationality, but it follows logically from their status orientation and from their social insight, coupled of course with the temperament necessary to bridge the gap between perception and action.

Upward-mobiles become "joiners," carriers of many institutionalized values, some of which are inevitably opposing. But not being seriously involved, they accommodate themselves without strain. Their lack of involvement is symbolized by frequent use of a vague, essentially "liberal" (eighteenth-century style) rhetoric of consensus. Social issues can be manipulated to whatever advantage is sought at the moment. They can be rugged enterprisers or believers in big government. They can inject whatever meaning they wish into words,

[52]Aileen E. Ross, "Philanthropic Activity and the Business Career," *Social Forces,* Vol. 32, pp. 275–278. Copyright by The Williams & Wilkins Company. Reprinted by permission of the publisher.

because, like Humpty Dumpty, they know that words mean whatever one chooses them to mean. They can express "democratic" values when necessary for rank-and-file appeal; they can admit the need for social progress and deplore the barriers of tradition. But they can also damn Washington and the muddled liberals. Given America's conservative social values, they lean toward social values that are conservative. "Progressive conservatism" is their hallmark. They play the tunes the audience demands, and when asked for their favorite, reply that they love them all.

Here upward-mobiles may seem to diverge from the authoritarian types who hold rigidly to conventional power-oriented values. Insofar as reality is distinguished from rhetoric, however, they remain faithful to convention and power. Their "liberalism" is merely part of the personal discipline that enables them to avoid unprofitable causes, anger, and resentment. But their essential skill is the ability to use an objective social reality, namely, a semantic confusion and the decline of traditional values, in a manipulative and rational way. Their conclusion that sophistry is often preferred and preferable to sincerity ensures a high probability of functional behavior. They know too that a pervasive optimism nourishes the human desire to find answers and certainty where neither exists.

Their insight informs them that individualism languishes in a bureaucratic situation where imprecise standards and group efforts are common. *By changing the conditions of work, bureaucratic structure has tended to change the character of work.* This differentiated, group-work milieu diffuses individual contributions, making evaluation difficult. There is on the one hand less inducement for individual effort and at the same time more opportunity to secure unwarranted rewards from a collective product. Reward is found less in the intrinsic value of work than in hierarchical roles of coordination which become valued as organizations become larger. Moreover, since those in such roles often control valued by-products of work such as income and recognition, the upward-mobile assumes disproportionate influence.

Here again the displacement of goals may be seen. For the upward-mobile, the manifest goals of the organization may become instrumental. The ability to identify strongly with collective goals and to assume a posture of selfless service is functional in the organizational society. Personal rewards and power may appear as mere by-products which one reluctantly accepts because they are necessary to dignify the role and the organization. Any resultant inequality is rationalized in operational terms. Quite simply, unequal rewards are necessary to inspire and to validate unequal contributions. Here again the whole trend toward subjective evaluations of individual performance is apparent, for example, loyalty by itself is highly valued in bureaucratic systems. As the official in charge of the State Department's security program put it, "An ounce of loyalty is worth a pound of brains."

Such aspects of the upward-mobiles' behavior may be explained by their essentially bifurcated role, one divided between a system-maintenance and a productivity orientation. The former tends to become paramount because of the critical need to maintain their power base within the organization. If this is lost, they obviously will have great difficulty marshalling the resources necessary to bring forth the substantative product that provides the reason for the organization's existence. This imperative may explain why elites so often seem to be occupied with ceremonial and honorific activities.

The most significant item in the personality of upward-mobiles is their respect for authority. Since the organization is essentially a system of authority relations, individual perceptions of authority are critically related to adjustment. An easy acceptance of authority eases interpersonal relations. In a study of 2,179 first-year recruits at West Point, psychiatrists found that respect for authority and idealization of one's father were critical factors differentiating successful from unsuccessful cadets. Concerned because a portion ranging from 20 to 25 percent of their carefully selected men failed to complete the first year of training, the academy gave detailed personal-history questionnaires to three first-year classes. These were supplemented by four-hour interviews with each cadet. The study found that successful cadets had "a closer, more gratifying relationship with the father . . . an admiration and respect for the father, and acceptance of him as an authority figure." Such cadets were able to "identify with the male role," and as a result, they adjusted well to classmates and to the stern officers who direct the academy. On the other hand, unsuccessful cadets were seldom close to their fathers and did not admire them. They were often anxious, unsure of their masculinity, and unable to sustain the authority-laden relationships of the military system.[53]

It is important to note that the upward-mobiles' authority relations with their fathers are not authoritarian. They admire and accept their authority relations with their fathers but this relationship is not autocratic. As one careful study of 1,455 public and parochial high school students found, "the data have reinforced the proposition that a democratic structure of parental authority is more conducive to

[53]United States Military Academy, *Adaptation to West Point: A Study of Some Psychological Factors Associated with Adjustment at the United States Military Academy* (West Point: 1959), pp. 31–39; James Bierli and Robin Lobeck, "Acceptance of Authority and Parental Identification," *Journal of Personality*, Vol. 27, pp. 74–86; L. Hart, "Maternal Childrearing Practices and Authoritarian Ideology," *Journal of Abnormal and Social Psychology*, Vol. 55, pp. 232–237.

achievement behavior . . . than one of autocratic authority."[54] The crucial point is probably that such childhood socialization instills in the individual the capacity to accept authority easily, encouraging a functional accommodation to the complex authority structure of bureaucracy.

Selective attrition in the military also occurs along political lines: "25 per cent of the entrants to a recent West Point class reported having liberal political views, 43 per cent reported middle-of-the-road and 32 per cent reported that their political views were conservative." Yet during the first year at West Point, "42 per cent of the resignees were from the liberal group, 33 per cent from the middle group, and 25 per cent from the conservative group."[55]

These findings suggest again the critical relationship between bureaucratic accommodations and attitudes toward authority. The "authoritarian personality," who may be equated with the upward-mobile, divides people into those who are weak and those who are strong. He or she needs certainty and admires strength. Successful executives regard their superiors as friendly models, while at the same time they view their subordinates with detachment. The upward-mobile's ability to make decisions that give priority to organizational over personal goals is also related to respect for authority.[56]

This valence toward authority is functional in both personal and organizational terms. We have seen that individuals have a strong need to impute superior ability to those who exercise authority over them. This "security operation" validates both the authority relationship and the act of submission. The latter may produce tension because of democratic values and the fear of authority that socialization instills in some individuals; but the typical upward-mobile finds it easy to legitimate such relationships. They justify his perception of the organization as a rational system in which authority, status, and income *must* be unequally distributed. The achievement of the organization's goals and the recognition of individual differences in ability require it. He easily accepts authority from those above while exercising it over those below himself. Individuals who score high on the F scale are more likely to choose strong, dominant leaders; whereas those who score low on the F scale prefer leaders who diagnose situations, ask

[54]Richard A. Rehberg, Judie Sinclair, and Walter E. Schafer, "Adolescent Achievement Behavior, Family Authority Structure, and Parental Socialization Patterns," *American Journal of Sociology,* Vol. 75, p. 1024.

[55]Gary Spencer, "Methodological Issues in the Study of Bureaucratic Elites: A Case Study of West Point," *Social Problems,* Vol. 21, p. 92.

[56]Elliot G. Mishler, "Personality Characteristics and the Resolution of Role Conflicts," *Public Opinion Quarterly,* Vol. 17, pp. 115–135.

for expressions of opinion, and interpret their own actions to the group.[57]

The bureaucratic situation nicely accommodates such authoritarian needs. Hierarchy is so constructed that a chain of command runs throughout the organization. Ideally, the "pecking order" insures an unbroken line of control from the highest office to the lowest. Individuals must play a dual role of super-and subordination. They must be able to move facilely from one role to the other. Although some tension may result, the high submission and dominance needs of the typical upward-mobile probably ease this accommodation. In effect, personality and role are mutually reinforcing.

Bureaucratic settings probably attract those who have such perceptions of authority. As a system of interlocking subhierarchies, they permit the indulgence of many degrees of authority at many levels. This psychic income is not limited to elites but percolates down to the lower levels. Only the private of the organizational army is virtually powerless. Moreover, the indulgence permitted by such a structure is increased by both small group structures and informal power centers with similar hierarchies and similar satisfactions. If status is to be satisfying, there must be hierarchy and someone to validate it. The bureaucratic situation provides both. Thus it seems to attract those who need certainty and authority-prescribed relationships.

The upward-mobiles' easy acceptance of authority and their typically advantaged educational experience often reflect advantaged social origins. Such conditions, in turn, may provide another useful career orientation which the psychiatrist, Robert Coles, has called the attitude of "entitlement." In research on highly advantaged children, Coles found that parents, teachers, and subsequent authority figures characteristically gave preferential treatment to such children because of their origins, and that such socialization tended over time to inculcate in the children the belief that they fully merited special dispensations as they moved through childhood into youth. One may speculate that such a self-image might prove quite useful in a bureaucratic career setting, easing any strain that might be evoked by advancement on extra-meritocratic grounds or by the accumulation of unearned status increments. Such patterns of behavior have heretofore been thought to be confined to societies that have a true aristocratic heritage, but Cole's work suggests that they may also be found in egalitarian milieux.

Their respect for authority and the entitlement ethic may help upward-mobiles reconcile any moral conflict arising from the injustice

[57]William Haythorn et al., "The Behavior of Authoritarian and Equalitarian Personalities in Groups," *Human Relations,* Vol. 9, pp. 67–69.

that organizations must at times commit. If the good of the organization is assigned the highest value, individual values must be subordinated to it. As the experience of Ernest Fitzgerald, Air Force cost analyst, fired by Richard Nixon in 1970, following his testimony before the Proxmire subcommittee investigating waste in the Defense Department shows,[58] when individual and organizational interests collide, it is the individual who must submit. Upward-mobiles' orientation enables them to submerge, diffuse, or rationalize any attending moral issue. Both their mobility claims and their personal values ease the problem of making such "tough-minded" decisions. A correlation exists between ambition and lack of faith in people. As one study found, whereas only 38 percent of those who thought it important to get ahead had high faith in people, 62 percent of those who felt that "getting ahead" was "not very important" had high faith.[59]

Obviously, the capacity for rationalizing injustice varies among individuals. Idealization of power, personal ambition, psychological insecurity, attitudes toward authority, value patterns of introversion and extroversion—all in various combinations play a part. But we may assume that upward-mobiles possess an exceptional ability to accept the inequities that unequal collective and individual power bring. Like that of most people, their attachment to individualism is an abstraction that does not always survive translation into concrete, personal terms. The limited utility of this principle in a pragmatic society contributes further to the tendency to look the other way when injustice occurs.

There is a well-known relationship between personal values and occupational choice. Here again there is a gap between the ideal-typical academic and the administrative mind. In his study of occupational choice and "faith in people," Rosenberg found that occupations such as teaching and science ranked at the top, whereas "self-interested" vocations such as business, finance, and public relations, ranked at the bottom.[60] The latter were chosen by people who had high mobility drives and low faith in people. The "aggressive" personality type, who "respects only the powerful and the successful," was found to be more self-confident and manipulative. Significantly, he chose "organizing-administrative" occupations.[61] The "detached" type who was "deeply concerned with his independence . . . and fundamentally resistant to coercion or domination of any sort," chose art, architecture, and

[58]Clark Mollenhoff, "Presidential Guile," *Harpers,* June 1973, pp. 38–42.

[59]Morris Rosenberg, "Faith in People and Success-Orientation," in Paul Lazarsfeld and Rosenberg, eds., *The Language of Social Research* (Glencoe, Ill.: Free Press, 1955), p. 159.

[60]Ibid., p. 27.

[61]Ibid., pp. 40, 46.

natural science as occupations."[62] Obviously, such characterizations refer only to general tendencies; they cannot be applied in individual cases.

Despite their facile role playing upward-mobiles are apparently relatively unwavering in their devotion to power. This item is also part of the authoritarian cluster that seems useful in defining them. Among the changing requirements of success and personality that confront them, this value remains constant. Here again there is a danger in exaggerating their rationality, but they seem to have an exceptional capacity for realistic appraisals and action. They think in terms of power and are sensitive to the long-range consequences of their actions. They know what they want and how to get it. Few reflections about what "might have been" disturb their preoccupation with the main chance. As a result, their jobs and the organization will often be viewed instrumentally, as a means of personal ascendancy.

In part, this ethic is forced upon them by the changing structure of participation in many fields. Such changes are nicely illustrated by the big foundations, such as Ford and Carnegie, which have considerable influence over the intellectual marketplace. Their activities in financing research and other university programs tend to restructure academic work and opportunity. By supporting research in selected areas they can modify the structure, the premises of recruitment and rewards, and the self-image of the university. They are providing new avenues for upward-mobiles whose forte is to understand the implications of such changes and to bend them to their advantage. By giving most of their funds to the prestige universities, which already have the most money and research facilities, they are solidifying the intellectual status quo.[63]

These conditions have bred a new academic role—the research entrepreneur (often called the vice-president for research) whose function is to get money from those who have it. To do so they must develop an extraordinary sensitivity to the desires of foundation executives and trustees. As these desires become the framework for shaping the interests and skills of the university in its search for financial support, the familar displacement of goals follows. Does the director of the relevant foundation division prefer quantitative or qualitative, rigorously defined or cosmic projects? The entrepreneurs know, or they will soon find out. Faculty recruitment is also influenced by the research-grant-producing potential of the candidates. And major rewards tend to go to those who get grants, actively seek

[62] Ibid., p. 42.

[63] As William H. Whyte, Jr., concludes, "They are not countering the bureaucratization of research, they are intensifying it." "Where the Foundations Fall Down," *Fortune*, November 1955, p. 141.

them, or at least endorse the system of grant getting. The academic upward-mobile's energies are devoted to designing projects that meet the foundations' major interests and values, which are "wide ranging; but characteristically they are critical examinations of prevailing orthodoxy."[64]

Similar observations can be made concerning the federal government's vast university research programs, which are almost exclusively devoted to physical science except for a very small amount of social research, much of which is militarily relevant. Among the disquieting implications here is the impact upon the university's ability to maintain some balance between the claims of physical science and of social science, and between teaching and research, and to preserve a rough equality in working conditions and rewards between physical-science faculties and those whose skills and interests are technologically irrelevant. Also challenged is the university's autonomy in matters of program development, in recruitment, and in the definition of its essential purpose. For example, the by-products of federally sponsored research often include a requirement that faculty members in physical-science departments be able to meet the security requirements of the government, whose grants are usually contingent upon clearances for everyone involved. Thus the university is obliged to share with outsiders, whose knowledge of university traditions and the conditions of productive research is likely to be limited, its right and obligation to determine the qualifications of its members. When, as today, something like 50 percent of the total budget of the private universities comes from federal research funds, the implications for the autonomy of higher education become apparent. More recently, as indicated earlier, the federal government's "Equal Opportunity" program has brought Health, Education, and Welfare directly into the faculty and student recruitment process.

The work, work place, interests, and skills of intellectuals are thus shaped. Grants mean personal and institutional prestige, freedom from professionally unrewarding teaching, leverage vis-à-vis the administration, and often, fresh opportunities to do meaningful work. But the suggestive point here is the impact of social change upon academic work, including new frontiers for the upward-mobile type.

At the same time, some of the frontiers are constricting. Like other people, potential upward-mobiles are faced by the sobering fact that the advantages of education, economic security, and social skill are often retained within the families who have achieved them. Social and economic differences rather than intellectual ones often differentiate

[64] Ibid., p. 140.

university from nonuniversity youth. And even twenty years ago the social mobility theme was losing ground in view of the fact that more often than not corporation executives were the sons of corporation executives.[65] While higher education increasingly challenges wealth and family as the main avenue of mobility, it too is correlated with income and class expectations. In 1955, top executives in business had twelve times the amount of education of their age group in the entire male population,[66] and a disproportionate number were from families of "medium" and "wealthy" incomes.[67]

By 1975, the situation remained much the same. Indeed, a remarkable continuity tends to persist at the very apex of bureaucratic structures. For example, the social origins of those who directed the major economic sectors of American society remained virtually unchanged during the first three-quarters of the 20th century. These economic elites demonstrated the talent for survival traditionally ascribed to them by modern elite theorists from Mosca to Pareto to C. Wright Mills.[68]

Despite claims that ownership and management had been separated, presumably creating a hiatus between the power and values of owners and high executives, as well as the Galbraithian illusion that a "technosphere" of upper-level managers and technicians now exerts decisive influence in corporate decision making,[69] evidence indicates that those who controlled the American economy had changed very little and, indeed, had actually become more homogenous. Profit-making remained their lodestar, as it had of the entrepreneurial giants who preceded them.

Executives at the very top of the American corporate hierarchy have apparently become *more alike* in terms of social class, ethnicity, educational backgrounds, age, religion, and work experience in only a single corporation.[70] A survey of 444 executives, based on *Who's Who* and *Poor's Register of Directors and Executives* reveals the following trends. Using type of university attended (private, public, none), as an index of family class status, 58 percent were found to come from "affluent families," 41 percent from middle-income, and less than 1 percent from poor families. The latter was an even smaller proportion, moreover, than from earlier studies. It may be, however, that the

---

[65]Newcomer, *The Big Business Executive,* pp. 60–61.

[66]Ibid., p. 146.

[67]Ibid., p. 63.

[68]For a clear analysis of elite theories, see Geraint Parry, *Political Elites* (New York: Praeger, 1969).

[69]Galbraith, *The New Industrial State,* 2nd rev. ed.

[70]Frederick D. Sturdivant and Roy D. Adler, "Executive Origins," *Harvard Business Review,* Vol. 54, pp. 125–132.

index used to determine family origin in 1975, differing as it does from earlier studies, underestimates the proportion of executives who rose from poor families. All earlier studies agree that about 85 percent of the top men (no women were included) were Protestants, about 60 percent of whom were Episcopalian, Presbyterian, and Congregationalists. No change occurred here, except that a very much smaller proportion of respondants were prepared to reveal their religious preference, compared with their earlier peers. The slight hardening of class-based criteria is apparent in the steady continuity of executives of Episcopalian faith and the disadvantage of Roman Catholics, remaining under 10 percent and Jews who rose only marginally from about 2 to 3 percent to 5 percent.[71] Thus the substantial upward-mobility documented by Blau and Duncan[72] occurred in the middle and lower-upper reaches of the technical-managerial class, whereas the criteria for admission to the positions at the very apex seem to have remained much the same. Indeed entry into this rarefied sanctuary has apparently become slightly less open, not only in the United States, but in Britian and Canada as well.[73]

Politically, the 70 percent of executives who had reported Republican affiliation since 1900 had risen by 1975 to 85 percent. As with their religion, a very high proportion refused to indicate their political ties.

The role of higher education has always been critical in corporate success and by 1975, the trend was even more pronounced. In 1900, 40 percent of executives had some college; by 1950, just over half; by 1955, three-quarters; and by 1975, fully 96 percent had been to college. Moreover, almost half of the latter had done graduate work and over 40 percent of these held graduate degrees, 15 percent of which were in law, 11 percent MBA's and 7 percent Ph.Ds.

More important perhaps is the extent to which their education was concentrated in a few prestigious universities. Only one public institution, University of Michigan, was in the first ten, as it had been since 1900. The social and occupational advantages gained by education in such schools is clear. Harvard, Yale, Massachusetts Institute of Technology, Columbia, and Princeton along with Michigan dominate the first ten, those cited most frequently. Cornell surfaced in 1950,

---

[71]Research using a national sample indicates that religiously based differential mobility among Protestants and Catholics (with social class controlled) still exists, despite theoretical assumptions that urbanization and secularization have reduced such variations. See Elton Jackson, W. S. Fox, and H. J. Crockett, Jr., "Religion and Occupational Achievement," *American Sociological Review*, Vol. 35, pp. 48–63.

[72]Blau and Duncan, *The American Occupational Structure*, especially chs. 11 and 12.

[73]Roger K. Kelsall et al., *Graduates: The Study of an Elite* (London: Methuen and Co., 1972), and Wallace Clement, *The Canadian Corporate Elite* (Toronto: McClelland & Stewart, 1975).

remained in until 1964, but dropped out by 1975. Pennsylvania broke in in 1950 and has remained in since. Stanford did not make the grade until 1964 and survived in 1975. Despite such formidable competition, one suspects that the prestige and connections conferred by a Harvard Business School degree remain unmatched as legitimating insignia in the corporate world. Its penumbra, moreover, is cross-national; the Harvard MBA enjoys a similar mystique in the Canadian industrial milieu and indeed, such influences tend to be even greater in a more ascriptive society.[74]

The single area in which a significant change has occurred, length of time in a single company, reflects the tendency toward larger limits and increased bureaucratization of the conditions of occupational participation. In 1900, less than 10 percent of the leading industrialists worked in only one corporation; by 1925, the proportion rose to 27 percent; by 1950 it was 31 percent; and by 1975 it had risen to 42.5 percent. While it apparently remains true that many executives switch from one company to another, about two-thirds of those who occupy the highest corporate positions have worked with only one company other than the one they are now with.[75]

These data on the advantaged social class origins of upward-mobiles in industrial bureaucracies are critical theoretically because they indicate that their mobility is the result of social origins, as well as the personal psychological variables emphasized here. Motivational effects are obviously critical, but appropriate social origins appear to be even more salient.[76] Some careful research suggests that the major in-

[74]See Robert Presthus, *Elites in the Policy Process* (New York and London: Cambridge University Press, 1974). See also Clement, *The Canadian Corporate Elite.*

[75]*Fortune,* May 1976, p. 177. This study of 500 directors of the leading industrial corporations and 300 in major banks, life insurance, retailing and utilities companies concludes that "today's chief executive represents a significant break with previous generations. He is more apt to come from a middle-class background than his predecessors" (p. 172). Insofar as the inference is that recruitment of such positions has become more open, I do not think the data support the conclusions, since fully 86 percent are college graduates and almost three-fourths are forty-five years of age or over and hence went to college at a time when entry was more socially selected, three-fourths own $100,000 or more of their company's stock, and receive salaries ranging from $97,000 to $209,000 per year. Moreover, and perhaps more importantly, their class of social origin is based upon the respondant's personal judgment of his family's status. Finally, the main drift of the article, written by a *Fortune* editor, seems at times mildly self-serving, e.g., "One of the *hoariest myths* about the corporate officer is that he comes from a wealthy, or at least upper-middle class background, and thus has a special advantage in getting to the top." Italics added (p. 174). This is precisely what Miller, Warner and Abegglen, Newcomer, Mills, and more recently, Blumberg, and Sturdivant and Adler, found, respectively, in the following studies: *Men in Business* (Cambridge: Harvard University Press, 1962); *The Big Business Executive* (New York: Columbia University Press, 1955); *Big Business Leaders in America* (New York: Harper & Row, 1955); *The Power Elite* (New York: Oxford University Press, 1959); *The Megacorporation in American Society* (Englewood Cliffs, N.J.: Prentice-Hall, 1975); and "Executive Careers."

[76]See, for example, Kelsall's comprehensive survey of graduates of British universities, which found that educational achievement was critical in occupational mo-

fluence of psychological factors on mobility is in encouraging the extended education required to prepare for a successful career. Precareer education is the critical factor. As one study concludes, "the achievement-related motivations of adult males play a modest role in the post-education socioeconomic career." Again, "if motivations and other personality dimensions do function as 'key' intervening variables in the processes of achievement in American society, then perhaps they constitute important determinants of the number of years of schooling obtained by men, generally, and by certain religio-ethnic subgroups, specifically."[77] Psychological motivations, in effect, seem to be a part of preorganizational experience, impelling Protestants to better prepare themselves educationally for upward-mobility than Catholics, and among Protestant sects, for those of Anglo-Saxon origin to obtain more education and thus higher occupational levels than other Protestants.

These studies suggest that the pattern of corporate career mobility is changing mainly in that independent business experience has been replaced by long service in a single organization as the common path to success. Whereas two-thirds of the major business executives in 1900 had had independent experience, by 1950 only 11 percent could claim so.[78] And, as Newcomer concludes, "The proportion whose entire business career had been limited to the company they head had increased from seven percent for the 1900 executives to twenty-two percent for the 1950 executives."[79] By 1975, as seen earlier, it was 42 percent. Such developments place an even greater premium on bureaucratic qualities of discipline, loyalty, and the long-run view. Above all, they dramatize the need for interpersonal skills that can weather the strains of extended association with the same superiors and subordinates.

Such demands may prove extremely trying. The upward-mobile must reconcile many conflicting roles and interests. Permissive authority relations require a discipline that cannot always survive the tensions of a competitive, power-oriented milieu. When tension does occur, the upward-mobiles' preference for dominance may demand expression. However, if our analysis is accurate, they will usually muster the required discipline. As Burleigh Gardner says, successful

---

bility up to the near-the-top level, but at that point advantaged social origins tended to assume a major role, *Graduates: The Sociology of an Elite.*

[77] David Featherman, "The Socioeconomic Achievement of White Religio-Ethnic Subgroups: Social and Psychological Explanations," *American Sociological Review,* Vol. 36, p. 221.

[78] Newcomer, *The Big Business Executive,* p. 148.

[79] Ibid.

executives "know what they are and what they want." They also have "techniques for getting what they want within the framework of their desires and within the often narrow possibilities of their own organization."[80] Their determination to make the most of such "narrow possibilities" explains much about the upward-mobiles' behavior. Their rationality encourages them to make the most of what they have, both for immediate personal satisfactions and for the enhancement of their own image of being qualified for further mobility.

Despite any conflict between their personalities and their roles, upward-mobiles are characterized by an ability to overcome doubt and ambivalence. They do not need perfect causes, and their devotion to prestige and power characteristically enables them to reach a satisfactory personal accommodation. This is putting the matter too negatively, however; it is clear that they find the bureaucratic situation congenial, and that they can often adapt with relatively little strain.

[80]Gardner, "What Makes Successful and Unsuccessful Executives," p. 118.

PATTERNS OF | 7
ACCOMMODATION:
INDIFFERENTS

Our second ideal type of accommodation in the bureaucratic situation is one of indifference. Security, prestige, and power are the values that mediate accommodation, and people act in ways that seem to secure them. Such values have been endorsed by society's authority figures, and since we all hope to gain some measure of security and prestige, the behavior of such figures often becomes a model for our own. Although anxiety reduction is probably the main impetus for such emulation, the ways of reducing it vary with the individual and with the situation. Status anxiety may push some of us into compulsive success striving, while others displace this need upon other values. Upward-mobiles regard organizations as excellent instruments for satisfying their claims, but indifferents are more likely to define them as calculated systems of frustration. They refuse to compete for the rewards they promise.

Indifference or withdrawal is the typical pattern of accommodation for the majority of organization people. The indifferents are found mainly among the great mass of waged and salaried employees who work in a bureaucratic setting. In 1975 such employees made up almost 90 percent of the labor force, divided almost equally into blue- and white-collar workers. By a very rough estimate, we can say that some 40 to 45 million of them—something less than half the wage-earning labor force—now work in such organizations. Moreover, this vast reservoir of potential indifferents is probably increasing. From 1950 to 1975 for example, while the number of managers, proprietors (including farm), and officials decreased by about 25 percent, professional and technical workers increased by over 100 percent, and the number of clerical and sales workers by about two and one-half times.

It is not to be inferred that all of these employees are indifferents, nor can anyone determine precisely the number who are. Both logic and empirical research, however, suggest that a considerable proportion of them have been disenchanted by the structural conditions of their work and work place. Since these conditions have been covered in detail, let us merely outline them here as a framework for the following analysis:

1. The bureaucratic worker's role is as a waged or salaried employee who is not directly sharing in either the ownership or the profits of the organization. In the past twenty-five years, for example, the number of "self-employed workers" (nonagricultural) increased only from 5,155,000 to 8,891,000. During the same period, the number of "private wage and salary workers" increased from 30 million to almost 80 million. Government workers almost tripled, rising from 5,726,000 in 1950 to 15,000,000 in 1975.[1]

2. Centralized power and decision making in large-scale organizations have shut employees out from real participation and influence over the decisions that affect them. As Edwin G. Nourse, former head of the Council of Economic Advisers, says, "Responsibility for determining the direction of the nation's economic life today and of furnishing both opportunity and incentives to the masses centers upon some one or two percent of the gainfully employed."[2]

3. The size and impersonality of organizations and the standardized, *process-determined* nature of their work encourage dissatisfaction by reducing the education and skill demands, and consequently the prestige, of both white- and blue-collar jobs. "Skilled" work is rather hard to define. But if "craftsmen, foremen, and kindred workers" can be called "skilled," we find that their relative proportion of a greatly expanded labor force has remained precisely the same between 1950 and 1975, at just over 13 percent. Meanwhile, the chances of entry and survival in a business of one's own have been reduced by the difficulty of securing capital and the growth of huge national and multinational enterprises whose resources make them highly resistant to competition and economic cycles.

4. Opportunities for higher education, perhaps the major instrument of social mobility, remain unequal. As C. Wright Mills noted in 1951, "The son of an unskilled laborer has 6 chances out of 100 of ever getting into a college; the son of a professional man has better than a 50–50 chance."[3] Lloyd Warner concludes, "Of the 580 boys and girls in a thousand who reach the third year of high school, about

---

[1] U.S. *Statistical Abstracts.*

[2] Cited in C. Wright Mills, *White Collar* (New York: Oxford University Press, 1951), p. 81, p. 276.

[3] Ibid., p. 276.

half are taking a course which leads to college. One hundred and fifty enter college, and 70 graduate. These are average figures for the country as a whole."[4] By 1972, Christopher Jencks and his colleagues found that their index of income and occupational status correlated strongly (.55) with educational achievement.[5]

5. Finally, the recent and probably transitory shift of attention and energy from work to recreation and leisure probably encourages occupational ambivalence. The decline of the Protestant Ethic, which deified work and accumulation, brings with it a reevaluation of the whole vocational bargain, subtly reinforced by the suspicion that one's life chances have been exaggerated in any case. Thus work tends to become an instrument for buying off-work satisfactions.

Do these conditions really inspire disenchantment and indifference? Are those observers correct who argue that the *embourgeoisement* of American workers has overcome any disaffection stemming from their powerless role in the industrial structure?

The indifferents are those who have come to terms with their work environment by withdrawal and by a redirection of their interests toward off-the-job satisfactions. They have also been put off by the work itself, which has often been downgraded by machine processing and by assembly-line methods. This dual basis for indifference must be recognized. In industrial psychology the main effort has been to compensate for the deadening effect of work by providing a happy work place. Less attention has been given to alienation from the job itself. Here, despite the social mobility that has often attended increased levels of education, science and technology have often brought a "degradation of work" by lowering or displacing its skill requirements.[6] John Porter writes of "examples of stripped down, simplified skills in automated office work." Bank tellers no longer need to add, but simply push bank books into computer terminals; library clerks run optical scanners over electronically sensitized labels attached to the books and thereby activate the entire recording of the circulation process. One wonders now about the usefulness of a graduate degree in library science and questions how much formal training is actually necessary for library technologists—a new job to emerge from our educational machinery. And so we might proceed

---

[4]Ibid., p. 268.

[5]Christopher S. Jencks et al., *Inequality* (New York: Basic Books, 1972), p. 138; see also, Raymond Boudon, *Education, Opportunity, and Social Inequality* (New York: Wiley, 1973); *Harvard Educational Review, Equal Educational Opportunity* (Cambridge: Harvard University Press, 1969).

[6]Harry Braverman, *Labor and Monopoly Capital: The Degradation of Work in the Twentieth Century* (New York: Monthly Review Press, 1974).

through a wide area of clerical and white collar work to find jobs which require fewer skills nowadays than formerly. Cooks in restaurants become thawer-outers and secretary-typists become automated word processors.[7]

The attending personal disenchantment has been aggravated by the continued rise of "credentialism," which tends constantly and artificially to raise the educational requirements for jobs. The motivation for artificial upgrading reflects in part cooperation between the universities and the worlds of business and industry, which derive mutual benefits from the system of certification which provides (along with improved performance in some cases) a bureaucratic apparatus of control over occupational selection, rewards, punishments and, essentially, the avenues of social mobility.

Upgrading, as a result, is often a statistical artifact of occupational census categories. Highly skilled occupations downgraded by the machine process continue to be classified as "skilled"; factory operatives on production lines are designated as "semi-skilled," despite the tenuous differences between their role and that of laborers; and a most questionable example of upward mobility by students of the subject is sons of farmers who become unskilled or semi-skilled urban workers. Instead, such a change probably represents a decline in both skill requirements and social status as farmers move from the class of independent owners to urban wage earners.

Consequences of these conditions include personal disenchantment among workers. We are not speaking here of pathological behavior but of modes of accommodation that often seem basically healthy. The typical indifferent has rejected majority values of success and power. While the upward-mobile strives for such values, realizable today mainly through big organizations, the indifferent seeks that security which the organization can also provide for those who merely "go along." Such security-seeking varies according to the demands of personality. Some individuals may have been taught to expect more than life can reasonably offer, and anxiety and frustration follow as their unrealistic claims are discounted. Others may have learned to expect less and refuse to accept or compete for success values; such perspectives have been found to be characteristic of individuals from working-class backgrounds. They are probably encouraged by such bureaucratic conditions as hierarchy, oligarchy, and specialization.

The indifferent reaction, then, is the product of class, technological, organizational, and personal influences. Organizational factors seem to aggravate class-induced expectations of limited mo-

---

[7]John Porter, "Education and the Just Society," Paper read at York University, Toronto, February 2, 1977, pp. 4–5.

bility. As James Quinn and Herbert Shepard found, over 40 percent of a random sample of 2,157 workers in all types of occupations "never want to be promoted and never expect to be."[8] The resulting accommodation may also reflect personal failures of nerve and energy, bad luck, and so on. But, essentially, indifference is manifested in a psychic withdrawal from the work arena and a transfer of interest to off-work activities. The employees "go through the motions," paying lip-service to organizational values, but they no longer retain any real interest in the organization, or in work for its own sake.

This accommodation may occur in two stages: disenchantment and indifference. The former characterizes those who come into the organization with great expectations. They are determined to climb. But when bureaucratic and personal limitations blunt their hopes, they become disenchanted. Over a period of time, it seems, this reaction works itself into indifference. On another level, we are dealing with indifference as an initial orientation. Such individuals, usually of working- or lower-middle-class origin, have been taught not to expect very much. Both early socialization and work experience reinforce this perception of their life chances. And both disenchantment and indifference counter the organization's claims for loyalty, predictability, and hard work.

Attitudes toward mobility, however, are complex and contradictory. At the popular level one finds an uncritical acceptance of the American dream of unlimited mobility for those who have what it takes. In social science, however, some observers accept this belief while others insist that mobility is considerably more limited. Since research supporting either view can be found, both interpretations have apparently been influenced by the historical context in which they occurred. During the Depression years the pessimistic view dominated; following the post–World War II years of prosperity, some observers regarded mobility more happily; today, however, as the work of Coleman, Jencks, Illich, and others indicates, the drift is again rather pessimistic, mainly because of the manifest failure of public education

---

[8]*The 1972–73 Quality of Employment Survey,* p. 209. For data regarding the association between social class and individual attitudes toward achievement, see William H. Sewell, Archie O. Haller, and Murray A. Straus, "Social Status and Educational and Occupational Aspirations," *American Sociological Review,* Vol. 22, pp. 67–73; David McClelland, *The Achieving Society* (New York: Free Press, 1961); B. Rosen and R. G. D'Andrade, "The Psychosocial Origins of Achievement Motivation," *Sociometry,* Vol. 22, pp. 185–218. The extent to which women's job aspirations are limited by sex-typing of occupations is traced in J. W. Grimm and R. N. Stern, "Sex Roles and Internal Labor Market Structures," *Social Forces,* Vol. 21, pp. 690–705.

to significantly erase the advantages of social class in the mobility equation.[9]

The problem is defined somewhat by discrete class attitudes toward mobility. Roughly speaking, white-collar people retain faith in the "high-mobility" ideal. On the other hand, blue-collar workers may pay homage to mobility, but their expectations are usually transferred to their children. Among the white-collar class there is no doubt that science and technology have created a new lower-middle class of office and sales people who have moved up from "manual" families. Mass production and liberal credit have helped validate their middle-class image by making widely available the material goods that partly define class status.

Moreover, class is a psychic as well as an objective social phenomenon. Most Americans, it seems, are not class conscious in the way that Europeans, with their feudal legacy, continue to be. A *Fortune* survey found that almost 80 percent of an American sample defined themselves as being of the "middle class." Richard Centers found that 51 percent of his sample called themselves "working class," which seems to indicate some class sensitivity,[10] but this response might also be interpreted to mean the absence of any Marxian connotation of "working class." Pragmatic Americans might very well reason: "Yes, I work for a living, therefore I am obviously a member of the 'working class.'"

But our concern is less with class than with mobility, and here the evidence has been carefully summarized. Once again, however, one encounters the problem of determining what the data really mean, since the same evidence can be interpreted in different ways. For example, Warner and Abegglen's survey of the origins of big business leaders found that 31 percent were descended from fathers who were also big business leaders.[11] Only 5 percent had fathers in skilled and semiskilled occupations. These leaders, in effect, were drawn from

---

[9] Among others, see the previously cited work of R. and H. Lynd, L. Warner, C. W. Mills, and A. B. Hollingshead, all of whom either wrote during, or experienced, the Depression of the 1930s; Natalie Rogoff: *Recent Trends in Occupational Mobility* (Glencoe, Ill.: Free Press, 1953); perhaps P. Blau and O. D. Duncan, *American Occupational Structure*, provides the best scholarly basis for the post–World War II optimism; on the contemporary pessimism, see James Coleman, *Equality of Educational Opportunity* (Washington, D.C.: 1966); Jencks, *Inequality: A Reassessment of the Effect of Family and Schooling in America;* and Ivan Illich, *De-Schooling Society* (New York: Harper & Row, 1971).

[10] Richard Centers, "The American Class Structure: A Psychological Analysis," in Guy E. Swanson, Theodore M. Newcomb, and Edwin L. Hartley et al., eds., *Readings in Social Psychology* (New York: Holt, Rinehart & Winston, 1952).

[11] W. Lloyd Warner and James C. Abegglen, *Occupational Mobility in American Business and Industry* (Minneapolis: University of Minnesota Press, 1955).

existing elites some eight times more often than would have been expected had succession been random. This suggests that mobility at the top of our social structure is highly restricted, but Joseph Kahl cautions, as follows: "These figures can be interpreted to indicate that American society is either relatively closed or relatively open, depending upon one's expectations. The statement that sixty-nine percent of the business elite were recruited from other levels suggests considerable openness. On the other hand, the statement that the business elite was recruited from its own ranks 7.75 times oftener than randomly suggests that American society is relatively closed."[12]

Kahl has a generally optimistic view of mobility. He concludes that "between one-half and three-quarters of the men who are in professional, clerical, or skilled jobs, have climbed relative to their fathers"; from 1920 to 1950, moreover, "total mobility" (the combined effects of technological change, individual effort, reproduction, and step-by-step progress) was enjoyed by a full 67 percent of the entire labor force; and even in the proprietorship category where the proportion of self-employed in the entire labor force has been sharply reduced, he estimates that only 4 percent have been downwardly mobile.[13] This estimate is based upon a National Opinion Research Center study of 1947, in which 1,334 sons were asked to indicate their fathers' occupations.

But other research is less optimistic. Natalie Rogoff, for example, found that mobility among her sample of Indianapolis men was no greater in 1940 than it had been in 1910.[14] She concludes, moreover, that no more men crossed the critical blue-collar–white-collar line in the later period. Her findings refer only to "individual effort," however, and to "step by step" mobility. Technological advances during the period would presumably have increased mobility by opening up large numbers of semiskilled, skilled, and administrative jobs. Census figures show that the number of professional jobs has increased by some five times since 1900.

A comparison of the 1952 Warner-Abegglen study and a similar one by Taussig and Joslyn in 1928 shows that recruitment to top business positions from businessmen families decreased from 9.67 to 4.73. Yet recruitment from professional groups, clerks and salesmen, farmers and laborers increased either very little or not at all.

Despite such rather pessimistic conclusions, other, more rigorous evidence indicates that social mobility in the United States has his-

---

[12]Joseph A. Kahl, *The American Class Structure* (New York: Holt, Rinehart & Winston, 1957), p. 269.

[13]Ibid., pp. 272, 260–261, 262.

[14]Rogoff, *Recent Trends in Occupational Mobility.*

torically been the highest in the Western world and that it remains quite high today.[15] This condition reflects three special historical circumstances: technological expansion, immigration, and differential fertility rates among class strata. Mechanization and rationalization of production reduced the relative need for physical labor and brought a secular increase in the proportion of the labor force in white-collar occupations, thus fostering upward mobility.[16] Meanwhile, millions of immigrants moved into the lower levels of the work hierarchy, freeing sons of men in these strata to move upward. Finally, the lower birth rates of the white-collar class and the expanding market for clerical, sales, and managerial occupations permitted disadvantaged workers to fill such places. Two of these three historical conditions have been significantly modified, i.e., immigration and differential fertility. Technological progress continues but at a slower pace and often with the result of simplifying tasks rather than raising the skill level of the work force.[17] Despite these changes, Peter Blau and Otis Duncan conclude that "the rates of upward mobility in the United States are still high."

To what are these high rates attributed? External migration is duplicated *within* the United States.[18] As we saw earlier, the farm population has steadily decreased as a proportion of the total labor force. Not surprisingly such recruits are among those who have experienced most mobility. Differential fertility rates, it seems, will tend to persist, despite some leveling off. This is because essentially *Gesellschaft* orientations (calculating, contractual, possessive) will continue to be strong among white-collar families in America, given the social rewards of success, resulting in limited child-rearing. At the same time, Blau and Duncan suggest, psychological inducements will continue to encourage higher fertility among blue-collar families. This is because such parents tend to compensate for any lack of material success by displacing their commitments to their families. Less happily, "the unsuccessful find a substitute in the authority they exercise in their role as fathers over a number of children."[19] This suggestive hypothesis rests upon findings that have usually shown that parents in working-class families tend to use more authoritarian patterns of socialization than middle-class parents. However, there is

---

[15]For an excellent analysis using census data, see Blau and Duncan, *The American Occupational Structure.*

[16]Ibid., p. 426.

[17]Ibid.

[18]Ibid., p. 426.

[19]Ibid., p. 428.

some indication that such differentials have narrowed in the recent past.

Another positive force is held to lie in universalistic and rational criteria of action and recruitment in the United States. Following Durkheim, greater specialization and differentiation of work provide increased opportunity for mobility; achievement rather than ascription becomes the basis for class status; discrimination against minorities lessens. Here again, compared with European societies, the United States remains a miracle of universalism, yet the opportunity for higher education, which is the major instrument of social mobility, remains greatly influenced by class status. Children in professional families have many times the chance to enter university compared with those from working-class homes. In addition, one suspects that universalism is not immune to intergenerational decomposition. Parents who have achieved occupational success and social mobility pass on their advantages to their children, regardless of their inherent talents. Although they are a small and exceptional proportion of the labor force, longitudinal studies of the social origins of top-level corporate executives indicate, for example, that there has been little change during the past several decades. Such people come from highly advantaged family backgrounds. Indeed, studies in both the United States and Canada indicate that people in such dominant positions are acutally becoming more similar in terms of their social backgrounds.[20]

As Sturdivant and Duncan note:

> The rather surprising result of all this digging through library materials and comparing of data is that the executives of 1975 form a *more* homogeneous group than those from earlier time periods. Indeed, a more uniform profile is reflected than the one of the supposedly 'conforming 1950s.' In addition to being exclusively male and Caucasian, predominantly Protestant, Republican, and of eastern U.S. origin, from relatively affluent families, and educated at one of a handful of select universities, as had been the case in the past, the executives in our sample share some new characteristics. Most significantly, the executives are closer together in age, and more of them have little or no work experience outside their companies.[21]

---

[20]For data on Canada, see Wallace Clement, *The Canadian Corporate Elite* (Toronto: McClelland Stewart, 1975) and his *Continental Corporate Power* (Toronto: McClelland Stewart, 1977). Of course, this condition is less unexpected in Canada which has been less of an egalitarian, technologically vibrant society than the United States.

[21]Sturdivant and Adler, "Executive Origins," p. 127.

Despite such sobering assessments, and contrary to some sociological research, there is impressive evidence that mobility rates in the
United States remain the highest among Western countries. Table 7.1
indicates the movement of manual, working-class, and middle-class
men into elite strata in eleven countries:

Table 7.1. Movement from Specified Origins into Elite[a] Destinations:
International Comparisons*

Country	Percent of All Men in Elite	Working Class into Elite		Manual Class into Elite		Middle Class into Elite	
		%	Mobility Ratio	%	Mobility Ratio	%	Mobility Ratio
Denmark	3.30			1.07	.32	4.58	1.39
France I (Bresard)	8.53	4.16	.49	3.52	.41	12.50	1.46
France II (Desabie)	6.12	1.99	.33	1.56	.25	10.48	1.71
Great Britain	7.49			2.23	.30	8.64	1.15
Italy	2.77	.48	.17	.35	.13	5.76	2.08
Japan	11.74			6.95	.59	15.12	1.29
Netherlands	11.08			6.61	.60	11.55	1.04
Puerto Rico	13.79	11.42	.83	8.60	.62	23.17	1.68
Sweden	6.66	4.43	.67	3.50	.53	18.09	2.72
United States (OCG)	11.60	10.41	.90	9.91	.85	20.90	1.80
West Germany	4.58	1.55	.34	1.46	.32	8.28	1.81

SOURCE: S. M. Miller, "Comparative Social Mobility," *Current Sociology*, Vol. 9, pp. 69–80, except for Sweden (G. Carlsson, *Social Mobility and Class Structure* p. 93), Italy (J. Lopreato, "Social Mobility in Italy" *American Journal of Sociology*, Vol. 71, p. 314), and the United States (OCG).

[a]"Elite" here is equivalent to Miller's "Elite I and II" for data taken from Miller and Carlsson, to Lopreato's "Ruling Class" for Italy, and to "Professional, Technical and Kindred" for the United States.

*Adapted from Blau and Duncan, *The American Occupational Structure*, p. 434.

Only in Puerto Rico among working-class men is the rate of mobility higher than in the United States. The chances of manual sons to
rise are greatest in the United States, and among middle-class sons it
is greater than in most countries, but not all. Underprivileged Americans from manual origins have a particularly good opportunity to
move into the elite stratum: 10 percent achieve this status, higher
than in any other country.[22] Blau and Duncan conclude with an
explanation of democratic stability in the United States that rests
upon social mobility and economic opportunity rather than upon the
somewhat nebulous claim that political integration and commitment

[22]Blau and Duncan, *The American Occupational Structure:* "It is the underprivileged class of manual sons that has exceptional chances for mobility into the elite in this country," p. 435.

are critical in achieving this end.[23] Both the ideal and the reality of upward social mobility, made possible by the combination of historical, structural factors and universalistic values seem to provide a more objectively based foundation for democratic stability in this country.

The weight of evidence suggests that the American dream remains viable, despite the political and economic disenchantments of the past two decades. Clearly, despite the strictures of environmental groups and "no growth" advocates such as the Club of Rome, continued mobility depends upon a sustained, if reduced, rate of economic growth. If it continues, the slowdown in population growth and immigration may take up the resultant slack in employment opportunities. Great strides toward meeting the much-bruited energy problem can be made by curbing the built-in waste in consumption styles in the United States. Apparently, self-discipline cut the total demand for electric power from a typical annual growth of some 6 percent to just over 1 percent in 1975–1976. Car manufacturers have rather quickly begun producing engines that cut gas consumption significantly.

Nevertheless, if social mobility continues at a satisfactory rate, it clearly occurs in a changed context. Rather than self-employment, which historically has been viewed as the most satisfying and viable form of upward movement, it is clear that individual mobility now more typically occurs as an employee in one or another giant institution. And even here, as Blau and Duncan conclude, "There is much upward mobility in the United States, but most of it involves relatively short distances upward."[24] Mobility, that is, often occurs within the several steps of a single occupational stratum. In white-collar work, for example, there is a great distance in income and prestige between the bottom and the top of the scale.

Such evidence indicates the difficulty of comparing data from studies that differ in point of time, method, and definition. For our purposes, however, quantitative rates of mobility must be set against qualitative changes brought about by the conditions of work in bureaucratic organizations. The essential change has been from a rather competitive system in which mobility often hinged upon the impartial dictates of the market to a highly structured, rule-and-certificated system in which mobility often rests upon educational achievement and the ability to please one's superiors. When aligned with concentration and consequent disparities in economic power, this condition fosters anxiety and dependency. In this context, one may move upward objectively, but the subjective consequences in terms of

[23]Ibid., pp. 439–441.
[24]Ibid., p. 420.

autonomy, self-realization, and influence upon the organization's policies remain much the same. The grinding reality persists: regardless of an individual's functional skill and achievement, control of the organization, its objectives, and its rewards remain largely in the hands of its hierarchical elite.

Many qualitative issues arise. Did the occupational categories mean in 1900, 1928, and even 1950 what they mean today? What kinds of changes have occurred in the relative status and prestige of jobs during the past half-century? Are the payoffs in income, satisfaction, and independence of a contemporary "professional" or a "skilled worker" really comparable with those of his counterparts in 1900? What about the vast number of farm proprietors who have turned to unskilled and skilled work in industry? While their income may be higher, what is their relative condition with regard to independence and morale? It is impressive, as noted, that students of mobility tend to undervalue farm proprietorship, while accepting movement from unskilled or skilled work into business proprietorship as a valid index of upward mobility.

We saw earlier, too, that a great deal of mock mobility has been achieved by upgrading the titles of socially devalued jobs. Janitors become custodians; reporters become journalists; clerks become administrators; secretaries become executive assistants; salesmen become sales executives; the large banks create innumerable vice-presidencies. Do these psychic emoluments skew the statistics on mobility compiled by the Census Bureau and the National Opinion Research Center? When American success values mean that the very admission of nonmobility is a self-indictment, how much confidence can be placed in the answers of individuals about their own or their father's occupational status? We know that respondents often exaggerate their education, knowledge, and income. Perhaps most important, when higher education has become so critical a factor in mobility, we must certainly ask how equal educational chances are in our society. Although great strides have been taken since World War II, the answer is not entirely reassuring.

Not only can it be shown that educational opportunity is unequal, but difficulties of entry and survival in the entrepreneurial field provide less opportunity for economic independence and for real gains in personal autonomy as contrasted with the built-in dependency of most bureaucratic work roles. We have seen that huge capital requirements restrict entry in industry, while high failure rates (combined with a chronic capital shortage) make small business a precarious venture. Meanwhile, manual workers who rise may find that white-collar status has been downgraded as mechanization reduces the skill demands of their jobs, and as the unionized blue-collar workers equal and may surpass them in pay and fringe benefits. Nor have the professions remained immune to organizational demands. Increasingly, the conditions of professional work are bureaucratically determined. As noted earlier, there is now a thriving union movement among universities and colleges, which supports some research that shows a proletarianization of white-collar workers. However symbolic of the contemporary drift toward egalitarianism, the union ethos brings in train the crystallization of bureaucratic norms and values. In sum, modern technology and the structural characteristics of organization have so modified the conditions of work and the work place that we cannot assume any nice comparability between occupations and mobility in the past with that of today.

Turning to the indifferents' accommodation to the bureaucratic situation, we find that they are typically of working-class or lower-middle-class origin. This implies a distinctive style of early socialization.[25] Not only will they rarely have been inculcated with the desire to excel, but class status and limited education have not usually prepared them for the graceful acceptance of authority which has become so critical for organizational mobility. Whereas middle-class child training has emphasized self-direction, respect for authority, and the muffling of aggression, lower-class socialization has stressed conformity and been rather more tolerant of fighting, truancy, haphazard toilet training, and the like.

Some of these differences are apparently narrowing, but only in selected areas. Physical punishment is probably no longer used more frequently by working-class parents.[26] Since World War II middle-class parents have become more permissive regarding aggression, thumbsucking, toilet mistakes, and sex play. On the whole, however, it seems that social class and attending differences in occupational values and experience are transmitted to children. As one summary of research concludes, "By and large, the middle-class mother expects more of her child than her working-class counterpart."[27] Middle-class

---

[25]"There is a remarkable parallel between the occupational conditions characteristic of each social class and the values espoused for their children by parents of that social class," Melvin L. Kohn, *Class and Conformity* (Homewood, Ill.: Dorsey, 1969), p. ix. Also Kohn and Carmi Schooler, "Occupational Experience and Psychological Functioning," *American Sociological Review*, Vol. 38, pp. 97–118; James D. Wright and Sonia Wright, "Social Class and Parental Values for Children," *ibid.*, pp. 527–537; and Kohn, "Comments on Wright and Wright," *ibid.*, pp. 538–548.

[26]Howard S. Erlanger, "Social Class and Corporal Punishment in Children: A Reassessment," *American Sociological Review*, Vol. 39, pp. 65–85.

[27]Urie Bronfenbrenner, "Socialization and Social Class Through Time and Space," in Eleanor E. Maccoby et al., eds., *Readings in Social Psychology* (New York: Holt, Rinehart & Winston, 1958), pp. 400–405, 424. Also, Arthur Davis and Robert J. Havighurst, "Social Class and Color Differences in Child Rearing," *American Sociological*

children, it seems, are put under more pressure to accept responsibility, to take care of themselves earlier, and to do better and go farther in school. There seems little reason to change substantially the following generalizations, set down two decades ago: "Middle-class socialization, in comparison with working-class socialization, is conscious, rational, deliberate and demanding. Relatively little is left to chance and 'just-growing.' Middle-class parents are likely to be concerned and anxious about their children's achievement of age-graded 'norms,' and this anxiety is likely to be communicated to the child. They are more geared to a timetable, to the future as well as the present. The child is constantly aware of what his parents want him to *be* and to *become*. He learns early to take the long view and become habituated to the self-discipline and effort necessary to meeting parental expectations."[28]

Such findings are directly related to accommodation in the bureaucratic situation, with its authority-structured context and attending behavioral demands. The indifferent type seems especially disadvantaged. The facile assumption of a "professional mask," the stifling of anxiety, resentment, and irritation, the personal discipline required when seniority and dependence upon the man above are common criteria for mobility and when long service in a single organization has become typical, the ability to play a variety of roles—such qualities are not characteristic of the typical working-class indifferent.

When it occurs, moreover, upward-mobility is often bought at great cost. W. N. Christensen and L. E. Hickle, Jr., of Cornell University Medical School found that executives of working-class origin experience a great deal more psychosomatic illness than their middle-class colleagues. One hundred and thirty-nine executives on the lower rungs of big corporations, who differed with respect to education (fifty-five were college graduates, eighty-four high school only), were studied over a three-year period. The high-school graduates had twice the number of illnesses and ten times the risk of death. Many more of them showed signs of premature cardiovascular disease.

Review, Vol. 11, pp. 698–710; Kurt B. Maye, *Class and Society* (New York: Random House, 1955); Harold W. Pfautz, "The Current Literature on Social Stratification," *American Journal of Sociology*, Vol. 48, pp. 397–418.

[28] Albert K. Cohen, *Delinquent Boys* (Glencoe, Ill.: Free Press, 1955), p. 98. In a study of New Haven, August B. Hollingshead and Fredrick C. Redlich found significant class differences, including different expectations as to educational achievement and, among Class 11 (upper-middle class) families, an expressed need "for a 'good education' for their children . . . by parents who attribute their success to education or who believe their mobility strivings are limited by the wrong kind or amount of education; . . . many of these parents project their strivings for higher status upon their children." Hollingshead and Redlich, *Social Class and Mental Illness* (New York: Wiley, 1958), p. 89.

Neither heredity nor personal habits were significant. Both groups were of white, northern-European stock. The crucial factor was *stress,* which was related in turn to the different class backgrounds of the men. University graduates were from "substantial middle-class families" and assumed their executive roles easily. This accommodation is nicely consonant with research by the psychiatrist Robert Coles on overprivileged children who early on develop a "norm of entitlement," fostered by the preferential treatment they received from teachers, clerks, policemen, and others.[29] On the other hand, the high-school graduates were sons and daughters of immigrant families with lower incomes. They married earlier, had more domestic problems, and did more "do-it-yourself" jobs at home. The researchers concluded: "Their relative ill health might well be regarded as the price they pay for getting ahead in the world."

The discrete socialization patterns of middle- and lower-class families have other different utilities in the bureaucratic situation. Miller and Swanson found that middle- and working-class youth from bureaucratic families differed significantly in their use of defenses against conflict. Working class boys *denied* their failures,whereas middle-class boys typically used repression and self-criticism as defenses. Repression is more functional because "this mechanism facilitates socially adjustive behavior."[30] Denial tends to be dysfunctional because it permits the individual to distort experience to the extent where failure may even be turned into success. The working-class youths' tendency toward denial inhibits their ability to make the kinds of *realistic self-appraisals* required to meet bureaucratic claims for discipline, rationality, and adaptability. By the time they become aware of such handicaps, it is often too late to change deep-seated security operations.

Upward-mobiles, on the other hand, will usually be of middle- or upper-class origin. They may be neurotically ambitious, because children of these strata are subject to intense pressure to succeed. More amenable to group norms, they accept prevailing values of success and prestige. They want to rise, and their mobility expectations are high. As we have seen, studies of mobility show that such expectations have a firm basis in reality. It is perhaps fortunate that the size and diversity of modern organizations can accommodate several levels of expectation.

The indifferents' rejection of status and prestige values often insures a felicitous accommodation. Since job satisfaction is a product of

---

[29]Robert Coles, *Children of Crisis* (Boston: Little, Brown, 1978).

[30]Donald R. Miller and Guy E. Swanson, *Inner Conflict and Defense* (New York: Holt, Rinehart & Winston, 1960), p. 232.

the relation between aspirations and achievement, they are often the most satisfied of organization people.[31] Their aspirations are based on a realistic appraisal of existing opportunities. They reject the status anxiety, the success striving, the self-discipline, and the conformity demanded of self and family that confront the upward-mobile. "I [37-year-old steelworker] got chewed out by my foreman once. He said, 'Mike, you're a good worker but you have a bad attitude.' My attitude is that I don't get excited about my job. I do my work but I don't say whoopee-doo. The day I get excited about my work is the day I go to a head shrinker. How are you gonna get excited about pullin' steel? How are you gonna get excited when you're tired and want to sit down?"[32]

In this sense, indifferents are the most "normal" of individuals. Emancipated from the puritan heritage that honors work and accumulation, escaping the commitments of the "true believer" and the anxiety of the neurotic striver, they receive big dividends in privacy, tranquillity, and self-realization through their *extravocational* orientation. To some extent they deflect bureaucratic claims by limiting their aspirations and transferring them elsewhere. Their off-the-job activities rarely reinforce their occupational role. Unlike the upward-mobile, whose social life is often harnessed to career claims, they separate their work experience from a more meaningful personal area. Work becomes a tool with which they buy satisfactions totally unrelated to work. They may regard their paid vacation as the most satisfying thing about their jobs. Whereas 45 percent of nonmanual employees (professionals, business executives, and upper-white-collar individuals) report an "unqualified preference for work," only 27 percent of active union members share this preference. While 54 percent of the latter have "an unqualified preference for leisure," only 27 percent of the nonmanuals do.[33]

Even at professional and managerial levels, technological and organizational control have made work somewhat more like factory production. Thus indifference is becoming a more likely pattern of accommodation for white- as well as for blue-collar workers. Disenchantment with work that has become routinized, yet demands manipulation in the "personality market," is visible in both groups. This condition has important qualitative implications for mobility as

[31] For a careful study of the relationship between selected "work values" and job satisfaction, see Arne Kalleberg, "Work Values and Job Rewards," *American Sociological Review*, Vol. 42, pp. 124–143.

[32] Terkel, *Working* (New York: Avon Books, 1975), p. 2.

[33] Seymour M. Lipset and Joel Gordon, "Mobility and Trade Union Membership," in Bendix and Lipset, eds., *Class, Status and Power* (Glencoe, Ill.: Free Press, 1953), pp. 495-496.

white-collar people who have risen from "manual" families do not find their rise paying off in the expected independence and occupational challenge. Even in such highly skilled work as university teaching, the feeling of being "just a number" may exist, particularly in the huge state universities. As C. Wright Mills says: "If white-collar people are not free to control their working actions, they, in time, habitually submit to the order of others and, insofar as they try to act freely, do so in other spheres. . . . If there is a split between their work and play, and their work and culture, they admit that split as a commonsense fact of existence. If their way of earning a living does not infuse their mode of living, they try to build their real life outside their work."[34]

This separation of work from "personal" life underlies the indifferents' perception of the bureaucratic situation. Aware of their essentially commercial nexus with the organization, they resist the image of themselves as commodities. Although they must accept the economic bargain, selling their skills and energy for forty hours a week, the remaining time is jealously guarded as their own. Since they are relatively immune to the organization's values, loyalty is not included in the bargain. In some cases, indifference approaches hostility as noninvolvement becomes a form of retaliation for their instrumental role. In mass-production industries, retaliation may take such forms as deprecating the product ("If people only knew how these things were made, they would never buy them"). The product may be regarded as a symbol of "profits," which appear immoral when the "real producers" work for wages.

Attitudes toward authority also affect involvement. Those who fear or hate authority find identification difficult; the sharp differentiation of authority in organizations aggravates this condition. As we have seen, such feelings reflect one's experiences with authority from infancy onward. Here again, selective perception is at work, compelling some individuals to experience superiors as threatening, thereby reinforcing their fear of authority. However, this kind of anxiety seems rarely characteristic of upward-mobiles or of indifferents. The former regard their superiors as friendly models; their particular brand of anxiety is fear of failure. The latter, who neither expect nor want anything from the organization, are immune to its discipline.

This conception of indifference conflicts with the "human-relations" view which defines organizations as "cooperative systems" composed of many intimate work groups which meet individual needs for identification. While small groups undoubtedly meet such needs, it seems equally clear that their members do not necessarily identify

---

[34]Mills, *White Collar.* pp. 227–228.

with the larger organization. With rare exceptions, the influence of any given individual on this level is inconsequential, and he knows it. As the Hawthorne studies found, the small group often plays a *protective* role, shielding its members from real or imaginary threats of management.[35] Small-group relations are often compensatory and negative; they may even underscore the employee's estrangement from the larger organization. A study of the automobile industry concludes: "When the worker discussed his relations with other workers and reported social interaction, such as joking, gossiping, or general conversation, he mentioned them chiefly as a fortunate *counterbalance and compensation* for the disliked features of his job."[36]

Indifferents recapture their identities by withdrawing; by withholding part of themselves, they experience a certain autonomy. Like the consumer who refuses to patronize chain stores because of small-business values, they take a stand, however quixotic. Withdrawal is encouraged by the instrumental role of the worker, whose assignment, level of output, status, and income are largely determined by technical demands, by the *work process*. Supervisory jobs, on the other hand, tend to encourage identification because the work is more responsible and less stereotyped, permitting greater freedom of action. Nevertheless, even the attitudes of those who do identify with the organization are as often competitive as they are cooperative. The upward-mobiles' desire for personal success sometimes outweighs the claims of group acceptance.

Indifference and withdrawal are also encouraged by the corrosion of friendship in bureaucratic society. As we have seen, organizational roles require the manufacture of affection, the ready smile, the "human-relations" approach—often animated by a manipulative ethic. Yet, when everyone suspects that everyone is insincere much of the time, disenchantment encourages the resort to the "professional mask" and the separation of work from one's "personal" life. One's "real" self is revealed only to family and intimate friends. Emotional commitments at work that may expose one to frustration or to exploitation are avoided. This accommodation is encouraged by the tendency to carry both status and business interests into off-the-job social relations. In the upward-mobile's one-track world, this mode is unquestioned; but the indifferent's eight-to-five orientation inhibits similar behavior.

Speaking very generally, the ubiquity of indifference seems to be associated with the routinization of work and with the limits on eco-

---

[35] Fred J. Roethlisberger and William J. Dickson, *Management and the Worker* (Cambridge: Harvard University Press, 1941).

[36] Charles R. Walker and Robert H. Guest, *The Man on the Assembly Line* (Cambridge: Harvard University Press, 1952), p. 142. Italics added.

nomic independence in an employee society. Over time, smaller opportunities probably make for smaller expectations. If size breeds oligarchy and co-optation, which then outline the conditions of personal mobility, the very structure of complex organizations encourages indifference. Blocked in traditional avenues requiring traditional skills, the individual seeks other channels of self-expression. Oligarchic leadership patterns, the restructuring of competition, and the bewildering complexity of decision making in organizations reduce the motivation and the chance for involvement, deflecting energies into off-work channels.

Reduced opportunities for real participation, as distinguished from the mock participation seen, for example, in stock-holders' meetings, underlie the indifferent reaction. As Clarence B. Randall insists: "We entice him [the stock-holder] to the annual meeting with every blandishment at our command . . . but when it comes to the exercise of the prerogative of ownership, we do not vouchsafe him the opportunity of making even one little cross on a piece of paper once a year in token recognition of the fact that we work for him."[37]

In view of mass education and the efficiency of the mass media, one might have assumed that participation would have increased, but the facts suggest otherwise. Voting participation, for example, ranges from about 25 percent in local contests to something just over 50 percent in recent presidential elections. As V. O. Key has shown, throughout the South a constellation of factors including tradition, class, race, and poverty has traditionally made politics a highly minoritarian craft. From 1920 to 1946, only in North Carolina and Louisiana did the average proportions of all citizens over twenty-one voting in primaries to nominate senators and governors exceed 30 percent.[38] (Republican and third-party inroads have changed this situation somewhat; for example, whereas in 1950 only 5 percent of Southern Congressmen were Republican, by 1972 the proportion had increased to 31 percent.[39]) By 1973, following Vietnam and Watergate, even children who a decade earlier had identified political authority figures in terms of unrestrained approval were expressing negative reactions: "Politicians are seen as more selfish, less intelligent, more dishonest, and less likely to keep their promises."[40]

[37]Clarence B. Randall, "The Myths of Communication," *Dun's Review,* Vol. 75, p. 39.

[38]Vladimar O. Key, *Southern Politics* (New York: Alfred A. Knopf, 1949), pp. 504–505.

[39]Everett Carll Ladd, Jr. and Charles D. Hadley, *Transformations of the American Party System* (New York: Norton, 1975), p. 146.

[40]F. Christopher Arterton, "Impact of Watergate on Children's Attitudes Toward Authority," *Political Science Quarterly,* Vol. 89, p. 274.

It seems clear that America is less a nation of "joiners" than is generally assumed, and, indeed, that withdrawal from political and community affairs is common.[41] Studies of group membership in New York City show that 60 percent of working-class and 53 percent of white-collar workers do not belong to even a *single* organization;[42] in Erie County, Ohio, less than fifty percent of the population belong to voluntary groups;[43] and in their study of a small New England town of 17,000, Warner and Lunt found that only 41 percent belonged.[44] In 1962, H. H. Hyman and C. R. Wright found similarly that 57 percent of American adults belonged to no organizations, while only 4 percent were members of four-or-more organizations, not including unions.[45]

Indifference may reflect a deeper value change in which traditional success aspirations collide with the demand for economic security and a maturer view of work. For example, the preference of some university graduates for careers in big, risk-free corporations rather than entrepreneurship may signal a tacit redirection of values based in part upon an awareness of economic realities. Such changes are apparent in the emerging themes of the mass media. As C. Wright Mills observes, a "literature of resignation . . . fits in with all those institutional changes involving the goal of security."[46] As the periphery of individual choice contracts, traditional success models of wealth and power are challenged by themes of spiritual and emotional maturity.

The new emphasis is also suggested by the competition over employee benefit programs in which private enterprise has now overcome government's historic advantage. Workers' preoccupation with security and fringe benefits suggests a realistic appraisal of bureaucratic conditions of work. The pervasiveness of this ethos is indicated by the expanding movement toward unionization in universities. The results are similar: the acceptance of an employee society and the weakening of traditional success images.

[41]Cf. Robert S. Gilmour and Robert B. Lamb, *Political Alienation in Contemporary America* (New York: St. Martin's Press, 1975), pp. 103–107; Bernard Barber, "Participation and Mass Apathy in Associations," in Alvin W. Gouldner, *Studies in Leadership* (New York: Harper & Row, 1950); Joan Foskett, "Social Structure and Social Participation," *American Sociological Review*, Vol. 20, pp. 431–438.

[42]Moira Komarovsky, "Voluntary Associations of Urban Dwellers," *American Sociological Review*, Vol. 11, pp. 686–698.

[43]Paul Lazarsfeld, Bernard Berelson, and Hazel Gaudet, *The People's Choice* (New York: Columbia University Press, 1944), p. 145.

[44]W. Lloyd Warner and Paul S. Lunt, *The Social Life of a Modern Community* (New Haven: Yale University Press, 1941).

[45]Herbert H. Hyman and Charles R. Wright, "Trends in Voluntary Association Membership of American Adults," *American Sociological Review*, Vol. 36, p. 205.

[46]Mills, *White Collar*, p. 285.

Noninvolvement as a typical pattern of accommodation is encouraged by size itself. A survey of some 100,000 workers in the Sears Roebuck empire found that "mere size is unquestionably one of the most important factors in determining the quality of employee relationships; the smaller the unit the higher the morale and vice versa."[47] In the factory both the character of the work and the process-determined interpersonal relations are often unsatisfying. "As a result of overspecialization a very large number of employees in American industry today have been deprived of the sense of performing interesting, significant work." Similarly: "Where jobs are broken down too finely we are more likely to have both low output and low morale."[48] Other studies show a similar relation between size and output,[49] absenteeism (morale),[50] and motivation.[51] In each case the result is negative: absenteeism increases while output and incentive tend to decline.

Indifferents thus tend to find their real satisfactions in extravocational activities. While the upward-mobile "carries his job home with him," indifferents separate their work from their "personal" experiences, and work is often repressed as something unpleasant. The pay check is what counts. "Studies agree beyond doubt that persons at the lower end of the socio-economic scale are more likely . . . to emphasize the *economic* aspects of work, whereas those at the upper end more typically stress the *satisfaction* they find in work itself."[52] Indifferents, then, are among the large number of employees who reject advancement because of the added responsibility it entails. They prefer to be left alone; instead of advancement they desire security.

The indifferents' interpersonal relations at work are generally satisfactory. Since there is little danger that they will become either a "speed king" or a "chiseler," they are not perceived as threatening by their colleagues. Since neither the organization's rewards nor its sanctions are very compelling, the attitudes of indifferents toward authority are generally uncomplicated. Their lack of ambition insures a large measure of psychic independence. Unlike upward-mobiles who

[47]James C. Worthy, "Organizational Structure and Employee Morale," *American Sociological Review*, Vol. 15, p. 173.

[48]Ibid., pp. 174–175.

[49]R. Marriott, "Size of Working Group and Output," *Occupational Psychology*, Vol. 23, pp. 47–57.

[50]D. Hewitt and J. Parfit, "A Note on Working Morale and Size of Group," *Occupational Psychology*, Vol. 27, pp. 38–42.

[51]H. Campbell, "Group Incentive Pay Schemes," *Occupational Psychology*, Vol. 26, pp. 15–21.

[52]Elizabeth L. Lyman, "Occupational Differences in the Value Attached to Work," *American Journal of Sociology*, Vol. 61, p. 138.

strain to be "on top" in every situation, or the "ambivalents" who suffer from unrealistic claims and comparisons of themselves and their jobs with idealized alternatives, indifferents conclude that people, jobs, and organizations are not much different. They adjust themselves accordingly.

While the personal qualities that permit indifferents to accommodate without undue strain vary individually, we can assume that some constant values are at work. Clearly, they are not driven by exceptional needs for power and success, since these would require intense involvement if they were to be achieved through the organization. Feeling no compulsion to control their work environment, they do not see the work situation as an instrument for manipulation. Since they are quite literally not going anywhere, they escape the status pressure and the manipulation of self and others often required for organizational success. The bureaucratic struggle may be observed with detachment. The capacity to be aware of majority values, to understand their fascination for others, yet to escape becoming personally involved is often a major item in their personalities.

But we must not give them too much credit for maturity since their accommodation may rest upon a naïve unawareness of the ways and rewards of power. It may simply reflect class and family backgrounds that failed to include great expectations among their motivating claims. If so, another rationalization becomes available. In our society where the mobility claims of parents are often transferred to children, indifferents can similarly displace their ambitions. This alternative undoubtedly provides a necessary cathartic, because idealized career hopes tend to result in a great deal of personal anxiety and frustration.

We can expect, as a result, that the indifferent's career expectations are realistic. Surveys of experienced workers suggest that success claims are generally revised downward in recognition of bureaucratic and personal constrictions. A confluence of class and structural factors encourages this result. In mass production industries, technology and organization tend to compress both income range and promotional opportunities. As Walker and Guest found, "The introduction of conveyors and machine hand tools have narrowed the wage distance between the day laborer's job and that of the skilled craftsman . . . the individual work operations have either been so mechanized or so fractionalized . . . that craft skills have been virtually eliminated. One result of this technological development has been wage standardization."[53]

[53]Walker and Guest, *The Man on the Assembly Line*, p. 153.

Moreover, promotional opportunities are limited. As Quinn and Shepard found, one-third of various types of workers (by far the largest single proportion) said they could not be promoted because there were no positions available.[54] In an automobile plant with 6,000 workers Chinoy found "only ten or twelve openings" occuring each year.[55] Guest found only one foreman's job opening each year for 120 automobile workers.[56] They conclude that such conditions result in a wholesale lowering of aspirations. Even within big unions, organized to offset the loss of power and of skill pride attending automation, the ordinary worker becomes part of a mass constituency providing numerical support and legitimation for decisions made by others.

Meanwhile, the sharp rise in university attendance[57] may exaggerate the extent to which increased mobility follows increased education. For not only is it true that as educational levels have risen, the educational requirements for many jobs have also risen; but it is not realized (especially by those who have "worked their way through" and thus assume that anyone can do the same) that *social barriers* as well as economic ones prevent many talented youngsters from developing their abilities. The President's Committee on Education Beyond High School found, in 1956, that only half of the most intelligent high-school graduates entered college. It seems that the primary factor differentiating college from noncollege youth is often class, not intelligence.[58] Lower-middle- and working-class children who aspire to university training often have neither the support nor the background of family expectation that insure the necessary encouragement. Indeed, both their parents and their social peers may actively oppose what they regard as presumptuous aspirations. As James S. Coleman's extensive research suggests, family environment is probably the most critical factor in academic achievement.[59]

Although the number of college graduates in the United States rose from 15,000 in 1890 to 900,000 in 1975, and although federal educational grants for veterans after World War II and Vietnam were a great step forward, such gains do not necessarily result in a comparable degree of increased mobility. This is partly because graduates

[54]*The 1972–73 Quality of Employment Survey*, p. 210.

[55]Eli Chinoy, *Automobile Workers and the American Dream* (New York: Random House, 1955), p. 44.

[56]Robert H. Guest, "Work Careers and Aspirations of Automobile Workers," *American Sociological Review*, Vol. 19, p. 157.

[57]See Martin Trow, "The Expansion and Transformation of Higher Education," *International Review of Education*, Vol. 18.

[58]Jencks, *Inequality*, pp. 19–23, 37–41, 138–141.

[59]James S. Coleman et al., *Equality of Educational Opportunity* (Washington, D.C.: Dept. of Health, Education, and Welfare, 1966).

from families that already enjoy relatively high status are highly over-represented. Basing his conclusion on the best evidence available, the President of the *American Sociological Association* (1971) could say: "To the extent that our data are representative they furnish solid documentation for the claim that there is substantially reduced opportunity for higher education in America for those of lower socioeconomic origins and for women, and that this inequality cannot be explained by differences in academic ability."[60] Since social mobility today often requires extended university training, it can be seen that unequal educational chances tend to crystallize social and occupational statuses.

This conclusion is reinforced by evidence that decisive mobility now occurs mainly among individuals who move from an employee status to one of self-employment. "The greatest social mobility occurs in the form of shifts into 'own business,' and shifts into the white-collar occupation and sales rank next. These are the occupations of most of those who manage to pass from manual to nonmanual work."[61] Although it is clear from the shocking rate of business failures (almost one thousand per month in 1975) that such shifts are often temporary, they provide a basis for loyalty to the entrepreneurial ethos. "To run a business of one's own is still a much-cherished ideal. But with the growth of large-scale organizations in all parts of American society it has lost some of its meaning, although its ideological appeal has not necessarily been weakened thereby. Many still cherish it, though their own careers show little evidence that 'private enterprise' has had much significance for them personally."[62]

The social framework for such conclusions is explicit in the following summary from a study of worker attitudes in local unions.

The steady rise in the size of the business unit, the larger amount of capital required, and the high proportion of failures among small business enterprises have made it increasingly difficult and hazardous for a wage earner to attempt to enter many lines of business. Acceptance of relatively permanent wage-earning status is apt to be accompanied by a greater acceptance of the need for group action to protect and advance one's interests in the employment relationship. Workers tend to settle early in life for the security of a

---

[60]William H. Sewell, "Inequality of Opportunity for Higher Education," *American Sociological Review*, Vol. 36, p. 797. See also Blau and Duncan, *The American Occupational Structure*, who conclude that the number of years of education attained by a child depends upon the social class status of his father as much today as it did a half-century ago.

[61]Lipset and Gordon, "Mobility and Trade Union Membership," p. 457.

[62]Ibid., p. 458.

steady job, depending upon their mounting seniority to shield them against the hazards of the layoff. The aspirations of factory workers are scaled down to industrial realities; for everyone who dreams of a business of his own, there are many who hope to move up to a better-paying job at a somewhat higher level of skill or responsibility or at most a foreman's position. [Moreover], most of those who dream of a business of their own . . . project their hopes for upward social mobility upon their children, hoping that an education superior to their own will open the doors to professional status, to managerial positions, or at least to white-collar employment.[63]

Although workers want to be independent and retain hopes of owning their own business, it is clear that they often accept the principle behind existing patterns of control in industrial society.[64] Some indicate that if *they* were running *their* own business, they would not want workers telling them what to do. Apparently, workers can accept the logic of big organization but at the same time reject the instrumental position they play in it. Shut out from meaningful participation, yet unable to break away, indifferents become resigned, using their jobs as a means to security and off-work enjoyment where frustrated status claims can be bought in the wish-fulfilling world of entertainment and consumption. "For the great majority of automobile workers, the only meaning of the job is the pay check, not in anything connected with the work or the product."[65]

Contrary to the *embourgeoisement* thesis that blue-collar workers are becoming middle class, it seems that they are often isolated from white-collar clericals and managers.[66] Their own lack of higher education often makes it diffcult for them to socialize their children in ways that prepare them for success in managerial and professional settings. The critical factor in this equation may be their position in the production system.[67]

[63]Joel Seidman et al., *The Worker Views His Union* (Chicago: University of Chicago Press, 1958), p. 257.

[64]For research indicating that many blue-collar workers retain faith in the American ideology of social mobility through hard work, often resulting in extreme antagonism against protesting students and special concessions to blacks, see H. Edward Ransford, "Blue Collar Anger: Reactions to Student and Black Protest," *American Sociological Review*, Vol. 37, pp. 333–346.

[65]Walker and Guest, *The Man on the Assembly Line*, p. 157.

[66]Recent findings, however, suggest that a proletarianization of *white-collar* workers is occurring, bringing them closer to manual workers than to middle-class workers. Sociometric analysis supports the same finding. Cf. Reece Vanneman, "The Occupational Composition of American Classes: Results from Cluster Analysis," *American Journal of Sociology*, Vol. 82, p. 783.

[67]Graham Mackenzie, *The Aristocracy of Labor* (London: Cambridge University Press, 1973), pp. 4–7, 162–175.

As C. Wright Mills has shown, the structural influences that strain blue-collar identification are also at work among white-collar workers. Their disenchantment is aggravated by higher mobility claims nourished by education and the precious white-collar self-image. Despite some equalization of white- and blue-collar status and income, this idealized image persists, preserved by youth and by the preferential status that our society gives to those who work with their heads instead of their hands.

Industrial sociologists have turned blue-collar workers inside out, but we know less about white-collar attitudes toward work and self. Analysis has been made difficult by the number and diversity of groups included under the white-collar rubric. This is a highly fluid and variable class ranging from dependent, salaried professionals to precarious sales and clerical people. As Mills says:

> The three largest groups of the white-collar spectrum are office workers (forty percent), school teachers (twenty-five percent), and salespeople (twenty-five percent). The remaining ten per cent is made up of managers. . . . [These people range from] almost the top to almost the bottom of modern society. [They are not a horizontal layer within society, but] a new pyramid within the old pyramid [of society]. Their characteristic skills involve the handling of paper and money and people. They are expert in dealing with people transiently and impersonally; they are masters of the commercial, professional, and technical relationships. . . . They live off the social machineries that organize and coordinate the people who make things. . . . The organizational reason for the expansion of the white-collar occupations is the rise of big business and big government, and the consequent trend of modern social structure, the steady growth of bureaucracy. In every branch of the economy, as firms merge and corporations become dominant, free entrepreneurs become employees, and the calculations of accountant, stastistician, bookkeeper, and clerk . . . replace the free "movement of prices" as the coordinating agent of the economic system.[68]

This class works mainly in big organizations. And its members are, in a sense, exceptionally vulnerable to its structural conditions because, as we have seen, their aspirations have been higher than those of blue-collar workers. Moreover, at the higher levels they have enjoyed considerable autonomy in their work place. The narrowing of job alternatives and the fusing of the differences in pay and status between themselves and unionized workers have brought a special

[68]Mills, *White Collar*, pp. 64–65, 68–69.

disenchantment. Since it is statistically impossible for the vast majority of them to cash in their success claims, theirs is an indifference of frustration, rather than of resignation as in the blue-collar class. As Mills concludes:

> The chance to rise has been affected by the shape-up of white-collar jobs. Their concentration into larger units and their specialization have made for many blind alleys, lessened the opportunity to learn about "other departments," or the business as a whole. The rationalization of white-collar work means that as the number of replaceable positions expands more than the number of higher positions, the chances of climbing decrease. Also, as higher positions become more technical, they are often more likely to be filled by people from outside the hierarchy. So the ideology of promotion—the expectation of a step-by-step ascent—no longer seems a sure thing.[69]

At the same time, and despite the contrary evidence cited earlier, it seems that most white-collar people continue to receive considerable psychic income from their favored prestige position as compared with industrial workers. Indeed, we may assume that as the indexes that set them off are reduced by unionization and decreased skill demands, prestige becomes more valued. We know that status needs can be met in many ways, including identification with a powerful organization. The very opportunity to wear a white collar is rewarding and provides an opportunity for borrowing the prestige and authority of superiors in the hierarchy. Equally important, white-collar individuals have had significantly more education than either businessmen or industrial workers. As Mills found, they had an average school achievement of twelve years, compared with only eight years for the other two groups.[70] Bureaucratic work conditions are undermining this prestige advantage, however, suggesting that indifference and a turn toward off-work satisfactions may become more common among all levels of the white-collar class.

What does the evidence show about changing work attitudes in the white-collar world? So far, our problem has been easy, since research shows clearly that blue-collar workers are often alienated from their work and their work place. While some evidence suggests that about 75 percent of all types of workers will answer "Yes" to the question, "Are you satisfied with your job?", this seems unconvincing. The question as stated is just too simple. Moreover, there are both psychological and social pressures against a negative answer. "There

[69]Ibid., pp. 274–275.
[70]Ibid., p. 246.

is a certain naïveté in expecting frank and simple answers to job-satis-faction questions in a society where work is so important a part of one's self that to demean one's job is to question one's very competence as a person."[71] Indeed, as we have seen, the whole trend in bureaucratic work is to upgrade ordinary jobs by verbal magic, to compensate for the erosion of skill demands and satisfaction in work with status benefits.

A more sophisticated index of job satisfaction is one which asks workers whether they would continue in the same kind of work if they inherited enough money to live comfortably without working:[72]

Occupational Group	Affirmative Replies (percent)
Professionals	68
Sales	59
Managers	55
Skilled manuals	40
Service	33
Semi-skilled operatives	32
Unskilled	16

Two points seem especially salient here. Professionals who rank at the top typically work in the least bureaucratized settings. Even if their work place is highly structured, the less routinized nature of their work and the extended education or training required to perform it give them more control over their work role. Also, the scale is nicely articulated with occupational prestige rankings. Such rankings are based upon the amount of education required and the income gained from the work. Both criteria seem to be central in de-termining job satisfaction. Research on assembly line workers indi-cates the weight of the first index: individuals sometimes put down their work role, saying in effect, "Anybody can learn this job in six weeks."

The indifferent's accommodation to work in a bureaucratic setting may involve alienation. Unfortunately, the term is often defined in different ways in research.[73] A typical connotation is the sense of powerlessness. At other times, the term is used to mean a rejection of the political "rules of the game" as being illegitimate or, more broadly,

[71] Robert Blauner, "Work Satisfaction and Industrial Trends in Modern Society," in Walter Galeson and Seymour M. Lipset, eds., *Labor and Trade Unionism: An Interdisci-plinary Reader* (New York: Wiley, 1960), p. 355. This selection is a survey of research on job satisfaction in both blue- and white-collar worlds.

[72] Nancy C. Morse and Robert S. Weiss, "The Function and Meaning of Work and the Job," *American Sociological Review*, Vol. 20, p. 197.

[73] For attempts to clarify the concept, see Melvin Seeman, "On the Meaning of Aliena-tion," *American Sociological Review*, Vol. 24, pp. 783–791 and Ada W. Finifter, "Dimen-sions of Political Alienation," *American Political Science Review*, Vol. 44, p. 389–410.

in Durkheim's conception of *anomie*, a rejection of social norms generally. Again, in the Marxian sense, the term may mean a generalized estrangement of workers from their work and a feeling of isolation based upon their relationships to the instruments of production. Sometimes the term is applied to the mode of alienation as contrasted with the institutional target it is directed against.

The table presented above is typical in that it fails to differentiate the occupational contexts in which job satisfaction was measured. Research on alienation in various occupational settings has overcome at least part of this problem. Robert Blauner, for example, controlled for technology and found that assembly-line workers ranked highest on "alienation," defined rather broadly as a lack of control of immediate work processes, a feeling of *meaninglessness* because of specialization and the inability of the worker to see the end product of his work, *normlessness* as far as the larger society is concerned, and *self-estrangement* in the sense that work is no longer perceived as fulfilling in itself, but is instead merely a means to some remote end.[74] Using a variety of industries, Blauner found a linear rise in alienation as technology advanced from craft to machine-tending to assembly line through to continuous process (highly automated) work. The finding suggests again that the extent of control retained by the worker is a critical factor in accommodation, since craft types of work are obviously more individualized than assemblyline technologies.

A shortcoming of the research, however, was that everyone working in the same factory was grouped together, despite the fact that different technologies existed to carry out the various stages of production. This limitation was confronted by a study of alienation that attempted to differentiate among occupational types and between alienation directed toward one's organization and toward the larger society.[75] Contrary to earlier studies, it was found that alienation, defined as perceived powerlessness, was not related at either organizational or societal level to occupational type, even within companies.[76] Apparently other factors such as earlier socialization or organizational size are more important than occupational type in determining worker alienation.[77] The study also found that levels of alienation were the same at both the organizational and societal levels. Contrary to the Marxian thesis that alienation from work occurs first and is then projected upon the larger society, the results reinforce our

[74]Robert Blauner, *Alienation and Freedom* (Chicago: University of Chicago Press, 1964), pp. 15–31.

[75]David E. Payne, "Alienation: an Organizational-Societal Comparison," *Social Forces,* Vol. 53, pp. 274–282.

[76]Ibid., p. 281.

[77]Ibid.

thesis that preorganizational socialization plays a significant role in accommodation in the work place.

In white-collar jobs, satisfaction is probably encouraged by higher educational levels, by clean, pleasant, working conditions, and by the chance to borrow status from the organization ("I am with U.S. Steel"), superiors, customers, and the like. A study of nurses found that "about two thirds select work as the preferred source of personal satisfaction."[78] Moreover, 55 percent of the nurses found satisfying personal relations on the job. The nurses' attitudes also relate to their associations with doctors, who not only have great prestige with nurses but also tend to have a democratic working relationship with them, in which "banter and joking . . . cancel out status differences."[79]

When one turns to professional work, such psychological factors become even more significant. Not only are professionals unusually sensitive to status symbols,[80] but there is a public expectation that they will enjoy their work. We saw earlier that individual behavior is largely the result of our perceptions of the expectations of others. A social role is usually defined as a series of expected behaviors. "The professional is expected to be dedicated to his profession and have an intense intrinsic interest in his area of specialized competence; the white-collar employee is expected to be 'company' oriented and to like his work; but the loyalty of the blue-collar worker is never taken for granted."[81]

There is little doubt that white-collar work provides an opportunity for satisfaction and the fulfillment of status claims. School teachers like their summer vacations and the opportunity to travel. They may even like teaching. Office workers enjoy their pleasant office, clean work, and steady pay. The intensity of the private secretarys' identification with their bosses, their delight in sharing and ramifying the boss' authority, deserve extended inquiry. Receptionists borrow the prestige and quiet opulence of their well-appointed office in a big firm; sales clerks on upper Fifth Avenue deal with the finest people, even though their salaries are no better than their peers on Thirty-Fourth Street. The expense accounts of salespersons insure both psychic and economic dividends. The "dedicated professional" is a com-

---

[78]Lloyd H. Orzack, "Work as a 'Central Life Interest' of Professionals," *Social Problems*, Vol. 7, p. 132.

[79]Ruth L. Coser, "Authority and Decision-Making in a Hospital," *American Sociological Review*, Vol. 23, p. 61.

[80]J. L. Resnick, "The Emerging Physician," in J. Gerstl and G. Jaccʾs, eds., *Professions for the People* (New York: Wiley, 1976), pp. 182–185. Among lawyers, see Erwin O. Smigel, *Wall Street Lawyer* (Bloomington: University of Indiana Press, 1969).

[81]Blauner, *Alienation and Freedom*, p. 343.

mon stereotype, based upon rigorous training, self-government as to achievement and behavior, and considerable independence in deciding when and how the work will be done.

But, although professionals and white-collar individuals often identify closely with work and the organization, both logic and evidence suggest that they too are disenchanted by increasing bureaucratization.

Logically, one can argue that job satisfaction and prestige are bound up with the degree of control that one exercises over the work process. As Robert Blauner says: "The fact that work inherently involves a surrender of control is probably what makes the relative degree of control in work so important an aspect of job attitudes."[82] Unskilled workers are found at the bottom of every job-satisfaction scale, for they tend to work on the assembly-line type of job in which they have virtually nothing to say about the work process.

✓ On the other hand, independent professionals, who appear at the top of most job satisfaction scales, have long enjoyed a maximum of control over the conditions of their work. Ideally, their time is their own to allocate. There is no hierarchy of authority over them. Theirs is the authority of knowledge, reinforced in the case of law and medicine by powerful associations which determine the conditions of training and of practice, protect them, and preserve inviolate the "official secrets" on which their authority rests. Their status and training mean that their competence is assumed until proven otherwise. In the independent professions, such as medicine, they work for themselves. Theoretically, there is no limit to their income, which is derived from fees assigned on the basis of judgments which they again have some latitude in making. They tend to work by themselves and for themselves.

✓ We can thus assume that the degree of control over one's work and the lack of direct supervision are primary factors in job satisfaction. But the essence of bureaucratic work is the replacement of individual control by the control of the work process. Even in some highly skilled fields, work is evaluated by supervisors; "work measurement" is a hallmark of bureaucracy. This is so whether the product is turned out by people or by machines. As we have seen, organizations are systems of roles graded by authority that seek to insure uniformity and predictability. Everything tends to follow rational prescriptions. The penetration of such logic into most work areas has enthroned collective judgments. On every hand, organizations fix the conditions of participation, limiting individual discretion by rules, certifications, and tacit expectations of many kinds.

---

[82]Blauner, *Alienation and Freedom*, p. 20.

Such demands tend to undercut traditional self-images in professional as well as in blue-collar fields. "The contemporary professional is increasingly an 'organization man' subject to job standardization, procedures, personal policies, and other structural coercions."[83] The effects are to level work roles, to lump people together as employees, and to standardize their incentives, rewards, and evaluations. Scientists and university professors, for example, seem especially susceptible to the indifference syndrome because their expectations of autonomy in their work and work place are higher than those of many groups. Yet they often work in bureaucratic work places. As the following analysis suggests, the attending substitution of hierarchical authority for skill authority proves especially disenchanting.

In discussing academic work, it is important to differentiate as follows. While there are almost 1,200 accredited, four-year universities and colleges in the United States, only a very small proportion, certainly not over 3 percent, can be called first-rate. Among this group there is an inner core of some twenty distinguished schools, including mainly those in the Northeast and a handful of small, private colleges scattered around the country. Moreover, while these schools include two or three state universities, the latter suffer from certain inherent problems that encourage indifference among their faculties. Such problems include their great size and their respect for size. More important is their ultimate subordination to the common denominator of understanding of their regents and state legislatures. Neither group is likely to know much about academic traditions and values, nor do they ordinarily come to know personally faculty members who might help overcome the gap in understanding. Although both public and private universities report that legislatures and politicians are the greatest single source of pressure upon their administrations, such pressures, as might be expected, increase with size and are relatively more frequent in the public universities.[84]

As a result, such institutions are constrained in social and political fields; they tend to build up strong physical science and professional schools, which are either innately conservative or whose subject matter is rarely controversial.[85] A dramatic example of the resulting differences in autonomy between the best state and private universities occurred during the mid-1950s when the House Un-American

[83]Orzack, "Work as a 'Central Life Interest' of Professionals," p. 132.

[84]Paul Lazarsfeld and Wagner Theilens, *The Academic Mind* (Glencoe, Ill.: Free Press, 1958), pp. 180–183.

[85]Everett C. Ladd and Seymour M. Lipset, *The Divided Academy* (New York: McGraw Hill, 1975), pp. 57–79.

Activities Committee was flourishing. Whereas Harvard in the Furry case and Cornell in the Singer case could apparently refuse to surrender to the Committee their right and obligation to determine the qualifications of their faculty, the University of Michigan felt obliged to welcome the Committee, and subsequently fired two instructors whose political views were suspect.[86] Similarly, the University of California was subjected to a loyalty oath conflict which disrupted its internal affairs for several years.

Such events symbolize the conflict between bureaucratic (and community) demands for control and orthodoxy and the demands of research and teaching for autonomy. Organizational logic is often insensitive to subtle matters of spirit, which is precisely a major area of difference between the good private and the good public universities. Their libraries, faculties, and physical plants are not substantially different (indeed, the state universities usually have superior physical plants); but they tend to be distinct in terms of academic traditions, bureaucratic rules, faculty influence, and the priorities they assign to quality, faculty influence, and research productivity, as over against public opinion, "community service," and conformity.

It must be said, however, that any greater academic freedom in the prestigious private schools has its ironic side, for their faculties seem to include a significant proportion of conservative social scientists, much of whose work tends either to be sympathetic to conventional values and often unconcerned with existing power disequilibria. Perhaps this condition reflects the symbiotic association of such institutions with government, corporate, and foundation worlds. As the record indicates, they have been very closely tied to government during the post–World War II years. They have supplied much of the brainpower and loyalty required to rationalize and carry through cold war imperatives. They have received the lion's share of research grants, which were often ultimately related to military ends. Yet, even though some 70 percent of American social scientists consider themselves "liberal," and Jews who are generally more "liberal" than their Protestant-Catholic colleagues are "heavily represented on the faculties of Ivy League schools. . . ,"[87] the leading social scientists at

[86]Some evidence suggests that the distinction being made here may require some qualification. Apparently, some tension arose between *raisons d'état* and traditional academic preferences for individual political autonomy in at least two cases of faculty appointment and tenure at Harvard during the McCarthy era. For documentation, see Sigmund Diamond, "Veritas at Harvard," *New York Review of Books*, pp. 13–17, April 28, 1977. Diamond states, "I myself had the offer of a job at Harvard withdrawn for political reasons" (13). McGeorge Bundy, former dean at Harvard, replies to Diamond in ibid., May 26, 1977, pp. 42–45; and Professor Robert Bellah of the University of California-Berkeley attests to a similar experience with Bundy in ibid., July 14, 1977, pp. 39–41.

[87]Everett C. Ladd and Seymour M. Lipset, ibid., pp. 80, 90, 150.

such schools include many well-known "conservatives."[88] Perhaps it is suggestive that the majority of Republicans at prestige schools classify themselves as "liberals."[89]

Obviously, the terms "liberal" and "conservative" have become highly ambiguous,[90] but it seems valid to argue that many leading social scientists at Harvard are "conservative" in the sense that they tend to manifest a generally positive view of the status quo; a rather tentative appreciation of change; some ambivalence about the erosion of ascriptive student recruitment by meritocratic criteria[91]; and a quiet concern with family background, tradition, and the value of experience. Certainly, the political roles of Henry Kissinger, McGeorge Bundy, and Walt Rostow suggest that some recruits from prestige institutions have little difficulty accommodating the cynical

[88]Although any such listing is unfortunately apt to be somewhat invidious, it is interesting that Harvard social scientists, for example, would include such talented political "conservatives" as the former *Fortune* writer Daniel Bell, Karl Deutsch, Samuel Huntington, George Homans, Seymour M. Lipset (now at the Hoover Institute), Talcott Parsons, and David Riesman. Certainly, there are no iconoclasts among them. Similarly well-known "conservatively-oriented" scholars would also include McGeorge Bundy and Henry Kissinger.

[89]Charles E. Noll and Peter Rossi, "General Social and Economic Attitudes of College and University Faculty Members," University of Chicago: National Opinion Research Center, 1966, p. 21. Cited in Ladd and Lipset, p. 141.

[90]The extent to which *noblesse oblige* remains a part of "conservative" ideology is clear in the following peroration by Peregrine Worsthorne: "It is in this field that socialist thinking is so weak, because of its original—perfectly understandable at the time—orientation toward the needs of the underprivileged. As a result, there is no socialist interest in, or understanding of, the other side of the coin: the problem of social engineering as it applies to the creation of the right kind of political and administrative leadership. For this vastly important purpose, crude egalitarianism is manifest nonsense, since it wholly fails to recognize the value of, say, the public schools as training grounds for the qualities of leadership which a socialist system requires; the need for cohesion and mutual trust in a governing élite, which can perhaps best be guaranteed if its members come from the same kind of social background; the value to society of there being a certain hereditary stratum with an age-old tradition of public service; the connection between political independence of mind and the security that comes from private affluence; the need to guarantee the right mixture at the top of new men and old, so that the defensive harshness of those who have struggled to "make it" should be mitigated by the relaxed assurance of those born to the purple; the undoubted psychological fact that most people prefer to be ruled, not by their equals, but by their superiors, whose style and manner commands respect; the relevance of glamour, panache, and colour to the arts of governing, none of which is likely to flower except in privileged soil; the impossibility of upholding authority in the State unless those who wield it are encouraged to do so with pride and glory, without always having to apologise for being high and mighty; and, most important of all, the fundamental dependence of free institutions on there being a social class which associates their defence with the survival of its own privileges, and is therefore prepared to defend them with that special ferocity which is only generated when selfishness is added to idealism." "Who's Left, What's Right?", *Encounter,* March 1977, p. 31.

[91]See, for example, Nelson W. Aldrich, Jr., "Harvard on the Way Down," *Harpers,* March, 1976.

realism that often characterizes politics in the real world.[92] In sum, whereas academic freedom may indeed be more secure in such milieux, there is some evidence that it is less necessary.

While the universities remain our major centers of creativity and disinterest, and while some of them nourish the freedom required to continue this role, organizational logic has made deep inroads. Here again, bureaucratic values and methods have been applied to an inapposite area. Not only is the American university president an innovation that European universities have never found any need for, but as scientist Robert A. Millikan says: "There has developed . . . a semi-military form of organization with lines of authority and responsibility clearly marked. Let me call it the Pentagon philosophy of organization, and let me recognize the fact that wherever *action* is more important than *wisdom*, as in military operations and to a lesser extent in American business, it represents at any rate a natural, if not a necessary, mode of organization."[93]

The resulting subordination of highly skilled and learned men has been responsible for a considerable amount of alienation (defined here in perhaps its most common connotation as a sense of powerlessness among faculty members). As one reported in the *New York Times Magazine*: "The truth of the matter is that the teachers in our large universities are the low men on the totem pole. The administrators look down their noses at the faculty. . . ." In their study of 375 academic men in nine first-rate institutions, Caplow and McGee similarly found an "extraordinary high incidence of conflict reported . . . and [a] widespread dissatisfaction of professors with the workings of academic government."[94]

This alienation is aggravated when both status and economic rewards tend to go to an administrative group which despite its remoteness from the essential purpose of the university typically symbolizes it before the public.[95] Let me say again that this condition is less characteristic of the prestige schools. But the latter, unfortunately, are extremely limited in number. In the vast majority of larger institu-

[92]For a perceptive analysis of the values, norms, and political behavior of elites (a substantial proportion of whom were Ivy League graduates) during the Kennedy-Johnson era, see Halberstam, *The Best and the Brightest*, especially chaps. 4, 6, 9, 12, and 16. See also Roger Morris, *Uncertain Greatness: Henry Kissinger and American Foreign Policy* (New York: Harper & Row, 1977), and Anthony Lewis, "A Matter of Character," *New York Review of Books*, October 27, 1977, pp. 8–10.

[93]Robert A. Millikan, *The Autobiography of Robert A. Millikan* (Englewood Cliffs, N.J.: Prentice-Hall, 1950), p. 225.

[94]Caplow and McGee, *The Academic Marketplace*, pp. 42, 181.

[95]For a mildly exaggerated account of administrative-faculty tensions, see Robert Presthus, "University Bosses: the Executive Conquest of Academe," *New Republic*, February 20, 1965, pp. 20–24; a useful analysis of the structural factors that account for the administrator's ambiguous role in the university is Terry Lunsford, "Authority and Ideology in the Administered University," *American Behavioral Scientist*, Vol. 11, pp. 5–14.

tions, bureaucratic patterns dominate. Hierarchy again places control of the distribution of authority, prestige, and income in administrative hands. Speaking of the effects of this distribution of power, Logan Wilson says: "Those who dispense largesse are certain to make dependents, if not create disciples; for much of the academician's immediate welfare, irrespective of his technical competence, depends on administrative policy and how he fits into the scheme of things."[96]

While it is customary for faculty members to deplore administration, recent world events raise questions about the efficacy of the present system of administrative control. As Oskar Morgenstern says:

> The universities must provide a new leadership and take the initiative. No one else can. There will have to be much soul searching and a pushing back of mushrooming administrations. The scholars and the scientists themselves will have to run the universities where they do not do it already—and there are precious few where they do even to a limited extent. Teaching will have to be raised to higher levels. . . . It is not enough to provide money. *The milieu in which the sciences and arts will flourish is infinitely more important.* . . . The fact is that the universities, which should provide the ideal milieu, do not do so, and no one else can. *They have not evolved an organization conducive to the unfettered growth of intellectual life. This is the really serious matter.*[97]

The disparity between administrative and faculty salaries, between the two styles of life, and between the two levels of status income in such terms as office and secretarial facilities also nourishes disenchantment. It is not uncommon to find world-famous scholars stuck off in some garretlike office, while those in the administrative stream enjoy the accoutrements of executives in the business world, upon which administrative pay and perquisites are patterned. In 1975 the average salary of university presidents was over 33,000 dollars higher than the median income reported for medical doctors. Moreover, a smaller share of the educational dollar now tends to go to the faculty. "What is especially striking is the large proportion of the increased costs to be charged to nonacademic salaries: though nonacademic employees were only two-thirds as numerous as faculty members, their pay rose so much more that they contributed one-third more to the inflation of outlays for institutions of higher learning than did faculty salaries."[98]

[96]Wilson, *The Academic Man*, p. 90. Here again, Veblen was the first to analyze the implications of administrative-business control of our universities, *The Higher Learning in America* (New York: Viking, 1918).

[97]Morgenstern, *The Question of National Defense* (New York: Random House, 1959), pp. 182–186.

[98]Seymour E. Harris, "Faculty Salaries," *Bulletin of the American Association of University Professors*, Vol. 43, p. 587.

Some observers insist that people would not have become professors had they not been timid in the first place; but evidence suggests that size, conformity demands, and bureaucratic conditions of work encourage anxiety and alienation (defined here as a sense of powerlessness) among them. Here again, our concern is mainly with the larger universities, some thirty of which in 1970 had over 30,000 students each, and about 10 percent of which contained 50 percent of all professors. These institutions meet the size criterion for "big organizations," and they include the quality universities and the productive scholars who set the standard for the rest. What is the nexus between size and faculty-administrative relations? In their survey of 2,451 social scientists in 165 institutions, Lazarsfeld and Theilens found that 51 percent of faculty members in "very small" colleges reported "unusually good relations between faculty and administration." Only 21 percent did in the "very large" group.[99] A similar but less marked analogy appeared regarding "good relations among faculty members," which ranged from 5 percent in small schools to 33 percent in the large.[100]

Although size and anxiety, concerning attacks from community groups and administrative support against them, were less dramatically related, apprehension still increased with size. Fully 50 percent of faculty members in "large" institutions were anxious, as compared with 37 percent in "small" schools. In large Catholic universities, 38 percent reported apprehension, while in small ones only 14 percent did.[101]

Interpersonal theory is helpful in explaining tensions between faculty and administration. An individual's perceptions of others, that is, his evaluation of their motives, is largely a function of his own personality. Sullivan, it will be recalled, defined personality as a "self-system," a style of behavior that had proved successful in one's interpersonal relations. Lazarsfeld and Theilens found three major attitudes among professors that characterized their unhappy relations with administrators.[102] First was the assumption on the part of administrators that the teacher is in the wrong when outside complaints occur. Teachers who felt their administrations were distrustful also felt a sense of powerlessness in their dealings with the administration. Some felt that resignation was their only weapon. An economics professor at a large Midwestern university, who felt that his superiors could hire and fire at will, says: "The administration of the university

---

[99]Lazarsfeld and Theilens, *The Academic Mind*, p. 25.
[100]Ibid.
[101]Ibid.
[102]Ibid., pp. 228–229.

so arranges it that the faculty doesn't know the answers to these questions—we never know why a man isn't hired, never know why a man left."[103] Finally, faculty members harbored guilt feelings over their compromises of principle in dealing with the administration. The objective validity of these perceptions is less significant than is the fact that they are believed to be true and are the basis for action.

These differing values complicate relations between professors, who are often "people-oriented," and administrators, who are usually (and perhaps necessarily) concerned with controls, techniques, and financial considerations. Each define situations and motivations differently. Each has a somewhat different "self-system," reflecting his or her discrete personal needs and values. They do not understand each other, or perhaps they understand each other too well.

The existing disparity in self-perceptions rests on other evidence. In their study of nine elite universities out of some forty major ones in the United States, Caplow and McGee conclude:

> The vast majority of personal problems reported in the interviews have less to do with long-range career opportunities than with the immediate working situations. The typical professor, if such there be, suffers from his acceptance of an ideology which is incongruous with his situation. He tends to see himself as a free member of an autonomous company of scholars, subject to no evaluation but the judgment of his peers. But he is likely to find himself under the sway of a chairman or dean or president whose authority is personal and arbitrary. . . . Academic authority is exercised largely by means of the personal control which the administrator has over the salary, rank, and prerogatives of the working professor. This control is essentially illegitimate. It serves in default of a workable system of academic government. . . . The violent opposition between the academician's image of himself as a kind of oligarch, independent of lay authority, and the galling subjection which he actually experiences is presumably responsible for the combination of private resentment and public submissiveness that so often characterizes the faculty attitude toward administrators.[104]

Perhaps the embattled professor is an "inner-directed" anachronism, maintaining a perception of himself that has rarely been viable in American universities.

But a more impressive index of alienation is the number of academic men who leave university work for industry, private research groups, or the foundations. Unfortunately, little is known about this

[103]Ibid., p. 229.
[104]Caplow and McGee, *The Academic Marketplace,* pp. 228–229.

point. Universities are reluctant to reveal their turnover figures, salaries, and hiring practices since these may seem to reflect adversely upon their internal policies.[105]

In their survey of academia, which leaves one between laughter and tears, Caplow and McGee describe turnover in prestige schools as excessive. They attribute it in part to the "internal dissension and low morale which follow the appointment of outsiders on unduly favorable terms."[106] This situation reflects the common policy of attracting new faculty members by substantial pay increases and related inducements such as limited teaching duties and liberal research time. In what seems a rather harsh indictment, they conclude that "this practice provides a perpetual incentive for everyone on the academic ladder to circulate among institutions. The result is a vicious circle whereby the appointment of outsiders on unduly favorable terms causes dissatisfaction among the staff members in place, so that some of them seek their fortunes elsewhere, which requires more new appointments to be made by means of extra inducements, which has a further unsettling effect upon the remaining members of the staff."[107] As we shall see in a moment, however, such rotation can also provide a certain measure of freedom to those who practice it.

Caplow and McGee also trace the displacement of values from teaching to publishing ("No one gives a damn if you can teach"), the mania for prestige, and persistent administrative inroads upon faculty autonomy. The domination of academic policy by trustees, who rarely know much about education, and by presidents, who are selected by the trustees in their own image, also contributes to faculty alienation. Ironically, this exclusion of the faculty may actually increase their productivity by driving the creative minority into furious work as a compensation. The result, of course, is to further exclude them from questions of educational policy with which they are well qualified to deal.

The weakness of academicians in a society which honors knowledge and innovation is ironic. It rests upon several structural and per-

---

[105]Some evidence of this reluctance is offered by Caplow and McGee, who found in their survey of nine leading U.S. universities that the presidents of the state schools responded promptly to their requests for cooperation, but the five private schools proved more difficult. One of them, rated among the best in the world, never answered their letter requesting help. The president of this institution later refused to countenance any such research not done by alumni. A second private school president refused for technical reasons. And the three remaining prestige schools required detailed explanations and assurances before they consented to cooperate fully. At one of these, the researchers were requested not to discuss faculty salaries at the institution. Ibid., pp. 33–35.

[106]Ibid., p. 228.

[107]Ibid., p. 235.

sonality factors. Certainly their debility is in direct proportion to their frequent failure to think and act collectively in an organizational society. Professors have been well defined as people who think otherwise. In part this posture stems from the nature of academic work, which has traditionally been highly individualistic. The productive scholar's is a lonely role. Criticism of majority values and conventional wisdom requires and reinforces this isolation and this dependence, and often disqualifies the scholar for success on the organization's terms. Personality plays its role too, since we may assume that a self-selection process occurs whereby a substantial proportion of those who resist majority values are likely to find themselves in university teaching and research.

But much of the academics' weakness rest upon their jejune status as employees rather than as independent professionals. Their hired-hand role excludes them from significant university affairs, particularly those relating to community issues and major educational policy. Insofar as long tenure is a requisite of political influence, their nomadic role has a similar consequence.

The problem and a possible solution have been well put by A. M. Carr-Saunders:

> The status of the free-lance worker has long been envied; he calls no man master. It has long been customary to express regret for the relative decline in numbers of persons with this status, and at the same time to say that it is inevitable. Under large-scale organization this decline in one sense is inevitable, but it does not follow that the positions of the salaried and wage-earning workers must remain as they now are. At present there goes with the employed status a sense of dependence; that is so because organizations have been permitted to gain control. . . . [But] the man who belongs to a profession which has won for itself prestige and a position of dignity, may pass from the service of one organization to that of another. Though he remains salaried all his life, he takes his stand upon his proved competence and experience; he serves one client after another much as does a free-lance worker. He is attached primarily to his profession, whence he goes out, as occasion may offer, to render his services in some co-operative organization, and whither he returns. The difference between the position of such a man and that of an ordinary salaried worker is not to be found in their respective legal situations; the difference is subtle, but it is vital.[108]

[108]Alexander M. Carr-Saunders and Paul A. Wilson, *The Professions* (Oxford: Oxford University Press, 1933), pp. 503–504.

The difference between the "ordinary salaried worker" and the professional has become subtle indeed. As we have seen, the effect of bureaucratic work is to reduce such distinctions, to rationalize, and to level off both people and tasks. Status anxiety and the attempts to personalize work through "human relations" attests both the intensity of this claim and the attempts to blunt it. Structure and control tend to overcome spirit and purpose. Not only are professors defined as employees, but many of them accept this definition. Few academic people have the prestige or the security to resist as individuals, and both academic work and temperament have until now discouraged the main practical alternative—collective action.

Such action is now appearing in the form of faculty unions. Until quite recently the major agent of faculty representation at the university level was the American Association of University Professors. Founded in 1915, the Association has usually been regarded as a professional body, with both the advantages and the limitations that entails. The Association's attitude toward unionization is probably well expressed by the following comments of a chapter president at Boston University:

> Unions cannot offer tenured professors great job security, since the instances of tenured faculty being fired are almost non-existent. . . . The only faculty group a union could really help are the junior, nontenured members, who tend to be exploited both on salary and working conditions, as well as having little job security. Unions might well lead to a higher percentage of these junior members being continued permanently in employment, but at a substantial price—the watering down of academic standards.[109]

The Association's major positive activity has been a program of sanctioning, exercized after lengthy on-the-spot investigations, in academic freedom cases in which faculty members have been removed without due cause or due process. Such investigations have occasionally resulted in offending institutions being placed upon a "censored institutions" list and publicized in the Association's monthly *Bulletin*. At times, the threat of such action has undoubtedly been useful to the individual harassed or dismissed under questionable circumstances. In the few cases where major universities have been censored it seems that they have reacted with dismay and attempted to take whatever actions are necessary to be removed. The Association's role has been largely restricted however to more routine yet significant problems of work and pay among their clientele group. Since

[109]Banks McDowell, Jr., "Should University Faculties Be Unionized," *Boston Globe*, June 18, 1972.

professors have suffered an extended secular decline in real income, it seems that the Association has not been entirely effective in this context. Nor can it apparently do much about changing occupational opportunities and supply and demand questions in the profession. As a result, individual bargaining has remained the usual pattern of negotiation in the higher learning.

For such reasons and no doubt influenced by the generalized militancy of the 1960s and the inroads of inflation upon middle-class living standards, some members of the profession have recently turned to traditional union structures to gain their ends. Much of the impetus has come from younger faculty members and graduate students of a left, often neomarxian persuasion who tend to conceptualize the university and their role in it in terms quite different from those traditionally apposite in American universities. The class consciousness long characteristic of Western European and Latin American institutions has often provided an alternative model. Alienation (defined as powerlessness) has apparently been a central incentive, manifested in a rejection of hierarchical forms of both administrative and faculty authority, in which seniors judge their junior colleagues and bring them into permanent tenure status on a co-optative basis. Both the structure and the principle underlying it are widely rejected, it seems, as younger men and women find it difficult to believe that disinterested judgments can be made regarding such vital career decisions. To some extent, a certain amount of normative projection is occurring, in that the adversary ethos of a new generation of academics compels them to ascribe a similar orientation to their predecessors.

A profile of prounion academics tends to include a disproportionate number of individuals under thirty-five, without tenure, ranking somewhat lower than modal antiunionists on productivity as measured by research and publications in their respective professional journals, with a tendency to define themselves as "teachers" rather than "intellectuals,"[110] to be in place at less prestigious institutions, to be more "left" politically, and often less inclined to define the university professionally as a place in which objective scholarship can occur than as an instrument of social change. It is not possible, apparently, to similarly categorize such individuals according to disciplinary preference, except perhaps that the professional schools of law, medicine, engineering and business probably include the largest proportion of antiunion faculty members.

It seems accurate to say that a union "movement" is now underway in North America. In Canada, the organic, corporatist nature of the

---

[110]See Everett C. Ladd and Seymour M. Lipset, *Professors, Unions, and American Higher Education* (Berkeley: Carnegie Commission on Higher Education, 1973).

political culture has eased the acceptance of unionization, although the older, more self-conscious universities have not yet shown interest in the trend.

To the extent that unionization tends to occur in marginal institutions, any assumed dysfunctions may be reduced, since the emphasis upon seniority, bureaucratic standardization, rule by committee, and increased politicization of the university often ascribed to such milieux will only be confirmed by unionization. Whether the movement is another significant step along the path to the iron cage of history cannot be determined. It may be significant, however, that one of the few institutional sectors of modern society devoted ideally at least, to individual autonomy, systematic skepticism and innovation has been invaded by an interest whose incentives often seem foreign to such values.

The bureaucratic assumptions and conditions of work underlying unionization will almost surely encourage indifference in the university, which has traditionally been among the least structured of work environments. Nevertheless, with the possible exception of a few prestige schools, the universities now have a significant proportion of indifferents in their faculties. This is explained in part by the high expectations of academic people for autonomy, a personal need which brought some of them to the university in the first instance.

Typical indifferents tend to reject the organizational bargain which promises authority, status, prestige, and income in exchange for loyalty, hard work, and identification with its values. Instead, they separate their work from the "meaningful" aspects of their lives, which include recreation and leisure activities. In speaking of "accomplishing something for the day," they are often referring to what they plan to do after work. If indifferents remain committed to their work, they will sometimes distinguish between it and the organization. If they are college instructors, they may assume a "cosmopolitan" view in which their interests, loyalty, and future are seen as bound up with their profession, rather than with the particular school in which they happen to find themselves.[111]

The indifferent posture also mediates preorganizational influences of class and education that failed to honor success and the repression of unprofitable opinions. The tension between such influences and the organization's claims encourages withdrawal, the rejection of majority values, and a refusal to compete for them. In so defining the work bargain, workers often reveal a realistic perception of themselves and their life chances. This accommodation may be en-

[111]Alvin W. Gouldner, "Cosmopolitans and Locals: Toward an Analysis of Latent Social Roles," *Administrative Science Quarterly*, Vols. 2, 3, pp. 281–306, 444–480.

couraged by advancing age, as experience results in a narrowing of career expectations and some loss of the incentive and energy required to achieve them.

One result of this mode of accommodation seems to be alienation (again defined as powerlessness) from political and community affairs. Indifferents tend to reject their company, their union, their political party, and other voluntary organizations. The mass character of society, the remoteness of its organizations, and one's resulting feelings of helplessness are among the psychological bases for alienation. Oligarchy, for example, probably encourages alienation by excluding most employees from real participation. The need for skilled leaders, the difficulty of getting the word to large numbers of people, the leaders' drive for power and continuity in office, the complexity of decisions, the need and the desire for secrecy in negotiations with other power groups—all tend to restrict active participation.

Today, as C. Wright Mills concludes, most people do not shape the decisions that affect them; they are shaped by the decisions. In industry, technology and the work process determine the worker's role. In education, remote boards of trustees and, more recently, faculty unions set down the conditions of work. In the big industrial unions, "pork choppers" deal with management and control union government. In national politics, by a most generous estimate of their influence some 3,000 delegates to the two presidential nominating conventions "decide" who will run for president,[112] while the number determining who runs for Congress is probably much smaller. Meanwhile, in the presidential election of 1976, at least, only 52 percent of adult citizens voted.[113] In big government, civil servants serve at least three masters: the politician-as-legislator, the administration in power, and the hierarchy of officialdom in which they work. Such conditions make indifference the most common pattern of bureaucratic accommodation.

---

[112] In 1976 there were 2,259 delegates to the Republican convention and 3,008 to the Democratic. Actually, of course, congressmen, governors, big city mayors, and presidential hopefuls and their organizational entourage usually control these delegates.

[113] For data on such aspects of electoral behavior as voting, efficacy, and alienation, see Nathaniel Beck and John Pierce, "Political Involvement and Party Allegiances in Canada and the United States," in Robert Presthus ed., *Cross-National Perspectives: The United States and Canada* (Leiden: Brill and Co., 1977), pp. 23–43.

PATTERNS OF | 8
ACCOMMODATION:
AMBIVALENTS

Only ambivalence remains to be discussed as a mode of accommodation. In this chapter the social context, personality, and behavior of the disenchanted minority of whom this mode is characteristic will be set against organizational patterns of authority, status, and small groups. In both personal and organizational terms, the self-system of ambivalents is generally dysfunctional. Creative and anxious, their values conflict with bureaucratic claims for loyalty and adaptability. While the upward-mobile finds the organization congenial, and the indifferent refuses to become engaged, ambivalents are a small residual category who can neither reject its promise of success and power, nor play the roles required to compete for them. While upward-mobile anxiety is usually adaptive, ambivalent anxiety tends toward the neurotic.[1] In the bureaucratic situation, the ambivalent is a marginal person with limited career chances.

One important qualification is required. Despite their inability to meet bureaucratic demands, the ambivalent types play a critical social role, namely, that of providing the insight, motivation, and the dialectic that inspire change. The upward-mobile honors the status quo and the indifferent accepts it, but ambivalents are always sensitive to the need for change. Their innovating role is often obscured because the authority and money needed to institutionalize change remain in the hands of organizational elites. Nevertheless, few ideals or institutions escape their critical scrutiny. In their view custom is no

---

[1]The distinction between adaptive anxiety and neurotic anxiety is widely accepted in psychology. Among others, see Karen Horney, *Neurosis and Human Growth* (New York: Norton, 1950); and *The Neurotic Personality of our Time* (New York: Norton, 1937); Rollo May, *The Meaning of Anxiety* (New York: The Ronald Press, 1950); Frieda Fromm-Reichmann, *An Outline of Psycho-Analysis* (New York: Random House, 1955); Roy Grinker, *Psychosomatic Research* (New York: Norton, 1953); Sullivan, *Interpersonal Theory of Psychiatry* and *Conceptions of Modern Psychiatry*.

guarantee of either rationality or legitimacy. This perception is sharpened by their inability to accept charismatic and traditional bases of authority; rationality alone provides a compelling standard.

Certain personality traits underlie the ambivalent's critical posture. Unlike the upward-mobile and indifferent types who either endorse or merely tolerate their essentially instrumental condition, the ambivalents' adjustment is directly influenced by their sensitivity to any restrictive consequences of science, technology, and organization for the individual. They would probably agree with Simmel's judgment:

> I see the most capacious and far-reaching collision between society and the individual, not in the aspect of particular interests but in the general form of the individual life. Society aspires to totality and organic unity, each of its members constituting but a component part. The individual as part of the society has to fulfill special functions and employ all his strength; he is expected to modify his skills so that he will become the best-qualified performer of these functions. But this role is opposed by man's bent toward unity and totality as an expression of his own individuality.[2]

In Simmel's terms, this evolution is very broadly from a "subjective spirit" to an "objective" one. Functional specialization and hyperorganization, the products of capitalism and the national state, in effect transform the ambivalent into a stranger. The evolution, traced by Tönnies and Durkheim, from the security and intimacy of *Gemeinschaft* society to the impersonal, rationalized *Gesellschaft* order characteristic of modern western industrial society, are central to the alienation (that is, estrangement) of the ambivalent.

The ambivalent is typically an introvert, with intense intellectual interests and limited interpersonal facility. Unlike the upward-mobiles, who stress action, objectivity, and easy interpersonal relations,[3] ambivalents are often subjective and withdrawn. Introversion has been found to be related to neurosis; anxiety and depression are common ailments.[4] Ambivalents have high aspirations, complicated by habitual underrating of their own performance. Compared with extroverts, their intellectual interests seem to be narrow and deep, ac-

[2]Georg Simmel, *The Sociology of Religion*, trans. E. Fischoff (Boston: Beacon Press, 1963), p. 48. Cited in Robert Nisbet, *The Sociological Tradition* (New York: Basic Books, 1966), p. 306.

[3]Hans J. Eysenck, *The Dimensions of Personality* (London: Routledge and Kegan Paul, 1947), p. 160.

[4]In a study of 3,083 factory workers, for example, R. Fraser found that about 30 percent suffered from minor and disabling neuroses, and that this condition was commonly associated with a "decrease in social contacts," a characteristic behavior of introvert types, *The Incidence of Neuroses Among Factory Workers* (London: H.M.S.O. Report No. 90, 1947).

curacy and persistence are highly developed, and verbal facility and intelligence are often markedly superior.[5]

Ambivalents ordinarily play a specialist, "cosmopolitan" role. They honor theory, knowledge, and skill. Socialization as an independent professional often blinds them to legitimate organizational needs for control and coordination. Believing explicitly that both motivation and expertise come from within, they resist bureaucratic rules and supervision. Attempts to impose standards from without are seen as presumptuous and denigrating. As a result, there is always a gap between their self-perception as independent professionals and the galling realization, punctuated daily by the organization's authority and status differentiations, that they are really employees. Their skill-based authority is not always recognized, even though it is perfectly clear that their technical judgments have been decisive. The managerial façade with which they are confronted confirms their belief that hierarchical authority is often specious. This tension between authority based upon skill and that based upon hierarchical position is aggravated by the tendency of the organization's elites to employ subjective criteria of seniority and obedience. In sum, the bureaucratic situation is often inapposite to the ambivalent's personal and professional values.

The heart of the ambivalent reaction is a tenacious self-concern. Most events are perceived by ambivalents in terms of themselves; personal goals are usually primary. Their own experiences and skills seem unique; and when their career expectations prove unrealistic, as they sometimes do, they may invoke humanistic themes to buttress their claims for preference. Unable to achieve distinction on the organization's terms, they may adopt idiosyncratic alternatives, a reaction encouraged by the contemporary erosion of qualitative standards. If they aspire to artistic achievement, they may assume a bohemian role, characterized by eccentric modes of dress and idiosyncratic romantic liaisons. If inadequate discipline or talent frustrate their intellectual claims, they may again enlist compensatory substitutes. But since majority values usually prove irresistible, such behaviors often prove unsatisfactory. Sensitive, emotionally undisciplined, individuals in a collectivized society, they are perpetually out of step.

So much has been said about neurosis in contemporary society that it seems necessary here to review only its immediately relevant aspects. Some psychiatrists maintain that the success and adjustment claims of our society encourage neurotic behavior, manifested in personal anxiety and a pathetic reliance upon others to tell us what we

[5] Eysenck, *The Dimensions of Personality*, p. 160.

are worth.[6] On the one hand, the demands of society for conformity without conviction provide for a built-in anxiety as individuals seek approval by simulating approved styles. On the other, their need for self-expression impels deviant behavior that nourishes anxiety because they are unable to sustain the resulting censorship. As they resist majority values, yet cannot rise above them, an interminable conflict may ensue in which they oscillate between defiance and submission. Not only is such behavior inimical to bureaucratic claims for loyalty and consistency, but we may assume that it is aggravated by the organization's authority, status, and group systems which sharpen the disparity between the demands of the organization and the inability of ambivalents to honor them.

It follows that their perceptions of interpersonal relations will sometimes be distorted. As Harry Stack Sullivan observes of the neurotic type who personifies extreme ambivalence:

> [His] delusion of unique individuality cuts off all communion. . . . We see quite a number of people in whom effectual development of personality was arrested at this stage; the later matured needs for intimacy . . . having then been tortured into strange channels of maladaptive expression, and the artistic-magical interpersonal behavior evolved in delusions of reference, of persecution, and of grandeur, or along an uncertain course in which other people are treated as troublesome units more or less useful to a flaming ambition.[7]

On the other hand, as Freud showed early on, anxiety is often functional because it helps individuals identify and accept authoritative stimuli.[8] The ambivalent types might therefore seem more adaptable because they are more anxious. But while a certain amount of anxiety eases learning and performance, particularly of simple tasks, a point

---

[6]Horney, *The Neurotic Personality of our Time;* May, *The Meaning of Anxiety;* Erich Fromm, *The Sane Society* (New York: Holt, Rinehart & Co., 1955).

[7]Harry Stack Sullivan, "A Note on the Implications of Psychiatry for Investigations in the Social Sciences," *American Journal of Sociology,* Vol. 42, pp. 848–861; how neurotic tendencies are inculcated in middle-class children by the contradictory family requirement that the child be obedient and loving *within* the family, while exhibiting aggression and independence *outside* the home is analyzed in A. W. Green, "The Middle-Class Male Child and Neurosis," in Arnold M. Rose, ed., *Mental Health and Mental Disorder* (New York: Norton, 1955), pp. 341–357; Fromm also finds the origin of neuroses in child-family relations in which the parents' imposition of "irrational authority" generates conflict usually ending in defeat for the child: "the scars left from this defeat . . . are to be found at the bottom of every neurosis," from "Individual and Social Origins of Neurosis," in Rose, ed., *Mental Health,* 287.

[8]Sigmund Freud, *Inhibitions, Symptoms, and Anxiety,* ed. and trans. by J. Strachey (London: Hogarth Press, 1926).

of diminishing returns soon occurs. Anxiety then distorts perception and encourages dysfunctional reactions.[9]

Insofar as the ambivalents' level of anxiety is too high, their adaptability to the bureaucratic situation is impaired. Too intense a self-concern blurs the signs and signals which permeate a complex social system. Here again, an analogy from animal behavior is instructive in suggesting the utility of the study of primate social organization for an understanding of human behavior. As Edward Wilson writes:

> Intelligence is the prerequisite for the most complex societies in the vertebrate style. Individual relationships are personalized, finely graduated, and rapidly changing. There is a premium on the precise expression of mood. Higher primates have extended the basic mammalian tendency away from the use of elementary sign stimuli and toward the perception of gestalt, that is, toward the simultaneous summation of complex sets of signals. . . . The monkey or ape more consistently [than fish or birds] tends to act on the appearance of the entire body, the posture, and the history of previous encounters with the individual confronted. There is also a tendency to utilize information from more than one sensory modality. At close range, visual and auditory signals are compatible and can be blended with tactile cues to form composite signals that convey messages redundantly and with greater exactitude. . . . In addition to monitoring multiple signals, higher primates evaluate the behavior of many individuals within the society simultaneously. The animal lives in a *social field*.[10]

[9]Evidence on the effect of anxiety upon performance is not entirely consistent. In highly routinized tasks, anxiety apparently improves performance, while in complex, difficult, and spontaneous kinds of activities, anxiety inhibits effectiveness. Grinker concludes: "If anxiety is mild, it is stimulating and facilitates increased and efficient action or thought. If it becomes too intense, disruptive effects ensue, calling forth emergency substitutive mechanisms of defense or, in greater degrees, differentiated regressive behavior." *Psychosomatic Research* (New York: Norton, 1953), p. 170. It seems that anxiety may also produce very high mobility drives, without providing the behavioral qualities required to satisfy them. Sullivan calls many of the security operations that individuals develop to ease anxiety "excess baggage" that hinders mature personality development, however useful it may be in allaying anxiety. For a summary of research on this subject, see Richard S. Lazarus et al., "The Effects of Psychological Stress upon Performance," *Psychological Bulletin*, Vol. 49, pp. 293–317; also, John W. Thibaut and Harold H. Kelley, *The Social Psychology of Groups* (New York: Wiley, 1959), pp. 56–58; and Sullivan, *Interpersonal Theory of Psychiatry*, pp.168–171, 190–192, 373–375; Roy Grinker and S. Spiegel, *Men Under Stress* (Philadelphia: Blakiston, 1945); Raymond B. Cattell and Ivan H. Scheier, *The Meaning and Measurement of Neuroticism and Anxiety* (New York: The Ronald Press, 1961); J. Taylor, "The Relationship of Anxiety to the Conditioned Eyelid Response," *Journal of Experimental Psychology*, Vol. 41, pp. 81–92; K. W. Spence and J. A. Taylor, "The Relation of Conditioned Response Strength to Anxiety in Normal Neurotic and Psychiatric Subjects," ibid., Vol. 45, pp. 265–272; G. Mandler and Seymour B. Sarason, "A Study of Anxiety and Learning," *Journal of Abnormal and Social Psychology*, Vol. 47, pp. 166–173.

[10]Edward Wilson, *Sociobiology: The New Synthesis* (Cambridge: Harvard University

Even though, as Wilson maintains, ambivalence is "a way of life in social creatures," adaptation to an even more complex environment must be especially difficult for the ambivalent type who often carries a heavy load of anxiety, aggravated by an inability to deal easily with the shifting authority relations found in bureaucratic structures.

At the very least, it undercuts the outward show of strength, control, and serenity required for bureaucratic success. Research indicates that extreme anxiety can inhibit learning and adaptation. A recent five-year study of young psychiatric residents found that the highly anxious ones had considerable difficulty in helping their patients. They were unable, for example, to accept the distrust and anger of some patients and tended as a result to abandon therapy in favor of tactics calculated to ward off hostility.[11] Another study indicated that "free-floating" anxiety was typically accompanied by perceptual distortion and self-deprecation.[12]

Anxiety's effects are particularly apparent in the ambivalent's reaction to authority. We saw earlier, for example, that the remoteness of decision making in big organizations could result in distorted perceptions of the power and expectations of superiors followed by extreme and often pathetic efforts to anticipate their will. When anxiety approaches this level, it becomes dysfunctional by definition.

Some research suggests that adaptive anxiety is largely an upper- and middle-class phenomenon. Hollingshead and Redlich, for example, show that neuroses are associated with class: "In classes I and II, some sixty-five percent of the patients are diagnosed as neurotic; in class III the percentage drops to forty-five, in class IV to approximately twenty, and in class V to ten percent."[13] While other research indicates that anxiety does not vary from class to class,[14] it is significant that the *kinds* of anxiety experienced by each class may vary.[15] Hollingshead and Redlich found that relatively milder and nonorganic neuroses were proportionally higher among the upper two classes, whereas incapacitating neuroses such as antisocial,

---

Press, 1975), pp. 516–517.

[11]D. H. Buie and P. G. Myerson, "Problems Which Interfere with Learning in Psychiatric Residents," *British Journal of Medical Psychology*, Vol. 49, pp. 55–63.

[12]A. Bond and M. Lader, "Self-Concepts in Anxiety States," *British Journal of Medical Psychology*, ibid., pp. 275–279.

[13]Hollingshead and Redlich, *Social Class and Mental Illness* (New York: Wiley, 1958), pp. 222, 223–229, ch. 8.

[14]T. A. C. Rennie and Leo Srole, "Social Class Prevalence and Distribution of Psychosomatic Conditions in an Urban Population," *Psychosomatic Medicine*, Vol. 18, pp. 449–556.

[15]For a catalogue of typical anxiety-producing situations used in research, see F. C. Richardson and D. L. Tasto, "Development and Factor Analysis of a Social Anxiety Inventory," *Behavior Therapy*, Vol. 7, pp. 453–462.

hysterical, and phobic reactions, in which individuals "act out" their destructive behavior, were substantially more common among classes IV and V. Such diagnoses may however reflect class bias on the psychiatrist's part. It is significant too that obsessive-compulsive neuroses, often characteristic of upward-mobile types, are concentrated in classes I and II. On the other hand, hysterical reactions, which paralyze work and self-discipline, occur six to twelve times as frequently in classes IV and V as in classes I, II, and III.[16]

This suggests that the kinds of anxiety most useful for organizational adjustment tend to occur disproportionally among upper- and middle-class individuals. At the same time, *within* these classes different kinds of anxiety have different implications for individual accommodation. For example, depression, which is characteristic of highly intelligent, anxious introverts, declines steadily from class I to class V. This form of neurosis is at the top of the rank order of personality disturbances among Cornell University students. As we have tried to show, the excessive doubt and guilt symptomatic of depression-prone individuals are dysfunctional for mobility in the bureaucratic situation. Ambivalents seem to be particularly susceptible to such stigmata.

In view of the compelling status needs, the intellectual orientation, and the marked educational achievement often characteristic of the introverted type, we may assume that our ambivalents are typically of middle-class origin. However, their socialization has apparently not included the respect for hierarchical success which seems to be crucial for bureaucratic mobility. "Success," probably the dominant value in our society, is usually defined in terms of competitive, personal achievement, with references that are mainly economic, but that also include almost any other value that can nourish self-esteem. But here again, ambivalents find it difficult to pay the price of success. Asked why he never achieved dramatic financial success, a New York stockbroker replies: "I just wasn't . . . I wasn't facile enough. I was bright enough to do the things I had to do to make a good living, but I really didn't come up with a big score. . . . Well, there was a limit to what I was prepared to do to make money in a crazy way. But that's no good. You're supposed to do *everything* you have to do to make money. I guess at some point there's a limit. You either demean yourself or change yourself or something happens where you become something else."[17]

Such conditions generate anxiety as people strive for the unrealistic

[16] Hollingshead and Redlich, *Social Class and Mental Illness*, pp. 223–226.
[17] Terkel, *Working*, pp. 438–439.

heights often set for them by well-meaning authority figures. Meanwhile chance, lack of opportunity, and irrelevant or anachronistic personal skills frustrate many claims. Since youth itself is a substitute for achievement, and since extended education is often the major instrument of success, the day of reckoning may be long postponed. But the very knowledge that new ways to prestige and power are available for those with skill and nerve encourages anxiety, lest opportunity pass one by.

As this idealized image of success flourishes, and many fail, self-punitive mechanisms are encouraged, ramifying inferiority feelings and in some cases providing a satisfying instrument of masochism. Generous self-assessments may be used to ease individual security needs, but such generally prove unsatisfying because individuals have been taught to rely mainly on someone else's judgment to validate their own. Anxiety is increased as they turn elsewhere to find out what they are worth, and attempt to play the roles that will enhance their market utility. Because a social theory of unlimited opportunity encourages neurotic claims and frustrations, and because uncertainty is related to not knowing just where one fits or how long one will be there, both the ideal and the reality of high mobility tend to evoke anxiety. The popularization of activities that once insured distinction, such as higher education, foreign travel, and class-laden recreations such as golf, may also sharpen the search for alternative indexes of superiority. Indeed, the declining status value of such instruments and the difficulty of inventing new ones may provoke a subtle demoralization. Conspicuous consumption, great expectations, and trading on the achievement of parents may provide temporary respite, but somewhere around the age of forty an accounting must be made. Status anxiety then becomes common, resulting in prestige claims whose ingenuity is matched only by their pathos.

Having outlined the social basis of ambivalence, we can now turn to its organizational aspect. The ambivalent's reaction may be clearer if we think of the organization as a system of highly circumscribed roles. Such roles are partly the result of personal accommodations to the bureaucratic situation, worked out in the context of its systems of authority, status and small groups. They also reflect the more or less institutionalized set of behaviors associated with a given position in the organization. Since satisfactory accommodations depend in part upon the number of behavioral alternatives available, this situation limits the probability that idiosyncratic individual needs will be met. While such needs will vary in terms of personality, individual growth often requires the opportunity for multiple choices and acceptance of the responsibility for their outcome. In the case of ambivalents, the bureaucratic situation evokes role strain because it tends to prescribe and to severely limit the range of accommodations.[18] Such conditions violate their permissive values and expectations, which resist the organization's claims for order and consistency. They are rarely able to bargain effectively in an arena which inhibits spontaneity by design.

As we have seen, authority is allocated disproportionately in organizations. It clusters around the top and decreases at an increasing rate as one descends the hierarchy. Its gradations are clearly marked. Specialists with idealistic value preferences, typical ambivalents find it difficult to accept the legitimacy of this system. They cannot believe that those who have the largest shares of authority really merit it in terms of talent, wisdom, or morality. In this context, psychological tests and interviews of managers in several companies found "no relationship between intelligence and aptitude and individual success as defined by their ranks or by their salaries."[19] Such evidence suggests that the ambivalent's reservations are not entirely imaginary.

On a philosophical basis, ambivalents find it equally hard to believe that objectively superior solutions to problems exist. They reject the organization's "one-best-way" ethos. They know enough about risk and uncertainty to conclude that decision making at best is highly tentative. If solutions were known, there would be no need for decisions. They may thus find it quixotic that anyone should pretend to have very much knowledge, let alone superior knowledge. Thus the very legitimacy of the authority system is questioned; neither its legal-rational nor its charismatic bases carry much weight. Perhaps, they agree, it is necessary to have someone in command, but it seems naïve to impute superior qualities to him. Furthermore, they do not need certainty, nor yet authoritative individuals to interpret reality for them. They do not believe that they or anyone else is master of their fate.[20] This tolerance for ambiguity permits them to live with a highly tentative view of people and events.

---

[18]William J. Goode, "A Theory of Role Strain," *American Sociological Review*, Vol. 25, pp. 483–496.

[19]Frederick Herzberg et al., *The Motivation to Work* (New York: Wiley, 1959), p. 129.

[20]Contrast with this the following description of a management group: "Beneath the surface and rarely verbalized as a formal code of belief, lies a basic faith in the American conception that a man can help shape his environment and, more specifically, that a man can to a considerable degree determine his own life chances. . . . Nine out of ten give a categorical or qualified 'yes' to the question, 'Do you feel that fate is pretty much in your own hands?' A typical answer is, 'It's almost completely. What happens to me is the result of the way I conduct myself. I may get a little help along the way but it's up to me and nobody else.'" John and Ruth Useem, "Social Stresses Among Middle-Management Men," in E. G. Jaco, ed., *Patients, Physicians, and Illness* (Glencoe, Ill.: Free Press, 1958), p. 86. On the other hand, such evidence is challenged by the anxiety and lack of control manifested by some high-level executives. As one corpora-

Their most important dysfunction is a distorted, often fearful perception of authority. The resulting anxiety is a constant handicap in dealing with their superiors and their coworkers. As we have seen, perhaps the most significant item in bureaucratic mobility is one's attitude toward authority. Is the authority system perceived as threatening, or as the natural result of size, specialization, and task-oriented relationships? Here again the ambivalent is disadvantaged. While the upward-mobile has a close bond with his father and accepts authority easily, ambivalents tend to view authority figures as threatening, probably because of rejection or dominance by their fathers but also because authority figures personify conventional values which they resist.[21]

Empirical studies suggest that upward-mobiles and ambivalents have different perceptions of authority. Each has a distinctive cluster of attitudes. Stegner found, for example, that "persons accepting authority . . . show a conservative orientation, hostile to labor unions, endorsing war as a policy, nationalistic, intolerant of minority groups, and leaning to forceful solutions of social problems."[22] Moreover, there is "a trend for pro-authority subjects to have a conscious idealization of parents."[23] We may recall that among the West Point cadets successful adjustment was positively related to respect for authority and idealization of the father.

The ambivalent type, on the other hand, tends to resist and to fear authority. Clearly, if one accepts authority, one must believe that there are answers, and that certain persons have them. Yet, as we have seen, ambivalents regard truth as relative and changing. They believe, with Oliver Wendell Holmes, Jr., that absolute truth is for others to discover. Such skepticism is ill-suited to the organization's demands for loyalty and discipline and respect for the competence of those who direct it.

---

tion president described his role, "Most corporations I've been in, they were on the New York Stock Exchange with thousands of stockholders. The last one—whereas I was the president and chief executive, I was always subject to the board of directors, who had pressure from the stockholders. I owned a portion of the business, but I wasn't in control. I don't know of any situation in the corporate world where an executive is completely free and sure of his job from moment to moment." Terkel, *Working*, p. 530.

[21] Adorno et al., *The Authoritarian Personality;* B. K. Ruebush, "Interfering and Facilitating Effects of Test Anxiety," *Journal of Abnormal and Social Psychology,* Vol. 60, pp. 205–212.

[22] Ross Stegner, "Attitudes Toward Authority," *Journal of Social Psychology,* Vol. 40, p. 210; "One of the most striking features of work-role flexibility [of middle managers] is what we have termed 'tolerance of irrational authority.'" Management-oriented types can apparently justify wide deviations in the authority exercised by their superiors, including "an ability to relate oneself to a superior whose decisions may not appear sound. . . ." Useem, "Social Stresses Among Middle-Management Men," p. 87.

[23] Stegner, "Attitudes Toward Authority," p. 210.

Learning theory tells us that socialization results in generalized attitudes. This means that the authority system will tend to evoke the anxiety residual from all of one's past conflicts with authority. If a legacy of antiauthority attitudes exists, it is easily called into action. Meanwhile, these same authority symbols impel positive reactions in the upward-mobiles and, indeed, in all those whose dependency needs have been amply gratified. Internalized attitudes to authority thus have both anxiety-producing and anxiety-reducing functions; personality is the mediating factor. Here again ambivalents are torn between the conflicting needs of self-realization and the security bought with dependency and submission. And once again, their reactions are often contrary to organizational needs.

As we have seen, upward-mobiles view those above them as friendly models, while ambivalents regard them as threatening figures having the power to disadvantage them. Their interpersonal relations become difficult both for themselves and their superiors, who are much less interested in them than they think. They will be embarrassed by the ambivalents' rejection of the friendly patina that colors their relationship. Whether their reaction takes the form of passive resistance, resigned acceptance, or eager submission, ambivalents are bound to disrupt the desired smoothness. If they present signals of appeasement, the senior may resent the fact that the relationship now rests on hierarchy rather than on commonsense, precedent, or their own wisdom. Submissiveness marks again the inability of ambivalents to accept the need for the kind of nimble role playing which insures that such relations seem permissive at the same time they nicely accommodate the authority structure of the situation. Although upward-mobiles learn to play such roles facilely, the ambivalent is often disqualified by self-consciousness and by awkward notions about equality, compounded at times by inconsistent needs to reduce anxiety by submission.

As biosocial research demonstrates, submission has deep roots in animal behavior and is related not only to survival but to altruism as social behavior becomes more complex. The rewards of submission are dramatically apparent in the ritualized combat seen among some carnivores. Among African wild dogs, for example, it is common for the victor in combat to spare the life of his antagonist. This seems to occur at the point when the latter signals his surrender by an open-mouth grimace, a lowering and turning of the neck, followed by a belly-up groveling motion of the body which exposes him even more fully to further bites.[24] Typically, at this point the attack eases or

---

[24]Wilson, *Sociobiology*, pp. 128–129. See also Lorenz, *On Aggression* (New York: Harcourt, Brace, 1967), pp. 40–45.

stops. Among male mantis shrimp, even though one blow from their hammer-shaped second maxillipeds could tear their opponent apart, they are careful to aim only at the heavily armored tail segment of their opponent. Wilson concludes that there are two purposes for such ritualized aggression: mercy is good for the species, permitting the largest number of individuals to remain healthy; and such behavior facilitates kin selection since it permits someone to win fights without eliminating the genes shared with others by common descent.[25] Submissive behavior is also visible in a less power-oriented context, as seen for example in the pecking order among barnyard fowl.

In organizations, the acceptance of hierarchical authority and power may be a rough equivalent of such behaviors. Elites are similarly altruistic in rewarding graceful submission to their authority. It is also suggestive that commands are typically expressed in an interrogative mood. The relationship between authority and organizational roles has been carefully studied among hospital aides.[26] Dividing their subjects into "custodial" (authoritarian) and "humanistic" (equalitarian) types on the basis of thematic apperception tests, Pine and Levinson found the orientation toward work and behavior of each type discrete. While humanistic types had a permissive view of authority, custodials tended to be authoritarian. "Whether the hospital authority is male or female, the custodial aide tends to conceive of him (her) as a traditional, autocratic, masculine leader."[27] Although some hostility may be expressed indirectly, he tends to "accept and idealize the authority of the doctor." He also idealizes his parents and may view the doctor as a father-figure.

Each type has a different conception of patients. Custodial aides regard them as aggressive trouble makers who could "snap out" of their illness if they really tried. Humanistic aides, on the other hand, are generally more permissive and feel personally involved with the doctors in the therapeutic process. They believe that their job enables them to understand themselves better. They accept the view that there is a "basic identity" between some personality aspects of those who are normal and those who are mentally ill. Both types, moreover, have discrete views about treatment: custodial-authoritarians believe

[25] Ibid., p. 129.

[26] Fred Pine and Daniel J. Levinson, "Two Patterns of Ideology, Role Conception and Personality among Mental Hospital Aides," in M. Greenblatt, D. J. Levinson, and R. H. Williams, eds., *The Patient and the Mental Hospital* (Glencoe, Ill.: Free Press, 1957), pp. 209–215; regarding the phenomenon of adult personality change in an occupational context, see Howard S. Becker and Anselm L. Strauss, "Careers, Personality, and Adult Socialization," *American Journal of Sociology*, Vol. 62, pp. 253–263.

[27] Pine and Levinson, "Two Patterns," p. 212.

in somatic methods such as shock therapy, while humanistic-equalitarians prefer psychological methods.

In the context of organizational demands and modal interpersonal styles, it seems that the custodials severely repress their aggressions; they are more disciplined in their interactions with others. Humanists, on the other hand, often express such impulses directly and verbally. They are also more inclined to admit inadequacy or fears. Custodial types sharply differentiate right from wrong. They tend to have conventional values, while humanistic types "have more individualized value systems."

We have seen that discipline, strength, the honoring of majority norms, and respect for authority are functional values in bureaucratic work places. Such values enable one to repress any aggression built up by elite monopolization of authority, prestige, and status. By definition, only a few individuals can secure large amounts of the latter.

In this context, and contrary to the assumptions of utopian critics of bureaucracy, the organization must inevitably fail to satisfy the claims of many of its members. The frustration and hostility which result make great self-discipline a necessity in those who hope to qualify for a larger share of rewards. Frustration and hostility may also result in a great deal of ritualized behavior whose main function is to deny the existence of aggression.[28] Significantly, when social distance between individuals in the organizations is narrowed, such ritualized behavior tends to disappear. For example, during combat, equalitarian relations between officer and man are at a peak. The combat situation permits the enlisted man to displace his hostility from the officer to the enemy. In a bureaucratic setting, however, ritual behavior remains common, demanding considerable personal discipline and tact.

We cannot account for one exception in the hospital aide findings, namely, that humanistic-equalitarian aides apparently have easier authority relations with both doctors and nurses. "Doctors and [humanistic] aides are friendly. They both seem to be at ease."[29] This behavior is not characteristic of the ambivalent type, who seems to experience considerable difficulty handling authority relations. Despite this, the humanistic aides challenge the doctors and the hospital more freely than the custodials, which indicates that even though their interpersonal relations with superiors may be less structured, they are less prone to accept authority uncritically. In general, the findings suggest again that personality directly affects organizational role, and that the bureaucratic situation provides opportunities to in-

---

[28]Yehudi A. Cohen, "Some Aspects of Ritualized Behavior in Interpersonal Relations," *Human Relations*, Vol. 11, pp. 195–216.

[29]Pine and Levinson, "Two Patterns," p. 214.

dulge authoritarian preferences. They also suggest that the tendency of the ambivalent-humanistic types to be freely aggressive, to criticize authority, to admit personal fears and inadequacy, and to stress personal value systems can be dysfunctional. Specifically, such values may make it difficult for them to accept bureaucratic norms as the basis for their actions. In the language of ethology, their genes have inferior adaptive value in the bureaucratic situation.

Ambivalents tend instead to substitute their own subjective, "tender-minded" preferences. It is well known that personality affects the resolution of role conflicts. In terms of issues involving organizational norms and individual-family values, individuals high in conformity and "external" security values find it easier to make decisions that affect personal friends adversely.[30] Here is a suggestive distinction between those who prosper in bureaucratic settings and those who do not. As we have seen, the ability to identify with the organization's manifest goals and to act accordingly is a typical upward-mobile value. On the other hand, "universalism" (the tendency to use objective, achievement-oriented criteria in decisions affecting individuals) is "associated with the rejection of authority, a permissive view of dissent, an acceptance of one's own impulses, and an objective appraisal of one's parents."[31] Such values are likely to be characteristic of our ambivalent type.

Their inability to accept the organization's authority system compels ambivalents to reject its status system also. As we have seen, status is closely articulated with authority. Those at the top enjoy disproportionate amounts of status, and deflation sets in quickly as one descends the hierarchy. While the manifest function of status is to reward differences in ability and achievement, one of its critical latent functions is to validate authority. The system draws upon the common human need to legitimate dependency by imputing superiority to those upon whom one is dependent.[32] Moreover, when status differentials are earned, that is, when they represent objective dif-

---

[30]Elliot G. Mishler, "Personality Characteristics and the Resolution of Role Conflicts," *Public Opinion Quarterly*, Vol. 17, pp. 115–135. S. A. Stouffer and Jackson Toby, "Role Conflict and Personality," in Talcott Parsons and Edward Shils, eds., *Toward a General Theory of Action;* Greenblatt, Levinson, and Williams, eds., *The Patient and the Mental Hospital*, pp. 197–208.

[31]Mishler, "Personality Characteristics," p. 124.

[32]Such formulations suggest why, in the long run, it may be suicidal for an organization or a society to utilize ascriptive bases of recruitment and reward. Any resulting cynicism and displacement of individual energy must surely reduce operational capabilities. In many institutional contexts, of course (including universities and government) such dysfunctional consequences are muted by the collective, subjective nature of the production process and the product which may confound the use of objective performance standards.

ferences in skill, achievement, and contributions to the organization, the system may enjoy widespread support. "The status system constitutes a form of currency with which members upon whom the group is highly dependent may be paid off. . . . When a consensus exists about status this currency has a dependable, common value, being regarded in very much the same way by each member and thus having high interpersonal comparability." "Status congruency," the belief that individuals in a group are fairly and objectively ranked, is related to organizational morale. "As congruency increases, the [air force] crews show higher friendship ratings, greater mutual trust, greater intimacy, and (most remarkably) *less* perception of rank differences within the crew."[33]

Bureaucratic structure may thus reduce anxiety and conflict by universalistic definitions of authority and status. However, a principal consequence of bureaucratic norms is to smooth out differences in individual productivity. Democratic ideology has also played its part by challenging our traditional norm of equality of opportunity with one of equality of condition. Such leveling effects of bureaucratic work induce status anxiety as people try to find ways to recapture their individuality. The routinization of work evokes intense efforts to personalize one's job. Also relevant is the impulse to compensate for any loss of pride in skill attending the mechanization of many jobs.[34] Bureaucratic structure may thus aggravate status anxiety by its specialization and anonymity, encouraging a preoccupation with indexes, however trivial, that can validate minute differentiations in prestige and income. If ambivalents could accept the status system and their position in it, their anxiety would indeed be eased, but both restrict their discretion in favor of collective goals. Accommodation is viewed as a surrender of their individualistic values. Not only are the organization's rules and rewards the instruments of authority, but they symbolize an ordered system which challenges the ambivalent's preference for complexity and spontaneity.

In sum, ambivalents cannot honor the status system. Although they recognize that felicitous status relations are a bureaucratic necessity, they often reject the compromise required to play the status game. Acutely aware of status differentials, they object to the blurring of objective evaluations of people and work that the system brings. Their professional values insist that status gradations "should" precisely differentiate skill and achievement, but it is clear that considerable dis-

---

[33]Thibaut and Kelley, *The Social Psychology of Groups*, pp. 232, 233. See also, Jeanne Erikson, William D. Pugh, and E. K. Erik Gunderson, "Status Congruity as a Predictor of Job Satisfaction and Life Stress," *Journal of Applied Psychology*, Vol. 56, pp. 523–525.

[34]E. L. Trist and K. W. Bamforth, "Some Social Psychological Consequences of the Long-wall Method of Coal-getting," *Human Relations*, Vol. 4, pp. 3–38.

placement has occurred. Status rewards often mediate dependability, seniority, and interpersonal alliances. In the words of one ambivalent: "After I saw the least competent man promoted because he was friendly with the chief, I was through. I wasn't up for promotion myself, but I didn't have the feeling I would get a fair shake when I would be. The first chance I had several months later I resigned and left for a new job."[35]

Placing the highest value upon creativity and individuality, normally specialist qualities, yet knowing that the big rewards go to those in hierarchical roles, the ambivalent rebels against the existing system. As Herzberg concludes in a study of 200 professional engineers and accountants in nine industrial companies, when dissatisfaction was reported, it was not associated with the work itself but with the conditions, that is, the bureaucratic situation in which the work was done. The effects of hierarchy upon orientations toward work are further documented by his conclusion that accountants, who worked in a more structured situation, were significantly more concerned with status and personal advancement than engineers who valued work achievement more highly.[36]

The disenchantment of ambivalents is based in part upon what seems to them an illegitimate ascription of authority and status to position rather than to knowledge. The status hierarchy inhibits their work by encouraging competitive relationships, which often make the job to be done almost secondary. Their idealistic orientation makes it hard for them to accept the common displacement of values from the work itself to the politics of organizational survival. In trying to work on an objective, task-oriented basis, ambivalents often find themselves in conflict with hierarchical status barriers. A study of professionals in a hospital concluded: "There is the constant attempt in interpersonal relations to break through the logical administrative setup or the realistic hierarchies and to deal with one another as individual personalities."[37] The effort to penetrate such barriers requires "political" and interpersonal skills that ambivalents do not always have. Rarely willing to admit that such complications are operationally necessary, they often attribute them to ritualistic demands for clearance and coordination that serve mainly to validate hierarchical status.

Such attitudes tend to paralyze their interpersonal relationships, which are often characterized by excessive candor and a devotion to "principle" when indirection would suffice. Others are embarrassed

[35] Herzberg et al., *The Motivation to Work*, p. 88.
[36] Ibid., pp. 101–102.
[37] Morris B. Loeb, "Role Definition in the Social World of a Psychiatric Hospital," in Greenblatt et al., eds., *The Patient and the Mental Hospital*, p. 18.

by their iconoclasm and their insistence upon analyzing every nuance of their relationship, stripping it of spontaneity, warmth, and charisma. Their egocentricity, which often masks a gnawing uncertainty, insures further distortion. Their peers resent their inability to concede that they have problems too. This is ironic since they often have a real concern for others. Meanwhile, they cannot believe that others really like and respect them for themselves. Karen Horney observes: "As long as we do not love ourselves, we cannot possibly believe that others can love us."[38] Ambivalents conclude that if they are not respected for themselves, other, less worthy motives must be involved. Thus their anxiety is fed and their interpersonal relations clouded by uncertainty about the motives of their work companions.

As we have seen, the ability to play contradictory roles gracefully is a critical bureaucratic skill. The main reason for executive failure is rarely technical or professional incompetence, but the inability to "get along" with others. One must be able to shift nicely from dominance to dependency. Although the organization's structured field usually defines appropriate behavior, considerable versatility may be required in situations where the relative status of actors is muted, tentative, or unknown. Transactions with peers may evoke tension among upward-mobiles, but dealing either up or down is relatively simple. (Such variations may account for the widely differing perceptions of an executive held by those at various levels in the hierarchy. In effect, each is interacting with a different person.) Ambivalents, however, lack such adaptability. Regardless of the role, they play themselves.

The small group in which they work similarly demands identifications and loyalties that ambivalents are not always able to give. In organizations, many groups compete for resources that are inevitably scarce. Their competitive chances rest upon the ability to close ranks and to present a united front against other factions. Group solidarity in turn is based upon consensus among its members. Each must accept the group's motivating values and its allocations of authority, prestige, and affection. In this context, the small group presents a structural and psychological frame quite like that of the larger organization. It socializes its members, using the tactics of learning, reward, and reinforcement. It disciplines those who dissent, denying them recognition and empathy. Like the larger system, its authority, status, and prestige are nicely ranked in terms of the degree to which each individual has internalized its values.[39] Here too, the ambivalent reac-

[38]Horney, *The Neurotic Personality of Our Time*, p. 45.

[39]George Homans, *The Human Group* (New York: Harcourt, Brace, 1950), p. 141; O. J. Harvey and C. Consalvi, "Status and Conformity to Pressures in Informal Groups," *Journal of Abnormal and Social Psychology*, Vol. 60, pp. 182–187; Peter Blau, "A Theory of Social Integration," *American Journal of Sociology*, Vol. 45, pp. 545–556.

tion proves disqualifying. Chronic "outsiders," they have learned anxiety defenses that often stress skepticism, rejection, and distrust.[40] Their rewards include a feeling of uniqueness and the flaunting of the conventional values that saturate organizations. The often precious distinctions of rank, status, and seniority, and the essentially manipulative interpersonal drift of organizations leave them between anger and despair.

This temperamental inability to identify with group values frustrates the hopes for mobility and autonomy that their idealism and ambition have led them to expect. The majoritarian ethos of organizations repels them. They will not understand that if they are to compete, organizations must deal in averages. Their standards and their product must suit the majority. They must seek control through hierarchy. Both their ends and their instruments must be collectivized. However, ambivalents confuse the ideal of individual autonomy with the reality of such political and technological barriers to self-realization. Each time these untenable hopes are dashed, they are disenchanted. A less rigid perception might include hope in its calculus, but ambivalents often see their own position and that of the organization as going from bad to worse. Insofar as their own mobility is concerned, they are correct. The closer individuals come to realizing in their behavior the norms of the group as a whole, the higher will be their rank, and in turn the greater their influence.[41]

This generalization holds in many contexts. In the United States Senate, for example, members seem to be divided into an elite "inner club" and those who remain outside.[42] The critical standard for membership in the club is the acceptance of the traditional values and behavioral norms of the Senate. Those who conform most closely to its folkways are likely to be the most influential members of the Senate, as measured by their ability to get their bills passed. This Senate type who "cares more for the esteem of like-minded colleagues than any other type of approval,"[43] shares many of the values of our

[40]Timothy Leary, *Interpersonal Diagnosis of Personality* (New York: The Ronald Press, 1956), pp. 269–276; for clinical data on group reactions to nonconformists, see D. Stock et al., "The Deviant Member in Therapy Groups," *Human Relations*, Vol. 11, pp. 341–372; Dorwin Cartwright and Alvin Zander, *Group Dynamics* (Evanston: Row, Peterson & Co., 1953); for literary and philosophical portraits of the "outsider," see also Albert Camus, *The Stranger* (New York: Alfred A. Knopf, 1946), and Colin Wilson, *The Outsider* (Boston: Houghton Mifflin, 1956).

[41]Homans, *The Human Group*, pp. 141,145,169, 257.

[42]Donald R. Matthews, *U.S. Senators and Their World* (Chapel Hill: University of North Carolina Press, 1960), and *The Social Background of Political Decision-Makers* (Garden City, N.Y.: Doubleday, 1954), ch. 3; William S. White, *Citadel: The Story of the U.S. Senate* (New York: Harper & Row, 1956).

[43]Ralph K. Huitt, "The Outsider in the Senate: An Alternative Role," *American Political Science Review*, Vol. 50, p. 571. It is significant that Huitt does not regard the

upward-mobile. He is above all "a prudent man, who serves a long apprenticeship before trying to assert himself, and even then talks infrequently. . . . More than anything else, he is a Senate man, proud of the institution and ready to defend its traditions and perquisites against all outsiders. He is a legislative workhorse who specializes in one or two policy areas . . . he is a conservative, institutional man, slow to change what he has mastered at the expense of so much time and patience."[44] Here again, note the acceptance of typical upward-mobile values of seniority, authority, group norms, and continuity.

On the other hand, the ambivalent role seems nicely comparable to that historically played by "outsiders" in the Senate. Iconoclasts are a small minority. In recent times, perhaps the following might be included: Joseph Clark, Gaylord Nelson, Lee Metcalf, George McGovern, and most recently James Abourezk (a Lebanese-American), who has engaged in direct combat what he calls "the powerful Jewish lobby" in the United States. Such senators may consciously elect *not* to become members of the inner club. Their disengagement is not necessarily a matter of personal or social disability, but is the result of deliberate choice. However, temperament again underlies this accommodation: "the outsider feels impelled to stand for principle absolutely, preferring defeat on those terms to half-a-loaf. He likes to tell people what they should and frequently do not want to hear. He is never so confident of his opinions as when he holds them alone. He is as comfortable alone against the crowd as the Senate type is in the bosom of the club."[45] Unlike the latter who is a "local," the ambivalent-outsider plays a "cosmopolitan" role: he "typically looks elsewhere—to his constituents and to his ideological allies across the nation."[46] The cost of this independence may be high, however, for he rarely exerts great and continuing influence within the Senate.

Here again the interpersonal phenomenon of becoming "locked into" relationships may be seen. The ambivalents' rejection of group values tends to result in a progressive worsening of their relations with its members.

What the individual experiences as estrangement from a group of which he is a member tends to be experienced by his associates as

---

"outsider" as a deviant type, but rather as an "alternative type, for whom the Senate has historically had considerable tolerance." To some extent, however, this conclusion neglects one well-documented aspect of group behavior, namely, the fact that both acceptance and influence are normally a function of the individual's internalization of majority group values.

[44]Ibid., pp. 566–567.

[45]Ibid., p. 571.

[46]Ibid.

repudiation of the group, and this ordinarily evokes a hostile response. As social relations between the individual and the rest of the group deteriorate, the norms of the group become less binding for him. For since he is progressively seceding from the group and being penalized by it, he is the less likely to experience rewards for adherence to the group's norms. Once initiated, this process seems to move toward a cumulative detachment from the group, in terms of attitudes and values as well as in terms of social relations.[47]

The ambivalents' accommodations prove disqualifying in another way: they may prevent them from developing a rational perception of bureaucratic interpersonal relations. They fail to understand that size, rationality, and anonymity inspire "universalistic," tough-minded choices. When General Cummings says: "The army works best when you're frightened of the man above you and contemptuous of your subordinates," ambivalents lose contact.[48] Not only are they temperamentally incapable of admitting that action is often immoral, they cannot avoid defining people as individuals. Partly as an anxiety reaction, but also because they believe individualism cuts both ways, they cannot make decisions that affect others adversely without undue personal strain. Always on the lookout for evidence that will document their "tender-minded" orientation, they idealize human relationships. They have never learned that many individuals want structured relationships and find in their dependency a cue that reinforces their own preference for hierarchy and their need to believe that its gradations are the result of merit.

In an organizational society where individuals are often viewed instrumentally, personal influence is often achieved by combination and compromise. One must, for example, join some interest group if one's will is to be felt in the modern political arena. One must accept its values and its collective mandate. But here again, the ambivalent's values often prove disqualifying. He resists organized "causes" because they are imperfect and require what he regards as a "sacrifice of principle." Disdaining half a loaf, ambivalents usually end up with nothing. As a result, their preconceptions about their personal impotence are reinforced. Withdrawal serves a self-confirming function. It also reinforces their neurotic tendencies. Significantly, withdrawal is often associated with neurotic disturbances. J. A. C. Brown says: "If this need [for group acceptance] remains unsatisfied, nothing else can

[47]Robert K. Merton and Andrea S. Kitt, "Reference Group Theory and Social Mobility," in R. K. Merton and P. F. Lazarsfeld, eds., *Continuities in Social Research* (Glencoe, Ill.: Free Press, 1950), p. 94.

[48]Norman Mailer, *The Naked and the Dead* (New York: Signet, 1950), p. 152.

compensate for its lack. Loss of status leads to social isolation, and is one of the commonest causes of neuroses."[49]

The difficulties experienced in interpersonal relationships are often aggravated by frustration. Since a classical generalization of social psychology is that aggression mediates frustration,[50] we may assume that the ambivalent's behavior will often be unpredictable and aggressive. As we have seen, ritualistic behavior and the concentration of culturally valued rewards at the top evoke frustration and hostility among some members of the organization. Unsatisfied claims for success and power skew the behavior of ambivalents from an effusive bonhomie to a failure to honor ordinary social amenities. Lacking a sense of proportion, they often take a stand on the basis of principle over relatively insignificant issues. This tendency to do the right thing at the wrong time may be aggravated by an insistence upon a degree of frankness that paralyzes human relations. They may also retain quaint and passionate beliefs about the relevance of objectivity in human affairs and the importance of hard work and merit in career success. Here they often fail to distinguish between what is and what they think ought to be. Indeed, they usually operate in an "ought" framework, providing themselves with an idealistic and not infrequently irrelevant standard that proves once again that everything is usually for the worst.

Such a self-system makes ambivalents somewhat tragic figures in the bureaucratic setting. On the one hand, they want success yet resist paying the price in collectively validated behavior. On the other, they disdain success, as popularly defined, yet feel that their individuality must be validated by others. Unable to reject or to raise above majority values, they are also unable or unwilling to play the roles required to achieve them. While the upward-mobile is sustained by status rewards and great expectations, and the indifferent accommodates by limiting his aspirations, the ambivalent is chronically disturbed. While upward-mobile anxiety seems to reflect mainly a fear of failure, the latter's fear mirrors ethical conflict, arising, for example, from bureaucratic claims for tough-minded decisions. Although incapable of playing the roles required for success, ambivalents badly need success to validate their intense need for recogni-

[49]J. A. C. Brown, *The Social Psychology of Industry* (Baltimore: Penguin Books, 1954), p. 281; a similar relation between isolation and neuroses was found by Fraser, *The Incidence of Neurosis.* Authorities believe that neuroses of one kind or another provide the largest single cause of problem workers, amounting to 20 to 40 percent of all patients referred to industrial physicians. Moreover, from 30 to 60 percent of all individuals who consult doctors are estimated to be suffering from psychoneuroses.

[50]John Dollard et al., *Frustration and Aggression* (New Haven: Yale University Press, 1939).

tion. Although majority values must be honored, they are temperamentally incapable of accepting them. They demand self-realization; they want to count, to put their ideas into practice. Yet in complex organizations such demands are often honored only through the disciplined muting of individual claims.

Ambivalents evaluate themselves by the same quixotic standards they set for others and build up more anxiety by their inevitable failure to measure up. Since (unlike the upward-mobile) they demand immaculate causes, they are immobilized a good deal of the time. Their inability to identify with the organization not only disqualifies them for success on its terms, but aggravates their anxiety as its leaders exchange loyalty to the organization for its rewards. If they were self-sufficient enough to reject such claims, the conflict might be resolved. If they could adopt unconventional behaviors without disqualifying strain, they would probably be less neurotic. If they had the upward-mobile's facility for "positive thinking," the organization might provide them security through recognition. Finally, if they were exceptionally productive they would personify Rank's "creative artist," who can rise above majority values. But the ambivalents' conflict is always the conflict between such values and the idiosyncratic alternatives they enlist to dramatize their individuality.

Such efforts to escape their cramping environment take several forms. They may develop a compulsive interest in their work, not so much for its intrinsic value, but as a means of obtaining sufficient recognition to set them off from the rank and file. Creative work is difficult for them, however, since they are often hypercritical of their own efforts. Moreover, their anxiety makes them afraid to project their ideas upon a world often perceived as hostile. They may seek easier ways of differentiating themselves and securing the independence that will permit escape from the bureaucratic mold. Unusual mannerisms or the cultivation of those who are successful may follow as they attempt to borrow status and clip a security dividend. But they are usually inhibited by a fundamental anxiety which may provoke extreme variations of behavior, from rebellion in an effort to validate their autonomy to submission which reduces anxiety. Toward the pathological end of the continuum, they may hope that something cataclysmic will break the monotony of their unsatisfying role. They may even entertain fantasies such as the well-known "magic helper" delusion, which insures that they receive preferential treatment. In this they are attempting to escape the stereotyping that often occurs in complex organizations.

Empirical research generally supports the relationship posited here between the ambivalents' ambiguous work role and their often dysfunctional anxiety and "alienation," defined as a sense of estrangement and/or powerlessness. Among so-called Type-A individuals, who are intense and highly committed to their work, a positive relation has been found between role stress and anxiety, resentment, and depression.[51] Similarly, role ambiguity has been found to be positively related to powerlessness and, not surprisingly, negatively related to job satisfaction.[52]

The ambivalent's unhappy accommodation is intensified not only by the organization's acquisitive demands but also by its structure and procedure, which seek control by limiting individual discretion. Collective goals and values always have priority. By ascribing specific roles with limited jurisdiction, bureaucratic structure aims at predictability, which necessarily assumes control. This creates a situation unalterably opposed to the ambivalent's needs for autonomy. We can now restate an earlier hypothesis: ambivalents find bureaucratic structure uncongenial because their value preferences deny its functional requirements. The latter include an uncritical acceptance of the legitimacy and rationality of the organization; the supremacy of its manifest goals; the honoring of tradition and precedent; structured, authoritative interpersonal relations; and collective decision making.

Unlike the indifferent, however, who ignores or displaces such claims, they can neither reject them nor find work situations in which they would seem less compelling. One might assume that they would seek an unstructured environment in small business or the "independent" professions of law, medicine, and university teaching. But the possibilities are limited because in these callings, too, bureaucratic settings often provide the main avenue for cashing in personal claims. Skill is no longer enough. Large, prestigious law firms, for example, now "want men who also have pleasing personalities, are from the 'right' schools with the 'right' social backgrounds, have a 'cleancut' appearance, and are endowed with tremendous stamina."[53] The dysfunctions of size are suggested by the recruitment themes of such firms, which play down the common anxiety of law graduates that they will be forced to specialize too soon, will fail to receive "proper training," or will "get lost" in the large organization. A related indication of bureaucratization is the gentlemen's agreement among law firms that they will not lure people away from another office, nor will they exceed the "going rate" of beginning salary. The highly spe-

[51]Robert D. Caplan and Kenneth W. Jones, "Effects of Work Load, Role Ambiguity, and Type-A Personality on Anxiety, Depression and Heart Rate," *Journal of Applied Psychology*, Vol. 60, pp. 713–719.

[52]W. Clay Hamner and Donald C. Tosi, "Relationship of Role Conflict and Role Ambiguity to Job Involvement Factors," *Journal of Applied Psychology*, Vol. 59, pp. 497–499.

[53]Erwin O. Smigel, "The Impact of Recruitment on the Organization of the Large Law Firm," *American Sociological Review*, Vol. 25, pp. 56–66.

cialized "law factory"; the state university with its utilitarian ethic and programs; medicine's demand for cohesion, as evidenced, for example, by the compulsory subscription policy of the American Medical Association in its long campaign against "socialized medicine"; the union movement among university faculties; "equal opportunity" norms in recruitment in law and medical schools—all underscore the changing conditions of professional work.

Fundamentally destructive reactions may follow. Disenchanted by unrealized claims for status, frustrated by an alien environment, the ambivalents' perceptions may become distorted. The organization's elite may appear to be unrestrained Machiavellians. The normal disenchantments of life may be perceived as evidence of conspiracy, particularly since chance no longer fits into their calculations. Here again their error is in generalizing from an individualized perception of a partial truth. The obvious rationality of the elite, its preoccupation with the "political" consequences of its actions, and its fairly patent manipulations suggest clearly enough that probability has indeed been harnessed; but ambivalents conclude that it has been eliminated. As Freud observed, such distortions meet their own needs in two ways: they escape a painful reality, which might show that their failure is really their own fault, and they can exploit the neurotic claim, perhaps by using it to rationalize their inability to work productively.[54]

Contrary to the Indian proverb, "It isn't how much one can do, but how much he cares," the ambivalents' tragedy is that they care too much, but can do too little. Alienated by bureaucratic conditions and by their own distortions of them, they find little satisfaction in work. The psychic security which identification with the organization would provide is denied them. Since they have little faith in either its rationality or legitimacy, both tend to be foreclosed. In some cases, and at great cost, a compulsive effort to escape anonymity and futility may result in achievement that brings the recognition they need. But such solutions are unlikely in a milieu whose ground rules stress seniority, co-optation, and conformity.

These formulations suggest that, unlike the other role types posited here, the survival chances of the ambivalent model are not very sanguine. Indeed, if technological imperatives and a declining position in the international power spectrum push America even further along the road to collectivism, ambivalents may become the first prisoners in the "iron cage of history." We turn to this highly speculative question in our final chapter.

---

[54]Sigmund Freud, *Introductory Lectures on Psychoanalysis* (New York: Norton, 1935).

THE FUTURE | 9
OF ORGANIZATIONS

In this final chapter some predictions will be made about organizations of the future. Since any changes in the structure, values, and norms of organizations will affect the survival potential of our three role models, some judgments about such consequences will also be made. Clearly, the erosion of traditional authority structures and values among youth has affected the role and prestige of typical upward-mobiles. Their status as widely legitimated models has been challenged by the decline of work as a central life incentive for many Americans. In the process, a powerful disciplinary force in our competitive society has been weakened.

For a closer look at such issues, we will begin with an analysis of social change including the conditions that seem to inspire it. Then, the implications of the new organizational structures proposed by so-called futurists will be set against the deterministic assumptions of the Weberian conclusion regarding the inevitable expansion of bureaucracy at the expense of human values. Finally, a very brief review will be offered regarding the consequences of the Weberian model for the three types of individual accommodation.

Organizational change, it seems, essentially reflects modifications in the larger socioeconomic milieu. Organizations shape their own environment to some extent, but the critical agents of change are probably exogenous, often international in scope and of a scale that usually compels both organizations and individuals to play a reactive role. As Marx and Weber argued, such changes are typically generated by the "dynamism of material interests." In some cases, of course, the ideological component is central, *viz.* the Russian Revolution, or it may provide the rationalizing façade, but the decisive underlying force is more likely to involve "hard" variables. In our time, the emerging energy crisis, the declining power of the United States in the international arena, and the political and economic desperation of third-world nations are among the factors that condition organizational change. Against such vast and pervasive imperatives, contemporary pleas for "open organizations" in the name of democratic values, equal opportunity, feminism, distributive justice, and the like seem weak, however compelling normatively. Ironically, the popular currency of such utopian claims may rest substantially upon some of the very conditions they are directed against: for example, the high overhead costs of the publishing industry which demand a sustained flow of novel materials.

Such assumptions suggest that the future of organizations is more likely to be some variation of Weber's "iron cage" of history than the "open systems" milieu advocated by futurologists. I am aware that this assumption that continuity is more common than change constitutes, often unknowingly, a bias toward the status quo. My essential argument, nevertheless, is that "change" will occur but in the direction of solidifying and expanding both the formal structure of modern bureaucracy and its behavioral norms. Economic scarcities and technological imperatives will provide the major incentives.

An important theoretical aspect of social change is the extent to which institutions resist change, and perhaps, particularly bureaucratic institutions.[1] Here, the economic concept of "sunk costs" is relevant and generalizable at a rather high level of abstraction, in part because the currencies involved in such commitments are so infinitely varied. They encompass not only the "trained incapacity" seen among highly skilled workers and professionals, but subjective values of empathy, friendship, settled relationships, status congruency, long-nourished influence, and power relationships. Such contingencies militate against the acceptance of organizational change. Equilibrium in bureaucratic settings is likely to be sought by co-opting change, by submerging it into time-honored, comfortable patterns.

A related characteristic of organizations which bears upon social change is their regenerative metabolism.[2] While physiological decomposition changes their human components, organizations maintain continuity by the systematic replacement and socialization of recruits co-opted by existing elites, in effect by perpetuating the bureaucratic norm that positions, not individuals, are the critical factor in achieving the organization's goals. For such reasons, continuity exerts a decisive influence in the evolution of organizations.

A related facet of social change is the assumption of unidimensionality, the conception that societies and their institutions have a

---

[1] See Amitai Etzioni, *The Active Society* (New York: Free Press, 1968), for this and other theoretical aspects of social change. For constraints more directly related to organizations, see Michael P. Smith, "Barriers to Organizational Democracy in Public Administration," *Administration and Society*, Vol. 8, pp. 275–315.

[2] Kenneth McNeil and James D. Thompson, "The Regeneration of Social Organizations," *American Sociological Review*, Vol. 36, pp. 624–637.

built-in tendency to evolve in the same direction. Here again, my assumption is that such is most likely to be the case.

It seems that social scientists have an occupational bias toward change. The premium on creativeness in scientific work and priority probably underlies this drift. Another "causal" factor may be the pervasive technological emphasis upon innovation and built-in obsolescence seen in captialist societies. The relentless impetus toward economic growth provides a critical incentive which spills over into the intellectual world. The weight of this influence is increased by familiarity with the work of such great European social theorists as Marx, Weber, Durkheim, and Tönnies, which leaves one with the impression that most of our seminal ideas were set down long ago. This conception of critical time-bound bursts of intellectual and scientific innovation may be relevant to our own time in the specific areas of physics and medicine; future generations may look back upon the 20th century as a period of striking achievement, much like the golden age of Greece or the Renaissance.

Selective perception may also be at work in judgments regarding the rate and the direction of social change. Post–World War II experience in the Middle East, for example, has inspired quite opposing conclusions regarding the amount and the rate of change occurring there.[3] Whether the observed rate of change is "fast" or "slow" is in part a subjective judgment.

In the case of modern bureaucratic organizations, judged from a utilitarian rather than a normative perspective, the attitudes we bring to them about change must be influenced by the fact that they have been generally effective in handling large-scale operations in most sectors. Despite his ultimate pessimism, Weber regarded bureaucracy as the best instrument yet designed for carrying out such activities. Judged only from an operational point of view, for example, one must be impressed by the dispatch, flexibility, and centralized control exhibited by multinational corporations in adjusting to such exogenous imperatives as high labor costs in North America and Europe and the opportunity for markets in third-world countries. It seems, however, that this adaptation was powered by an exquisitely detailed use of bureaucratic controls, by a magnification of bureaucratic instruments rather than by new organizational forms.

[3]For the judgment that dramatic change has occurred, essentially because of rural accessibility to modern instruments of communication, see Daniel Lerner, *The Passing of Traditional Society* (Glencoe, Ill.: Free Press, 1958); for the opposing view, also based on personal experience in the area, see Robert Presthus, "Weberian and Welfare Bureaucracy in Traditional Society," *Administrative Science Quarterly*, Vol. 6, pp. 1–24 and "The Social Bases of Bureaucratic Organization," *Social Forces*, Vol. 38, pp. 103–109.

Another theoretical assumption that requires mention is the view that change is typically a manifestation of instability and integration. This assumption has often been implicit in the work of structural functionalists and essentially "conservative" scholars such as Talcott Parsons and Robert Nisbet.[4] Yet, ameliorative social change has often proved stabilizing, as seen in political behavior, for example, the New Deal innovations and civil rights legislation in the United States and the extension of the franchise and the incorporation of new merchant elites into the landed aristocracy in Britain.

The concept of "sunk costs" may also be put in terms of rather specific environmental constraints against change. These have been called macrophenomena and compared with what Emile Durkheim called "social facts."[5] Such facts cannot be distributed among individuals; they tend to be aggregate values for groups or populations. While some observers argue that individuals and organizations have considerable effect upon such exogenous structures, my view, as suggested earlier, is that organizations and individuals more typically adapt to them. An analogy may be drawn here with the process of individual socialization in which existing cultural norms and values are typically decisive. A useful way of thinking about such constraints is to regard them as "external pressures toward inertia." They include the following factors:

1. Legal and fiscal barriers to entry and exit from markets (broadly defined) are numerous. Discussions of organizational behavior typically emphasize barriers to entry (state licensed monopoly positions, etc.). Barriers to exit are equally interesting. There are an increasing number of instances in which political decisions prevent firms from abandoning certain activities. All such constraints on entry and exit limit the breadth of adaptation possibilities.

2. Internal constraints upon the availability of information are paralleled by external constraints. The acquisition of information about relevant environments is costly particularly in turbulent situations where the information is most essential. In addition, the type of specialists employed by the organization constrains both the nature of the information it is likely to obtain . . . and the kind of specialized information it can process and utilize.

[4]Cf. Robert H. Lauer, "The Scientific Legitimation of Fallacy: Neutralizing Social Change Theory," *American Sociological Review*, Vol. 36, pp. 881–889.

[5]See Gudmund Hernes, "Structural Change in Social Process," *American Journal of Sociology*, Vol. 82, pp. 515–518.

3. Legitimacy constraints also emanate from the environment. Any legitimacy an organization has been able to generate constitutes an asset in manipulating the environment. To the extent that adaptation (e.g., eliminating undergraduate instruction in public universities) violates the legitimacy claims, it incurs considerable costs. So external legitimacy considerations also tend to limit adaptation.

4. Finally, there is the collective rationality problem. One of the most difficult issues in contemporary economics concerns general equilibria. If one can find an optimal strategy for some individual buyer or seller in a competitive market, it does not necessarily follow that there is a general equilibrium once all players start trading. More generally, it is difficult to establish that a strategy that is rational for a single decision maker will be rational if adopted by a large number of decision makers. A number of solutions to this problem have been proposed in competitive market theory, but we know of no treatment of the problem for organizations generally. Until such a treatment is established we should not presume that a course of action that is adaptive for a single organization facing some changing environment will be adaptive for many competing organizations adopting a similar strategy.[6]

The political culture of a given nation may also provide external constraints on organizational adaptability. In the context of interest group activism, in the political arena, for example, the United States and Canada provide suggestive discontinuities, reflecting the laissez-faire individualism of the United States and the organic corporatism of Canada.[7] The former encourages felicitous interest group adaptation in the form of the quick mobilization of new interest groups to meet social and political innovations. The activating rationale is that those who do not organize have only themselves to blame if governmental largesse goes to other, more resourceful clients. In Canada, corporatism fosters the notion that society is comprised of essentially cooperative groups and that governmental elites will allocate public resources equitably, without much need for direct intervention by groups. An allied value, part of Canada's British legacy, is deferential patterns of authority, which foster the belief that leaders should enjoy considerable autonomy because they have superior qualifications and wisdom. Such conditions partially explain why the political activism

[6]Michael T. Hannan and John Freeman, "The Population Ecology of Organizations," *American Journal of Sociology*, Vol. 82, p. 932. Reprinted by permission of the University of Chicago Press.

[7]Robert Presthus, *Elites in the Policy Process*, pp. 30–39, 301, 315.

and adaptability of Canadian interest groups lag well behind that of the United States.[8]

Deeply-held philosophical conceptions regarding education and recruitment may also encourage organizational continuity. In British government, for example, the adaptability of the administrative class, the some 4,500 senior civil servants who play critical roles in public policy making, has been seriously impaired by what is often called the "generalist" conception of administrative behavior.[9] This preference holds that a broadly-educated amateur, with proper "leadership qualities," including poise, confidence, forensic skills, and a liberal education, is fully competent to advise modern political leaders on complex policy issues. This somewhat anachronistic view is based upon classical values, probably stemming from the Greco-Roman ideal of the universal genius, personified by Leonardo da Vinci. Despite recent efforts to modify the recruitment assumptions that define this appreciation, very little change has occurred, in good part because of the internal opposition of members of the administrative class itself. This latter condition may be regarded as an internal constraint.

Such internal factors aggravate the kinds of exogenous constraints outlined earlier. Here again, they have been nicely summarized as follows:

1. An organization's investment in plant, equipment and specialized personnel constitutes assets that are not easily transferable to other tasks or functions. The ways in which such sunk costs constrain adaptation options are so obvious that they need not be discussed further.

2. Organizational decision makers also face constraints on the information they receive. Much of what we know about the flow of information through organizational structures tells us that leaders do not obtain anything close to full information on activities within the organization and environmental contingencies facing the subunits.

3. Internal political constraints are even more important. When organizations alter structure, political equilibria are disturbed. As long as the pool of resources is fixed, structural change almost always involves redistribution of resources across subunits. Such redistribution upsets the prevailing system of exchange among

---

[8]Ibid.

[9]Among others, see Max Nicholson, *The System: The Misgovernment of Modern Britain* (London: Hodder & Stoughton, 1967); the "Fulton Report," The Civil Service (London: HMSO, 1968–69), especially Vol. 3 (1) and (2); Timothy Balough, "The Apotheosis of the Dilettante," in Hugh Thomas, *The Establishment* (London: New English Library, 1962); Kelsall et al., *Graduates: The Sociology of an Elite*.

subunits (or subunit leaders). So at least some subunits are likely to resist any proposed reorganization. Moreover, the benefits of structural reorganization are likely to be both generalized (designed to benefit the organization as a whole) and long-run. Any negative political response will tend to generate short-run costs that are high enough that organizational leaders will forego the planned reorganization. . . .

4. Finally, organizations face constraints generated by their own history. Once standards of procedure and the allocation of tasks and authority have become the subject of normative agreement, the costs of change are greatly increased. Normative agreements constrain adaptation in at least two ways. First, they provide a justification and an organizing principle for those elements that wish to resist reorganization (i.e., they can resist in terms of a shared principle). Second, normative agreements preclude the serious consideration of many alternative responses. For example, few research-oriented universities seriously consider adapting to declining enrollments by eliminating the teaching function.[10]

The types of constraints generated by an organization's own history must also include the conceptual opacity cited by Thomas Kuhn in his description of the process of scientific revolutions. Despite the rapidity of technological change, it seems that individuals develop commitments to established ways of conceptualizing problems. Only when the scientist has been able to overcome such intellectual sunk costs, when he has "learned to see the world in a different way . . ." is scientific innovation possible.[11] Examples are legion. Copernicus' rejection of the Ptolemaic paradigm in the sixteenth century provides a well-known case. During our time, the discovery of the jet aircraft engine, based upon an entirely new conception of propulsion, met with considerable resistance from aeronautical experts.[12] In foreign aid programs, the diffusion of both technological and intellectual innovation has been similarly confounded by the inapposite norms and values of host countries.[13] As Gunnar Myrdal has shown, traditional class structures, anticolonial ideologies, caste systems that inculcate contempt for manual work and create sharp divisions among social groups, restrictions on women's rights, the colonial fixation on cheap

[10]Hannan and Freeman, "The Population Ecology of Organizations," pp. 931–932. Reprinted by permission of the University of Chicago Press.

[11]Thomas Kuhn, *The Structure of Scientific Discovery* (Chicago: University of Chicago Press, 1962), p. 52; pp. 68–69.

[12]Sir Frank Whittle, *Jet: Story of a Pioneer* (London: Muller, 1953).

[13]Among others, see Robert Presthus, "The Social Bases of Bureaucratic Organization," pp. 103–109.

labor and its corollary low productivity—are among the vast number of barriers to change in poor countries.[14]

The constraints upon social, institutional, and ideological change seem almost as compelling in rich societies, if only because the *status quo* provides unprecedented levels of economic security and welfare benefits. Confronted with the choice between full employment and zero growth, most Americans will choose the former, however reluctantly. Without accepting his essential thesis, one can find in Herbert Marcuse a useful statement of the extent to which contemporary society co-opts change. "The containment of social change is perhaps the most singular achievement of advanced industrial society; the general acceptance of the National Purpose, bipartisan policy, the decline of pluralism, the collusion of Business and Labor within the strong State testify to the integration of opposites which is the result as well as the prerequisite of this achievement."[15] As a result, both history and the functional needs of society tend to make most proposals for change appear utopian and even elitist insofar as they oppose the overwhelmingly egalitarian drift of Western society.

It seems quite plausible that, as well as being agents of change, modern complex organizations are equally well suited and disposed toward suffocating it. I would suggest that the federal government seems best described as a system that is running us; consider for example, as the Comptroller General informs us, that almost *three-quarters* of the President's budget is beyond his control, fixed by previous commitments. Beyond this, for what have been called "routine technologies"—those in which exceptions in the processes involved in changing the raw materials with which an organization deals are unusual and in which the degree to which search is logical and analytic—the ideal-typical bureaucracy is probably the "socially optimum form."[16] As Charles Perrow concludes, "To call for decentralization, representative bureaucracy, collegial authority, or employee-centered, innovative or organic organizations—to mention only a few of the highly normative prescriptions that are being offered by social scientists today—is to call for a structure that can be realized only with a certain type of technology, unless we are willing to pay a high cost in terms of output."[17]

[14]Gunnar Myrdal, *Asian Drama: An Inquiry into the Poverty of Nations* (New York: Pantheon, 1968), esp. Vol. I, ch. 3.

[15]Herbert Marcuse, *One-Dimensional Man: Studies in the Ideology of Advanced Industrial Society* (Boston: Beacon Press, 1964), p. xxi.

[16]Charles Perrow, "A Framework for the Comparative Analysis of Organizations, *American Sociological Review*, Vol. 32, pp. 194–208.

[17]Ibid., p. 204.

Such imperatives must be set against the prescriptions of utopian critics of bureaucracy. In the presence of such social, institutional, and technological constraints upon social and organizational change, the formulations of contemporary advocates of far-reaching changes in organizational structure seem rather utopian. However appealing in their democratic-humanism, they will probably not be very influential. Among the reasons is the assumption that social change can be effected by essentially normative appeals. Their approach is often essentially ideological. More important, they seem to focus upon the structure and processes of organizations, with insufficient attention to the output and economic imperatives that provide the *raison d'être* of most organizations. As John McLeish writes, "*In the last analysis* the mode of production is primary, ideology secondary; the economic basis will have its way."[18] Or as Malinowski said, "Man does not live by bread alone, but he lives primarily by bread."

Organizations, in effect, have a critical functional role to play in modern society. All else being equal, their survival potential rests upon their capacity to fulfill this role. Their internal structure and the individual and small-group interactions upon which advocates of change often focus, are necessarily subordinate to this larger end. In a rich society, the day of reckoning may be long postponed, but organizations must eventually meet some test of collective functionality and economic survival. This imperative has now appeared among rich Western governments, and its ultimate claims have perhaps only been so long deferred by vast borrowing, most notably in our time by Britain and Canada.

Such emerging constrictions upon national wealth and attending tolerance for experimentation suggest that some of the proposed modifications face hard going. For example, the "open organizations" model posits the free exchange of work roles. This prescription would dispense with bureaucracy. As Warren Bennis states, "In today's world [bureaucracy] is a prosthenic device, no longer useful. For we now require organic-adaptive systems as structures of freedom to permit the expression of play and imagination and to exploit the new pleasures of work."[19] While its objective is certainly reasonable, this assumption ignores the very specialization that gives modern organizations much of their rationality and effectiveness. Perhaps such a scheme could be introduced in assembly line systems, but there the

---

[18]John McLeish, *The Theory of Social Change* (London: Routledge and Kegan Paul, 1969), p. 12.

[19]Warren Bennis, *Changing Organizations* (New York: McGraw-Hill, 1966), p. 14. For similar prescriptions, see among others, Ernst F. Schumacher, *Small is Beautiful: Economics as if People Mattered* (New York: Harper & Row, 1975), and Frank Marini, ed., *Toward a New Public Administration* (Scranton: Chandler Publishing Co., 1971).

boredom and exquisite segmentation of tasks obviate the intended goal. How such an innovation would affect collective outcomes in universities, hospitals, symphony orchestras, armies, or government hierarchies is problematic at best. At the micro level, such a variable structure would be widely acceptable on humanistic and ideological grounds, but its larger operational consequences for productivity would probably be chaotic.

Here, the assumption seems to be that modern man can dispense with science and technology. But, as Weber said, "this is impossible" and he was writing in 1904.

> Fashion and the zeal of the *literati* would have us think that the specialist can to-day be spared, or degraded to a position subordinate to that of the seer. Almost all sciences owe something to dilettantes, often very valuable view-points. But dilettantism as a leading principle would be the end of science. He who yearns for seeing should go to the cinema, though it will be offered to him copiously to-day in literary form in the present field of investigation also. Nothing is farther from the intent of these thoroughly serious studies than such an attitude. And, I might add, whoever wants a sermon should go to a conventicle. The question of the relative value of the cultures which are compared here will not receive a single word. It is true that the path of human destiny cannot but appall him who surveys a section of it. But he will do well to keep his small personal commentaries to himself, as one does at the sight of the sea or of majestic mountains, unless he knows himself to be called and gifted to give them expression in artistic or prophetic form. In most other cases the voluminous talk about intuition does nothing but conceal a lack of perspective toward the object, which merits the same judgment as a similar lack of perspective toward men.[20]

A related proposal would transform existing hierarchical structures in organizations, attempting to broaden participation and collective decision making by easing communication and status barriers. The argument is that individuals "will be differentiated not vertically according to rank and role but flexibly according to skill and professional training."[21] Under such a system, moreover, executives would become "linking pins" between various temporary groups, organized upon a "problems to be solved" basis rather than along traditional hierarchical lines. Such modifications could probably be made and certainly they would ease some of the dysfunctions outlined

---

[20]Max Weber, *The Protestant Ethic and the Spirit of Capitalism*, trans. Talcott Parsons (New York: Scribner's, 1958), p. 29.

[21]Bennis, *Changing Organizations, p. 12.*

throughout this analysis. Hierarchical structures do inhibit communication and obvious disparities may at times be seen between an individual's position and his or her contribution to the organization's goals.

Nevertheless, ethological and anthropological research suggest that status rankings and social class differentiations tend to characterize most social collectivities, including informal small groups. To this extent, bureaucratic rankings are essentially a manifestation of phylogenetic factors. One suspects that individuals would still be "vertically differentiated" under the proposed setting. It is instructive, meanwhile, that democracies in crises often turn to hierarchical patterns of operation, even in such fields as physical science where one might have thought such conditions were inapposite. During World War II, for example, some 30,000 scientists in the Office of Scientific Research and Development were controlled by about "thirty-five men in senior positions" who generally ran things according to "convenient, authoritarian military liaisons."[22]

More important, perhaps, is the ethological evidence cited earlier that hierarchy is not only ubiquitous, it is often useful. Some examples were cited earlier, but the generalization could rest on Weber's dictum that one of the main causes of bureaucratic rationalization is simply large populations. It is virtually impossible to order an apparatus that must serve a huge clientele without the differentiations of skill and authority that define hierarchy. The evidence supporting the existence and utility of hierarchy among living creatures is impressive indeed. Hierarchy is typically found among colonial microorganisms, invertebrates, insects, vertebrates, and mammals, including humans, at both social and organizational levels.[23]

The nice dichotomy assumed by utopians between differentiation according to rank and role, on the one hand, and skill and professional training also seems overstated. It denies the fact that, whatever violations of this principle may occur, compared with any Western society, the United States has been substantially more meritocratic.[24] The probability that rank and skill will tend to be equitably articulated, in effect, is relatively great, all else being equal.

[22] Vanevar Bush, *Modern Arms and Free Men* (New York: Simon and Schuster, 1949), pp. 6–7 and "The Great Science Debate," *Fortune,* June 1946, p. 236.

[23] Edward Wilson, *Sociobiology: The New Synthesis* (Cambridge: Harvard University Press, 1975).

[24] Rawls argues against the principle of meritocracy, but it is important to note that his analysis is hypothetical and not primarily concerned with the functional needs of society. "Among the essential features of this situation is that no one knows his place in society, his class position or social status, nor does anyone know his fortune in the distribution of natural assets and abilities, his intelligence, strength, and the like. I shall even assume that the parties do not know their conceptions of the good or their special psychological properties. The principles of justice are chosen behind a veil of ignorance." John Rawls, *A Theory of Justice* (Cambridge: Harvard University Press, 1971), pp. 11–17, 106–107.

Sigmund Freud once maintained that the discovery of tobacco was the essential virtue of America, but he might have given equal homage to our much-honored achievement orientation and the reality and promise of upward social mobility.[25] If it can be shown, moreover, that inequities in authority, prestige, and income culminate in compensating benefits for everyone, the fact of hierarchy in the organizational society seems to meet even the most astringent conditions of justice.[26]

Finally, the proposed temporary organizational setting probably assumes too high an expectation that work can be pleasurable, other than for a minority of highly educated, internally-directed individuals. Instead, most tasks in modern organizations and industry will probably remain routine and unchallenging, as part of the price paid for the rationalization of production and high productivity. No one denies the resultant individual costs, but the prior goal remains the collective product. We turn next to some of the conditions underlying the assumption that continuity is more likely to occur than radical change in bureaucratic structures.

Following Max Weber, I shall argue that sunk costs of ideology and economic organization will tend to push American society further along toward the iron cage of history. Perhaps the greatest social scientist of this century, Weber's ideas are well known, and we will confine ourselves to some of his contributions in the area of social change as it affects bureaucratic organization. It is difficult to separate these formulations, however, from those set down in Weber's most famous work, *The Protestant Ethic and the Spirit of Capitalism*. One theme from this work relates directly to bureaucracy, namely, Weber's finding that capitalism provided the genesis of both rationality and bureaucracy. These two forces were regarded as irresistible. They fed on themselves and would ultimately, in Weber's pessimistic judgment during his later years, undermine subjective, individual values and human spontaneity. Throughout his writings one finds evocative phrases that symbolize this conviction: "the routinization of charisma," "the new house of enslavement," "benevolent feudalism" (relating specifically to America), "inescapable universal bureaucratization," "the tide of materialist forces," "petrified society," "plebiscitory leader-democracy," "the icy objectivity of business."

His world view is clearly apparent in these words from *Science as a Vocation:*

It is the fate of our times, with its characteristic rationalization, intellectualization, and above all, disenchantment of the world, that

---

[25] For careful evidence of the comparatively high rate of social mobility in the United States, see Blau and Duncan, *The American Occupational Structure* (New York: Wiley, 1967).

[26] Rawls, *A Theory of Justice*, pp. 14–15.

precisely the ultimate and most sublime values have disappeared from public life, either into the shadow realm of mystical life or into the brotherliness of direct relationships between individuals. It is not accidental that our highest art is intimate rather than monumental, nor is it chance that today, only within the smallest circles of community, from man to man, in *pianissimo* does that Something pulsate which earlier, as prophetic *pneuma* (spirit) went through the great communities like a fire storm and fused them together.[27]

Weber's apocalyptic vision of the future, as Wolfgang Mommsen suggests,[28] stems in part from the influence of Nietzsche. The special sense of responsiblity accorded to great men, themes of power (Macht) and dominance (Herrschaft), German cultural nationalism, and the need for charismatic leaders to break through the confining web of bureaucracy—all seem to reflect some of Nietzsche's dicta.[29] More directly, Mommsen cites Weber's paraphrase of Nietzsche in the *Sociology of Religion*. Regarding the pervasive thrust of a triumphant capitalism, Weber states:

No one yet knows who will inhabit that abode and whether this prodigious development may end in entirely new prophets arising or in a mighty rebirth of ancient thoughts and ideals—or if neither happens, in a mechanized petrification decked out with a sort of obsessive self-importance. Then indeed could it be said of these "ultimate" men of that stage of cultural development: "Technicians without souls, sensualists without hearts—this nothingness imagines it has climbed to a level of humanity never reached."[30]

In the end, Weber concluded that "mechanized petrification" was the most likely outcome.

The essential impulse in this historical drift was rationalization, which destroyed the distinction between means and ends and indeed became at times irrational, as in the situation where the mere accumulation of wealth became the primal incentive. Although Weber notes that the movement from traditional forms of authority and charismatic legitimacy through to bureaucratic dominance did not occur linearly, he appears to believe that the major path of history leads in this direction. Here, and despite his desperate efforts to avoid prophecy and remain scientifically neutral, he reminds one of Marx.

[27]Cited in Arthur Mitzman, *The Iron Cage: An Historical Interpretation of Max Weber* (New York: Alfred A. Knopf, 1970), p. 228.

[28]Wolfgang Mommsen, "Max Weber's Political Sociology and His Philosophy of World History," *International Social Science Journal*, Vol. 17, pp. 35–45.

[29]In this context, see Ilsa Dronberger, *The Political Thought of Max Weber* (New York: Appleton, Century, Crofts, 1971).

[30]Max Weber, *The Sociology of Religion* (Boston: Beacon Press, 1964), Vol. 1, p. 204.

Both assume a certain historical necessity, but whereas Marx is optimistic in his view that human exploitation will ultimately be overcome, Weber sees the great forces of capitalist rationality as leading to the constriction of individual autonomy.

Regarding our earlier comments on the internal versus the external components of social change, Weber believed that its foremost agent, rationalization, rose from both sources. War and migration are among the major exogenous forces cited as change agents in the economic sphere. Internally, bureaucratic elites are seen as extending their power through specialization and a monopoly of knowledge of the rules. Weber saw the rise of rationalization everywhere, in law, exchange relations in the marketplace, the theory and use of money, military technology, factory organization, monasticism in the early church, the bureaucratization of political parties, the administration of charity, and the ordering of bureaucratic recruitment and processes. In the political arena, its triumph was seen in "the complete disappearance of ideological substance in the American parties, but the greatest example, of course, is the age-old connection between capitalist interests and the expansion of political communities."[31]

Capitalism and its drive for profit maximization provide the primary source of rationalization. Characteristic types of rational economic action are cited as follows:

1. The systematic allocation as between present and future of utilities, on the control of which the actor for whatever reason feels able to count. (These are the essential features of saving.)

2. The systematic allocation of available utilities to various potential uses in the order of their estimated relative urgency, ranked according to the principle of marginal utility.[32]

"Economic organization," for Weber, encompassed "not only business corporations, cooperative associations, cartels, partnerships, and so on, but all permanent economic establishments (*Betriebe*) which involve the activities of a plurality of persons, all the way from a workshop run by two artisans to a conceivable communistic organization of the world."[33] The scope attributed to economic incentives was virtually Marxian: "Groups that are not somehow economically determined are extremely rare."[34]

Rationality, for Weber, meant essentially a calculated relationship between means and ends. "Rational technique is a choice of means

[31]Max Weber, *Economy and Society*, G. Roth and C. Wittich, eds. (New York: Bedminster Press, 1968), Vol. I, pp. 345–346.

[32]Ibid., p. 71.

[33]Ibid., p. 74.

[34]Ibid., p. 341.

which is consciously and systematically oriented to the experience and reflection of the actor, which consists, at the highest level of rationality, in scientific knowledge."[35] Rationality becomes the "catalytic agent" in the evolution from earlier patrimonial to bureaucratic forms of dominance.[36] In its economic context, it is divided into formal and substantive components. The former "will be used to designate the extent of quantitative calculation or accounting which is technically possible and which is actually applied." The latter "is the degree to which the provisioning of given groups of persons (no matter how delimited) with goods is shaped by economically oriented social action under some criterion (past, present, or potential) of ultimate values (*wertende Postulate*), regardless of the nature of these ends."[37]

An integral aspect of rationalization was the secular historical tendency toward centralized control in most fields of activity. Here again, Weber's debt to Marx is clear:

> The relative independence of the artisan or cottage outworker, of the landowning peasant, of the holder of a benefice, of the knight and the vassal depended on the fact that he himself owned the tools, supplies, financial means, or weapons with whose help he pursued his economic, military, or political function and from which he lived during his performance. Contrariwise, the hierarchical dependence of the worker, salesman, technician, academic assistant, *and* state official and soldier rests on the fact that those tools, supplies, and financial means which are indispensable for organization and economic existence are concentrated in the hands of either the entrepreneur or the political lord. . . . The "separation" of the worker from the material means to his activity takes many forms; he is separated from the means of production in the economy, from the means of war in the army, from the material means of administration in public administration, from the means of research in the university institute and laboratory, from the financial means in all of them. It is the decisive foundation common to the capitalist private enterprise and to the cultural, political, and military activities of the modern power state.[38]

In effect, the dynamics of rationalization include specialization of individuals and institutions; the techniques of commerce, the eradica-

---

[35] Ibid., p. 65.

[36] Cited in Mitzman, *The Iron Cage*, p. 234.

[37] Mitzman, p. 85.

[38] Max Weber, *Gesammelte Politische Schriften* (Tubingen, 1958), p. 309. Cited in Mitzman, *The Iron Cage*, p. 184.

tion of traditional and charismatic forms of authority by legal-rational ones; the harnessing of rational calculation to the means and ends of virtually every type of social activity; the displacement of goal rationality to that of means; the increasingly technical and pragmatic basis of university education, as best seen perhaps in legal training; the tendency (not everywhere seen) of the nuclear family to dissolve in service to the demands of industrial development; and urbanization and the replacement of *Gemeinshaft*, community-oriented values by contractually based, economically relevant values and norms.

Set against the material hegemony and financial resources of modern industrial structures and the functional need for national economic growth to provide employment, all buttressed by the dominant values of materialism and success, which remain salient because they have no saturation value for those who accept them, the rationale of contemporary advocates of "open organizations" seems rather utopian. The majority of Americans are probably not economically secure enough to indulge second-level desires for intrinsically impeccable values of conservation, ecological sanity, and work that is challenging and worthwhile. Consumption styles and expectations have become so compelling that the continued production of often trivial products is probably required not only to maintain economic growth but to meet artifically inculcated demands. Necessities tend to become luxuries given the calculus of capitalist production. Functional demands for a reasonable level of effectiveness and productivity provide another constraint against attempts to set higher priorities for individual needs in work and the work place. For such reasons, we conclude that the movement toward new liberating departures in organizational structure and processes will have only a marginal impact.

There is a natural tendency for revisionists to set existing structures, processes, and values against some utopian alternative and to exaggerate the dispatch and ease with which social change can occur. A more realistic perception suggests that the eradication of social and ethnic inequalities is likely to be slow and tortured. The limited success of equal opportunity programs,[39] including the backlash from disenchanted majorities; the failure of British socialism despite a generally sympathetic and rational environment;[40] and the experiences of most African nations where political independence is quickly followed by economic despair—all suggest that capitalist

---

[39]For a review of such disenchantments, see Theodore Caplow, *Toward Social Hope* (New York: Basic Books, 1975), especially chs. 13 and 14.

[40]It is hard to believe today, for example, that Durkheim could have once regarded the political state as the "brains of the social organism."

systems, however imperfect, may be the best solution available in an imperfect world. The critical need of the new nations is to create wealth, and capitalism remains the instrument *par excellence* for this purpose. Certainly, the faith that government can bring a new competence and rationality to economic affairs rests heavily upon ideological assumptions, as opposed to systematic calculation of such common dilemmas as the impact of unrestrained public spending upon inflation and the distortion of priorities, seen for example in the defense production sector.[41] Perhaps inevitably, the egalitarian values of collective systems seem to sacrifice individualism in the service of welfare equality. Whether even the most powerful economic systems can sustain the resultant costs is now moot. We are told that the social security systems of all major Western nations are financially anomalous. Given such constraints, the probability seems great that rationalization will increase in line with the Weberian prophecy.

In this context, it is interesting to speculate about the future of the three bureaucratic types. Somewhat cavalierly, perhaps, one may dispense with the indifferents who will carry on with minimal commitment, transferring their essential concerns to off-work pursuits. The ambivalents, however, would seem to be less functionally suited to the bureaucratic society of the future. The latitude for dissent and normative concerns for distributive justice will probably decrease as economic and energy stringencies accumulate. Equally, the exhaustion of viable political alternatives to the present welfare-capitalist systems may further circumscribe the autonomy of ambivalents. If socialism has failed and the swift resolution of individual inequities proves illusory, while analyses of justice remain highly abstract,[42] the parameters of discussion and experimentation in new social forms, the special prerogative of ambivalent types, may shrink. Just as the devotion of many young Americans to equal opportunity failed when put to the test, that is, when limited employment opportunities brought them into direct competition with favored minorities, the revamping of satisfactory yet imperfect institutions seems more likely to be entertained.

Upward-mobiles, on the other hand, will probably continue to flourish in the emerging "benevolent feudalism." Nicely suited to the imperatives of the bureaucratic setting, they will continue to determine the allocation of disproportionate amounts of private and public resources. Their catalogue of personal attributes will continue

[41]Congress is anticipating a 60 billion dollar deficit in fiscal 1977, with a total budget of about 430 billion dollars.

[42]It is again suggestive that John Rawl's treatise on justice proceeds on an abstract and immaculate level; such presumably relevant realities as Vietnam and the rationality of national priorities are never mentioned. See *A Theory of Justice*, e.g., pp. 11–17.

to mesh nicely with the organization's demands for discipline, neutrality, technical expertise, collective decision making, the acceptance of the priority of collective ends, and proper respect for hierarchically defined estimates of personal worth.

On the larger stage, insofar as the power of technology as rational domination continues its global conquest, the upward-mobile should continue to flourish. Neither revolutionary nor conservative,

> he symbolizes a type which is becoming increasingly important in all belligerent countries: the pure technician, the classless bright young man without background, with no other original aim than to make his way in the world and no other means than his technical and managerial ability. It is the lack of psychological and spiritual ballast, and the ease with which he handles the terrifying technical and organizational machinery of our age, which makes this slight type go so far nowadays. . . . This is their age.[43]

Impervious to the counterpoise to technological imperialism symbolized by the recent wave of cultism, feminism, sexual freedom, and a generalized antiauthority drift, typical upward-mobiles will probably remain happy prisoners in the iron cage. Indeed, their autonomy and preferential status may be enhanced as socialization and alienation (a sense of powerlessness) tend to broaden the acceptance of bureaucratic structure and values among ordinary people. If Weber could conclude a half-century ago, when capitalism was comparatively unsophisticated, that the victory of bureaucracy was inevitable, it will not be unexpected that individuals will increasingly succumb to its pervasive strength in contemporary America.

[43] Albert Speer, *Inside the Third Reich* (New York: Macmillan, 1970), p. 344.

RESEARCH
POSTSCRIPT

Several attempts have been made to test some of the formulations set down in the present theory of accommodation.[1] As noted in the book, some of the posited characteristics of the upward-mobile type have been validated. These include the association between job satisfaction (predicted as typically "high") and a positive attitude toward promotion. Evidence also suggests that high needs for dominance (posited for upward-mobiles) is positively linked with strong preferences for promotion also attributed to upward-mobiles.[2] On the other hand, Dorothy Harlow found that the assumed positive association between promotional preference and low toleration for ambiguity did not appear and, indeed, a significant *negative* association was found.[3] In a subsample of graduate engineers in executive roles at several levels in their firms, however, Harlow found that among those above the median on job satisfaction, tolerance for ambiguity and promotional preference were negatively associated, as predicted in the theory of accommodation. She speculated that this relationship might have resulted from an identification with the authority structure of the organization or that tolerance for ambiguity is related more closely to authoritarianism through socialization in the work place rather than by socialization in the culture as a whole, as suggested by the theory.

Harlow's research was replicated by O'Reilly, Bretton, and Roberts, with very similar results, but with one interesting addition: a test of the extent to which upward-mobiles may validly be categorized as "locals," that is, as conceiving their roles to be primarily identified with their own organization, in contrast to an alternative "cosmopolitan" industry- or discipline-wide orientation. Using high preference for promotion as a criterion for upward-mobiles, a very strong

[1]Dorothy Harlow, "Professional Employees' Preference for Upward Mobility," *Journal of Applied Psychology,* Vol. 57, pp. 137–141; C. A. O'Reilly, G. E. Bretton, and K. H. Roberts, "Professional Employees' Preference for Upward Mobility: An Extension," *Journal of Vocational Behavior,* Vol. 5, pp. 139–145; Henry O. Pruden, "The Upward-Mobile, Indifferent, and Ambivalent Typology of Managers," *Academy of Management Journal,* Vol. 16, pp. 454–464.

[2]Harlow, "Professional Employees' Preference," p. 139.

[3]Ibid.

and significant correlation was found with commitment to the organization (.50 p > .001).[4]

Regarding job satisfaction, using two military aviation units (252 people), the authors found a strong positive relation (.32 p = > .001) between promotional preference and overall job satisfaction. No significant relation was found between promotional preference and tolerance for ambiguity, thus reinforcing Harlow's finding.[5] Finally, regarding tolerance for ambiguity and job satisfaction, no significant relationship was found, contrary to Harlow who had found a significant negative association between these two variables.[6]

Using a sample of 150 business managers, Pruden measured differences among upward-mobile, ambivalent, and indifferent types along the dimensions of job satisfaction, career anchorage (orientation toward one's career), alienation, cosmopolitanism, and organizational rank. Significant variations occurred on three of the five: career anchorage, alienation, and cosmopolitanism.

The upward-mobiles ranked as expected on all five dimensions, indifferents on four of five, and ambivalents on three of five. Several disparities appeared among the latter types. Ambivalents, for example, ranked "high" on organizational position, though the theory assumes that their personal attributes typically proved disqualifying. Indifferents ranked "high" on job satisfaction which seems anomalous but may reflect their low job commitment and consequent satisfaction. Indifferents also ranked "high" on cosmopolitanism which seems odd, yet it may reflect their lack of identification with their present organization. Pruden's research did not include such critical variables as attitudes toward authority (authoritarianism), tolerance of ambiguity, and intellectual orientation, for example, preference for simplicity versus complexity in art forms or "idealism" versus "pragmatism."[7]

Such findings are useful in increasing our understanding of the qualities that seem to be associated with personal success in a bureaucratic society. At a theoretical level, they provide some further evidence about the suggestive relations between bureaucratic structure and personality. Their practical significance is even clearer, given their implications for more intelligent and productive recruitment into authoritative roles in society. The costs of inept appointments at high organizational levels are obvious.

---

[4] O'Reilly, Bretton, and Roberts, "Professional Employees' Preference for Upward Mobility: An Extension," p. 144. For items and research procedure, see A. W. Gouldner, "Cosmopolitans and Locals: Toward an Analysis of Latent Social Roles," *Administrative Science Quarterly,* Vols. 2, 3, pp. 281–306; 444–480.

[5] O'Reilly, Bretton, and Roberts, p. 141.

[6] Ibid., pp. 143–144.

[7] Pruden, "The Upward-Mobile, Indifferent, and Ambivalent Typology."

It seems proper to suggest that these empirical researches require considerably more testing before we can feel reasonably secure about the utility and validity of the theory of accommodation set down in this work. In this context, several hypotheses will be offered below in a propositional form that permits empirical testing. The sources of several relevant scales will be included to provide appropriate indexes of such salient variables as toleration for ambiguity, easy acceptance of authority, and preference for conventionality. The operationalization of several of my rather loosely stated concepts and variables may also prove useful to colleagues and students who find the problem of organizational accommodation challenging.

Perhaps a word is in order about the suggested focus here upon upward-mobile types. Essentially, this is because they occupy the most strategic roles in modern organizations. On functional grounds, that is, they allocate most of the resources, money, authority, time, and legitimacy that organizational members require to perform their roles adequately. Such a rationale may prove disenchanting to some observers, underestimating as it does vital alternative goals of equity, justice, and individual self-realization for the majority of ordinary members of organizations. It can be justified only on scientific grounds that counsel one to suspend normative judgments about one's subject in the interest of analysis. The pervasiveness and power of bureaucratic norms and institutions also seem to demand hardheaded analysis in order to determine the functional requisites of this most strategic of modern instruments for meeting human needs.

Some Hypotheses for Further Research

Proposition: Individuals who occupy high-level positions in typical bureaucratic settings will tend to rank disproportionately high on certain attitudes that seem functional in such settings:

I   Upward-mobile types will tend to exhibit a "lower tolerance for ambiguity" than individuals who have lower preferences for advancement in bureaucratic settings:

> Achieved position in the organization of job satisfaction can be used as the independent variable while indexes from the Adorno Authoritarian scale, from variations in preference for abstract versus representational art forms, from "cognitive dissonance" theory, or from the index used in the Harlow and O'Reilly et al. research might also be useful.

II Upward-mobile types will tend to rank higher on deference toward authority than individuals who have experienced less organizational mobility, to ascribe high value to such mobility, and to rank higher on overall job satisfaction.

Indexes that may be useful for testing this hypothesis include patterns of emotional attachment to father, selected items from the Adorno scale, or items designed from various analyses of authority. See, for example, the fascinating work of Stanley Milgram, *Obedience to Authority* (New York: Harper & Row, 1974).

III Upward-mobile types typically exhibit higher dominance needs than those who rank lower on selected variables found to be associated with mobility in organizations, namely, achieved mobility, high job satisfaction, high deference toward authority, (possibly) low tolerance for ambiguity, and high "localism."

Potentially useful indexes here would include measures that differentiate individuals on such needs as (a) control in interpersonal situations (b) preference for occupational roles that seem to indulge high dominance needs—for example, military, medicine, teaching, and law enforcement (c) subjects' recollections of child-raising patterns that did/did not inculcate respect for authority (for useful theoretical suggestions, see R. A. Bierstedt, "The Problem of Authority," in *Freedom and Control in Modern Society* [New York: Van Nostrand, 1954], pp. 67–81; M. Rokeach, "Authority, Authoritarianism, and Conformity," in *Conformity and Deviation* [New York. Harper & Row, 1961], pp. 230–257).

In effect some of the hypotheses suggested in the book provide the basis for manageable projects, which could be useful in research training and, potentially, in adding to our knowledge of individual reactions to complex organizations. The practical implications for personnel recruitment and the probabilities of reasonably effective performance are clear as well. Equally important is the intrinsic interest one can find in testing hypotheses dealing with human behavior and the conditions of social mobility in American society.

About the Author

Robert Presthus, University Professor of Political Science at York University and former editor of *Administrative Science Quarterly,* has written widely in political and organizational behavior. He has received research grants and fellowships from the Social Science Research Council, Haynes Foundation, Ford Foundation, *Conseil des Arts du Canada,* National Science Foundation, National Institutes of Mental Health, and the Consortium for Comparative Legislative Studies. He has been on the editorial boards of *Theory and Decision, Comparative Politics,* and *Comparative Political Studies.* In 1956 he was research director of the United Nations Institute of Public Administration, Ankara, Turkey. In 1965 he gave the Southern Regional Conference lectures at the University of Alabama, and in 1978 he was Visiting Distinguished Professor of Political Science at Arizona State University. He has lectured at several American and European universities, and his articles have appeared in such journals as *American Political Science Review, Journal of Politics, Canadian Journal of Political Science, Administrative Science Quarterly, International Journal of Comparative Sociology, Social Forces, Public Administration Review, The Annals, American Academy of Political and Social Science, New Republic,* and *Nation.*

NAME INDEX

SUBJECT INDEX